Houghton Mifflin Math Steps

HOUGHTON MIFFLIN

Boston • Atlanta • Dallas • Denver • Geneva, Illinois • Palo Alto • Princeton

Grateful acknowledgment is given for the contributions of

Student Book

Rosemary Theresa Barry
Karen R. Boyle
Barbara Brozman
Gary S. Bush
John E. Cassidy
Dorothy Kirk

Sharon Ann Kovalcik
Bernice Kubek
Donna Marie Kvasnok
Ann Cherney Markunas
Joanne Marie Mascha
Kathleen Mary Ogrin

Judith Ostrowski
Jeanette Mishic Polomsky
Patricia Stenger
Annabelle L. Higgins Svete

Teacher Book Contributing Writers

Dr. Judy Curran Buck
  Assistant Professor of Mathematics
  Plymouth State College
  Plymouth, New Hampshire

Dr. Richard Evans
  Professor of Mathematics
  Plymouth State College
  Plymouth, New Hampshire

Dr. Mary K. Porter
  Professor of Mathematics
  St. Mary's College
  Notre Dame, Indiana

Dr. Anne M. Raymond
  Assistant Professor of Mathematics
  Keene State College
  Keene, New Hampshire

Stuart P. Robertson, Jr.
  Education Consultant
  Pelham, New Hampshire

Dr. David Rock
  Associate Professor,
    Mathematics Education
  University of Mississippi
  Oxford, Mississippi

Michelle Lynn Rock
  Elementary Teacher
  Oxford School District
  Oxford, Mississippi

Dr. Jean M. Shaw
  Professor of Elementary Education
  University of Mississippi
  Oxford, Mississippi

Copyright © 2000 by Houghton Mifflin Company. All rights reserved.

No part of this work may be reproduced or transmitted in any form or by any means, electronic or mechanical, including photocopying and recording, or by any information storage or retrieval system without the prior written permission of the copyright owner, unless such copying is expressly permitted by federal copyright law. Address requests for permission to make copies of Houghton Mifflin materials to School Permissions, Houghton Mifflin Company, 222 Berkeley Street, Boston, MA 02116.

Printed in the U.S.A.

ISBN: 0-395-98539-0

123456789-B-05 04 03 02 01 00 99

Contents

Unit 1	Introduction to Algebraic Thinking	1
Unit 2	Number Theory, Decimals, and Fractions	31
Unit 3	Measurement	73
Unit 4	Ratios, Proportions, and Percents	97
Unit 5	Applications of Percent	127
Unit 6	Data, Statistics, and Probability	151
Unit 7	Geometry	179
Unit 8	Integers and Rational Numbers	215
Unit 9	Algebra: Expressions and Equations	241
Unit 10	Using Formulas in Geometry	275
Unit 11	The Coordinate Plane: Graphs and Transformations	315

Tables of Measures 349

Glossary 352

UNIT 1 • TABLE OF CONTENTS

Introduction to Algebraic Thinking

Lesson	Page
1 Whole Numbers and Data	3
2 Expressions	5
3 Order of Operations	7
4 Solving Addition and Subtraction Equations	9
5 Solving Multiplication and Division Equations	12
6 **Problem Solving Strategy:** Write an Equation	14
7 Properties	16
8 Using the Distributive Property	19
9 Expressions with Exponents	22
10 Using Geometric Formulas	24
11 **Problem Solving Application:** Use a Formula	27
• Unit 1 Review	29
• Cumulative Review ★ Test Prep	30

Dear Family,

During the next few weeks, our math class will be studying some ideas from algebra. You can expect to see homework that provides practice with these skills. Here is a sample you may want to keep handy to give help if needed.

Evaluating Expressions

To find the value of the expression $7(8 - 5)^2 + 9$, you apply the order of operations. First perform operations inside parentheses, then simplify exponents, then multiply and divide in order from left to right, and finally, add and subtract in order from left to right.

$$
\begin{aligned}
7(8 - 5)^2 + 9 &= 7(3)^2 + 9 & &\text{First subtract inside the ( ).} \\
&= 7(9) + 9 & &\text{Then square the result.} \\
&= 63 + 9 & &\text{Multiply to simplify.} \\
&= 72 & &\text{Finally, add.}
\end{aligned}
$$

To find the value of $a \div b + 7 \cdot c$ when $a = 42$, $b = 6$, and $c = 3$, substitute for the variables in the expression. Then use the order of operations to evaluate the expression.

$$
\begin{aligned}
a \div b + 7 \cdot c &= 42 \div 6 + 7 \cdot 3 & &\text{Substitute for the variables.} \\
&= 7 + 21 & &\text{Then divide and multiply.} \\
&= 28 & &\text{Finally, add.}
\end{aligned}
$$

During this unit, students will continue to learn new techniques related to the study of algebra.

Sincerely,

We will be using this vocabulary:

mean the average of a set of data

median the middle point of the data set when they are arranged from least to greatest

mode the number(s) that occur most often in a set of data

variable a letter that is used to represent one or more numbers

order of operations the rules that define the established order in which the operations in an expression are to be evaluated

solve an equation find the value of the variable that makes the equation a true statement

exponent a number that tells how many times a base is used as a factor

evaluate an expression find the value of the expression

Name _____

Whole Numbers and Data

The **line plot** shows the number of hours that 32 students in Johnson Middle School spent reading last weekend. Which measure—range, mean, median, or mode—best represents the number of hours the typical student read?

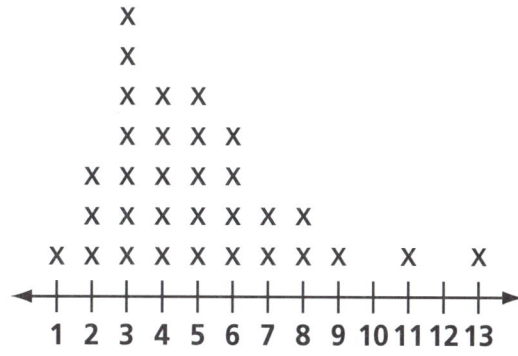

- The **range**, or spread, of the data is the difference between the least and greatest values.

  The range is $13 - 1 = 12$.

- The **mean**, or average, is the most commonly used *typical* value.

  To find the mean, find the sum of the data items divided by the number of pieces of data. There are 32 items of data.

  $$\frac{1 + (3 \cdot 2) + (7 \cdot 3) + (5 \cdot 4) + (5 \cdot 5) + (4 \cdot 6) + (2 \cdot 7) + (2 \cdot 8) + 9 + 11 + 13}{32} = \frac{160}{32} \text{ or } 5 \quad \text{The mean is } \mathbf{5}.$$

- The **median**, or the middle number, is the most typical measure when there are gaps and a few values (called *outliers*) that are much higher or lower than most data.

  When there are an odd number of data items, the median is the middle item. Since the number of data items is even, the median is the average of the two middle items, **4** and **5**.

  The median is **4.5**.

- The **mode**, or the number that occurs most often, is the most typical measure in data sets when several data points cluster around it.

  The tallest column is above the 3. The mode is **3**.

You can see in the line plot that the majority of data points cluster around the mode. You can say that the mode best represents the number of hours the typical student spent reading last weekend.

Use the data at the right to complete.

1. Make a line plot of the data in the table.

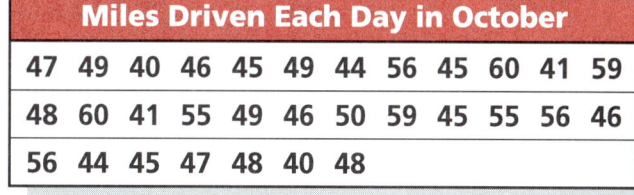

2. Find the mean, median, mode, and range for the data.

mean: 49 median: 48 mode: 45 range: 20

Unit 1 Lesson 1   **3**

Graphs are also used to display the relationships among the data. A bar graph is a good choice when you want to compare data that can be counted. Use the bar graph to answer the questions.

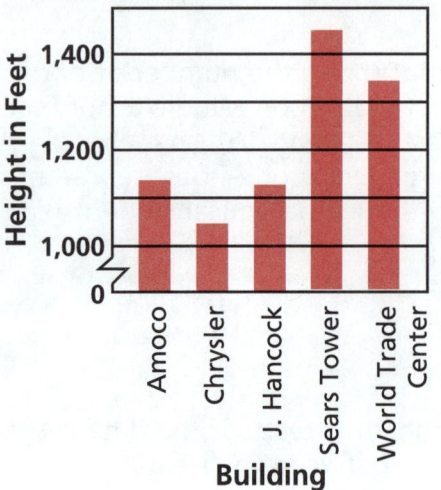

3. Each mark on the vertical axis represents how many feet? _____

4. Which two buildings are about the same height? _____

5. Is it true that the Sears Tower is about 4 times taller than the Chrysler Building? Explain.
_____

A line graph is more appropriate when you want to compare changes or trends over time. Use the line graph shown to answer the questions below.

6. Name the three warmest months.

_____

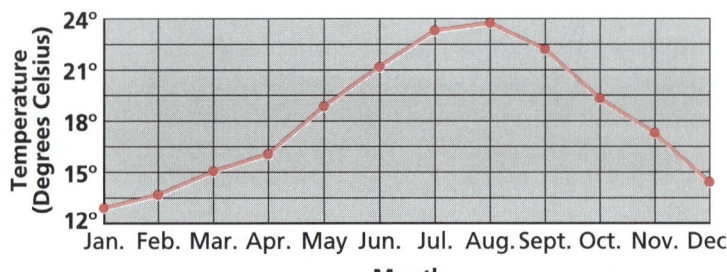

7. Find the temperature range.

_____

8. In what months is the average temperature below 18°C?

_____

Problem Solving Reasoning Which measure would best describe the data? Explain.

9. Price of a family home in the United States

_____

10. Number of raisins in a box

_____

11. Points scored per game during the season

_____

Test Prep ★ Mixed Review

12 Which is an equivalent fraction for $4\frac{1}{3}$?

A $\frac{8}{3}$ B $\frac{12}{3}$ C $\frac{13}{3}$ D $\frac{41}{3}$

13 $73,165 - 1,000 =$

F 63,165   H 73,065

G 72,165   J 73,155

Name _____

Solving Addition and Subtraction Equations

When you solve an equation, you use inverse operations to get the variable alone on one side of the equation. The questions below can be solved by writing an equation.

- What number can be added to **18** to get **47**?
- What number can be subtracted from **29** to get **12**?

Open equations contain a variable. To **solve an equation** means to find the value of the variable that makes the open equation true. Such a value is called a **solution.**

You can check your solution by substituting it into the original equation.

Solving an Addition Equation

Addition and subtraction are inverse operations. When you solve an equation, you use inverse operations to get the variable alone on one side of the equation. So to solve an addition equation, subtract the same number from both sides of the equation.

Solve. $n + 28 = 42$

1. Subtract **28** from each side. $n + 28 - 28 = 42 - 28$
2. Simplify each side. $n + 0 = 14$ $n = 14$

✓Check: $14 + 28 = 42$

Solve. $37 = m + 12$

1. Subtract **12** from each side. $37 - 12 = m + 12 - 12$
2. Simplify each side. $25 = m + 0$ $25 = m$

✓Check: $37 = 25 + 12$

Solve for the variable. Check your solution.

1. $y + 12 = 45$
y = 33
45 - 12 = 33

$h + 29 = 42$
h = 13
42 - 29 = 13

$c + 64 = 108$
c + 64 - 64 = 108 - 64
= 44
check 108 - 64 = 44

2. $74 = x + 25$
x = 49
74 - 25 = 49

$17 = b + 9$
b = 8
17 - 9 = 8

$67 = r + 65$
r = 2
67 - 65 = 2

3. $23 + h = 47$
h = 24
47 - 23 = 24

$83 = 75 + w$
w = 8
83 - 75 = 8

$72 = t + 15$
t = 57
72 - 15 = 57

4. $22 = a + 19$
a = 3
22 - 19 = 3

$61 = t + 48$
t = 13
61 - 48 = 13

$18 + k = 35$
k = 17
35 - 18 = 17

Unit 1 Lesson 4   9

Subtraction equations are solved in a similar way.

> **Solving a Subtraction Equation**
>
> To solve a subtraction equation, add the same number to both sides of the equation.

Solve.	$a - 15 = 22$	**Solve.**	$19 = t - 23$
1. Add **15** to both sides.	$a - 15 + 15 = 22 + 15$	1. Add **23** to both sides.	$19 + 23 = t - 23 + 23$
2. Simplify.	$a + 0 = 37$	2. Simplify.	$42 = t - 0$
	$a = 37$		$42 = t$
	✔ Check: $37 - 15 = 22$		✔ Check: $19 = 42 - 23$

When the variable is being subtracted, add the variable to both sides of the equation. Study these examples.

Solve.	$28 - x = 12$	**Solve.**	$15 = 42 - n$
1. Add x to both sides.	$28 - x + x = 12 + x$	1. Add n to both sides.	$15 + n = 42 - n + n$
2. Simplify.	$28 = 12 + x$	2. Simplify.	$15 + n = 42$
3. Subtract.	$28 - 12 = 12 - 12 + x$	3. Subtract.	$15 - 15 + n = 42 - 15$
4. Simplify.	$16 = x$	4. Simplify.	$n = 27$
	✔ Check: $28 - 16 = 12$		✔ Check: $15 = 42 - 27$

Solve. Remember to check your answer.

5. $k - 14 = 15$ $n - 9 = 17$ $d - 38 = 48$
   $k = 29$ $n = 26$ $d - 38 + 38 = 48 + 38$
   $29 - 14 = 15$ $26 - 9 = 17$

6. $44 = x - 18$ $11 = c - 18$ $31 = t - 8$
   $x = 62$ $c = 29$ $t = 39$
   $44 = 62 - 18$ $31 = 39 - 8$

7. $13 - y = 8$ $23 = 35 - z$ $12 = m - 11$
   $y = 5$ $z = 12$ $m = 23$
   $13 - 5 = 8$ $23 = 35 - 12$ $12 = 23 - 11$

8. $32 = a - 14$ $21 = t - 21$ $28 - d = 15$
   $a = 46$ $t = 42$ $d = 13$
   $32 = 46 - 14$ $21 = 42 - 21$ $28 - 13 = 15$

Name _____

Equations can be solved in **vertical format** instead of **horizontal format**.

Solve.

1. Subtract **24** from each side.
2. Simplify.

$$x + 24 = 73$$
$$-24 \quad -24$$
$$x = 49$$

✔Check: $49 + 24 = 73$

Solve.

1. Add **17** to each side.
2. Simplify.

$$x - 17 = 42$$
$$+17 \quad +17$$
$$x = 59$$

✔Check: $59 - 17 = 42$

Solve using the vertical format. Check your answer by substitution.

9. $m + 32 = 57$
   $-32 \quad -32$
   $m = 25$
   check: $25 + 32 = 57$ ✔

   $43 = y - 8$
   $+8 \quad +8$
   $y = 51$
   $43 + 8 = 51$

   $g - 17 = 18$
   $+17 \quad +17$
   $g = 30$
   $18 + 17 = 30$

10. $x + 72 = 81$
    $-72 \quad -72$
    $x = 9$
    $81 - 72 = 9$

    $54 = v - 17$
    $+17 \quad +17$
    $v = 71$
    $54 + 17 = 71$

    $48 = 22 + b$
    $-22 \quad -22$
    $b = 26$
    $48 - 22 = 26$

11. $n + 4 = 4$
    $-4 \quad -4$
    $n = 0$
    $4 - 4 = 0$

    $x - 23 = 23$
    $+23 \quad +23$
    $x = 46$
    $23 + 23 = 46$

    $t - 15 = 15$
    $+15 \quad +15$
    $t = 30$
    $15 + 15 = 30$

Problem Solving Reasoning — Decide whether Equation A or Equation B should be used to solve the problem. Then solve.

Equation A: $n + 15 = 32$ Equation B: $n - 15 = 32$

12. The difference between a number and **15** is **32**. What is the number? _____

13. The sum of a number and **15** is **32**. What is the number? _____

14. How are the equations in exercises **12** and **13** alike? How are they different?
_____

Test Prep ★ Mixed Review

15 What is the value of 4 in 9.546?

- A four
- B four tenths
- C four hundredths
- D four thousandths

16 What is the product of 9 and 0.5?

- F 0.045
- G 0.45
- H 4.5
- J 45

Unit 1 Lesson 4

Name _____

Solving Multiplication and Division Equations

You have solved addition and subtraction equations. Multiplication and division equations can be solved in a similar way.

> **Solving Multiplication and Division Equations**
>
> Multiplication and division are inverse operations.
> - To solve a **multiplication** equation, **divide** both sides of the equation by the same non-zero number.
> - To solve a **division** equation, **multiply** both sides of the equation by the same non-zero number.

Remember, to write the product of **5** and *x*, you can write **5x**.
Similarly, to write *x* divided by 5, you write $\frac{x}{5}$.

Solve. $7n = 42$
1. Divide each side by 7. $\frac{7n}{7} = \frac{42}{7}$
2. Simplify each side. $n = 6$

✓Check: $7(6) = 42$

Solve. $8 = \frac{d}{4}$
1. Multiply each side by 4. $4 \cdot 8 = 4 \cdot \frac{d}{4}$
2. Simplify each side. $32 = d$

✓Check: $8 = 32 \div 4$

Solve for the variable. Check your solution.

1. $5c = 85$ $12x = 156$ $84 = 3t$

2. $\frac{w}{7} = 12$ $\frac{p}{3} = 9$ $8 = \frac{m}{4}$ M=32
    W=84   P=27

3. $8h = 96$ $35r = 245$ $88a = 792$
    12   7   9

4. $\frac{a}{20} = 40$ $\frac{f}{56} = 4$ $3 = \frac{x}{13}$
    A=800   F=224   x=39

Name _____

Use the Write an Equation strategy or any other strategy you have learned to solve.

1. You have **5** hours to drive from City A to City B, a distance of **360** miles. If the speed limit is **65** miles per hour, will you be able to make it without breaking the law? Explain.

   Think: Are you finding a missing factor or a product? Which equation could you use to find the time t?

   $65t = 360$ or $t = 65 \cdot 360$

   _____

   _____

2. You have a collection of **22** key chains. Your aunt gives you her collection of key chains, so now you have **51**. How many key chains did your aunt give you?

   Think: Are you finding a missing addend or a sum? Which equation could you use to find the number of key chains n?

   $22 + 51 = n$ or $22 + n = 51$

   _____

   _____

3. You and **3** of your friends have lunch at the Pizza Palace. The bill, including tax and tip, is **$24**. If you share the cost equally, what will each of you pay?

   _____

4. The Pizza Palace offers **3** types of crust, **3** sizes of pizza, and **2** different cheese toppings. How many different cheese pizzas are possible?

   _____

5. How could you arrange **10** coins so that you have **5** rows with **4** coins in each row? Draw your solution.

6. How many circles will be needed for

   figure 4? _____ for figure 5? _____

   figure 1

   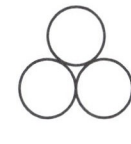
   figure 2

   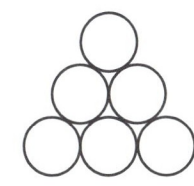
   figure 3

7. You are very excited that it will be your birthday in **24** days. Today is Tuesday. What day of the week is your birthday on?

   _____

8. Every member of the seventh grade class is allowed to bring a guest from another school to the dance. Every class member attends the dance and exactly half the students bring a guest. There are **108** students at the dance. How many are members of the seventh grade class?

   _____

Unit 1 Lesson 6   15

Name _____

Properties

In algebra and other math classes, you will find it helpful to use the number properties for addition and multiplication. Study the properties stated below.

	Arithmetic	Algebra
Commutative Property of Addition: The order of the addends does not change the sum.	$8 + 12 = 12 + 8$	$a + b = b + a$
Commutative Property of Multiplication: The order of the factors does not change the product.	$8 \cdot 12 = 12 \cdot 8$	$a \cdot b = b \cdot a$
Associative Property of Addition: The grouping of the addends does not change the sum.	$(4 + 5) + 7 = 4 + (5 + 7)$	$(a + b) + c = a + (b + c)$
Associative Property of Multiplication: The grouping of the factors does not change the product.	$(4 \cdot 5) \cdot 7 = 4 \cdot (5 \cdot 7)$	$(a \cdot b) \cdot c = a \cdot (b \cdot c)$

Computations can be made simpler by combining the properties with mental-math strategies.

Simplify: **18 + (94 + 12)**

Look for combinations of multiples of **10** or **100**.

	$18 + (94 + 12)$
1. Use the commutative property.	$18 + (12 + 94)$
2. Use the associative property.	$(18 + 12) + 94$
3. Simplify.	$30 + 94$
	124

Simplify: **25 · (7 · 4)**

Look for multiples of **10** or **100**.

	$25 \cdot (7 \cdot 4)$
1. Use the commutative property.	$25 \cdot (4 \cdot 7)$
2. Use the associative property.	$(25 \cdot 4) \cdot 7$
3. Simplify.	$100 \cdot 7$
	700

Name the property.

1. $g + t = t + g$ __CP of A__
2. $5 \cdot (6 \cdot 9) = (5 \cdot 6) \cdot 9$ __AP of M__
3. $(7 + 3) + 4 = (3 + 7) + 4$ __CP of A__

$3 + (5 + 4) = 3 + (4 + 5)$ __CP of A__
$7 \cdot 15 = 15 \cdot 7$ __CP of M__
$(x + y) + z = x + (y + z)$ __AP of A__

Use the properties to complete the equation.

4. $8 + 22 = \underline{22} + 8$
5. $(7 \cdot 15) \cdot 12 = 7 \cdot (\underline{15} \cdot 12)$
6. $\underline{} + 17 = 17 + 25$
7. $(\underline{38} + 62) + 29 = (62 + 38) + 29$

$3 \cdot \underline{7} = 7 \cdot 3$
$(m + \underline{r}) + t = m + (r + t)$
$(\underline{} \cdot 15) \cdot M = 4 \cdot (15 \cdot M)$
$k \cdot 12 = 12 \cdot \underline{k}$

16 Unit 1 Lesson 7

Name _____

Simplify by adding or subtracting like terms.

20. $4(6 + 2x)$ $2(8k - 4)$ $3(3a + 7)$

_____   _____   _____

21. $5b + 7b + 9$ $3x + 2y + 9x$ $6 - t + 9 + 4t$

_____   _____   _____

22. $2m + 6(3m + n)$ $4(2a + 5c) - 7c$ $5(x + 4y) + 2(2x + y)$

_____   _____   _____

Problem Solving Reasoning — Show how to use the distributive property to solve.

23. A store sold **64** video tapes on Thursday and **36** on Friday. Each video tape costs **$18**. What was the total video tape sales for both days?

_____

24. Cia worked **47** hours one week and **53** hours the next week. She earns **$9.00** an hour. How much did she earn in the two weeks?

_____

25. Joey, Henry, and Lena went to the bookstore. They each paid **$2** for the bus, **$7** for one book, and **$5** for a second book. How much did they spend altogether?

_____

26. Gina runs **8** laps at each practice session. She practiced **4** times last week and **5** times this week. How many laps has she run?

_____

Test Prep ★ Mixed Review

27 What is the value of the expression $2x - 2$ when $x = 3$?

A 8
B 4
C 3
D 1

28 If $\frac{x}{6} = 12$, $x = ?$

F 2
G 6
H 18
J 72

Unit 1 Lesson 8   21

Name _____ **Expressions with Exponents**

Exponents may be used when multiplying a number or a variable by itself.

An **exponent** tells how many times to use the **base** as a **factor**. The entire expression is called a **power**.

$4 \cdot 4 \cdot 4 = 4^3$ — exponent, power, factors, base

$x \cdot x = x^2$

Read as "4 cubed" or "4 to the third power"

Read as "x squared"

You can use exponents in evaluating and simplifying expressions.

Simplify 5^3.

$5^3 \rightarrow 5 \cdot 5 \cdot 5 = 125$

Simplify $3 \cdot 3 \cdot a \cdot a \cdot a \cdot b$ by using exponents.

$3 \cdot 3 \cdot a \cdot a \cdot a \cdot b \rightarrow 3^2 a^3 b = 9a^3 b$

Evaluate $2m^2$ for $m = 3$.

$2m^2 = 2 \cdot m \cdot m$
$= 2 \cdot 3 \cdot 3$
$= 18$

Simplify using exponents.

1. $6 \cdot 6 \cdot 6 \cdot 6$ _____ $4 \cdot 4$ _____ $7 \cdot 7 \cdot 7$ _____

2. $a \cdot a$ _____ $x \cdot x \cdot x \cdot y$ _____ $t \cdot t \cdot r \cdot r$ _____

3. $3 \cdot 3 \cdot x \cdot y \cdot y \cdot y$ _____ $9 \cdot m \cdot m \cdot n \cdot n \cdot n$ _____ $2 \cdot k \cdot k \cdot k \cdot k$ _____

4. $8 \cdot w \cdot 8 \cdot w \cdot 8 \cdot g$ _____ $x \cdot y \cdot x \cdot y \cdot x \cdot x \cdot y$ _____ $a \cdot b \cdot a \cdot b \cdot c \cdot a$ _____

Evaluate.

5. 3 squared _____ 8^2 _____   5 cubed _____

6. 10^1 _____   4 to the third power _____   2 to the fifth power _____

7. 1^{10} _____   7 to the second power _____ 10^4 _____

Evaluate for $a = 3$, $b = 7$, $x = 2$.

8. a^2 _____ x^3 _____ $2b^2$ _____

9. $a^2 \cdot x^3$ _____ $b \cdot x^4$ _____ $5x^3$ _____

22   Unit 1 Lesson 9

Name _____

You can now include powers in the rules for the Order of Operations.

> **Order of Operations**
> 1. Perform all operations inside grouping symbols first.
> 2. **Evaluate powers.**
> 3. Multiply and divide from left to right.
> 4. Add and subtract from left to right.

Evaluate: $3 + 5^2$

$3 + 5^2 = 3 + 25$
$ = 28$

Evaluate: $(9 - 7)^3 + 12$

$(9 - 7)^3 + 12 = 2^3 + 12$
$ = 8 + 12$
$ = 20$

Evaluate: $4(5^2 - 14)$

$4(5^2 - 14) = 4(25 - 14)$
$ = 4(11)$
$ = 44$

Evaluate for $a = 2$, $m = 3$, and $x = 5$.

10. $(1 + m)^2 =$ _____ $5 + a^2 - 8 =$ _____ $(x^2 + 1) \div 13 =$ _____

11. $4m - 2a =$ _____ $3(a + x) =$ _____ $4a^2 - 5 =$ _____

12. $7(4 - a) + 4x =$ _____ $10a - 6m =$ _____ $m^3 - x^2 =$ _____

13. $24 - (a + m + x) =$ _____ $4m^2 \div (2a) =$ _____ $x - m - a + 2 =$ _____

Problem Solving Reasoning — Solve.

14. The eighth power of a number divided by the fifth power of that number is **27**. What is the number? Hint: Write **27** as a power.

_____

15. A number squared and then multiplied by its cube is **32**. What is the number?

_____

16. Look at exercises **14** and **15**. Do you see a shortcut for finding products and quotients of expressions with like bases? Try it with other bases. Does it still work?

_____

Test Prep ★ Mixed Review

17 What is the median of the data 79, 64, 58, 60, 71?

A 66.4   C 58
B 64   D 21

18 What is the range of the data 79, 64, 58, 60, 71?

F 8   H 19
G 15   J 21

Using Geometric Formulas

The distance around a polygon is called its **perimeter**. The distance around a circle is called the **circumference**. The table shows the **formulas**, or general rules, you can use to find the perimeter of some common geometric figures and the circumference of a circle.

Figure	Formula	Example
Rectangle w = width l = length	$P = 2l + 2w$	5 in., 2 in. $P = 2l + 2w$ $= 2(5) + 2(2)$ $= 10 + 4$ $= 14$ in.
Triangle s = side	$P = s_1 + s_2 + s_3$	7 cm, 3 cm, 6 cm $P = s_1 + s_2 + s_3$ $= 3 + 7 + 6$ $= 16$ cm
Circle d = diameter r = radius $d = 2r$	$C = \pi d$ or $2\pi r$ Read π as pi. $\pi \approx 3.14$ or $\frac{22}{7}$ $\approx$ is approximately equal to	5 cm $C = 2\pi r$ $\approx 2(3.14)(5)$ ≈ 31.4 cm

---

Find the perimeter or circumference. Use 3.14 for π. The dashed marks in the figures show the sides that are equal in length, or congruent to each other.

1. 1 ft, 2 ft P = _____   5 mm P = _____   12 cm, 2 cm P = _____

2. 2 in., 8 in. P = _____   3", 4", 5" P = _____   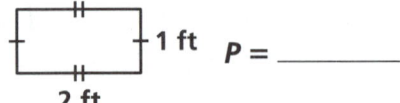 7 cm P = _____

3. 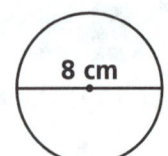 8 cm C ≈ _____   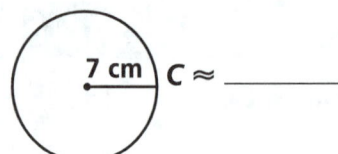 7 cm C ≈ _____   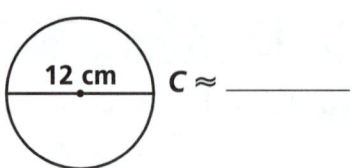 12 cm C ≈ _____

Name _____

The measure of how much surface is covered by a figure is its **area**. Some common units for area are the square inch (in.^{2}) and the square centimeter (cm^2). The table shows the formulas you can use to find the area of some common geometric figures.

Figure	Formula	Example
Rectangle w = width l = length	$A = lw$	8 in. × 4 in. $A = lw$ $= 8 \cdot 4$ $= 32$ in.^{2}
Triangle b = base h = height	$A = \frac{1}{2}bh$ or $\frac{bh}{2}$	8 in., 7 in. $A = \frac{bh}{2}$ $= \frac{7 \cdot 8}{2}$ or 28 in.^{2}
Circle d = diameter r = radius $\pi \approx 3.14$ or $\frac{22}{7}$ $d = 2r$	$A = \pi r^2$	4 cm $A = \pi r^2$ $\approx (3.14)(4)(4)$ ≈ 50.24 cm^2

Find the area of the figure. Use 3.14 for π.

4. 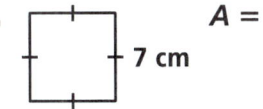 7 cm $A =$ _____

   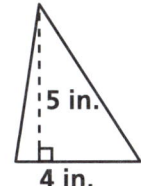 5 in., 4 in. $A =$ _____

   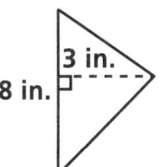 3 in., 8 in. $A =$ _____

5. 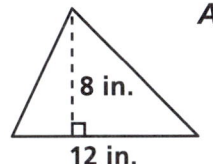 8 in., 12 in. $A =$ _____

   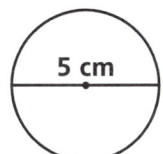 5 cm $A \approx$ _____

   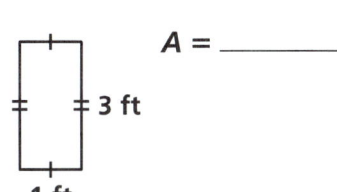 3 ft, 1 ft $A =$ _____

6. 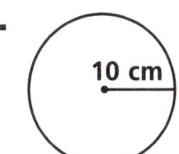 10 cm $A \approx$ _____

   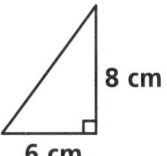 8 cm, 6 cm $A =$ _____

   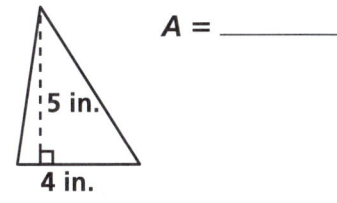 5 in., 4 in. $A =$ _____

7. 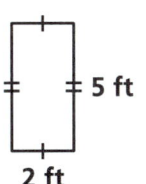 5 ft, 2 ft $A =$ _____

   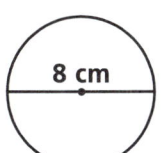 8 cm $A \approx$ _____

   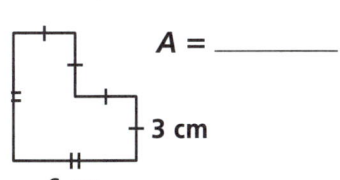 3 cm, 6 cm $A =$ _____

Unit 1 Lesson 10   25

Formulas are like any other equation in algebra. You can use them to find missing measures when the area or perimeter of a figure is known.

Find the length of the side of a square whose perimeter is 28 cm.

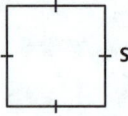

1. Write the formula.　　$P = 4s$
2. Substitute for P.　　$28 = 4s$
3. Solve the equation.　　$\dfrac{28}{4} = \dfrac{4}{4}s$
　　　　　　　　　　　$7 = s$

The length of a side is **7** cm.

Two sides of a triangle are **12** cm and **19** cm. Find the length of the third side if its perimeter is **42** cm.

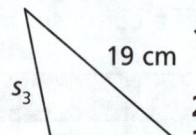

1. Write the formula.　　$P = s_1 + s_2 + s_3$
2. Substitute.　　$42 = 12 + 19 + s_3$
　　　　　　　　$42 = 31 + s_3$
3. Solve.　　$11 = s_3$

The missing side is **11** cm.

Write an equation to solve for the missing measure.

8. 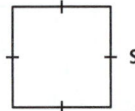　　$P = 96$ cm

　　$s = $ _____

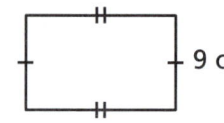

　　x

　　$P = 50$ cm

　　$s = $ _____

9. 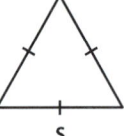　　$P = 48$ ft

　　$s = $ _____

　　9 cm

　　l

　　$A = 126$ in.^{2}

　　$l = $ _____

Draw a diagram to illustrate the figure. Then solve and check.

10. A rectangle with length **11** in. and width **8** in. has a square with side of **3** in. shaded in one corner. What is the area of the unshaded part of the rectangle?

_____

11. A rectangle has dimensions **5** cm by **8** cm. Another rectangle has dimensions that are twice as long. Compare the perimeters of both rectangles. Compare the areas of both rectangles. What do you observe?

_____

✓ Quick Check

Use the distributive property to evaluate.　　Work Space.

12. $4(t + 3)$ for $t = 7$ _____　　13. $z \cdot 3 - z \cdot 2$ for $z = 6$ _____

Write using exponents.

14. 7 to the fourth power _____　　15. $4 \cdot 4 \cdot x \cdot x \cdot x \cdot x \cdot y \cdot y$ _____

Find the perimeter or circumference and the area. Use 3.14 for π.

16. 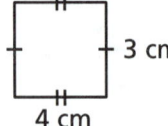　　17. 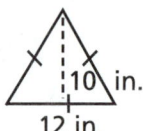　　18.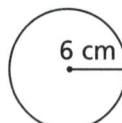

_____　　_____　　_____

Name _____

Problem Solving Application: Use a Formula

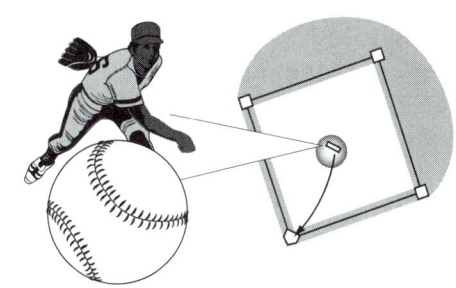

The announcer said that when the ball left the pitcher's hand it was traveling at **90** miles per hour. You can use the formula below to determine how much time the batter had to swing the bat.

- The distance (*d*) that the ball travels is equal to the rate (*r*) multiplied by the time (*t*).

    Formula: $d = rt$

- It is a little over 60 feet from the pitcher's mound to home plate.

Notice that there are different units of measure in the statement of this problem: miles and feet.

Tips to Remember:

| 1. Understand | 2. Decide | 3. Solve | 4. Look back |

- Ask yourself whether you have solved a problem like this before. Think about the relationships between the units of measure. What facts do you know that will help you solve the problem?
- Think about the strategies you have learned and use them to help you solve a problem.

Solve.

1. How many feet per hour is the ball traveling? (Hint: Use unit rates.)

Think: There are **5,280** feet in 1 mile, so **90** miles equals how many feet?

_____

_____

Answer _____

2. Use your answer from exercise **1**. How many feet per second is this?

Think: There are **3,600** seconds in 1 hour, so use this fact to rewrite your answer to exercise **1**.

_____

_____

Answer _____

3. Use the formula $t = \dfrac{d}{r}$ to decide if the batter has more or less than **1** second to swing the bat. Explain your answer.

_____

_____

Unit 1 Lesson 11

**Remember that a formula is another name for an equation.
Write a formula or use any other strategy to solve.**

4. Your school's football team scored **26** points last weekend. Use the information below to determine how many touchdowns were scored.

6-point touchdowns	?
1-point conversions	2
3-point field goals	2

   _____

   _____

5. Dominique made **11** two-point baskets, **2** three-point baskets, and **5** one-point foul shots. Use the information to determine how many points Dominique scored.

   _____

   _____

6. A car travels **2** hours at **65** miles per hour, **1** hour at **60** miles per hour, and **1** hour at **45** miles per hour. What is the total mileage?

   _____

   _____

7. The distance between two cities is **1,800** miles. If you drive at a constant **65** miles per hour, could you complete the trip in one day? Explain.

   _____

   _____

8. A bag of fertilizer covers **60** square feet. How many bags would be needed to cover a lawn that measures **25** feet by **20** feet? Remember — you can't buy a portion of a bag!

   _____

   _____

9. A rule of thumb for changing a Celsius temperature to a Fahrenheit temperature is "double the Celsius temperature and add **30°**." The radio announced it would be **26°C** today. Is this beach weather? Explain.

   _____

   _____

Extend Your Thinking

10. Consider the formula $d = rt$.
    distance rate time

    Use what you know about inverse operations and equations to write a formula to find a missing rate (r).

    _____

11. Look back at exercise **9**. Explain how to use the formula you wrote in exercise **9** to find an equivalent formula for changing a Fahrenheit temperature to a Celsius temperature.

    _____

Unit 1 Lesson 11

UNIT 2 • TABLE OF CONTENTS

Number Theory, Decimals, and Fractions

Lesson	Page
1 Comparing and Ordering Decimals	33
2 Rounding and Estimating Decimals	35
3 Adding and Subtracting Decimals	37
4 Multiplying Decimals and Powers of Ten	39
5 Dividing Decimals and Powers of Ten	42
6 Prime Factorization, Greatest Common Factor, and Least Common Multiple	45
7 Equivalent Fractions	47
8 Equivalent Fractions and Decimals	49
9 Comparing and Ordering Fractions	51
10 Adding Fractions and Mixed Numbers	53
11 Subtracting Fractions and Mixed Numbers	55
12 **Problem Solving Application:** Use a Diagram	57
13 Multiplying Fractions and Mixed Numbers	59
14 Dividing Fractions and Mixed Numbers	62
15 **Problem Solving Strategy:** Draw a Diagram	65
16 **Algebra •** Expressions with Fractions and Decimals	67
17 **Algebra •** Solving Equations with Fractions and Decimals	69
• Unit 2 Review	71
• Cumulative Review ★ Test Prep	72

Dear Family,

During the next few weeks, our math class will be learning and practicing addition, subtraction, multiplication, and division of decimals and fractions. You can expect to see homework that provides practice with these skills. Here is a sample you may want to keep handy to give help if needed.

We will be using this vocabulary:

numerator the top number in a fraction; names the number of parts being considered

denominator the bottom number in a fraction; names the number of equal parts in the whole

common denominator denominators of two or more fractions that are the same

common factor a number that divides two or more numbers evenly

simplest form a fraction whose numerator and denominator have only **1** as a common factor or a mixed number whose fraction is in simplest form

algebraic expression a group of numbers, variables, and addition, subtraction, multiplication, or division symbols

Multiplication of Mixed Numbers

To find the product $4\frac{2}{3} \times 1\frac{2}{7}$, you need to write each mixed number as a fraction. One way to do this is shown below.

$$4\frac{2}{3} = \frac{3 \times 4 + 2}{3} \rightarrow \frac{14}{3} \qquad 1\frac{2}{7} = \frac{7 \times 1 + 2}{7} \rightarrow \frac{9}{7}$$

Now it is possible to multiply. Before multiplying you can try to simplify by dividing a numerator and a denominator by a common factor.

$$\frac{14}{3} \times \frac{9}{7} = \frac{\overset{2}{\cancel{14}} \cdot \overset{3}{\cancel{9}}}{\underset{1}{\cancel{3}} \cdot \underset{1}{\cancel{7}}} \qquad \frac{2 \cdot 3}{1 \cdot 1} = \frac{6}{1} \rightarrow 6$$

During this unit, students will need to continue practicing all operations with both decimals and fractions.

Sincerely,

Name _____

Prime Factorization, Greatest Common Factor, and Least Common Multiple

A **prime number** is a whole number with exactly two factors, itself and **1**. For example, **2, 3, 5, 7, 11**, and **13** are prime numbers.

Composite numbers have more than two factors.

To write the **prime factorization** of a number means to write the number as the product of prime numbers.

Write the prime factorization of **36**.

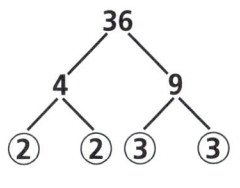
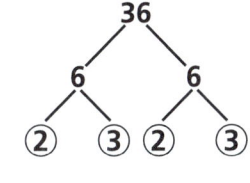

$36 = 2^2 \cdot 3^2$

Both **tree diagrams** give the same prime factorization. The circled numbers are all prime.

Write the prime factorization of **56**.

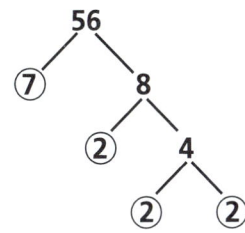

$56 = 2^3 \cdot 7$

Write the prime factorization of the number.

1. 16 = _____   10 = _____   24 = _____

2. 54 = _____   45 = _____   62 = _____

3. 50 = _____   18 = _____   70 = _____

4. 60 = _____   100 = _____   144 = _____

Write the product of the prime factorization.

5. $2^3 \cdot 3 =$ _____ $3^2 \cdot 7 =$ _____ $2 \cdot 3 \cdot 7 =$ _____

6. $2 \cdot 3^2 \cdot 5 =$ _____ $3^2 \cdot 11 =$ _____ $2^2 \cdot 5^2 \cdot 7 =$ _____

Unit 2 Lesson 6   45

The **greatest common factor (GCF)** of two numbers is the greatest number that is a factor of both numbers.

Find the greatest common factor of **24** and **36**.

Method 1: List each number's factors.

24: **1, 2, 3, 4, 6,** 8, **12,** 24

36: **1, 2, 3, 4, 6,** 9, **12,** 18, 36

The common factors are **1, 2, 3, 4, 6,** and **12**. The *greatest* of these factors is **12**.

Method 2: Find the product of all **common** prime factors.

$24 = 2 \cdot 2 \cdot 2 \cdot 3$ $\quad$ $36 = 2 \cdot 2 \cdot 3 \cdot 3$

GCF is $2 \cdot 2 \cdot 3 = 2^2 \cdot 3$, or **12**.

The **least common multiple (LCM)** of two numbers is the least number that is a multiple of both numbers.

Find the least common multiple of **20** and **24**.

Method 1: List each number's multiples.

20: 20, 40, 60, 80, 100, **120**, 140, . . .

24: 24, 48, 72, 96, **120**, 144, . . .

The least *common* multiple is **120**.

Method 2: Multiply the greatest power of each prime number that appears in either.

$20 = 2 \cdot 2 \cdot 5$ $\quad$ $24 = 2 \cdot 2 \cdot 2 \cdot 3$

LCM is $2 \cdot 2 \cdot 5 \cdot 2 \cdot 3 = 2^3 \cdot 3 \cdot 5$, or **120**.

Find the greatest common factor.

7. 16 and 40 _____   24 and 30 _____   18 and 24 _____   36 and 48 _____

8. 12 and 64 _____   24 and 52 _____   10 and 16 _____   44 and 66 _____

9. 42 and 63 _____   20 and 45 _____   28 and 34 _____   36 and 84 _____

Find the least common multiple.

10. 8 and 12 _____   12 and 16 _____   6 and 8 _____   15 and 20 _____

11. 9 and 12 _____   15 and 35 _____   3 and 15 _____   17 and 51 _____

12. 6 and 10 _____   12 and 30 _____   9 and 15 _____   24 and 36 _____

 Quick Check

Solve.   Work Space.

13. $7.2 \times 0.09 =$ _____   **14.** $0.021 \times 0.63 =$ _____

15. $0.3 \overline{)9.774}$ **16.** $1.2 \overline{)0.0054}$ **17.** $0.15 \overline{)85.5}$

18. Write the first five multiples of 16. _____

19. Write the prime factorization of 72. _____

20. What is the GCF of 12 and 16? _____

21. What is the LCM of 12 and 16? _____

Name _____

Equivalent Fractions

Fractions that represent the same number are **equivalent fractions**. You can multiply the numerator and the denominator of a fraction by the same non-zero number to find an equivalent fraction. This is because it is the same as multiplying by **1**.

Both of these models show $\frac{2}{3}$.

The ratio of shaded parts to total parts is equivalent.

$\frac{2}{3}$ is equivalent to $\frac{8}{12}$ because $\frac{2}{3} \rightarrow \frac{2 \cdot 4}{3 \cdot 4} = \frac{8}{12}$

$\frac{2}{3}$ is equivalent to many fractions.

$\frac{2}{3} \rightarrow \frac{2 \cdot 2}{3 \cdot 2} = \frac{4}{6}$, $\quad \frac{2}{3} \rightarrow \frac{2 \cdot 3}{3 \cdot 3} = \frac{6}{9}$, $\quad \frac{2}{3} \rightarrow \frac{2 \cdot 7}{3 \cdot 7} = \frac{14}{21}$

Name the fraction represented by the model. Then name an equivalent fraction.

1.

2.

Find the missing numerator.

3. $\frac{4}{5} = \frac{}{15}$ 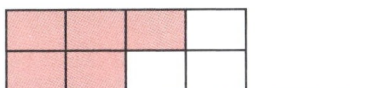 $\frac{5}{6} = \frac{}{42}$  $\frac{2}{3} = \frac{}{51}$ 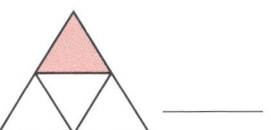 $\frac{11}{12} = \frac{}{60}$

4. $\frac{6}{7} = \frac{}{14}$ $\quad \frac{3}{4} = \frac{}{40}$ $\quad \frac{1}{5} = \frac{}{50}$ $\quad \frac{4}{15} = \frac{}{45}$

5. $\frac{1}{3} = \frac{}{21}$ $\quad \frac{3}{5} = \frac{}{45}$ $\quad \frac{7}{8} = \frac{}{32}$ $\quad \frac{2}{17} = \frac{}{51}$

6. $\frac{7}{8} = \frac{}{64}$ 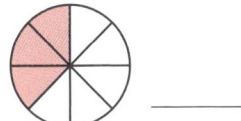 $\frac{7}{10} = \frac{}{20}$ 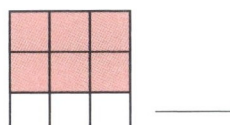 $\frac{4}{6} = \frac{}{72}$ 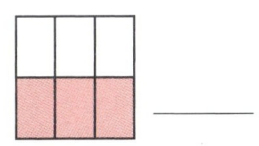 $\frac{7}{12} = \frac{}{48}$

Name five equivalent fractions for the fraction.

7. $\frac{3}{5}$ _____ $\frac{4}{9}$ _____

8. $\frac{1}{3}$ _____ $\frac{5}{6}$ _____

9. $\frac{2}{7}$ _____ $\frac{2}{3}$ _____

Unit 2 Lesson 7   **47**

The fractions $\frac{1}{2}$ and $\frac{2}{4}$ are equivalent. Of these two, $\frac{1}{2}$ is said to be in **simplest form**. A fraction is in simplest form when the greatest common factor of the numerator and denominator is **1**.

To write a fraction in simplest form, divide the numerator and denominator by their greatest common factor.

$\frac{8}{20} \rightarrow \frac{8 \div 4}{20 \div 4} = \frac{2}{5}$ *4 is the GCF of 8 and 20.*

$\frac{12}{36} \rightarrow \frac{12 \div 12}{36 \div 12} = \frac{1}{3}$ *12 is the GCF of 12 and 36.*

Write the fraction in simplest form.

10. $\frac{9}{12} =$ _____ $\frac{9}{18} =$ _____ $\frac{12}{14} =$ _____ $\frac{18}{36} =$ _____

11. $\frac{6}{9} =$ _____ $\frac{15}{24} =$ _____ $\frac{4}{20} =$ _____ $\frac{15}{25} =$ _____

12. $\frac{18}{24} =$ _____ $\frac{12}{30} =$ _____ $\frac{14}{20} =$ _____ $\frac{3}{51} =$ _____

13. $\frac{98}{100} =$ _____ $\frac{14}{35} =$ _____ $\frac{75}{135} =$ _____ $\frac{16}{32} =$ _____

Problem Solving Reasoning   Write the next three fractions in the pattern.

14. $\frac{2}{3} \; \frac{4}{6} \; \frac{6}{9}$ _____ $\frac{1}{4} \; \frac{2}{8} \; \frac{3}{12}$ _____ $\frac{3}{5} \; \frac{6}{10} \; \frac{9}{15}$ _____

15. $\frac{3}{4} \; \frac{6}{8} \; \frac{12}{16}$ _____ $\frac{5}{6} \; \frac{10}{12} \; \frac{20}{24}$ _____ $\frac{3}{7} \; \frac{6}{14} \; \frac{12}{28}$ _____

Test Prep ★ Mixed Review

16 $35.91 \div 0.19 =$

A 189

B 1.89

C 0.189

D 0.0189

17 What is the greatest common factor of 54 and 180?

F 2

G 6

H 9

J 18

48   Unit 2 Lesson 7

Name _____

Equivalent Fractions and Decimals

You can write one half as the fraction $\frac{1}{2}$ or as the decimal 0.5. They are equivalent. You can find equivalent fractions and decimals using the steps below.

Writing Fractions as Decimals
To write a fraction as a decimal, divide.

$$\frac{5}{12} \rightarrow 12\overline{)5.0000} \quad \begin{array}{r} 0.4166 \\ -48 \\ \hline 20 \\ -12 \\ \hline 80 \\ -72 \\ \hline 80 \end{array}$$

Remainder starts to repeat.

The decimal 0.41666 . . . is a **repeating** decimal. The three dots mean the pattern keeps repeating. You may write it $0.41\overline{6}$.

Other Example

$$\frac{3}{4} \rightarrow 4\overline{)3.00} \quad \begin{array}{r} 0.75 \\ -28 \\ \hline 20 \\ -20 \\ \hline 0 \end{array}$$

Remainder is 0.

The decimal 0.75 is a **terminating** decimal.

Writing Decimals as Fractions
To write a decimal as a fraction, use what you know about place value.

0.7 = seven tenths or $\frac{7}{10}$

Remember to simplify fractions when you can.

Other Examples

0.48 = 48 hundredths or $\frac{48}{100}$

0.325 = 325 thousandths or $\frac{325}{1,000}$

2.4 = 2 ones and 4 tenths or $2\frac{4}{10}$

Write the fraction as a decimal. Use bar notation to write repeating decimals.

1. $\frac{4}{5} = $ _____ $\frac{2}{3} = $ _____ $\frac{3}{8} = $ _____ $\frac{4}{9} = $ _____

2. $\frac{7}{10} = 0.7$ $2\frac{4}{8} = 2.5$ $\frac{1}{12} = 0.84$ $\frac{7}{20} = 0.3$

3. $\frac{4}{11} = 0.36$ $1\frac{1}{15} = 1.06$ $\frac{7}{30} = 0.23$ $2\frac{5}{18} = 2.27$

Write the decimal as a fraction or mixed number in simplest form.

4. 0.4 = $\frac{4}{10} = \frac{2}{5}$ 0.05 = $\frac{5}{100} = \frac{1}{20}$ 0.125 = $\frac{125}{1000} = \frac{1}{8}$ 0.3 = $\frac{3}{10}$

5. 0.06 = $\frac{6}{100} = \frac{3}{50}$ 1.29 = $1\frac{29}{100}$ 0.086 = $\frac{86}{1000} = \frac{43}{500}$ 0.72 = $\frac{72}{100} = \frac{36}{50} = \frac{18}{25}$

6. 1.15 = $1\frac{15}{100}$ 2.5 = $2\frac{5}{10} = \frac{5}{2}$ 1.85 = $1\frac{85}{100}$ 3.1 = $3\frac{1}{10}$

Unit 2 Lesson 8   49

Compare. Write <, >, or = to make a true sentence.

7. $\frac{6}{11}$ < $0.\overline{5}$ $\frac{5}{8}$ = 0.625 $\frac{11}{16}$ < 0.7 $\frac{8}{9}$ > 0.8

8. $\frac{7}{8}$ > 0.7 $\frac{2}{15}$ < $0.1\overline{3}$ $\frac{4}{5}$ > 0.4 $\frac{40}{100}$ < 0.4

Problem Solving / Reasoning — Write each fraction as a decimal. Use a bar to write the repeating decimals. Describe the patterns you observe.

9. $\frac{1}{9}$ $\frac{2}{9}$ $\frac{3}{9}$ $\frac{4}{9}$ $\frac{5}{9}$

.19, .29, .39, .49, .59

it added ten

10. $\frac{1}{11}$ $\frac{2}{11}$ $\frac{3}{11}$ $\frac{4}{11}$ $\frac{5}{11}$

.11, .14, .311, .411, .511

Added a hundred

11. $\frac{1}{3}$ $\frac{4}{3}$ $\frac{7}{3}$ $\frac{10}{3}$ $\frac{13}{3}$

12. $\frac{1}{6}$ $\frac{2}{6}$ $\frac{3}{6}$ $\frac{4}{6}$ $\frac{5}{6}$

13. How is the pattern with multiples of $\frac{1}{6}$ different from the other three patterns?

Test Prep ★ Mixed Review

14. What number is missing? $\frac{12}{15} = \frac{4}{x}$

A 3
B 5
C 12
D 15

15. What is the least common multiple of 24 and 30?

F 6
G 54
H 120
J 240

50 Unit 2 Lesson 8

Name _____

Problem Solving Application: Use a Diagram

You can use a diagram that represents information visually. In this lesson, diagrams are used to help solve problems.

Tips to Remember:

1. Understand   2. Decide   3. Solve   4. Look back

- Ask yourself if you have solved a problem like this before.
- Think about the relationships shown in the diagram. What information is displayed or represented by the diagram?
- Think about the strategies you have learned. Use them to help you solve a problem.

Assume that four friends live on the same straight east-west street. The following information is also known.

- Kareem lives **3.7** km from Amal.
- Anita lives between Amal and Kareem, and **1.2** km from Kareem.
- Barb lives closest to Amal, and **4.9** km from Anita.

Where Do They Live?

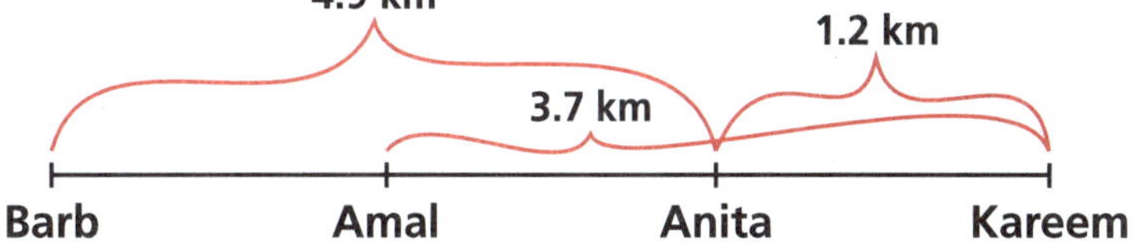

4.9 km | 3.7 km | 1.2 km

Barb — Amal — Anita — Kareem

Think: How does the diagram show each piece of information?

Solve. Use the diagram above.

1. Which two friends live the closest to one another? Explain your reasoning.

   Think: Do you have enough information to decide how far each friend lives from the other?

   _____

   _____

   Answer _____

2. Where does Emily live if she is the same distance to Barb as she is to Kareem? How far does she live from each?

   Think: Is there only one place that Emily could live? How can you find her distance to Kareem?

   _____

   _____

   Answer _____

Unit 2 Lesson 12   **57**

Solve.

3. A student survey showed that science was more popular than language arts, but not as popular as math. Social studies was the least favorite subject. Draw a diagram to show the subjects from least to most favorite.

4. Among the 22 girls in seventh grade, 6 play only basketball, 8 play only softball, and 5 play neither sport. Draw a diagram to show how many girls play both.

5. Joe goes a total of 2 blocks east and 2 blocks north to get from his house to the park. How many different routes can Joe take that are 4 blocks long? One route is shown.

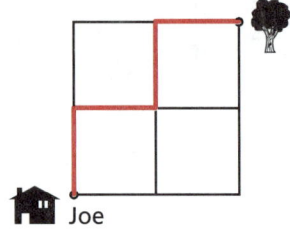

_____

6. Erin lives one block north of the park. How many different routes that are 5 blocks long can Carlos take to get to Erin's house? One route is shown.

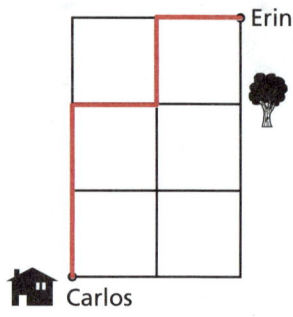

_____

7. A unit is divided in half. Then the half is divided in half. Suppose you continue to divide the smallest part in half. What would the next three fractional parts be called?

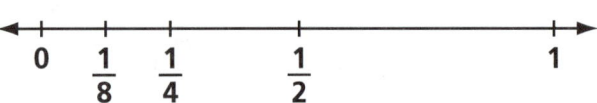

8. A unit is divided in thirds. Then one third is divided in thirds. Suppose you continue to divide the smallest part in thirds. What would the next three fractional parts be called?

Extend Your Thinking

$$\frac{1}{5} \times \frac{1}{5} \rightarrow \left(\frac{1}{5}\right)^2 = \frac{1}{25}$$

9. Look at the fractions you listed in problem 7. How could you write the fractions using exponents in the denominator? Describe the pattern.

_____

10. Look at the fractions you listed in problem 8. How could you write the fractions using exponents in the denominator? Describe the pattern.

_____

Name _____

Multiplying Fractions and Mixed Numbers

To multiply fractions or mixed numbers, no common denominator is needed. Look at the pattern:

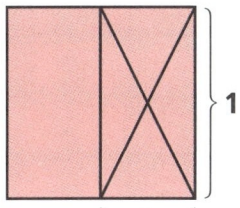
Think: $\frac{1}{2}$ of 1
$\frac{1}{2} \times 1 = \frac{1}{2}$

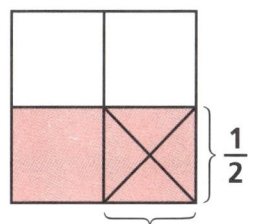
Think: $\frac{1}{2}$ of $\frac{3}{4}$
$\frac{1}{2} \times \frac{3}{4} = \frac{3}{8}$

Think: $\frac{1}{2}$ of $\frac{1}{2}$
$\frac{1}{2} \times \frac{1}{2} = \frac{1}{4}$

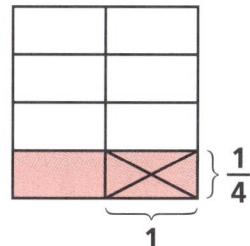
Think: $\frac{1}{2}$ of $\frac{1}{4}$
$\frac{1}{2} \times \frac{1}{4} = \frac{1}{8}$

Find $\frac{3}{7} \times \frac{4}{5}$.

1. Multiply the numerators.

$\frac{3}{7} \times \frac{4}{5} = \frac{3 \cdot 4}{7 \cdot 5} = \frac{12}{}$

2. Then, multiply the denominators.

$\frac{3}{7} \times \frac{4}{5} = \frac{3 \cdot 4}{7 \cdot 5} = \frac{12}{35}$

When each factor is less than **1**, the product is less than **1**.

Find $6 \times \frac{3}{4}$.

1. If one factor is a whole number, write it as a fraction with a denominator of **1**.

$6 \times \frac{3}{4} = \frac{6}{1} \times \frac{3}{4}$

2. Multiply the numerators. Then, multiply the denominators.

$\frac{6}{1} \times \frac{3}{4} \rightarrow \frac{6 \cdot 3}{1 \cdot 4} = \frac{18}{4}$

3. Simplify if necessary.

$\frac{18}{4} = \frac{9}{2}$

$\frac{9}{2} = 4\frac{1}{2}$

When a whole number and a fraction less than 1 are multiplied, the product is less than the whole number.

Write the product in simplest form.

1. $\frac{2}{3} \times \frac{5}{7} =$ $\frac{10}{21}$ $\quad$ $\frac{12}{13} \times \frac{1}{5} =$ $\frac{12}{65}$ $\quad$ $8 \times \frac{2}{5} =$ $\frac{16}{5}$

2. $\frac{7}{8} \times 5 =$ $4\frac{3}{8}$ $\quad$ $\frac{3}{4} \times \frac{8}{9} =$ $\frac{24}{36} = \frac{2}{3}$ $\quad$ $\frac{14}{15} \times 2 =$ $1\frac{13}{15}$

3. $\frac{6}{10} \times \frac{4}{5} =$ $\frac{25}{50} = \frac{12}{25}$ $\quad$ $7 \times \frac{3}{5} =$ $4\frac{1}{5}$ $\quad$ $\frac{1}{2} \times \frac{1}{2} =$ $\frac{1}{4}$

Unit 2 Lesson 13   59

Sometimes you can simplify before multiplying.

Find $\frac{3}{4} \times \frac{1}{9}$.

1. Divide a numerator and a denominator by a common factor before multiplying.

$$\frac{\cancel{3}^1}{4} \times \frac{1}{\cancel{9}_3}$$ Divide by 3.

2. Multiply.

$$\frac{1}{4} \times \frac{1}{3} = \frac{1}{12}$$

Find $3\frac{7}{8} \times 3\frac{1}{5}$.

1. Round to the nearest whole number to estimate.

$3\frac{7}{8} \times 3\frac{1}{5}$

close to 4, close to 3

4×3

The product is close to **12**.

2. Rewrite mixed numbers as fractions.

$$3\frac{7}{8} \times 3\frac{1}{5} = \frac{31}{8} \times \frac{16}{5}$$

3. Divide a numerator and a denominator by a common factor. Then multiply.

$$\frac{31}{\cancel{8}_1} \times \frac{\cancel{16}^2}{5} = \frac{62}{5}$$

4. Simplify. Check that your answer is reasonable.

$$\frac{62}{5} = 12\frac{2}{5}$$

The actual product is close to the estimate. The answer is reasonable.

Round to the nearest whole number. Estimate the product.

4. $4\frac{1}{5} \times 5\frac{1}{3} =$ _____ $\frac{3}{8} \times 3\frac{4}{5} =$ _____ $\frac{5}{6} \times \frac{7}{8} =$ _____

Try to simplify before multiplying. Write the product in simplest form.

5. $\frac{1}{2} \times \frac{2}{5} =$ _____ $\frac{5}{6} \times \frac{3}{20} =$ _____ $\frac{5}{12} \times 108 =$ _____

6. $4\frac{1}{5} \times 5\frac{1}{3} =$ _____ $10 \times 1\frac{3}{5} =$ _____ $3\frac{1}{4} \times 2\frac{2}{3} =$ _____

7. $3\frac{3}{4} \times \frac{2}{7} =$ _____ $5\frac{1}{5} \times \frac{4}{13} =$ _____ $\frac{3}{4} \cdot \frac{15}{18} \cdot \frac{16}{20} =$ _____

60 Unit 2 Lesson 13

Write the product in simplest form.

8. $\frac{2}{3} \times \frac{9}{16} =$ _____ $2\frac{1}{2} \times 3\frac{1}{3} =$ _____ $7\frac{1}{2} \times 1\frac{3}{5} =$ _____

9. $3\frac{1}{8} \times 4 =$ _____ $\frac{7}{8} \times 2 \times 1\frac{1}{4} =$ _____ $6 \times 4\frac{1}{3} =$ _____

Problem Solving Reasoning Solve.

10. Try both problems. Would you rather multiply fractions or decimals? Explain.

$4\frac{1}{2} \times 2\frac{1}{4} =$ _____ $4.5 \times 2.25 =$ _____

11. Explain to your friend why you do not multiply mixed numbers as shown.

$2\frac{4}{5} \times 6\frac{1}{3} = 12\frac{4}{15}$

Quick Check

Write the sum or difference in simplest form.

12. $1\frac{3}{8}$
$+ 2\frac{6}{8}$

13. $\frac{7}{12}$
$+ \frac{2}{3}$

14. $3\frac{5}{6}$
$+ 5\frac{7}{10}$

15. $4\frac{1}{5}$
$- 3\frac{3}{5}$

16. $\frac{3}{4}$
$- \frac{1}{3}$

17. $2\frac{2}{5}$
$- 1\frac{1}{2}$

Work Space.

Write the product in simplest form.

18. $\frac{2}{3} \times \frac{7}{8} =$ _____   **19.** $4 \times \frac{5}{6} =$ _____   **20.** $3\frac{1}{3} \times 2\frac{2}{5} =$ _____

Dividing Fractions and Mixed Numbers

Reciprocals
Two numbers are **reciprocals** if their product is **1**.

$\frac{1}{4}$ and **4** are reciprocals

because $\frac{1}{4} \times \frac{4}{1} = \frac{4}{4}$ or **1**.

$\frac{2}{5}$ and $2\frac{1}{2}$ are reciprocals

because $\frac{2}{5} \times \frac{5}{2} = \frac{10}{10}$ or **1**.

$4\frac{1}{3}$ and $\frac{3}{13}$ are reciprocals

because $\frac{13}{3} \times \frac{3}{13} = \frac{39}{39}$ or **1**.

Dividing Fractions

To divide fractions, multiply the first fraction by the reciprocal of the second fraction.

Divide: $\frac{6}{8} \div \frac{3}{8}$

$\frac{6}{8} \div \frac{3}{8} \rightarrow \frac{\cancel{6}^2}{\cancel{8}_1} \times \frac{\cancel{8}^1}{\cancel{3}_1} = 2$

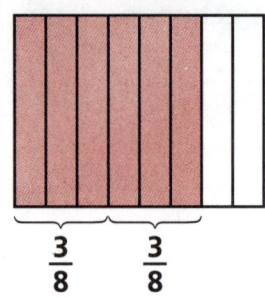

There are two groups of $\frac{3}{8}$ in $\frac{6}{8}$.

Divide: $\frac{5}{9} \div \frac{2}{3}$

$\frac{5}{9} \div \frac{2}{3} = \frac{5}{\cancel{9}_3} \times \frac{\cancel{3}^1}{2}$ or $\frac{5}{6}$

reciprocals

Divide: $\frac{4}{5} \div \frac{8}{15}$

$\frac{4}{5} \div \frac{8}{15} = \frac{\cancel{4}^1}{\cancel{5}_1} \times \frac{\cancel{15}^3}{\cancel{8}_2} \rightarrow \frac{3}{2} = 1\frac{1}{2}$

reciprocals

Write the quotient in simplest form.

1. $\frac{7}{9} \div \frac{2}{3} =$ _____ $\frac{6}{7} \div \frac{4}{7} =$ _____ $\frac{3}{7} \div \frac{21}{5} =$ _____

2. $\frac{1}{5} \div \frac{1}{6} =$ _____ $\frac{1}{2} \div \frac{1}{3} =$ _____ $\frac{5}{7} \div \frac{10}{12} =$ _____

3. $\frac{3}{4} \div \frac{3}{8} =$ _____ $\frac{3}{8} \div \frac{3}{4} =$ _____ $\frac{2}{5} \div \frac{3}{10} =$ _____

4. $\frac{5}{6} \div \frac{5}{12} =$ _____ $\frac{5}{12} \div \frac{5}{6} =$ _____ $\frac{1}{3} \div \frac{1}{4} =$ _____

Dividing Mixed Numbers

To divide mixed numbers, rewrite each as a fraction first.

Divide: $2\frac{1}{3} \div 1\frac{2}{5}$

Round to the nearest whole number to estimate: **2 ÷ 1 = 2**

1. Rewrite as fractions.

    $2\frac{1}{3} \div 1\frac{2}{5} = \frac{7}{3} \div \frac{7}{5}$

2. Rewrite using multiplication and the reciprocal of the divisor.

    $\frac{7}{3} \div \frac{7}{5} = \frac{7}{3} \times \frac{5}{7}$

3. Multiply. Simplify first if you can.

    $\frac{\cancel{7}^1}{3} \times \frac{5}{\cancel{7}_1} = \frac{5}{3}$

4. Simplify.

    $\frac{5}{3} = 1\frac{2}{3}$

    So there are $1\frac{2}{3}$ groups of $1\frac{2}{5}$ in $2\frac{1}{3}$.

Other Example

Divide: $3\frac{1}{3} \div \frac{5}{9}$

Estimate: $3 \div \frac{1}{2} \rightarrow 3 \times 2 = 6$ $\quad 3\frac{1}{3} \div \frac{5}{9} \rightarrow \frac{10}{3} \div \frac{5}{9} \rightarrow \frac{\cancel{10}^2}{\cancel{3}_1} \times \frac{\cancel{9}^3}{\cancel{5}_1} = \frac{6}{1}$ or 6

So there are **6** groups of $\frac{5}{9}$ in $3\frac{1}{3}$.

Round to the nearest whole number. Estimate the quotient.

5. $4\frac{1}{3} \div 2\frac{1}{5}$ _____ $\quad 4\frac{7}{8} \div 2\frac{1}{2}$ _____ $\quad 10\frac{2}{3} \div 3\frac{1}{3}$ _____

6. $2\frac{1}{5} \div 4\frac{1}{3}$ _____ $\quad 5\frac{5}{6} \div 3$ _____ $\quad 8\frac{5}{8} \div \frac{7}{8}$ _____

Write the quotient in simplest form. Check that your answer is reasonable.

7. $3\frac{1}{3} \div \frac{5}{9} =$ _____ $\quad 2\frac{2}{5} \div 1\frac{2}{3} =$ _____ $\quad 1\frac{1}{2} \div 2\frac{2}{5} =$ _____

8. $2\frac{2}{3} \div \frac{8}{9} =$ _____ $\quad 4\frac{1}{2} \div \frac{1}{4} =$ _____ $\quad 1\frac{1}{4} \div 4\frac{1}{2} =$ _____

9. $5\frac{1}{4} \div \frac{7}{16} =$ _____ $\quad 2\frac{2}{3} \div 1\frac{6}{7} =$ _____ $\quad \frac{1}{2} \div 1\frac{1}{6} =$ _____

When you divide a whole number and a fraction, rewrite the whole number as a fraction with a denominator of **1**. Divide as usual.

Divide: $10 \div \frac{5}{6}$

$10 \div \frac{5}{6} \rightarrow \frac{10}{1} \div \frac{5}{6} \rightarrow \frac{\cancel{10}^{2}}{1} \times \frac{6}{\cancel{5}_{1}}$ or $\frac{12}{1}$ or 12

Divide: $4\frac{2}{3} \div 8$

$4\frac{2}{3} \div 8 \rightarrow \frac{14}{3} \div \frac{8}{1} \rightarrow \frac{\cancel{14}^{7}}{3} \times \frac{1}{\cancel{8}_{4}} = \frac{7}{12}$

Write the quotient in simplest form.

10. $\frac{3}{5} \div 3 = $ _____ $\qquad \frac{8}{11} \div 2 = $ _____ $\qquad 6\frac{1}{3} \div 6 = $ _____

11. $7 \div 1\frac{3}{4} = $ _____ $\qquad 18 \div \frac{9}{10} = $ _____ $\qquad 5 \div \frac{1}{10} = $ _____

12. $4\frac{1}{2} \div 4 = $ _____ $\qquad 4 \div 4\frac{1}{2} = $ _____ $\qquad \frac{1}{10} \div 5 = $ _____

Problem Solving Reasoning Solve.

13. You live $\frac{3}{4}$ mile from school. Tiffany lives 3 miles from school. How many times as far from school does Tiffany live than you?

_____

14. Todd has $12\frac{1}{2}$ feet of string. It takes $1\frac{1}{3}$ feet to make a key chain. How many can he make?

_____

Test Prep ★ Mixed Review

15 $\frac{9}{10} + \frac{1}{6} = $

A $\frac{32}{30}$

B $\frac{10}{60}$

C $\frac{9}{16}$

D $\frac{10}{16}$

16 Which is the correct order from least to greatest? $\frac{3}{4}$, 0.35, 0.78, $\frac{3}{5}$

F $\frac{3}{4}, \frac{4}{5}, 0.35, 0.78$

G $0.35, \frac{3}{5}, \frac{3}{4}, 0.78$

H $0.35, 0.78, \frac{3}{4}, \frac{3}{5}$

J $\frac{3}{5}, 0.35, \frac{3}{4}, 0.78$

Name _____

Problem Solving Strategy: Draw a Diagram

To solve some problems, you may want to draw a diagram to help you think about the many possibilities.

You can draw a picture. Label information you know. Analyze the information.

> **Problem**
>
> Placing toothpicks end-to-end, how many different rectangles can you make using 12 toothpicks? A rectangle with a length of 1 and a width of 2 is the same rectangle as one with a length of 2 and a width of 1.

❶ Understand   As you reread, ask yourself questions.

- What do you know about the toothpicks?
  You have **12** toothpicks.
  The toothpicks will be placed end-to-end to form a rectangle.
  The perimeter of the rectangle will be **12** "toothpicks."

- What information do you already know?
  A rectangle has **4** sides.

- What do you need to find? _____

❷ Decide   Choose a method for solving.

Try the Draw a Diagram strategy.

- What will your first diagram be?

- How many toothpicks are used in this rectangle? _____

❸ Solve   Draw additional diagrams to solve the problem.

Organize your approach so that you do not miss any rectangles and that you don't draw the same rectangle more than once.

❹ Look back   Check that you have answered the question.

How many different rectangles did you draw? List the length and width of each.

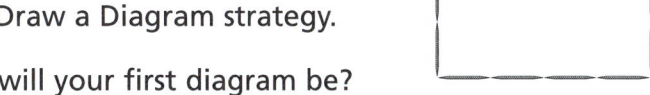

How did drawing a picture help you solve the problem?

_____

Unit 2 Lesson 15   **65**

Use the Draw a Diagram strategy or any other strategy you have learned to solve these problems.

1. What is the perimeter of each of the rectangles you drew on the previous page? What is the area of each rectangle?

Think: Do you have to compute the perimeter to complete the table?

Length	Width	Perimeter	Area

2. The diagram below shows the first four square numbers. What are the next two square numbers? _____

Think: Is there a pattern in the arrangement of dots and numbers?

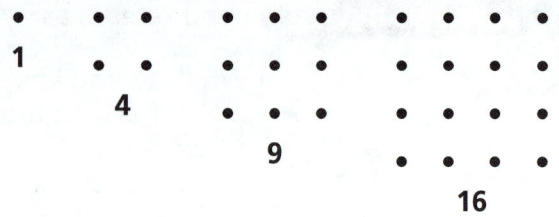

3. Before lunch there was $\frac{7}{8}$ gallon of milk in the refrigerator. After lunch there was $\frac{1}{4}$ gallon left. How much milk was drunk at lunch? _____

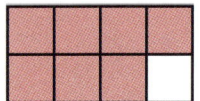

4. While helping to take inventory at the department store, Antonio worked $2\frac{1}{2}$ hours on Monday and $1\frac{3}{4}$ hours on Tuesday. How much longer did he work on Monday? _____

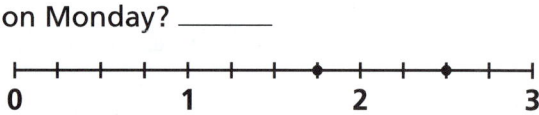

5. Your family buys a **3**-pound bag of Golden Delicious apples for **$2.29**. Your aunt bought a pound of Macintosh apples for **$.79** a pound. Which is the better buy? Explain.

_____

_____

6. In January, you measured **108.3** cm and your brother was **97.8** cm. In December, you were **111.7** cm and your brother was **101.1** cm. Who grew more during the year? Explain.

_____

_____

7. How many different squares are in this figure? (Hint: the squares can be different sizes.)

_____

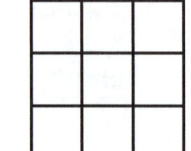

8. Is it possible to trace the figure shown without lifting your pencil from the paper, and without tracing over any line more than once?

_____

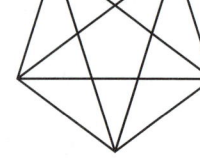

Name _____

Expressions with Fractions and Decimals

You reviewed operations with fractions and decimals in this unit.
You can simplify expressions with fractions and decimals just as you do expressions with whole numbers.

Order of Operations

1. Perform all operations within parentheses first.
2. Evaluate all powers.
3. Multiply and divide from left to right.
4. Finally, add and subtract from left to right.

Simplify: $\left(\frac{4}{5}\right)^2 - \frac{3}{10} \times \frac{2}{5}$

Original problem	$\left(\frac{4}{5}\right)^2 - \frac{3}{10} \times \frac{2}{5}$
Evaluate powers and multiply.	$\frac{16}{25} - \frac{3}{25}$
Subtract.	$\frac{16}{25} - \frac{3}{25} \rightarrow \frac{13}{25}$

Simplify: $3.4(8 + 2.04)$

Original problem	$3.4(8 + 2.04)$
Add inside parentheses.	$3.4(10.04)$
Multiply.	$3.4 \times 10.04 \rightarrow 34.136$

Simplify. Write answers in simplest form.

1. $4.2^2 - 3.1^2$ _____ $3(12.05 - 8.9)$ _____ $14.8 + 2.1 \times 4$ _____

2. $\frac{3}{5} + 4 \times \frac{1}{8}$ _____ $6\frac{2}{3} - 2\frac{1}{2} + 3$ _____ $\frac{4}{9} + \left(\frac{2}{3}\right)^2$ _____

3. $12.6 \div 0.2 \times 0.03$ _____ $(4 + 0.07)^2$ _____ $(12 - 5.5) \times \frac{1}{2}$ _____

4. $3(3^2 - 2.2) \div \frac{2}{5}$ _____ $\frac{3}{4} \div 1\frac{1}{2} + \frac{3}{4} \times 1\frac{1}{2}$ _____ $(2 + 3 \times 4)^2 - 24$ _____

To evaluate algebraic expressions, substitute for the variable and simplify.

Evaluate: $3.1x + 2x$. Use $x = 1.5$.		**Evaluate: $y^2 + 3y$. Use $y = \frac{3}{4}$.**		
Original problem	$3.1x + 2x$	Original problem	$y^2 + 3y$	
Substitute $x = 1.5$.	$3.1(1.5) + 2(1.5)$	Substitute $y = \frac{3}{4}$.	$\left(\frac{3}{4}\right)^2 + 3\left(\frac{3}{4}\right)$	
Multiply and add.	$4.65 + 3.0 \rightarrow 7.65$	Evaluate powers and multiply.	$\frac{9}{16} + \frac{9}{4}$	
		Add. Use the LCD of **16**.	$\frac{9}{16} + \frac{36}{16} \rightarrow \frac{45}{16} \rightarrow 2\frac{13}{16}$	

Evaluate. Let $a = 0.04$, $b = \frac{1}{3}$, and $c = 6$.

5. $\frac{c}{8} + 7$ _____ $5b + 1$ _____ $10a + 6.5$ _____

6. $a \div 8 \cdot c$ _____ $3.2c + 1.5c$ _____ $\frac{6}{5}b + \frac{3}{5}b$ _____

7. $2(a + c)$ _____ $b \cdot c + a$ _____ $200a - c$ _____

Problem Solving / Reasoning Solve.

8. Curtis simplified $0.8 \div 0.2 \times 0.04$ and got **10**. Latoya simplified and got **1.6**. Is either correct? Explain.

   _____

9. When Max evaluated a^2 for $a = \frac{4}{5}$ he got $\frac{8}{10}$. Explain how Max went wrong.

   _____

Test Prep ★ Mixed Review

10 What is the greatest common factor of 20, 28, and 36?

  A 2
  B 4
  C 8
  D 18

11 $5k + 7(k + 8) =$

  F $12k + 8$
  G 68
  H $12k + 56$
  J $68k$

68 Unit 2 Lesson 16

Name _____

Solving Equations with Fractions and Decimals

You have solved equations with whole numbers. You can solve equations with fractions and decimals as you do with whole numbers.

Properties of Equality

Equivalent equations can be formed by

- adding the same number to both sides of an equation.
- subtracting the same number from both sides of an equation.
- multiplying both sides of an equation by the same non-zero number.
- dividing both sides of an equation by the same non-zero number.

Solve: $n + \frac{2}{5} = \frac{3}{4}$

Original equation	$n + \frac{2}{5} = \frac{3}{4}$
Subtract $\frac{2}{5}$ from both sides.	$n + \frac{2}{5} - \frac{2}{5} = \frac{3}{4} - \frac{2}{5}$
Use an LCD of 20. Simplify.	$n = \frac{7}{20}$

Solve: $a - 2.7 = 9.04$

Original equation	$a - 2.7 = 9.04$
Add 2.7 to both sides.	$a - 2.7 + 2.7 = 9.04 + 2.7$
Simplify.	$a = 11.74$

Solve. Write the answers in simplest form.

1. $x - \frac{2}{3} = \frac{1}{4}$ _____ $n + \frac{4}{5} = 2\frac{1}{2}$ _____ $w - 2\frac{1}{5} = 6$ _____

2. $n + 3.8 = 10$ _____ $x - 2.06 = 6.1$ _____ $t + 0.4 = 8.1$ _____

3. $x + 10\frac{2}{3} = 15$ _____ $3.02 + h = 8$ _____ $x - 4.02 = 9.8$ _____

4. $w - 5.2 = .003$ _____ $m - 2\frac{2}{5} = 7\frac{1}{3}$ _____ $n - 4\frac{1}{2} = 8.5$ _____

Unit 2 Lesson 17 **69**

Some equations involve multiplication and division. Use what you know about reciprocals to solve them.

Solve: $\frac{4}{5}x = 8$

Original equation	$\frac{4}{5}x = 8$
Multiply by $\frac{5}{4}$.	$\frac{\cancel{5}}{\cancel{4}} \cdot \frac{\cancel{4}}{\cancel{5}} x = \frac{5}{4} \cdot 8$
Simplify.	$x = 10$

Solve: $\frac{n}{1.4} = 8.6$

Original equation	$\frac{n}{1.4} = 8.6$
Multiply by 1.4.	$\frac{\cancel{1.4}}{1} \cdot \frac{n}{\cancel{1.4}} = (1.4)(8.6)$
Simplify.	$n = 12.04$

Solve.

5. $\frac{c}{8} = 7.5$ _____ $5.2b = 17.68$ _____ $10a = 17.02$ _____

6. $\frac{1}{4}a = 5$ _____ $3n = 6\frac{3}{4}$ _____ $\frac{6}{5}b = \frac{12}{15}$ _____

7. $0.04a = 1.08$ _____ $2\frac{1}{2}x = 8.75$ _____ $\frac{n}{0.01} = 0.5$ _____

 Quick Check

Write the quotient in simplest form.

Work Space.

8. $\frac{3}{4} \div \frac{1}{2}$ $1\frac{1}{2}$ 9. $10 \div \frac{5}{6}$ 12 10. $2\frac{3}{4} \div 1\frac{1}{3}$ $2\frac{1}{16}$

Evaluate the expression for $a = 1.2$ and $b = \frac{3}{4}$.

11. $2(a + 3b)$ _____   12. $1.5a - 0.1b$ 2.87 13. $\frac{b}{6} + \frac{5}{6}a$ _____

Solve the equation.

14. $4.06 + j = 9$ $+4.06$ 15. $n - 1\frac{5}{8} = 3\frac{1}{6}$ $-1\frac{5}{8}$

16. $4k = 1\frac{2}{3}$ 17. $0.2a = 0.98$ $\div 0.2$

UNIT 3 • TABLE OF CONTENTS

Measurement

Lesson	Page
1 Metric Units of Length	75
2 Metric Units of Capacity and Mass	77
3 Metric Units of Area and Volume	79
4 **Problem Solving Application:** Too Much or Too Little Information	81
5 Customary Units of Length	83
6 Customary Units of Capacity and Weight	85
7 Customary Units of Area and Volume	87
8 **Algebra** • Temperature and Line Graphs	89
9 Time	91
10 **Problem Solving Strategy:** Make a Table	93
• Unit 3 Review	95
• Cumulative Review ★ Test Prep	96

Dear Family,

During the next few weeks, our math class will be studying units of measure in both the metric and customary systems of measure. This unit includes units of length, capacity, mass or weight, area, volume, time, and temperature. You can expect to see homework that provides practice with these skills. Here is a sample you may want to keep handy to give help if needed.

> **We will be using this vocabulary:**
>
> **meter** a standard unit of length in the metric system (A meter is a little longer than a yard.)
>
> **liter** a standard unit of capacity in the metric system (A liter is a little greater than a quart.)
>
> **gram** a standard unit of mass in the metric system (The mass of a raisin is about a gram.)
>
> **Celsius scale** a metric temperature scale in which the boiling temperature of water is **100°C** and the freezing temperature of water is **0°C**
>
> **Fahrenheit scale** a customary temperature scale in which the boiling temperature of water is **212°F** and the freezing temperature of water is **32°F**
>
> **24-hour clock** a clock scale that starts and ends at midnight; for example, **1430** means it is **14** hours and **30** minutes after midnight (**0000**), or **2:30** P.M.

Finding Equivalent Measures

To change from a larger unit of measure to a smaller unit of measure, you need to multiply.

2.5 square feet = ____?____ square inches

$2.5 \times 144 = 360$

> Think: 1 square foot = 144 square inches. Since a square inch is smaller in area than a square foot, you need more of them.

2.5 square feet = 360 square inches

To change from a smaller unit of measure to a larger unit of measure, you need to divide.

436.5 cm = __?__ m

$436.5 \div 100 = 4.365$

> Think: 1 m = 100 cm. Since a meter is longer than a centimeter, you need fewer of them.

436.5 cm = 4.365 m

During this unit, students will continue to learn new techniques related to problem solving and will continue to practice basic skills with fractions and decimals.

Sincerely,

Name _____

Metric Units of Length

The basic, or standard, unit of length in the metric system is the **meter (m)**. Look at the chart. Notice how the prefix of each unit of measure tells you how that unit is related to the meter. Notice, also, that each unit is **10** times greater than the next lesser unit.

Measurement	Symbol	Meaning	Familiar Approximations
kilometer	km	1,000 meters	11 football fields end to end
hectometer	hm	100 meters	little more than a football field
dekameter	dam	10 meters	width of a two lane street
meter	m	1 meter	height of a kitchen sink
decimeter	dm	0.1 meter	length of a new piece of chalk
centimeter	cm	0.01 meter	width of your index finger
millimeter	mm	0.001 meter	thickness of a dime

What metric unit of length (km, m, cm, or mm) would you use to measure the item?

1. distance from home to school _____   distance around your waist _____

2. thickness of a pencil eraser _____   distance run by a marathon runner _____

3. width of the head of a nail _____   your height _____

4. length of the school hall _____   thickness of this piece of paper _____

Circle the best estimate of the length of each item.

5. width of a textbook
   2 cm   20 cm   40 cm

6. thickness of a nickel
   2 mm   20 mm   40 mm

7. height of a doorknob
   1 m   2 m   3 m

8. distance from New York to California
   30 km   300 km   3,000 km

9. height of milk glass
   2 cm   5 cm   15 cm

10. length of average car
    1 m   5 m   10 m

Use the centimeter ruler to write equivalent measures.

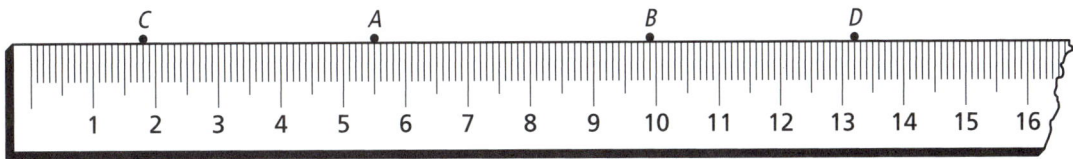

11. Point A = _____ cm = _____ cm _____ mm   Point B = _____ cm = _____ cm _____ mm

12. Point C = _____ cm = _____ cm _____ mm   Point D = _____ cm = _____ cm _____ mm

Unit 3 Lesson 1   75

Each metric unit of length is **10** times longer than the next shorter unit. To change from one metric unit of length to another, you multiply or divide by a power of **10**.

Larger to Smaller		Smaller to Larger
4 km = ___?___ m	km ↑ hm dam × m ÷ dm cm mm ↓	62 cm = ___?___ m
There are **1,000** m, or **10³** m, in every kilometer, so multiply by **1,000**. Move the decimal point **3** places to the **right**.		There are **100** cm, or **10²** cm, in every meter, so divide by **100**. Move the decimal point **2** places to the **left**.
4 km = 4,000 m  longer unit smaller number		62 cm = 0.62 m  shorter unit larger number

Complete.

13. 32 m = _____ cm   162 mm = _____ cm   500 cm = _____ m

14. 17 mm = _____ m   42 km = _____ m   7.3 cm = _____ mm

15. 8.2 m = _____ mm   16 m = _____ dm   3,500 cm = _____ m

16. 4.4 dm = _____ cm   80 m = _____ km   0.2 km = _____ m

17. 152 cm = _____ m   8.3 m = _____ dm   2.5 m = _____ cm

Problem Solving Reasoning Use what you know about units of length to solve.

18. Juanita used a meter stick to measure the width of her school desk. She recorded the width as **605** cm. Is this reasonable?

Explain. _____

19. Jacob walks **400** m around his block every morning. How many times would he need to walk around the block to walk **2** km?

_____

Test Prep ★ Mixed Review

20 Every 5th person gets a pen. Every 7th person gets a pencil. Every 21st person gets a pad of paper. Which person is the first to get all three?

   A the 735th   **C** the 105th

   B the 210th   **D** the 35th

21 What is the solution of the equation $a - 0.6 = 7.24$?

   F 7.84   **H** 7.18

   G 7.30   **J** 6.64

Name _____

Problem Solving Application: Too Much or Too Little Information

Some problems give more facts than you may need. In a problem with many facts, it helps to identify which information is necessary for solving.

- Jan has **32** bean bag animals.
- Jan has spent **$220** for the bean bag animals.

Which facts are extra?

_____

_____

> **Problem**
>
> In Jan's store, there are 32 bean bag animals on a 2-foot shelf. She keeps art supplies on a 3-foot shelf. Jan has spent a total of $220 on the bean bag animals. About what was the average cost of each bean bag animal?

In this lesson, you may also need to identify a missing fact that is necessary for solving.

Tips to Remember:

> 1. Understand   2. Decide   3. Solve   4. Look back

- Ask yourself: What do I know? What do I need to find?
- Organize facts in a list. Decide which facts are extra. Recheck your list as you solve. Is information missing?
- Think about the strategies you have learned and use them to help you solve a problem.

Cross out the extra information and then solve the problem. If the problem has information missing, list the fact or facts needed.

1. About what was the average cost to Jan for each bean-bag animal?

   Think: How many animals did she buy for $220?

   _____

   _____

   Answer _____

2. Mrs. Jaynes bought **3.4** pounds of chicken for **$6.28** and beef for **$4.93**. Which was the better buy?

   Think: What do you need to compare?

   _____

   _____

   Answer _____

Unit 3 Lesson 4

Cross out the extra information and then solve the problem. If the problem has information missing, list the fact or facts you need.

3. A can of peas usually costs **$0.49**. How much do you save on each **15** oz can of peas if you buy one dozen for **$5.52**?

_____

4. Pedro wants to buy a watch that costs **$140**. He works in the library after school. He earns **$15** per day, **$3.50** of which he saves toward the cost of the watch. How many workdays will it take for him to save **$140**?

_____

5. Sarah worked 5 days for her mom. She was paid **$77.50** for working **5** days. How much was she paid per hour?

_____

6. Forrest is **6** ft **4** in. and just bought a new pair of size **11** sneakers. He gave the clerk four **$20** bills to pay for the **$68** sneakers. His change was **$7.92**. How much was the sales tax on the sneakers?

_____

7. On Tuesday Eric picked up a prescription for **6** mL of medicine that cost **$12.30**. By Saturday he had finished the bottle. If he took the same amount of medicine each day, how many mL did he take each day?

_____

8. A warehouse charged a store **$48** for 2 cartons. The first carton contained eight **12**-ounce packages, while the other contained six **1** pound packages. All cartons with the same total weight have an equal cost. How much would the store pay for a carton that has **6**-ounce packages in it?

_____

Extend Your Thinking

9. Choose a problem in which a fact is missing. Suggest a reasonable amount for the misssing fact and then solve the problem.

_____

10. Explain your method for solving problem 6. Is there more than one way to solve the problem?

_____

Name _____   **Customary Units of Length**

This ruler measures to the nearest $\frac{1}{16}$-inch. Recall that sixteenths can be simplified to eighths, fourths, or halves.

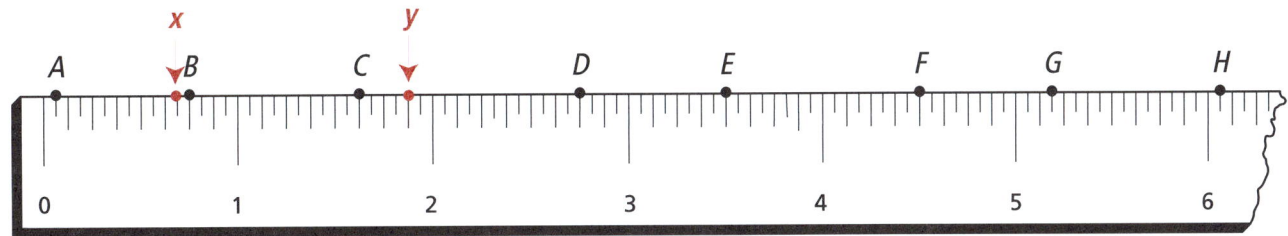

Every mark represents $\frac{1}{16}$ inch. So the distance from the zero point of the ruler to *x* is $\frac{11}{16}$ in. and to *y* is $1\frac{14}{16}$ in., or $1\frac{7}{8}$ in. You may need to regroup to add or subtract units of length.

Add: **3 ft 6 in. + 2 ft 9 in.**

- Add inches first. Regroup. Add feet.

$$\begin{array}{r} \overset{1}{3}\text{ ft 6 in.} \\ +\ 2\text{ ft 9 in.} \\ \hline 6\text{ ft 3 in., or } 6\tfrac{1}{4}\text{ ft} \end{array}$$

6 in. + 9 in. = 15 in.

Subtract: $9\frac{1}{4}$ ft − 6 ft 7 in.

- Regroup feet as inches. Subtract inches, then feet.

$$\begin{array}{r} \overset{8}{\cancel{9}}\text{ ft }\overset{15}{\cancel{3}}\text{ in.} \\ +\ 6\text{ ft 7 in.} \\ \hline 2\text{ ft 8 in., or } 2\tfrac{2}{3}\text{ ft} \end{array}$$

$9\frac{1}{4}$ ft = 9 ft 3 in.

Write the distance from zero to the given point in simplest form.

1. A _____   B _____   C _____   D _____

2. E _____   F _____   G _____   H _____

Write the sum or difference.

3. 7 ft 5 in. − 3 ft 2 in. = _____ ft _____ in.   5 ft 4 in. + 6 ft 5 in. = _____ ft _____ in.

4. 12 ft 9 in. + 4 ft 6 in. = _____ ft _____ in.   8 ft 5 in. − 2 ft 7 in. = _____ ft _____ in.

5. $2\frac{1}{2}$ ft − 1 ft 4 in. = _____ ft _____ in. $5\frac{1}{3}$ ft + 6 ft 9 in. = _____ ft _____ in.

Write the sum or difference. Express inches as part of a foot.

6. 3 ft + 7 ft 6 in. = _____ ft   4 ft 8 in. − 3 ft 2 in. = _____ ft

7. $5\frac{1}{4}$ ft + 3 ft 6 in. = _____ ft   9 ft − $2\frac{3}{4}$ ft = _____ ft

8. 6 ft 10 in. − 4 ft 1 in. = _____ ft   3 ft 8 in. + 5 ft 8 in. = _____ ft

To write a length using a different unit of measure, you need to know equivalent lengths.

Equivalent Lengths

12 inches = 1 foot
36 inches = 1 yard
3 feet = 1 yard
5,280 feet = 1 mile
1,760 yards = 1 mile

Larger to Smaller

$5\frac{1}{2}$ ft = _____?_____ in.

1 ft = 12 in., so **multiply**.

$5\frac{1}{2} \times 12 = \frac{11}{2} \times 12$ or 66

Then, $5\frac{1}{2}$ ft = 66 in.

Smaller to Larger

38 ft = _____?_____ yd

3 ft = 1 yd, so **divide**.

$$12\frac{2}{3}$$
$$3\overline{)38}$$
$$\underline{36}$$
$$2$$

Then, 38 ft = $12\frac{2}{3}$ yd.

Complete.

9. 6 ft = _____ in. $5\frac{1}{3}$ yd = _____ ft   6160 yd = _____ mi

10. 18 in. = _____ yd   48 in. = _____ ft $2\frac{1}{2}$ mi = _____ ft

11. 2.4 mi = _____ ft   10.5 yd = _____ in. $1\frac{1}{4}$ mi = _____ yd

12. 81 ft = _____ yd $12\frac{3}{4}$ ft = _____ in.   0.2 mi = _____ ft

Problem Solving Reasoning Solve.

13. Last year Becca's height was **4 ft 5 in.** This year her height is **57 in.** How much did she grow?

    _____

14. Jason needs **7 yd 2 ft** of molding. It sells for **$.68** per foot. How much will the molding cost?

    _____

Test Prep ★ Mixed Review

15 What is the solution to the equation $3k = 2.04$?

   A 6.12   C 6.012

   B 6.8   D 0.68

16 What is the volume of a small box that is 5 cm in width, 6 cm in length, and 4 cm in height?

   F 120 cm^3 H 120 cm

   G 120 cm^2 J 15 cm

84 Unit 3 Lesson 5

Name _____

Customary Units of Capacity and Weight

Customary units of capacity or liquid measure are fluid ounce (fl oz), cup (c), pint (pt), quart (qt), and gallon (gal). Unlike the metric system, these units are not related by powers of **10**.

Equivalent Measures

8 fluid ounces = 1 cup
16 fluid ounces = 1 pint
2 cups = 1 pint
2 pints = 1 quart
4 quarts = 1 gallon
32 fluid ounces = 1 quart

Larger to Smaller

5 qt = ___?___ fl oz

1 qt = 32 fl oz, so **multiply**.

5 × 32 = 160

Then, **5** qt = **160** fl oz.

Smaller to Larger

44 fl oz = ___?___ c

8 fl oz = 1 c, so **divide**.

$$8\overline{)44} \quad \begin{array}{c} 5\frac{4}{8} \\ \underline{40} \\ 4 \end{array}$$

Simplify. $5\frac{4}{8} = 5\frac{1}{2}$

Then, **44** fl oz = $5\frac{1}{2}$ c.

Complete.

1. 7 pt = _____ qt
2. $\frac{1}{2}$ c = _____ pt
3. 48 fl oz = _____ qt
4. $2\frac{1}{2}$ gal = _____ qt

24 fl oz = _____ c
$\frac{1}{2}$ c = _____ fl oz
3 qt = _____ c
$3\frac{3}{4}$ gal = _____ pt

3 qt = _____ gal
5 gal = _____ pt
5 pt = _____ fl oz
14 c = _____ qt

Write the sum or difference of the measures.

5. $2\frac{1}{2}$ c + $3\frac{1}{2}$ c + $\frac{3}{4}$ c = _____ c

6. 20 fl oz + 32 fl oz = _____ c

7. 64 fl oz + 32 fl oz = _____ qt

8. 3 qt − 1 pt = _____ fl oz

9. 3 gal 2 qt + 4 gal 1 qt = _____ gal _____ qt

10. 6 gal 1 qt − 2 gal 3 qt = _____ gal _____ qt

11. 5 qt 1 pt + 4 qt 1 pt = _____ qt _____ pt

12. 11 qt − 3 qt 1 pt = _____ qt _____ pt

Write true or false.

13. _____ A gallon of maple syrup equals **64** fluid ounces.

14. _____ Pouring **8** cups of milk is the same as pouring a half gallon of milk.

15. _____ Taking **2** fluid ounces of cough syrup **4** times a day for **4** days is equal to a quart.

Unit 3 Lesson 6   85

Customary units of weight are ounce (oz), pound (lb), and ton.

Equivalent Measures

16 ounces = 1 pound

2,000 pounds = 1 ton

Larger to Smaller

$3\frac{1}{2}$ lb = _____?_____ oz

1 lb = 16 oz, so **multiply**.

$3\frac{1}{2} \times 16 = \frac{7}{2} \times 16$ or 56

Then, $3\frac{1}{2}$ lb = 56 oz.

Smaller to Larger

56 oz = _____?_____ lb

Fact: 16 oz = 1 lb, so **divide**.

$16\overline{)56}$ → $3\frac{8}{16}$ Simplify. $3\frac{8}{16} = 3\frac{1}{2}$

Then, 56 oz = $3\frac{1}{2}$ lb.

Complete.

16. 6,000 lb = _____ tons   18 oz = _____ lb   4,500 lb = _____ tons

17. $\frac{1}{2}$ ton = _____ lb $2\frac{1}{2}$ lb = _____ oz $\frac{1}{4}$ ton = _____ oz

Write the sum or difference of the measures.

18. 5 lb 6 oz + 12 lb 4 oz = _____ lb _____ oz   8 lb 6 oz − 4 lb 8 oz = _____ lb _____ oz

19. $2\frac{1}{2}$ lb + $3\frac{1}{4}$ lb = _____ lb _____ oz   5 lb 12 oz − 3 lb 8 oz = _____ lb

Problem Solving Reasoning   Solve.

20. A bottling plant fills one hundred 20-fl oz bottles with spring water each minute. How many gallons of water are needed each hour?

_____

21. The combined weight of 45 crates, each with the same weight, is $3\frac{1}{2}$ tons. How many pounds does each crate weigh to the nearest pound?

_____

Test Prep ★ Mixed Review

22. What is the volume of water in a tank measuring 6 feet by 3 feet by 2 feet?

- **A** 11 ft
- **B** 18 ft²
- **C** 36 ft³
- **D** 36 ft²

23. The area of a tabletop is 4 square feet. What is the area in square inches?

- **F** 576 in.
- **G** 576 in.²
- **H** 48 in.
- **J** 48 in.²

Unit 3 Lesson 6

Name _____

Customary Units of Area and Volume

In the Customary System, area is measured in square feet. A square foot, written "sq ft" or "ft²," is a square whose sides are **1** foot long.

You know that **1** ft = **12** in., so the two squares at the right are the same size. Their areas are equal, so **1** ft² = **144** in.².

1 ft square, 1 ft × 1 ft, Area = 1 ft²

12 in. square, 12 in. × 12 in., Area = 144 in.²

Equivalent Measures

144 in.² = 1 ft²

9 ft² = 1 yd²

4,840 yd² = 1 acre

640 acres = 1 mi²

Larger to Smaller

5 ft² = ___?___ in.²

1 ft² = 144 in.², so **multiply**.

5 × 144 = 720

Then, **5** ft² = **720** in.².

Smaller to Larger

21 ft² = ___?___ yd²

9 ft² = 1 yd², so **divide**.

$$9\overline{)21} \quad \begin{array}{r} 2\frac{3}{9} \\ \underline{18} \\ 3 \end{array}$$

Simplify. $2\frac{3}{9} = 2\frac{1}{3}$

Then, **21** ft² = $2\frac{1}{3}$ yd².

Which unit would you use to measure the item?
Choose in.², ft², yd², acre, or mi².

1. classroom floor _____   your school grounds _____   store window _____

2. writing paper _____   your state _____   light switch cover _____

Complete.

3. 576 in.² = _____ ft²   0.75 acre = _____ yd²   35 yd² = _____ ft²

4. 5 yd² = _____ ft²   216 in.² = _____ ft²   18 ft² = _____ yd²

5. 3 acres = _____ yd²   0.5 mi² = _____ acres   3 ft² = _____ in.²

Write true or false.

6. _____ A field is **100** yd long by **60** yd wide, and its area is **18,000** ft².

7. _____ The area of a 6-inch square is $\frac{1}{4}$ ft².

8. _____ Linoleum that costs **$3.50** per square foot will cost **$10.50** per square yard.

Volume is measured using cubic units. A cubic foot, written "cu ft " or "ft³," is a cube whose edges are **1** foot long.

You know that **1** ft = **12** in., so the two cubes at the right are the same size. The volumes are equal, so **1** ft³ = **1,728** in.³.

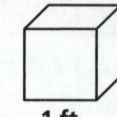
1 ft
Volume = 1 ft³

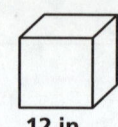
12 in.
Volume = 1,728 ft³

Equivalent Measures

1,728 in.³ = 1 ft³

27 ft³ = 1 yd³

Larger to Smaller

3 ft³ = _?_ in.³

1 ft³ = 1,728 in.³, so **multiply**.

3 × 1,728 = 5,184

Then, 3 ft³ = 5,128 in.³.

Smaller to Larger

144 ft³ = _?_ yd³

27 ft³ = 1 yd³, so **divide**.

$$27\overline{)144} 5\frac{9}{27}$$
$$\underline{135}$$
$$9$$

Simplify

$5\frac{9}{27} = 5\frac{1}{3}$

Then, **144** ft³ = $5\frac{1}{3}$ yd³.

Complete.

9. 2 ft³ = _____ in.³   3 yd³ = _____ ft³   72 ft³ = _____ yd³

10. 432 in.³ = _____ ft³ $4\frac{2}{3}$ yd³ = _____ ft³ $\frac{1}{12}$ ft³ = _____ in.³

Solve.

11. A dump truck holds **10** yd³ of sand. How many loads will it take to fill a hole that is **30** ft by **60** ft by **6** ft deep?

12. A **5**-acre parcel is subdivided into parcels of **440** yd². How many parcels will there be?

✓ Quick Check

Complete.

13. 4 ft 9 in. + 7 ft 6 in. = _____ ft _____ in.

14. $9\frac{1}{4}$ ft − 5 ft 8 in. = _____ ft _____ in.

15. 3 gal 2 qt + 6 gal 3 qt = _____ gal _____ qt

16. $4\frac{3}{4}$ lb + $1\frac{1}{2}$ lb = _____ lb _____ oz

17. 9.5 yd = _____ ft   18. 189 in. = _____ ft

19. 1.4 mi = _____ ft   20. 156 fl oz = _____ pt

21. $5\frac{3}{8}$ lb = _____ oz   22. $2\frac{1}{4}$ tons = _____ lb

23. 6 ft² = _____ in.²   24. 30 ft² = _____ yd²

25. 10 yd³ = _____ ft³

Work Space.

Name _____

Temperature and Line Graphs

Two common temperature scales are the **Celsius (C)** and **Fahrenheit (F)** scales shown at the right.

The boiling and freezing points on the Celsius scale are **100°** apart. These points are **180°** apart on the Fahrenheit scale. The temperatures *feel* the same, but the scale is different.

Celsius	Reference Points	Fahrenheit
100°	Boiling point	212°
37°	Body temperature	98.6°
32°	Hot summer day	90°
21°	A room in winter	70°
16°	Pleasant spring day	60°
0°	Freezing point	32°

The Celsius (C) and Fahrenheit (F) scales are both used in the United States. If you know the temperature in one scale, you can estimate what it will be in the other scale.

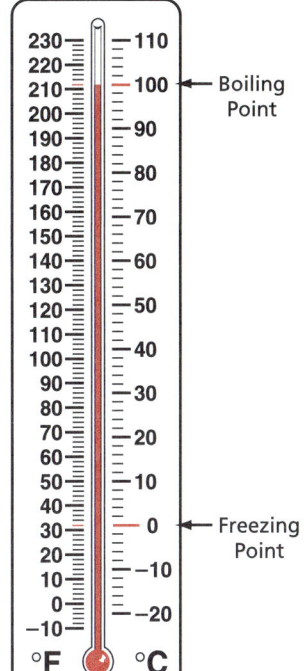

Celsius to Fahrenheit: Double, then add 30.

≈ means "is approximately equal to"

10°C ≈ 2 × 10 + 30
     ≈ 50°F

Fahrenheit to Celsius: Subtract 30, then divide by 2.

70°F ≈ (70 − 30) ÷ 2
     ≈ 20°C

Write true or false. Use the temperature scales above to help you.

1. _____ 20°C is colder than 20°F.   _____ You would swim at the beach at 35°F.

2. _____ You need a sweater at 40°C.   _____ You would swim at the beach at 35°C.

3. _____ You need a sweater at 40°F.   _____ 85°C is normal in Honolulu.

4. _____ It snows at 10°F.   _____ 30°C is normal winter weather in Chicago.

Complete. Estimate the Celsius or Fahrenheit temperature.

5. 80°F ≈ _____ °C   16°C ≈ _____ °F   72°F ≈ _____ °C

6. 22°C ≈ _____ °F   40°F ≈ _____ °C   28°C ≈ _____ °F

7. 90°F ≈ _____ °C   35°C ≈ _____ °F   66°F ≈ _____ °C

A **line graph** is best used to show trends, or changes in data over time.
One or more sets of related data can be shown on the same graph.

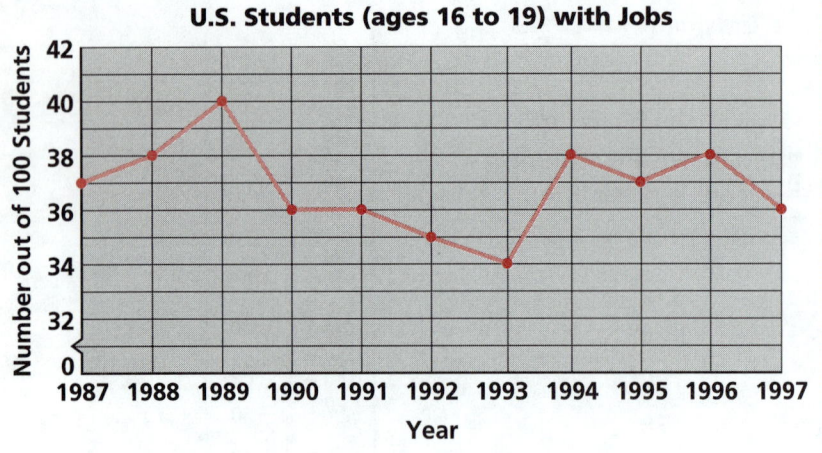

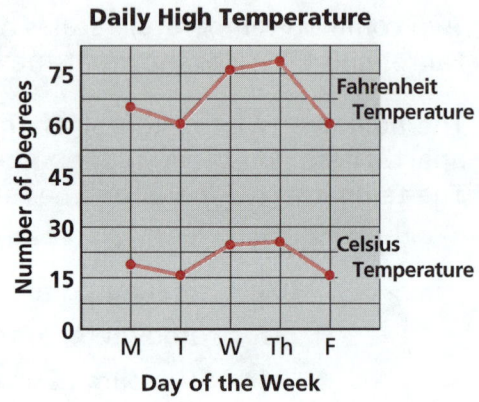

From the graph, you can see that in **1996**,
38 out of **100** students had jobs.

From the graph, you can see that
on Wednesday the temperature
was about **24**°C, or **76**°F.

Complete. Use the graphs above.

8. How many students out of **100** had jobs in **1990**? _____ In **1994**? _____

9. Between what two years was the decrease in students with jobs the greatest?

_____ The increase greatest? _____

10. What was the approximate temperature on Tuesday? _____°F and _____°C

11. Which line graph shows the greatest change in the number of degrees,

Fahrenheit or Celsius? _____

Problem Solving Reasoning **Solve.**

12. Ben is traveling to New York City in July. Which of these is a reasonable temperature to expect: **10°F, 85°F,** or **113°F**?

_____

13. Ashlea has a fever. Her body temperature is **2°** above normal. Which is more severe, **2°C** or **2°F**? Explain.

_____

Test Prep ★ Mixed Review

14. A container with a volume of 1 dm³ has a capacity of 1 L. What is the capacity in liters of a box that is 8 cm in width, 10 cm in length, and 5.5 cm in height?

  A 4.4 L   C 0.044 L

  B 0.44 L   D 0.08 L

15. Two gallons of juice will fill how many cups?

  F 8   H 32

  G 16   J 64

90 Unit 3 Lesson 8

Name _____

Time

You can write equivalent units of time in the same way that you write equivalent lengths, capacities, areas, and volumes.

Equivalent Measures

60 seconds (s) = 1 minute (min)
60 minutes = 1 hour (h)
24 hours = 1 day
7 days = 1 week (wk)
52 weeks = 1 year (yr)
365 days = 1 year
366 days = 1 leap year
10 years = 1 decade
100 years = 1 century

Complete. Use the equivalent measures in the table at the right.

1. 180 s = _____ min   73 days = _____ yr
2. 32 h = _____ days   60 days = _____ h
3. 8 days = _____ h   2,480 h = _____ days
4. 60 wk = _____ yr   8 decades = _____ yr
5. 3 wk = _____ days   22 min = _____ s
6. 24 h = _____ min   260 wk = _____ decade
7. 15 min = _____ s   2 yr = _____ days
8. 28 days = _____ wk   120 yr = _____ decades
9. 3 yr = _____ wk   150 yr = _____ centuries
10. 10 min = _____ hr   6 h = _____ day

Time Zones

The continental United States (not including Alaska and Hawaii) has four time zones. Each zone is one hour later than the zone to its west.

If it is 5 P.M. in New York, then it is 4 P.M. in Illinois, 3 P.M. in Colorado, and 2 P.M. in California.

Complete.

11. It is noon in IL. What time is it in MD? _____ In UT? _____ In OR? _____

12. A football game begins at 3 P.M. in NY. What is the starting time on television in CA? _____

13. It is midnight in NM. What time is it in NV? _____ In OK? _____ In FL? _____

14. It is 9 A.M. in NY, where Joe lives. He wants to phone his aunt in eastern KS.

    What time is it there? _____

15. It is 2:30 P.M. in OH. What time is it in CO? _____ In SC? _____ In TX? _____

16. How many hours time difference is there between MA and CA? _____

Unit 3 Lesson 9

The U.S. armed forces use a **24**-hour clock. The time of day is written as a four-digit number from **0000** (midnight) to **1200** (noon) to **2400** (midnight).

Examples
3:00 A.M.   0300
7:30 A.M.   0730
1:15 P.M.   1315
8:45 P.M.   2045

In **24**-hour time, the first two digits tell the number of hours after midnight. The last two digits tell the number of minutes after the hour.

Write the 24-hour time as A.M. or P.M. time.

17. 2120 _____   1314 _____   1000 _____   1610 _____

18. 2215 _____   0710 _____   1255 _____   2321 _____

Write the A.M. or P.M. time as 24-hour time.

19. 9:20 A.M. _____   3:40 P.M. _____   5:18 A.M. _____   11:00 P.M. _____

20. 2:30 P.M. _____   4:12 P.M. _____   4:45 A.M. _____   5:18 P.M. _____

Solve.

21. Maria boarded a bus at **0930**. She traveled for $3\frac{1}{4}$ hours. What time did she arrive? Write your answer in both A.M. or P.M. time and 24-hour time. _____

22. The Miscio family left Atlanta at **8:00** A.M. and arrived in Sacramento at **10:45** A.M. on a non stop flight. How long was the family in the air?

_____

 Quick Check

Complete. Estimate the Fahrenheit or Celsius temperature.   Work Space.

23. 60°F = _____ °C   **24.** 80°C = _____ °F   **25.** 35°F = _____ °C

Solve. Write the A.M. or P.M. time and the 24-hour time.

26. It is **2:30** P.M. in PA. What time is it in AZ, which is two time zones west of PA?

A.M. or P.M. time _____   24-hour time _____

27. It is **1730** at an air force base in OR. What time is it in TN, which is three time zones to the east?

A.M. or P.M. time _____   24-hour time _____

92   Unit 3 Lesson 9

Name _____

Problem Solving Strategy: Make a Table

To solve some problems, making a table can help you to organize information and to plan a solution strategy.

When you make a table, think about how you will label the rows and columns.

Problem

One year the Buccaneers won 16, lost 4, and tied 3 games. The next year they won 17, lost 5, and tied 1. In the third year, they won 15, lost 2, and tied 6. What is the team's three-year record? Which was their best year?

---

1 Understand   As you reread the problem, ask yourself questions.

- What was the team's record each year?

    First year: **16-4-3**
    Second year: **17-5-1**
    Third year: **15-2-6**

- What do you need to find? _____

---

2 Decide   Choose a method for solving.

Try the strategy Make a Table.

- Set up a table with a row for each year. Use columns for wins, losses, and ties.

	Wins	Losses	Ties
Year 1			
Year 2			
Year 3			

- How will you decide which year the team had the best record?

---

3 Solve   Answer the two questions.

- Add a "Totals" row to the table. Find the total number of wins, losses, and ties for the three years.

    _____

	Wins	Losses	Ties
Year 1			
Year 2			
Year 3			
Totals			

- Explain how you selected which year the team had the best record.

    _____

---

4 Look back   Ask if your answers make sense.

- Did others agree with which year the team had their best record?

    _____

Unit 3 Lesson 10

Use the Make a Table strategy or any other strategy you have learned.

1. The table shows the annual per person consumption (in gallons) of milk and soda. If the trend continues, what will be the consumption of milk and soda in **2000**?

	1985	1990	1995
Milk	26.4	25.3	24.2
Soda	24.6	26.8	29.0

Think: What patterns do you see? How can you extend these patterns?

_____

Answer _____

2. Trent made **3** rectangles. The first was **3.2** cm by **4.6** cm. He doubled these dimensions to make the second rectangle and tripled them to make the third rectangle. Find the area and perimeter of each and describe any patterns.

Think: How can you organize your results? Use a table.

_____

Answer _____

3. Describe the pattern and write the next three numbers in the pattern.

3, 7, 15, 31, _____, _____, _____

_____

_____

231, 23.1, 2.31, _____, _____, _____

_____

4. A deli offers a choice of ham, turkey, or roast beef and a choice of provolone or Swiss cheese in their meat-and-cheese sandwiches. How many different sandwiches can you make?

_____

_____

_____

5. Find two consecutive numbers whose product is **240**.

_____

6. Sarah is making a beaded necklace. She uses **2** red, **1** white, **3** blue and then starts over with the **2** red. If she continues this pattern, what color will the **28**th bead be?

_____

7. At **6:45** A.M. you begin an eight-mile hike. At **7:20** A.M. you have hiked one mile. If you hike at the same speed the entire day, when will you finish your hike?

_____

8. Ms. Bogardus is hanging mobiles in her classroom. Four of them will hang $2\frac{1}{2}$ feet from the ceiling. Three of them will hang down **18** inches. What is the shortest length of string (in yards) she will need?

_____

Name _____

Unit 3 Review

Circle the best estimate of the measure.

1. **Capacity:** cup of cocoa
   2.5 mL 25 mL 250 mL

2. **Mass:** hamburger patty
   150 g 1500 g 1.5 kg

3. **Temperature:** hot summer day
   30°C 80°C 140°C

Complete.

4. 24 cm = _____ mm

5. 1.3 cm = _____ m

6. 55 L = _____ kL

7. 2 L = _____ mL

8. 3.1 kg = _____ g

9. 5 mg = _____ g

10. 5.1 cm² = _____ m³

11. 0.2 cm² = _____ mm²

12. 254 cm² = _____ m³

13. 254 cm³ = _____ mm³

14. $4\frac{1}{2}$ ft = _____ in.

15. 120 in. = _____ yd

16. 12 lb = _____ oz

17. 9 pt = _____ qt

18. $2\frac{1}{2}$ c = _____ fl oz

19. $\frac{1}{2}$ ton = _____ lb

20. What is the area of a rectangle with dimensions $1\frac{1}{2}$ ft by 6 in.?

    Write your answer in square inches. _____

Write the approximate Fahrenheit temperature.

21. 20°C = _____

22. 32°C = _____

Express the 24-hour clock time as a 12-hour clock time using A.M. and P.M.

23. 0745 _____

24. 1820 _____

25. 1223 _____

It is 2:15 P.M. in time zone 1. What time is it in the other time zones? (Use the map on page 91.)

26. Zone 2 _____

27. Zone 3 _____

28. Zone 4 _____

Problem Solving Reasoning Solve.

29. The volume of a wheelbarrow is **3** cubic feet. A sandbox holds **3** cubic yards. How many trips will it take with the wheelbarrow to fill it? _____

30. The standard workday is **8** hours. Steve worked **12** days in a row and was paid **$648**. How much did he make per hour?

    _____

Cumulative Review ★ Test Prep

Name _____

Use these boxes to answer questions 1 and 2.

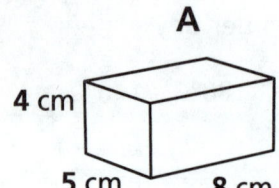

A

4 cm, 5 cm, 8 cm

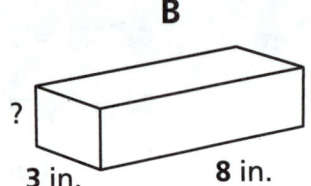

B

?, 3 in., 8 in.

1. What is the volume of box A?

A 160 cm
B 160 cm²
C 160 cm³
D 17 cm

2. The volume of box B is 48 in.³. What is its height?

F 2 in.
G 2 in.²
H 6 in.²
J 8 in.

Use these containers to answer questions 3 and 4.

0.52 Kg

20 Gal

3. What is the mass of sand in grams?

A 5,200 g
B 520 g
C 52 g
D 5.2 g

4. What is the volume of paint in pints?

F 40 pt
G 80 pt
H 160 pt
J 320 pt

5. Which is the quotient of $1\frac{1}{8} \div \frac{2}{16}$?

A 9
B $\frac{9}{64}$
C $\frac{1}{9}$
D $\frac{1}{32}$

6. The area formula for a triangle is $\frac{1}{2}bh$. What is the area of this triangle?

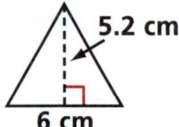
5.2 cm, 6 cm

F 90.6 cm²
G 15.6 cm
H 15.6 cm²
J 9.6 cm

7. These are the number of coins some students counted in their backpacks.

9, 7, 3, 8, 4, 5, 23, 7, 16

What is the mode of the coin data set?

A 20
B 9.1
C 6.5
D 7
E Not here

8. Evaluate for $a = 0.2$ and $b = \frac{3}{4}$.

$$2.8b + 3(a + b)$$

F 3.31
G 3.41
H 4.51
J 4.95
K Not here

9. Which shows the value of $\frac{2}{3} \times 1\frac{1}{5} + 7^2$?

A $49\frac{4}{5}$
B $33\frac{7}{15}$
C $7\frac{4}{5}$
D $\frac{4}{5}$

96 Unit 3 Cumulative Review

UNIT 4 • TABLE OF CONTENTS

Ratios, Proportions, and Percents

Lesson	Page
1 Ratios	99
2 **Algebra** • Unit Rates	101
3 **Algebra** • Solving Proportions	103
4 **Algebra** • Direct Proportion	105
5 **Algebra** • Inverse Proportion	107
6 **Problem Solving Application:** Is the Answer Reasonable?	109
7 Scale Drawing	111
8 Percents, Decimals, and Fractions	114
9 Fractional and Decimal Percents	117
10 Percents Greater than 100%	119
11 Estimating with Fractions, Decimals, and Percents	121
12 **Problem Solving Strategy:** Work Backward	123
• Unit 4 Review	125
• Cumulative Review ★ Test Prep	126

Dear Family,

During the next few weeks, our math class will be studying ratios, proportions, and percents. This includes setting up and solving proportions and using ratios and rates to solve problems. You can expect to see homework that provides practice with these skills. Here is a sample you may want to keep handy to give help if needed.

We will be using this vocabulary:

ratio a comparison by division of two quantities with like units, such as cups of flour and cups of sugar

rate a comparison of two quantities with unlike units, such as words per minute

unit rate a rate that compares a quantity to **1** such as **45** miles per **1** hour

proportion an equation that states that two ratios are equal

direct proportion a relationship between two quantities such that both increase simultaneously

inverse proportion a relationship between two quantities such that one quantity increases as the other decreases

scale drawing a picture or drawing that is an enlargement or reduction of another

percent a ratio that compares a number with **100**

Solving a Proportion

One way to solve a proportion is to use the Cross Products Property. In a proportion, if $\frac{a}{b} = \frac{c}{d}$, then $a \cdot d = b \cdot c$.

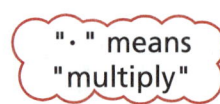
" · " means "multiply"

Example $\frac{9}{36} = \frac{5}{n}$

$5 \cdot 36 = 9 \cdot n$ Apply the Cross Products Property.

$\frac{\overset{20}{\cancel{180}}}{\cancel{9}} = \frac{9 \cdot n}{\cancel{9}}$ Divide each side by **9**.

$20 = n$ Simplify.

Using Percents

To find values such as **8.5%** of a number, students need to be able to write a percent as a fraction and as a decimal.

Example $8.5\% \rightarrow \frac{8.5}{100} = \frac{85}{1{,}000} \rightarrow 0.085$

During this unit, students will continue to learn new techniques related to problem solving and will continue to practice basic skills with fractions and decimals.

Sincerely,

Rates and Ratios

A **ratio** is a comparison by division of two like quantities.

Example:
Use *2 cups* of flour *to 1 cup* of sugar.
There are *2 girls to* every *3 boys* in the class.

Either of the two numbers in a ratio is called its **terms**.

Writing Ratios
A ratio is a comparison of **like** quantities. A ratio is usually written without units.

The ratio **2** girls to every **3** boys can be written in three forms:

$$2 \text{ to } 3 \quad \text{or} \quad 2:3 \quad \text{or} \quad \frac{2}{3}$$

Ratios are not written as mixed numbers.

Other Example: The ratio **64** points to **56** points is written:

$$64 \text{ to } 56 \quad \text{or} \quad 64:56 \quad \text{or} \quad \frac{64}{56}$$

A **rate** is a comparison of two unlike quantities.

Example:
She is driving *45 miles per hour*.
The sale price is *3 boxes for $10*.

We bought *2 pizzas for 5 people*.

Writing Rates
A rate is a comparison of **unlike** quantities. A rate is always written with units.

The rate **2** pizzas for **6** people is written:

$$\frac{2 \text{ pizzas}}{6 \text{ people}} \quad \text{or} \quad \frac{2}{6} \text{ pizza per person}$$

Rates are usually written in per unit form.

Other Example: The rate **6** classes each day is written:

$$\frac{6 \text{ classes}}{1 \text{ day}} \quad \text{or} \quad 6 \text{ classes per day}$$

Identify the comparison as a rate or ratio.

1. **3** inches per day _____
2. **15** rose bushes to **8** lily plants _____
3. **4** computers for each classroom _____

   22 students to **3** adults _____
   6 pounds seed to **100** square feet _____
   5 gal lemonade to **2** gal soda pop _____

Write each comparison as a rate.

4. **32** oz box for **$2.24** _____
5. **82** points for **4** games _____
6. **$35** for **2** hours _____

   68 miles per **2** gallons of gas _____
   30 points on each assignment _____
   8 campers in a cabin _____

Write each comparison as a ratio in two ways.

7. **4** infielders to **3** outfielders _____
8. **2** cardinals to **3** robins _____
9. **6** cups flour to **2** cups sugar _____

   16 girls to **14** boys _____
   3 blue cars for every **10** cars _____
   $5 to **$30** _____

Unit 4 Lesson 1

Like fractions, ratios can be simplified using multiplication and division. Before you simplify a ratio, you should always be sure that terms of the ratio are in the same unit.

Write the ratio of hours spent biking to hours spent studying in simplest form.

biking → 14 hours
studying → 6 hours

$\dfrac{14 \text{ hours}}{6 \text{ hours}} = \dfrac{14}{6} \rightarrow \dfrac{7}{3}$

(same units)

Write the ratio of width to length in simplest form.

4 in. ☐ 2 ft

It is usually easier to change the greater unit to the lesser unit.

(1 ft = 12 in.)

$\dfrac{4 \text{ inches}}{2 \text{ feet}} = \dfrac{4 \text{ inches}}{24 \text{ inches}} \rightarrow \dfrac{4}{24} \rightarrow \dfrac{1}{6}$

(different units)

Write the ratio in its simplest form.

10. 3 days to 1 week _____   45 pounds to 70 pounds _____   1 hour to 1 day _____

11. 1 pound to 32 ounces _____   3 months to 2 years _____   2 ft to 10 in. _____

12. 5 feet to 5 yards _____   4 dimes to 5 dollars _____   4 cups to 1 pint _____

13. 3 dollars to 5 dollars _____   40 min to 1 h _____   2 g to 50 mg _____

14. 25 cm to 1 m _____   8 hours to 3 days _____   3 yards to 2 feet _____

Problem Solving Reasoning Solve.

15. Tonya traveled a distance of 150 miles in 3 hours. Melba traveled a distance of 98 miles in 2 hours. Who was traveling at a greater rate of speed? Explain.

16. Lou typed 96 words in 2 minutes. Tara typed 126 words in 4 minutes. Rob typed 140 words in 5 minutes. Who is the fastest typist? Explain.

Test Prep ★ Mixed Review

17 The area of a lawn is 15 square yards. How many square feet is that?

A 5
B 45
C 90
D 135

18 For the following data, what does the value 10.5 represent?

13, 7, 8, 17, 10, 8

F mode
G median
H mean
J range

100   Unit 4 Lesson 1

Name _____

Unit Rates

If you can make **20** paper stars in **5** minutes, then you can make **4** paper stars in **1** minute.

$$\frac{20 \text{ stars}}{5 \text{ minutes}} = \frac{4 \text{ stars}}{1 \text{ minute}}$$

Rates are simplified by writing them as **unit rates,** that is, rates whose second term is a single unit. To find a unit rate, you need to divide to find an equivalent rate with a denominator of **1** unit.

You were paid **$28** for **4** hours of work. Write the hourly wage as a rate. Then, find the unit rate.

$$\frac{\text{amount paid}}{\text{time}} \rightarrow \frac{\$28}{4 \text{ h}} = \frac{\$28 \div 4}{4 \text{ h} \div 4} \rightarrow \frac{\$7}{1 \text{ h}}$$

The hourly wage is **$7.00** per hour.

You washed **50** plates in **8** minutes. Write this information as a rate. Then, find a unit rate.

$$\frac{\text{plates washed}}{\text{time}} \rightarrow \frac{50 \text{ plates}}{8 \text{ min}} = \frac{50 \text{ plates} \div 8}{8 \text{ min} \div 8}$$
$$= \frac{6.25 \text{ plates}}{1 \text{ min}}$$

You washed about **6** plates per minute.

Write the unit rate.

1. $\frac{360 \text{ words}}{5 \text{ minutes}}$ _____ $\frac{6 \text{ beanbags}}{\$4.00}$ _____ $\frac{96 \text{ students}}{3 \text{ classrooms}}$ _____

2. $\frac{2 \text{ cups}}{4 \text{ minutes}}$ _____ $\frac{2 \text{ bags}}{8 \text{ people}}$ _____ $\frac{42 \text{ yards}}{3 \text{ plays}}$ _____

3. $\frac{22.5 \text{ miles}}{4 \text{ hour}}$ _____ $\frac{4 \text{ tops}}{\$5.00}$ _____ $\frac{138 \text{ pages}}{12 \text{ minutes}}$ _____

4. **6** books for every **3** students   **9** bars of soap for **3** dollars

   _____ _____   _____ _____

5. **3** rulers for **3** students   **3** pounds for **12** people

   _____ _____   _____ _____

6. **$1.00** for **10** fish hooks   **45** people in **9** cars

   _____ _____   _____ _____

7. **60** hours in **6** weeks   **$21.35** for **7** feet

   _____ _____   _____ _____

8. **18** pine cones for **3** wreaths   **72** holes for **4** golf courses

   _____ _____   _____ _____

A **unit price** is the cost per unit of an item or service. Comparing unit prices can help you decide what is the better buy.

One brand of corn flakes comes in two different-sized boxes. The **15** oz box costs **$2.79**. The larger, **18** oz box costs **$3.29**. Which is the better buy, that is, which box has the lower cost per ounce?

You want to find the cost **per** ounce, so divide the cost by the number of ounces.

$2.79 for a 15 oz box

$$\frac{\$2.79}{15 \text{ oz}} \rightarrow 15\overline{)2.790}^{.186}$$

The unit price is about **$.186**, or **18.6¢**, per ounce.

$3.29 for an 18 oz box

$$\frac{\$3.29}{18 \text{ oz}} \rightarrow 18\overline{)3.2900}^{.1827}$$

The unit price is about **$.183**, or **18.3¢**, per ounce.

The **18** oz box is the better buy.

Find the unit price to the nearest tenth of a cent. Circle the item that is a better buy.

9. Foil: **$5.59** for **200** feet

    or **$2.39** for **75** feet

    Hot dogs: **8** for **$2.19**

    or **10** for **$2.79**

    Frozen yogurt: **0.5** gal for **$2.25**

    or **2** gal for **$8.00**

10. Potatoes: **10**-lb bag for **$1.99**

    or a **25**-lb bag for **$4.50**

    Cereal: **16**-oz box for **$3.49**

    or **20**-oz box for **$4.19**

    Apples: **3** dozen for **$4.80**

    or **6** for **90¢**

Problem Solving Reasoning   Solve.

11. John bought a quart of Mill's ice cream for **$2.99**. Amy bought a half-gallon of Mill's ice cream for **$4.69**. Who got the better buy? Explain. _____

12. Both you and your friend have weekend jobs. You were paid **$84** for **12** hours of work. Your friend was paid **$72** for **9** hours of work. Who has the higher hourly wage? Explain. _____

Test Prep ★ Mixed Review

13. What is the value of the expression $3 + 5 \times 7 - 2 \times 6$?

    A 26

    B 44

    C 240

    D 324

14. What is the greatest common factor of 72, 15, and 45?

    F 15

    G 9

    H 5

    J 3

Name _____

Proportions

A **proportion** is an equation that states that two ratios are equal. To solve a proportion, you find the value of the missing term, **n**.

$\frac{8}{5} = \frac{n}{25}$ proportion

Read the proportion as:
"**8** is to **5** as **n** is to **25**"

Here are two examples that show how to use mental math to solve proportions.

Solve: $\frac{8}{5} = \frac{n}{25}$

If the missing term is in the numerator, write both ratios with the same denominator. A common denominator of **5** and **25** is **25**, so rewrite $\frac{8}{5}$.

Multiply the numerator and the denominator by **5**. $\frac{5 \cdot 8}{5 \cdot 5} = \frac{n}{25}$

Simplify. $\frac{40}{25} = \frac{n}{25}$

The denominators both equal **25**, so **n = 40**.

Solve: $\frac{48}{n} = \frac{6}{9}$

If the missing term is in the denominator, write both ratios with the same numerator. Since **48** is a multiple of **6**, rewrite $\frac{6}{9}$ with a numerator of **48**.

Multiply both the numerator and the denominator by **8**. $\frac{48}{n} = \frac{6 \cdot 8}{9 \cdot 8}$

Simplify. $\frac{48}{n} = \frac{48}{72}$

The numerators both equal **48**, so **n = 72**.

Write the proportion as an equation. Sometimes the terms in a ratio are not whole numbers.

1. **8** is to **12** as **x** is to **48**   _____   **24** is to **26** as **2** is to **x**   _____   **9** is to **n** as **3** is to **12**   _____

2. **m** is to **20** as **4** is to **5**   _____   **18** is to **t** as **6** is to **7**   _____   **2.4** is to **2.8** as **w** is to **3**   _____

3. **a** is to **b** as **c** is to **d**   _____   **10** is to **15** as **100** is to **h**   _____   **8** is to $\frac{1}{2}$ as $\frac{3}{4}$ is to **x**   _____

Solve the proportion, that is, find the missing term.

4. $\frac{5}{3} = \frac{x}{12}$ _____ $\frac{n}{24} = \frac{5}{8}$ _____ $\frac{x}{10} = \frac{3}{5}$ _____

5. $\frac{8}{13} = \frac{t}{26}$ _____ $\frac{8}{m} = \frac{4}{3}$ _____ $\frac{28}{p} = \frac{7}{11}$ _____

6. $\frac{k}{9} = \frac{5}{3}$ _____ $\frac{8}{3} = \frac{n}{18}$ _____ $\frac{12}{15} = \frac{36}{x}$ _____

7. $\frac{m}{49} = \frac{3}{7}$ _____ $\frac{24}{m} = \frac{6}{6}$ _____ $\frac{x}{30} = \frac{8}{10}$ _____

Another way to solve proportions is to use **cross products** to write a related multiplication equation.

Cross Products Property

In a proportion, if $\frac{a}{b} = \frac{c}{d}$ then $a \cdot d = b \cdot c$

$\frac{7}{12} = \frac{m}{90}$

Cross multiply. $7 \cdot 90 = 12 \cdot m$

Divide each side by 12. $\frac{630}{12} = \frac{12 \cdot m}{12}$

Simplify each side. $52.5 = m$

Solve the proportion. Use the Cross Products Property.

8. $\frac{1}{3} = \frac{15}{n}$ _____ $\frac{5}{8} = \frac{x}{12}$ _____ $\frac{5}{6} = \frac{15}{t}$ _____ $\frac{n}{8} = \frac{108}{9}$ _____

9. $\frac{39}{13} = \frac{a}{24}$ _____ $\frac{16}{24} = \frac{18}{m}$ _____ $\frac{5}{6} = \frac{x}{432}$ _____ $\frac{105}{h} = \frac{5}{8}$ _____

Problem Solving Reasoning Solve.

10. Maria bought 2 pairs of socks for $5.50. Could she buy a dozen pairs for less than $35.00? Explain. _____

✓ Quick Check

Identify each comparison as a ratio or a rate. Then, write a simplified ratio or rate.

Work Space.

11. 14 miles in 5 hours _____

12. 24 feet to 16 yards _____

13. $85 to $40 _____

Write the unit rate.

14. 1,000 words in 80 lines _____

15. 3 notebooks for 8 students _____

16. $6.38 for 24 oz _____

Solve the proportions.

17. $\frac{3}{8} = \frac{n}{40}$ _____   18. $\frac{6}{n} = \frac{23}{16}$ _____   19. $\frac{5}{12} = \frac{8}{n}$ _____

104 Unit 4 Lesson 3

Name _____

Direct Proportion

Proportions are helpful in solving problems where both quantities increase simultaneously. There are different ways to set up the pairs of numbers in a problem as a proportion.

Lee is driving at **60** miles per hour. At this rate, how long will it take to go **150** miles?

Solution

You want to know *how long,* so the missing term is time.

Compare the distance in miles to the time it takes in hours to drive that distance.

Let *x* = hours needed to drive **150** miles at **60** mph.

$\dfrac{\text{distance}}{\text{time}} \rightarrow \dfrac{60}{1} = \dfrac{150}{x} \leftarrow \dfrac{\text{distance}}{\text{time}}$

Cross multiply. $60 \cdot x = 150$

Divide each side by **60**. $\dfrac{60 \cdot x}{60} = \dfrac{150}{60}$

Simplify. $x = 2.5$

It would take **2.5** hours to drive **150** miles.

Here is another example of setting up and solving a proportion.

If you work out on a stair climber for **5** minutes, you will use about **60** calories. How long will you need to exercise on the stair climber to use **420** calories?

Solution

Set up the proportion in greater to lesser order:

$\dfrac{\text{calories used}}{\text{minutes exercised}}$

Let *n* = number of minutes needed to use **420** calories.

$\dfrac{60}{5} = \dfrac{420}{n}$

Cross multiply. $60 \cdot n = 5 \cdot 420$

Divide each side by **60**. $\dfrac{60 \cdot n}{60} = \dfrac{2{,}100}{60}$

Simplify each side. $n = 35$

You would need to exercise for **35** minutes to use **420** calories.

Set up a proportion for each problem. Then, solve the problem.

1. A student got a job during school vacation. He earned **$82.50** for the first **3** days of work. If he continues to work at the same daily rate, how much will he earn after **5** days? _____

2. How far can a train travel in **45** minutes if it is traveling at **68** miles per hour? _____

3. How many gallons would a car use on a trip of **171** miles if it used **7** gallons on a trip of **133** miles? _____

In **direct proportion** problems, as one term increases, so does the other. When solving direct proportion problems, you can write more than one proportion.

Take another look at the problem. Another way to solve it is to set up the proportion to compare quantities with similar units, that is, calories to calories and time to time.

Solution

- Set up the proportion in lesser to greater order.

  Let n = number of minutes on the stair climber to use **420** calories.

- Notice that in each case, the resulting multiplication equation after cross multiplying is the same except for the order of the factors.

fewer calories / more calories → $\dfrac{60 \text{ cal}}{420 \text{ cal}} = \dfrac{5 \text{ min}}{n \text{ min}}$ ← less time / more time

Cross multiply. $60 \cdot n = 420 \cdot 5$

Divide each side by **60**. $\dfrac{60 \cdot n}{60} = \dfrac{2{,}100}{60}$

Simplify each side. $n = 35$

Write and solve a proportion for each problem. Remember there is more than one way to set up the proportion.

4. A jet flies **102.5** miles in **25** minutes. At that rate, how far will it go in **1.5** hours? _____

5. If $4\dfrac{1}{4}$ yards of cloth cost **$25.50**, then how much will **8** yards cost? _____

6. Mario can buy a dozen pencils for **$1.20**. How much will he pay for **100** pencils? _____

Problem Solving Reasoning Solve.

7. Raj charges **$8** for a half hour of computer instruction. How many hours of instruction can you get for **$100**?

   _____

8. Maddie puts aside **$3** for every **$5** she earns. How much will she need to earn in order to save **$200**?

   _____

Test Prep ★ Mixed Review

9. Nita runs 9 miles in the same time it takes Winnie to run 12 miles. What is the simplest form of the ratio 9:12?

   A 1:15   C 3:4
   B 1:33   D 3:8

10. What value of n makes $\dfrac{1}{5} = \dfrac{n}{45}$ a true proportion?

    F 40   H 5
    G 9   J 1

106 Unit 4 Lesson 4

Name _____   **Inverse Proportion**

Sometimes the relationship between two quantities is in **inverse proportion.** That is, as one term increases, the other decreases. For example, as the *speed* of a car *increases*, the *time* it takes to get to a destination *decreases*.

A car traveling on a straight road at the rate of **30** miles per hour takes **12** minutes to go a certain distance. How long will it take a car traveling at **40** miles per hour to go the same distance on the same road?

Solution

- Identify the variable for the missing term.

  Let x = time in minutes it takes the car traveling at **40** mph to go the same distance.

- Set up a ratio using the term in the situation that has the same unit of measure.

  Both x and **12** represent minutes, so write $\frac{x}{12}$.

- Set up both ratios of the proportion in the same order. Then solve.

  $\frac{x \text{ min}}{12 \text{ min}} = \frac{30 \text{ mph}}{40 \text{ mph}}$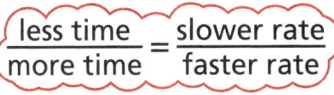
  $40x = 360$
  $x = 9$

  Decide: Which represents the lesser time, x or **12**? x should be less than **12** since it takes less time driving faster.

  It will take the car driving **40** mph **9** minutes to go the same distance as the car going **30** mph.

Write a proportion for each situation. Then solve the problem.

1. The scoutmaster thought he had enough food to feed **24** scouts at camp for **8** days. How long would the food last if **32** scouts arrived at the camp?

   _____

2. Working together, it takes Al and Marvin **3** hours to shell **20** quarts of peas. How long might it take to shell the peas if **3** more people joined them?

   _____

3. A committee of **7** students took **5** days of after-school time to decorate the auditorium for a school program. How many days would it have taken **10** students to do the same work?

   _____

4. At an average speed of **46** miles per hour, it takes about **7** hours for a truck driver to go from one end of a turnpike to the other. How long should it take the driver to travel the turnpike at an average speed of **60** miles per hour?

   _____

Unit 4 Lesson 5 **107**

Decide whether these are direct or inverse proportion problems. Then solve.

5. It takes Robin 2 hours to deliver about 50 newspapers. How long might it take her to deliver 75 papers?

   _____

6. It took 20 workers $2\frac{1}{2}$ days to repair a street.

   How long might the job have taken if only 15 workers had been working?

   _____

7. In Ohio the maximum speed limit was lowered from 70 miles per hour to 55 miles per hour. At one time, you could drive from Cleveland, OH to Columbus, OH in only 3 hours. How much time should you allow for this trip now?

   _____

8. A airplane traveling at 550 miles per hour took 4 hours to go 2,200 miles. With a tailwind, the speed of the plane increased to 560 miles per hour. How far would the plane travel in 4 hours at the greater speed?

   _____

9. Five parent volunteers spent 14 evenings helping paint the classrooms in the school building. About how many volunteers could have completed the same job in only 10 evenings?

   _____

Problem Solving Reasoning Solve.

10. Suppose you are baking 12 dozen cookies for a party. It takes 8 minutes to roll, cut, and place a **dozen** cookies on a small cookie sheet. How much total time could you save if you cut, roll, and place 18 cookies on a larger sheet in the same amount of time?

    _____

11. A candidate hired 15 people to make calls to registered voters before an election. In 4 days, the callers reached about 1,000 voters. At the same rate, about how many more voters could they have reached working for 6 days?

    _____

Test Prep ★ Mixed Review

12. What is the value of n in the proportion $\frac{3}{17} = \frac{n}{51}$?

    A 3　　　　C 17

    B 9　　　　D 37

13. It cost a company $260 to rent 4 meeting rooms at a hotel. What is the average cost per room?

    F $1,040　　H $65

    G $260　　　J $4

Name _____

Problem Solving Application:
Is the Answer Reasonable?

In order to look back to know if your answer is reasonable, you need to know some basic relationships between the common units of measure. If you know the number of seconds in a minute, you can decide whether this answer is reasonable or not by using dimensional analysis. **Dimensional analysis** is a procedure for applying unit rates in rewriting units of measure.

In this lesson, you may also need to set up and solve proportions.

> Lucine walks at a rate of 240 feet per minute. She says that she is walking at a rate of 40 feet per second. Is this answer reasonable?

Tips to Remember:

1. Understand   2. Decide   3. Solve   4. Look back

- Ask yourself: What do I know? What do I need to find?
- When you can, make a prediction about the answer. When you finish solving, ask "Is the answer reasonable?"
- Think about the strategies you have learned and use them to help you solve a problem.

Use dimensional analysis to solve. Check to see that your answer is reasonable.

1. How fast is Lucine walking in feet per second? Is she walking **40** feet per second?

Think: **1** minute = **60** seconds, so

$$\frac{240 \text{ feet}}{1 \text{ minute}} \times \frac{1 \text{ minute}}{60 \text{ seconds}} = \frac{\text{feet}}{\text{second}}$$

Answer _____

2. Mrs. Dodge plans to travel **200** miles at **60** miles per hour. Is **4** hours a reasonable time to allow? Explain.

Think: $200 \text{ miles} \times \frac{1 \text{ hour}}{60 \text{ miles}} = $ _____ hours

Answer _____

3. Paul has a yearly salary of **$34,000** and is paid weekly. He says that this works out at more than **$650** per week. Is his statement reasonable?

Think: **1** year = **52** weeks

Answer _____

4. Sally cycled a distance of **5** mi in **30** min and Hal cycled **8** km in **25** min. Sally claimed that her time was faster. Was her claim reasonable?

Think: **1** mi = **1.6** km

Answer _____

Unit 4 Lesson 6   109

Solve. Use dimensional analysis where appropriate. Is the answer provided reasonable?

5. Mr. Field checked the price of an **18** ounce box of corn flakes and found it was **$3.99**. A tag on the shelf said the unit price was **2¢** per ounce. Is this reasonable? Explain.

_____

_____

6. The exchange rate from United States dollars to Canadian dollars is **$1.00** to **$1.45**. Is it reasonable to expect more than **250** Canadian dollars for **150** U.S. dollars? Explain.

_____

_____

7. The area of a room that needs to be carpeted is **15** square yards. Is it reasonable to purchase **45** square feet of carpet to do the room? Explain.

_____

_____

8. A car is traveling at **60** miles per hour. Is this faster than **50** feet per second? Explain.

_____

_____

9. Can you earn **$500** in the next **3** weeks if you make **$5.25** per hour and work **6** hours per day, **5** days per week? Explain.

_____

_____

10. A recipe calls for $1\frac{1}{4}$ cup of milk. If you only have **one** quart of milk, is it reasonable to try to **triple** the recipe? Explain.

_____

_____

Extend Your Thinking

11. If the exchange rate were **1.45** U.S. dollars to **1** Canadian dollar, how much would you get for **150** U.S. dollars?

_____

_____

12. Explain your method for solving problem 8. Is there more than one way to solve the problem?

_____

_____

Name _____ **Scale Drawings**

A **scale drawing** is a picture or drawing in which the dimensions are proportional to the actual dimensions of an object. A scale drawing could be larger (an enlargement) or smaller (a reduction) than the actual object. Maps and blueprints are common examples of scale drawings.

The ratio of the measurements in the scale drawing to the actual measurements is called the **scale factor.** To find the actual size of an object, you can use the scale factor to write a proportion.

The blueprint has a scale factor of $\frac{1}{4}$ in. to **1** ft. What is the actual width of the bedroom?

Solution: Let x = width of the room in feet. Set up a proportion and simplify the fractions.

$2\frac{1}{2} = \frac{5}{2}$

feet   inches
↓   ↓

$\frac{1}{x} = \dfrac{\frac{1}{4}}{\frac{5}{2}}$

Think:
$\frac{1}{4} \times \frac{2}{5} = \frac{1}{10}$

$\frac{1}{x} = \frac{1}{10}$

$x = 10$

The bedroom is **10** feet wide.

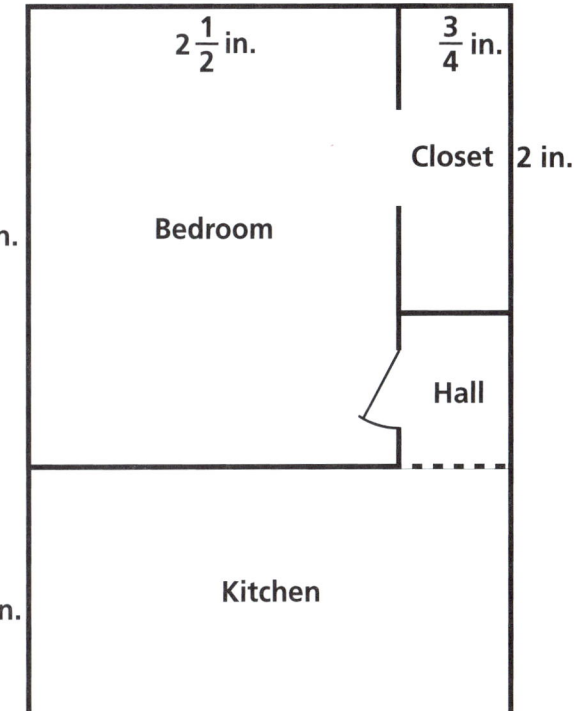

Use the blueprint to complete the table.

	Room	Blueprint Length	Actual Length	Blueprint Width	Actual Width
1.	Bedroom				
2.	Kitchen				
3.	Closet				
4.	Hall				

Use a scale factor of $\frac{1}{8}$ in. to 1 ft to find the actual length.

5. scale of $2\frac{1}{4}$ in. = actual length of _____   scale of $1\frac{1}{2}$ in. = actual length of _____

6. scale of $1\frac{3}{4}$ in. = actual length of _____   scale of $2\frac{5}{8}$ in. = actual length of _____

Unit 4 Lesson 7

If you know the scale of a map, you can use proportions to estimate the actual distance.

On the trail map, the distance from Benson's Cabin to Roaring Falls is **3.8 cm**. What is the actual distance between the two places?

Solution:

Let *x* = actual distance in km

The map has been drawn using a **scale** of **2 cm : 3 km**. Use the scale to set up the proportion:

$$\frac{2 \text{ cm}}{3 \text{ km}} = \frac{3.8 \text{ cm}}{x}$$

$$2x = 3 \cdot 3.8$$

$$\frac{2x}{2} = \frac{11.4}{2}$$

$$x = 5.7$$

The actual distance from Benson's Cabin to Roaring Falls is **5.7** km.

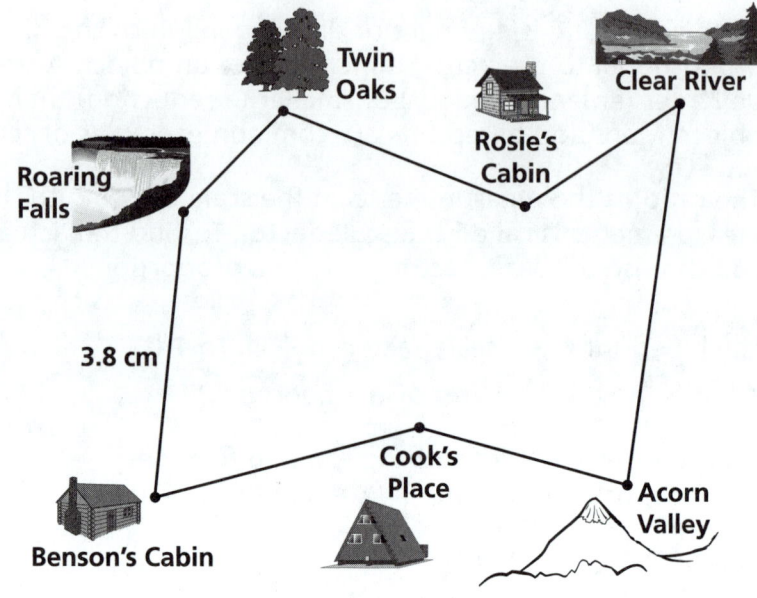

Scale: **2 cm = 3 km**

Use a metric ruler to measure each trail to the nearest tenth of a centimeter. Then, find the actual distance.

7. Benson's Cabin to Roaring Falls   scale _____   actual _____

8. Roaring Falls to Twin Oaks   scale _____   actual _____

9. Twin Oaks to Rosie's Cabin   scale _____   actual _____

10. Rosie's Cabin to Clear River   scale _____   actual _____

11. Clear River to Acorn Valley   scale _____   actual _____

12. Acorn Valley to Cook's Place   scale _____   actual _____

13. Cook's Place to Benson's Cabin   scale _____   actual _____

14. What is the actual roundtrip distance? _____

15. If you hike at a rate of **5 kilometers per hour**, approximately how long will the roundtrip take? _____

Name _____

Use a metric ruler to construct a scale drawing on the grid.

16. Measure the dimensions of the figure below in centimeters. Enlarge the figure by a scale factor of **3 : 1**; that is, draw all dimensions three times longer.

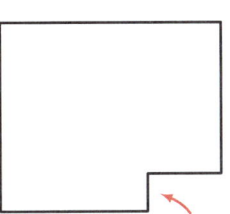

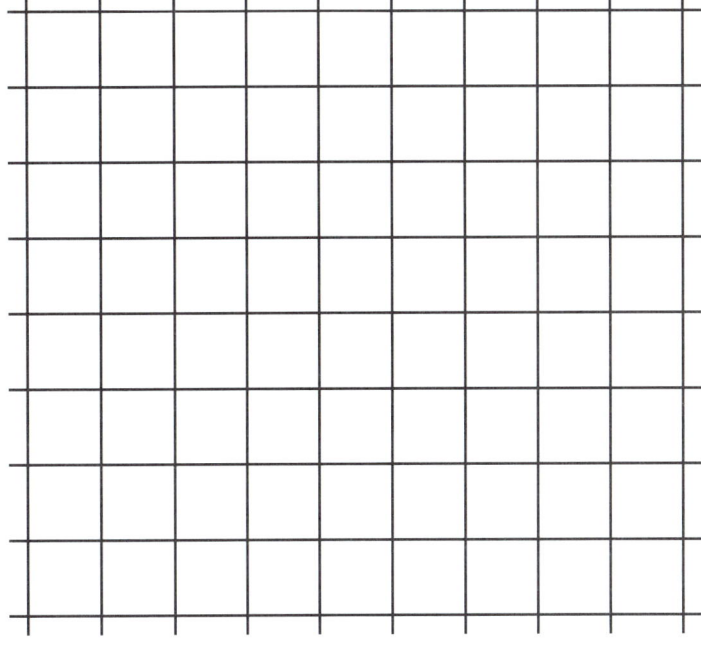

Use the figures in exercise 16 to complete.

17. What is the ratio of the perimeters of the enlarged and original figures? How is this ratio related to the scale factor?

_____

_____

18. What is the ratio of the areas of the enlarged and original figures? How is this ratio related to the scale factor?

_____

_____

 Quick Check

Decide whether the situation is a direct or inverse proportion. Then solve.

Work Space.

19. On the highway, a sports car averages **32** miles on a gallon of gas. The car went **512** miles on a tank of gas. About how much does the gas tank hold? _____

20. Working together, it takes **2** students about **3** hours to set up the cafeteria for a party. How long would it have taken if **3** more students had offered to help? _____

The scale on a map is $\frac{1}{4}$ in. = 3 mi. Complete the statement.

21. **6** in. on the map represents _____ mi.

22. _____ in. represents **15** mi.

Unit 4 Lesson 7

Name _____

Percents, Decimals, and Fractions

A **percent** is a ratio with a denominator of **100**. The symbol % means *per one hundred*. The square at the right contains **100** small squares. Each small square is **1%** of the whole square.

24 of the **100** little squares are shaded. So **24%** of the large square is shaded.

76 of the **100** little squares are unshaded. So **76%** of the large square is unshaded.

Complete. Do not use the same square more than once.

1. Shade **10%** of the squares gray. What percent of the grid is unshaded? _____

2. Put X's in **25%** of the squares. What percent of the grid remains blank? _____

3. Put O's in **15%** of the squares. What percent of the grid remains blank? _____

4. Using different colors, show **20%**; **8%**; **2%**; **5%**; **15%**

5. What percent of the grid remains blank? _____

6. Is the entire region marked or shaded? _____

Write the percent.

7. Mary's sweater is **80%** cotton. What percent is not cotton? _____

8. Jamal said his team won **80%** of their games. What percent did they lose? _____

9. If **93%** of your class has perfect attendance, what percent have been absent? _____

10. If **70%** of Earth's surface is water, what percent is not water? _____

11. So far, Mr. Quinn has planted **48%** of his farm in corn and **23%** in oats. What percent of the farm is not planted? _____

12. A survey showed that **45%** of the class likes peas, **32%** likes carrots, and **38%** like neither. What percent of the class like both peas and carrots? _____

Name _____

Percents can be written in more than one form.

Percent Form	Fraction Form	Decimal Form
50%	$\frac{50}{100}$	0.50

Study these examples of how to use the meaning of percent to change between percent and decimal form.

Writing a Percent as a Decimal

To change from a percent to a decimal, remove the % symbol and multiply by **0.01**. This is the same as moving the decimal point two places to the left.

Write the percent as an equivalent fraction in hundredths first.

Write **58%** as a decimal.

$$58\% \rightarrow \frac{58}{100} \rightarrow 0.58$$

Write **7.5%** as a decimal.

$$7.5\% \rightarrow \frac{7.5}{100} \rightarrow 0.075$$

Writing a Decimal as a Percent

To change from a decimal to a percent, multiply the decimal by **100** and write a % symbol. This is the same as moving the decimal point two places to the right.

Write the decimal as an equivalent fraction in hundredths first.

Write **0.42** as a percent.

$$0.42 \rightarrow \frac{42}{100} \rightarrow 42\%$$

Write **0.2** as a percent.

$$0.2 \rightarrow \frac{20}{100} \rightarrow 20\%$$

Write the percent as a decimal.

13. 15% = _____   65% = _____   7% = _____   90% = _____

14. 60% = _____   7.5% = _____   20% = _____   73% = _____

15. 11% = _____   1.2% = _____   12.5% = _____   8.75% = _____

Write the decimal as a percent.

16. 0.28 = _____%   0.13 = _____%   0.065 = _____%   0.80 = _____%

17. 0.92 = _____%   0.43 = _____%   0.5 = _____%   0.3 = _____%

18. 0.05 = _____%   0.64 = _____%   0.01 = _____%   0.4 = _____%

Unit 4 Lesson 8

Study these examples of how to change between percent and fraction form.

Writing a Percent as a Fraction

Write the percent as an equivalent fraction in hundredths first. Then simplify.

Write **64%** as a fraction.

$$64\% \rightarrow \frac{64}{100} = \frac{16}{25}$$

Write **5%** as a fraction.

$$5\% \rightarrow \frac{5}{100} = \frac{1}{20}$$

Writing a Fraction as a Percent

Write the fraction as an equivalent fraction in hundredths first.

Write $\frac{3}{4}$ as a percent.

$$\frac{3}{4} \rightarrow \frac{75}{100} = 75\%$$

Other Example
Sometimes you may need to write the fraction as an equivalent fraction in thousandths first.

Write $\frac{3}{8}$ as a percent.

$$\frac{3}{8} \rightarrow \frac{375}{1,000} \rightarrow \frac{37.5}{100} = 37.5\%$$

Write the percent as a fraction.

19. 24% = _____   60% = _____   15% = _____   45% = _____

20. 18% = _____   95% = _____   80% = _____   4% = _____

Write the fraction as a percent.

21. $\frac{65}{100}$ = _____ $\frac{19}{50}$ = _____ $\frac{1}{8}$ = _____ $\frac{3}{25}$ = _____

22. $\frac{3}{10}$ = _____ $\frac{6}{10}$ = _____ $\frac{1}{20}$ = _____ $\frac{11}{20}$ = _____

Problem Solving Reasoning   Solve.

23. On Monday, **4** students were absent from a class of **25** students. What percent of the students in the class were present on Monday? _____

24. Kayla got some money for her birthday. She spent **0.65** of her money on school supplies. What percent of her money is left? _____

Test Prep ★ Mixed Review

25. The scale on a map is 1 cm : 500 m. What is the actual distance between towns that are 10.5 cm apart on the map?

  A 47.6 m   C 5,250 m
  B 5,250 km   D 5,250 cm

26. A car went 84 miles in $3\frac{1}{2}$ hours? How can you express this rate as a unit rate?

  F 294 miles per hour   H $3\frac{1}{2}$ hours
  G 84 miles   J 24 miles per hour

Name _____

Fractional and Decimal Percents

Sometimes you need to use fractions or decimals to write a percent as an equivalent fraction in hundredths or thousandths.

Writing a Percent as a Decimal

To write a percent as a decimal, remove the % symbol and multiply by **0.01**.

Write $\frac{1}{3}$% as a decimal. $\left(\frac{1}{3} = 0.\bar{3}\right)$

$\frac{1}{3}\% \rightarrow 0.\bar{3}\% \rightarrow 0.33\bar{3} \cdot 0.01 = 0.0033\bar{3}$ or $0.00\bar{3}$

Writing a Decimal as a Percent

To write a decimal as a percent, multiply the decimal by **100** and write a % symbol.

Write **0.00825** as a percent.

$0.00825 \cdot 100 = 0.825\%$

Writing a Percent as a Fraction

To write a percent as a fraction, remove the % symbol, and multiply by $\frac{1}{100}$.

Write $7\frac{1}{4}$% as a fraction.

$7\frac{1}{4}\% \rightarrow \frac{29}{4}\% \rightarrow \frac{29}{4} \cdot \frac{1}{100} = \frac{29}{400}$

Writing a Fraction as a Percent

To write a fraction as a percent, multiply by **100,** and write a % symbol.

Write $\frac{2}{3}$ as a percent.

$\frac{2}{3} \cdot 100 \rightarrow \frac{200}{3} = 66\frac{2}{3}\%$

Write the percent as a decimal and a fraction.

1. 18.5% = _____   1.25% = _____   20% = _____ $22\frac{1}{2}$% = _____

2. $8\frac{3}{4}$% = _____   1.02% = _____ $6\frac{1}{2}$% = _____ $8\frac{1}{6}$% = _____

3. 62.4% = _____   0.1% = _____   0.5% = _____ $\frac{3}{4}$% = _____

4. 21.5% = _____ $19\frac{3}{4}$% = _____   99% = _____   0.99% = _____

Write the decimal or fraction as a percent.

5. 0.544 = _____% $\frac{5}{12}$ = _____% $\frac{1}{3}$ = _____% $\frac{3}{5}$ = _____%

6. 0.0125 = _____%   0.008 = _____%   0.955 = _____% $\frac{7}{40}$ = _____%

7. $\frac{7}{20}$ = _____% $\frac{7}{1000}$ = _____% $\frac{5}{6}$ = _____%   0.111 = _____%

8. 0.625 = _____% $\frac{1}{7}$ = _____% $\frac{4}{9}$ = _____%   2.5 = _____%

Unit 4 Lesson 9

Certain percents are used more often than others. Complete the following table of *benchmark* percents.

	Percent	50%		10%		5%		$66\frac{2}{3}$%
9.								
10.	Fraction		$\frac{1}{3}$		$\frac{1}{100}$		$\frac{3}{4}$	
11.	Decimal			0.25		0.2		0.15

Problem Solving / Reasoning Solve.

12. A baked potato has **25** units of Vitamin A. Nutritionists suggest that the average daily amount should be **5,000** units of Vitamin A. What percent of the daily recommended amount does a baked potato have? _____

13. You read in a newspaper that the bank offered an interest rate of $8\frac{5}{8}$% on a personal loan. What is the decimal form of this interest rate?

_____

14. Write $\frac{1}{8}, \frac{2}{8}, \frac{3}{8}, \ldots, \frac{8}{8}$ as percents. Describe the pattern that you observe.

_____
_____

15. A sign painter ran out of paint. What percent of the sign still needs to be painted? _____

 Quick Check

Write the percent as a decimal and a fraction.

16. 60%   **17.** 8%   **18.** 5.9%

_____   _____   _____

19. 0.2%   **20.** 8.5%   **21.** $66\frac{2}{3}$%

_____   _____   _____

Write the decimal or fraction as a percent.

22. $\frac{3}{4}$ **23.** 0.7   **24.** $\frac{19}{25}$

_____   _____   _____

25. $\frac{9}{40}$ **26.** 0.0175   **27.** $\frac{1}{200}$

_____   _____   _____

Work Space.

Name _____ **Percents Greater than 100%**

Percents greater than **100%** represent more than the whole. You may have scored more than **100%** on a test because of extra credit. You may have heard someone say, "I feel **200%** better!" The price of certain goods may have increased **350%**.

These are all examples of percents greater than **100%**. They are greater than **1**, and they may be written in decimal and fraction form.

Writing a Percent as a Decimal

To write a percent as a decimal, remove the % symbol and multiply by **0.01**.

Write **150%** as a decimal.

$150\% = 150 \cdot 0.01 \to 1.5$

Writing a Decimal as a Percent

To write a decimal as a percent, multiply the decimal by **100** and write a % symbol.

Write **3** as a percent.

$3 \cdot 100 = 300\%$

Writing a Percent as a Fraction

To write a percent as a fraction, remove the % symbol and multiply by $\frac{1}{100}$.

Write **225%** as a fraction or mixed number in simplest form.

$225\% = 225 \cdot \frac{1}{100}$
$= \frac{225}{100}$
$= 2\frac{25}{100} \to 2\frac{1}{4}$ (simplest form)

Writing a Fraction as a Percent

To write a fraction as a percent, multiply by **100**, and write a % symbol.

Write $\frac{5}{4}$ as a percent.

$\frac{5}{4} \cdot 100 \to \frac{500}{4} \to 125\%$

Write the percent as a decimal and a fraction or mixed number in simplest form.

1. 185% = _____   125% = _____   240% = _____ $225\frac{1}{2}\%$ = _____

2. 181% = _____   1,000% = _____ $6\frac{1}{2}\%$ = _____   380% = _____

3. 625% = _____   190% = _____   500% = _____   415% = _____

Write the decimal or fraction as a percent.

4. 5.4 = _____ % $\frac{15}{12}$ = _____ % $\frac{4}{3}$ = _____ % $\frac{6}{5}$ = _____ %

5. $\frac{8}{5}$ = _____ %   3.25 = _____ %   1.18 = _____ % $\frac{7}{6}$ = _____ %

6. 1.05 = _____ % $\frac{7}{3}$ = _____ %   222 = _____ %   4 = _____ %

Complete the following table of some *benchmark* percents.

	Percent	100%		225%		400%		$133\frac{1}{3}$%
7.								
8.	Fraction		$\frac{3}{2}$		10		$\frac{5}{4}$	
9.	Decimal			5		1.75		2

Complete. Write your answer as a fraction in simplest form, a decimal, or a percent.

10. Kate earned **$400**. She needed **$250** for a new CD player. What percent of the money needed is the money raised? _____

11. A bus will hold **60** people. There are **80** students who decided to go on the field trip. What percent of the bus capacity is the number of students wishing to go? _____

12. Kymea bought a pager two years ago for **$90**. Her sister just paid **30%** more for one. What fraction of Kymea's price was her sister's price? _____

13. A vitamin capsule provides **3** times the daily requirement of Vitamin C. What percent of the daily requirement is that? _____

Problem Solving Reasoning
Solve.

14. "Satisfaction guaranteed or double your money back." What percent of the cost of the item will you receive if you are not satisfied?

_____

15. Write $\frac{4}{4}, \frac{5}{4}, \frac{6}{4}, \ldots, \frac{10}{4}$ as percents.

Describe the pattern that you observe.

_____

_____

Test Prep ★ Mixed Review

16 Mia has 79¢. What percent of a dollar is that?

A 79%　　C 0.79%

B 7.9%　　D 0.079%

17 The scale on a map is 1 in. : 5 mi. How far apart on the map are towns whose actual distance from each other is $27\frac{1}{2}$ miles?

F $5\frac{1}{2}$ in.　　H $137\frac{1}{2}$ in.

G $22\frac{1}{2}$ in.　　J $5\frac{1}{2}$ mi

Name _____

Estimating with Fractions, Decimals, and Percents

Two numbers that form a basic division fact are **compatible numbers**. For example, **6** and **30** are compatible numbers because **30 ÷ 6 = 5**. You can use compatible numbers to estimate with percents.

Estimate $\frac{11}{16}$ of **389**.

1. Think: $\frac{11}{16}$ is close to $\frac{12}{16} = \frac{3}{4}$.

2. **389** is close to **400**, which is a compatible number with **4**.

3. $\frac{11}{16}$ of **389** ≈ $\frac{3}{4}$ of **400** → $\frac{3}{4}$ × **400** → **300**

   So $\frac{11}{16}$ of **389** is about **300**.

Estimate **42%** of **209**.

1. Think: **42%** is close to **40%** = $\frac{2}{5}$

2. **209** is close to **200**, which is a compatible number with **5**.

3. **42%** of **209** ≈ $\frac{2}{5}$ of **200** → $\frac{2}{5}$ × **200** → **80**

   So **42%** of **209** is about **80**.

Circle the correct answer.

1. 78% is closer to $\frac{1}{2}$ or $\frac{3}{4}$?   87% is closer to $\frac{1}{2}$ or $\frac{3}{4}$?   33% is closer to $\frac{1}{3}$ or $\frac{3}{10}$?

2. 61% is closer to $\frac{1}{2}$ or $\frac{2}{3}$?   21% is closer to $\frac{1}{4}$ or $\frac{1}{5}$?   72% is closer to $\frac{2}{3}$ or $\frac{3}{4}$?

3. 27% is closer to $\frac{1}{4}$ or $\frac{1}{3}$?   45% is closer to $\frac{2}{5}$ or $\frac{3}{5}$?   38% is closer to $\frac{1}{2}$ or $\frac{1}{3}$?

Find compatible numbers.

4. $\frac{3}{5}$ of 127 _____ $\frac{2}{3}$ of 797 _____ $\frac{1}{4}$ of 156 _____

5. $\frac{7}{16}$ of 45 _____ $\frac{27}{50}$ of 8,900 _____ $\frac{2}{7}$ of 342 _____

6. $\frac{1}{8}$ of 620 _____ $\frac{13}{16}$ of 902 _____ $\frac{8}{9}$ of 27 _____

Estimate. Record your method and your solution.

7. $\frac{3}{7}$ of 50 _____ $\frac{11}{34}$ of 62 _____ $\frac{2}{11}$ of 311 _____

8. $\frac{7}{12}$ of 53 _____ $\frac{2}{9}$ of 478 _____ $\frac{13}{16}$ of 212 _____

9. 0.55 of 515 _____   0.78 of 419 _____   0.62 of 41 _____

Unit 4 Lesson 11

You can also use rounding to estimate answers. Remember that dividing a number by **10**, or finding $\frac{1}{10}$ of a number, is the same as moving the decimal point one place to the left.

Estimate **15%** of **$48.92**.

15% of **$48.92** is close to **15%** of **$50**.

$$\begin{aligned} 10\% \text{ of } \$50 &= \$5.00 \\ + 5\% \text{ of } \$50 &= \$2.50 \\ \hline 15\% \text{ of } \$50 &= \$7.50 \end{aligned}$$

15% of **$48.92** is about **$7.50**.

Estimate **30%** of **$81.99**.

30% of **$81.99** is close to **30%** of **$80**.

$$\begin{aligned} 10\% \text{ of } \$80 &= \$8 \\ 10\% \text{ of } \$80 &= \$8 \\ + 10\% \text{ of } \$80 &= \$8 \\ \hline 30\% \text{ of } \$80 &= \$24 \end{aligned}$$

30% of **$81.99** is about **$24**.

Estimate.

10. 10% of 42 _____   10% of $834.75 _____   11% of 83 _____

11. 15% of 38 _____   15% of $139 _____   14% of 29 _____

12. 20% of $81.95 _____   20% of 72 _____   22% of $91.62 _____

13. 30% of $158.62 _____   50% of $482.99 _____   5% of 182 _____

Problem Solving Reasoning Solve.

14. Mr. Johnson's restaurant bill was **$87.89**. He wants to leave a **15%** tip. Explain how to estimate the tip.

_____

15. A video game that sells for **$38.99** is on sale at **20%** off. Explain how you would estimate the amount you would save.

_____

✓ Quick Check

Write the percent as a decimal and a fraction.

Work Space.

16. 60%   **17.** 400%   **18.** 350%

_____   _____   _____

Write the decimal or fraction as a percent.

19. 18   **20.** $\frac{9}{6}$ **21.** 1.09

_____   _____   _____

Estimate.

22. 9% of 38   **23.** 36% of 92   **24.** 22% of 41

_____   _____   _____

122 Unit 4 Lesson 11

Name _____

Problem Solving Strategy: Work Backward

To solve problems, you may need to work backward, using inverse operations to "undo" the operations that have been done.

Problem
You use your birthday money to go to a concert. You spend half of your money on the ticket, half of what you have left on a T-shirt, $3.00 on a program, and you have $8.00 left. How much money did you receive for your birthday?

---

1 Understand — As you reread, ask yourself questions.

- How much money did you have at the end?

    You had **$8.00** at the end.

- How much did you have just before your last purchase?

    You spent **$3.00** on a program, so you must have had **$11.00**.

- What do you need to find? _____

---

2 Decide — Choose a method for solving.

Try the strategy Draw a Diagram.

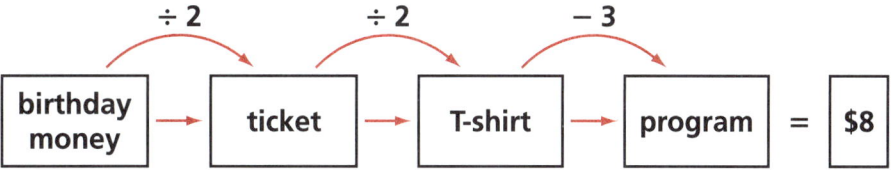

- How will you find how much money you began with?

---

3 Solve — Start at the ending amount and work backward.

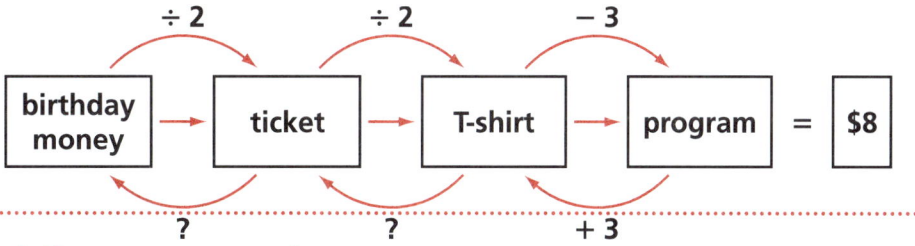

---

4 Look back — Ask if your answer makes sense.

- Check your answer.

- How did working backward help you solve the problem?

_____

Unit 4 Lesson 12 123

Use the Work Backward strategy or any other strategy you have learned to solve these problems.

1. Your friend likes number puzzles and says, "I'm thinking of a number. If you add **3** to my number, then multiply by **5**, and then subtract **4**, you will get **26**." What is your friend's number?

   Think: Start with **26** and work backward using inverse operations. What is the first operation you need to undo?

   _____

   Answer _____

2. You go to the movies and spend half your money on the admission. You spend **$6.00** for popcorn and large soda. You give your last **$3.00** to your friend. How much money did you have when you arrived?

   Think: Start with the **$3.00** and work backward using inverse operations. What is the first step you need to undo?

   _____

   Answer _____

3. The concert you attended was part of a **42** week tour that included **5** concerts per week. The concert promoter paid **$9,660,000** in expenses for shipping, insurance, and facility rental. What was the average expense per concert?

   _____

4. Concert promoters use ticket agencies to help sell their tickets. One agency has **2000** each of tickets at three different prices—**$18.50**, **$26**, and **$35**. If the agency adds a **$2.50** service charge to each ticket and sells all the tickets, how much money will the agency collect?

   _____

5. What will be the next figure in this pattern? Explain your reasoning.

   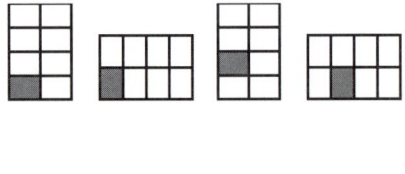

   _____

6. With **one** straight cut, you can cut a circle into **two** pieces. Shown are the results of using **one**, **two**, and **three** straight cuts. What is the greatest number of pieces you can make using **five** straight cuts?

      2   4   7

   _____

7. The sum of two consecutive numbers is **55**. The product of the same two consecutive numbers is **756**. What are the numbers?

   _____

8. You are scheduling a chess tournament for **6** members of the chess club. Each member must play a game against each of the other members. How many games will you schedule?

   _____

Name _____

Unit 4 Review

Write the comparison as a ratio in simplest form.

1. 18 girls to 16 boys _____
2. 6 cups flour to 2 cups sugar _____
3. 4 feet to 4 yards _____
4. 2 days to 6 hours _____

Write the rate as a unit rate.

5. 84 minutes for 6 pages _____
6. 371 miles for 14 gallons of gas _____
7. Determine the better buy: 6 apples for $1.25 or 8 apples for $1.50? _____

Solve.

8. $\frac{n}{36} = \frac{4}{9}$ _____
9. $\frac{3}{10} = \frac{x}{40}$ _____
10. $\frac{16}{18} = \frac{24}{m}$ _____
11. $\frac{8}{n} = \frac{2}{9}$ _____

12. You can purchase a **dozen** juices for $7.20. At that rate, what will 30 juices cost you?

13. Estimate what a 15% tip for a restaurant bill of $58.62 would be.

14. Using a scale factor of $\frac{1}{4}$ inch = 1 foot, what would the actual dimensions be for a scale measurement of $3\frac{1}{2}$ inches?

15. It would take Nigel 2 hours to paint 12 mailboxes. How long should it take if 2 friends help him paint the 12 mailboxes?

Write the percent as a decimal and a fraction in simplest form.

16. 80% _____
17. 42% _____
18. 250% _____
19. 65% _____
20. 20% _____
21. 120% _____

Write the decimal or fraction as a percent.

22. 0.15 _____
23. 0.205 _____
24. 0.005 _____
25. $\frac{3}{5}$ _____
26. $\frac{3}{25}$ _____
27. $\frac{7}{8}$ _____

Solve.

28. The speed limit on a highway is 55 mph. A speed sensor showed that a car went 900 ft in 8 s. Is the car traveling over the speed limit? Explain.

29. In the morning, 20% of the jars of salsa in a store were sold. In the afternoon, $\frac{7}{8}$ of what was left was sold. There are 14 jars left. How many jars were there at the start? How many jars were sold in the morning? In the afternoon?

Name _____

Cumulative Review
★ Test Prep

Use this picture for exercises 1 and 2.

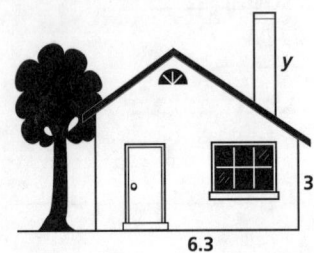 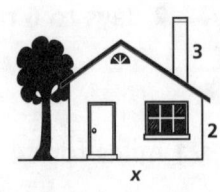

1 The smaller figure above is a scale drawing of the larger figure. What is the value of x?

A 2.1 units

B 4.2 units

C 6.3 units

D 9.45 units

2 What is the value of y?

F 4.5 units

G 3 units

H 2 units

J 1.5 units

3 What is the unit price of a CD in the special offer?

A $7.50

B $8.50

C $9.00

D $10.00

4 The ratio of boys to girls in the glee club is 15 to 9. If there are 24 girls, then how many boys are there?

F 40   H 30

G 35   J 15

5 Simplify: $4x - 2x \div x$

A 2

B $\dfrac{2}{x}$

C $4x - 2$

D $4 - 2x$

6 Which should you do first to solve the equation?

$$8x + 4 = 8$$

F Add 4 to both sides.

G Subtract 4 from both sides.

H Divide both sides by 8.

J Multiply both sides by 8.

K Divide both sides by x.

7 The ratio of girls to boys at Hill City High School is 7:6. There are 504 boys. How many girls are there?

A 432   C 517   E Not here

B 505   D 588

8 The advertisement for a medicine claimed there was a $\dfrac{9}{10}$ of a 1% chance that there would be any side effects. What is the decimal equivalent of $\dfrac{9}{10}$ of 1%?

F 0.009   H 0.9   K Not here

G 0.09   J 9.0

126   Unit 4 Cumulative Review

UNIT 5 • TABLE OF CONTENTS

Applications of Percent

Lesson	Page
1 **Algebra:** The Percent Equation: Solving for the Percentage	129
2 **Algebra:** The Percent Equation: Solving for the Base	131
3 **Algebra:** The Percent Equation: Solving for the Percent	133
4 **Problem Solving Strategy:** Conjecture and Verify	135
5 Percent of Increase or Decrease	137
6 **Algebra:** Discount	139
7 **Algebra:** List Price and Net Price	141
8 **Algebra:** Commission	143
9 **Algebra:** Simple and Compound Interest	145
10 **Problem Solving Application:** Use a Table	147
• **Unit 5 Review**	149
• **Cumulative Review ★ Test Prep**	150

Dear Family,

During the next few weeks, our math class will be studying the applications of percents. This will include solving percent equations, which will help to prepare for algebra. You can expect to see homework that provides practice with these skills. Here is a sample you may want to keep handy to give help if needed.

Solving a Percent Equation

A percent equation has three quantities. Knowing two of the three allows you to solve for the third.

Percent equation: $n\%$ of b = p

rate × base = percentage

A $58 sweater is discounted 15%. Find the discount and selling price.

The discount is 15% of $58.   Let d = discount.

d is 15% of $58	Write the percent equation.
$d = 0.15 \cdot 58$	Write 15% as a decimal.
$d = 8.70$	Simplify.

The discount is $8.70 and the selling price is
$58.00 − $8.70 = $49.30

During this unit, students will continue to learn new techniques related to problem solving and will continue to practice basic skills with fractions and decimals.

Sincerely,

We will be using this vocabulary:

percent equation $r\%$ of b is p

rate usually written as a percent, but can be a decimal or fraction

base the whole or entire amount; **100%** of the original number

percentage a part of the base expressed in the same units of measure as the base

percent change the ratio of the amount of change to the original amount

discount a percent of the list price of an item that the buyer does not pay

net price the price of an item after any discount to the list price, or original

commission a part of the selling price that is paid to the seller

simple interest
  interest = principal · rate · time

compound interest interest paid on interest that has been added to the principal

Name _____

The Percent Equation: Solving for the Percentage

There is a wide variety of applications for percents. You can solve problems involving percents using the **percent equation**.

For example, to find how much you will save on a sweater on sale for **20%** off the regular price, you can use the equation at right. In this problem you are solving for the **percentage**.

> Rate × Base = Percentage
> **20%** of **$40** is **n**

Rate: usually written as a percent, but can be a decimal or fraction	**Base:** the whole or entire amount—**100%** of the original number	**Percentage:** a part of the base expressed in the same units as the base

Find: 20% of $40

1. Write the percent equation.   20% of $40 = n
2. Write 20% as a decimal. $0.2 \cdot 40 = n$
3. Simplify. $8 = n$

So **20%** of **$40** is **$8.00**.

Find: $8\frac{1}{4}$% of 140

1. Write the percent equation. $8\frac{1}{4}$% of 140 = n
2. Write $8\frac{1}{4}$% as a decimal. $0.0825 \cdot 140 = n$
3. Simplify. $11.55 = n$

So $8\frac{1}{4}$% of **140** is **11.55**.

You can also use a proportion. Find **35%** of **$75**.

1. Write the percent as a fraction.

   35% → $\frac{35}{100}$

2. Write the proportion and solve.

   $\frac{35}{100} = \frac{n}{\$75}$

   $\$75 \cdot 35 = 100n$ So $n = \frac{\$75 \cdot 35}{100}$ or **$26.25**.

Write the percent as a decimal and as a fraction.

1. 12% = _____   6% = _____   30% = _____

2. 4.5% = _____   25.5% = _____   9.7% = _____

3. $15\frac{1}{4}$% = _____ $5\frac{1}{2}$% = _____ $33\frac{1}{3}$% = _____

Solve for the percentage.

4. 75% of 800 is _____   15% of 176 is _____   50% of 135 is _____

5. 40% of $82.50 is _____   90% of 946 is _____   17% of 68 is _____

6. 8% of 484 is _____   25% of $68.50 is _____   45% of $315 is _____

7. $9\frac{1}{4}$% of 200 is _____ $12\frac{1}{2}$% of 176 is _____ $52\frac{1}{4}$% of 20 is _____

8. $3\frac{1}{3}$% of 3 is _____ $4\frac{1}{2}$% of 1 is _____ $1\frac{1}{3}$% of 2 is _____

A percent can be written as a decimal or fraction. In most percent equations, the percent is written as a decimal to make multiplying easier. However, if the rate has a repeating decimal equivalent such as $33\frac{1}{3}\%$, it is easier to write the percent as a fraction.

Find $33\frac{1}{3}\%$ of 78.

1. Write the percent equation. $33\frac{1}{3}\%$ of $78 = n$
2. Write $33\frac{1}{3}\%$ as a fraction. $\frac{1}{3} \cdot 78 = n$
3. Simplify. $26 = n$

So $33\frac{1}{3}\%$ of 78 is 26.

Writing a Percent as a Fraction

$$8\frac{1}{3}\% = \frac{25}{3} \cdot \frac{1}{100}$$
$$= \frac{25}{300}$$
$$= \frac{1}{12}$$

Solve for the percentage.

9. $33\frac{1}{3}\%$ of 1,266 is _____ $8\frac{1}{3}\%$ of 180 is _____ $15\frac{1}{3}\%$ of 240 is _____

10. $16\frac{2}{3}\%$ of 360 is _____ $12\frac{2}{3}\%$ of 300 is _____ $66\frac{2}{3}\%$ of 1,500 is _____

11. $22\frac{2}{9}\%$ of 81 is _____ $6\frac{1}{9}\%$ of 270 is _____ $30\frac{1}{9}\%$ of 840 is _____

12. $8\frac{1}{6}\%$ of 300 is _____ $7\frac{1}{7}\%$ of 70 is _____ $3\frac{1}{6}\%$ of 36 is _____

13. $2\frac{2}{9}\%$ of 90 is _____ $9\frac{1}{6}\%$ of 60 is _____ $4\frac{1}{7}\%$ of 28 is _____

Problem Solving
Reasoning

14. Jericho answered **90%** of the questions correctly on the current events quiz. The quiz had **40** questions. How many did he miss?

_____

15. The ABC cereal company claims that one serving of their new cereal provides **two-thirds** of the daily requirement of vitamin A. The daily requirement is **42** mg. How many mg will you get by eating one serving of the new cereal?

_____

Test Prep ★ Mixed Review

16 What is the value of n in the proportion $\frac{5}{42} = \frac{n}{126}$?

  A 5
  B 15
  C 42
  D 89

17 You drive 175 miles in $3\frac{1}{2}$ hours. What is your unit rate?

  F 1 hour
  G 50 miles
  H 50 miles per hour
  J 58 miles per hour

Name _____

The Percent Equation: Solving for the Base

In the last lesson you used multiplication to solve for the percentage in the percent equation. To solve for the **base**, you need to divide.

> Rate × Base = Percentage
> **8%** of n is **20**

Suppose there are **20** people in the front row of a theater. This represents **8%** of the total audience. What is the total number of people in the audience?

Find: **8%** of what number is **20**?

1. Write the percent equation. **8%** of $n = 20$

2. Write **8%** as a decimal. $0.08 \cdot n = 20$

3. Divide each side by **0.08**. $\dfrac{0.08 \cdot n}{0.08} = \dfrac{20}{0.08}$

4. Simplify. $n = 250$

So, there are **250** people in the audience. Is the answer reasonable? Think: **10%** of **250** is **25**, so **8%** is reasonable.

Find: $12\tfrac{1}{2}$% of what number is **10.5**?

1. Write the percent equation. $12\tfrac{1}{2}$% of $n = 10.5$

2. Write the $12\tfrac{1}{2}$% as a decimal. $0.125 \cdot n = 10.5$

3. Divide each side by **0.125**. $\dfrac{0.125 \cdot n}{0.125} = \dfrac{10.5}{0.125}$

4. Simplify. $n = 84$

So, **10.5** is $12\tfrac{1}{2}$ % of **84**.

Check: $12\tfrac{1}{2}$% · **84** and **0.125** · **84** = **10.5**

Solve for the base.

1. **10%** of what number is **22**? _____   **15%** of what number is **9**? _____

2. **25%** of what number is **38**? _____   **30%** of what number is **36**? _____

3. $6\tfrac{1}{2}$% of what number is **5.2**? _____ $10\tfrac{1}{4}$% of what number is **41**? _____

4. **8.5%** of what number is **3.4**? _____   **30.2%** of what number is **151**? _____

5. **40** is **50%** of what number? _____   **60** is **75%** of what number? _____

6. **72** is **60%** of what number? _____   **5** is **20%** of what number? _____

7. **135** is **45%** of what number? _____   **65** is **25%** of what number? _____

8. **35%** of what number is **70**? _____   **12%** of what number is **48**? _____

9. **2.5%** of what number is **5**? _____   **3** is **4%** of what number? _____

You know that a rate such as $33\frac{1}{3}\%$ has this repeating decimal equivalent: $0.\overline{3}$. Instead of using the decimal, write the equivalent fraction in the percent equation and divide to solve for the base.

Recall that when you divide by a fraction you find its reciprocal and multiply.

Find: $33\frac{1}{3}\%$ of what number is 24?

1. Write the percent equation. $33\frac{1}{3}\%$ of $n = 24$

2. Write the percentage as a fraction. $\frac{1}{3} \cdot n = 24$

3. Divide each side by $\frac{1}{3}$. $\dfrac{\frac{1}{3} \cdot n}{\frac{1}{3}} = \dfrac{24}{\frac{1}{3}}$

4. Simplify. $n = 72$

So 24 is $33\frac{1}{3}\%$ of 72.

> Dividing by the fraction form of the percent is also useful when the percent is a common fraction such as $10\% = \frac{1}{10}$, $25\% = \frac{1}{4}$, or $50\% = \frac{1}{2}$. **Think:** Dividing by the fraction $\frac{1}{10}$ is the same as multiplying by 10.

Solve for the base.

10. $33\frac{1}{3}\%$ of what number is 45? _____ $33\frac{1}{3}\%$ of what number is 120? _____

11. $66\frac{2}{3}\%$ of what number is 36? _____ $66\frac{2}{3}\%$ of what number is 80? _____

12. 10% of what number is 17? _____   25% of what number is 29? _____

13. 300 is 50% of what number? _____   7 is 20% of what number? _____

Problem Solving / Reasoning

14. There were 18 people at the rehearsal, which is 90% of the cast. How many people are in the cast?

_____

15. The sign said everything was 25% off. Tori saved $8 on her purchase. What was the original price of the item?

_____

Test Prep ★ Mixed Review

16. The scale on a map is 1 cm:50 m. How far apart on the map are buildings whose actual distance from each other is 0.85 km?

    A 17 cm   **C** 850 cm

    B 85 cm   **D** 17 m

17. What is the percent equivalent of $\frac{9}{25}$?

    F 9%   **H** 25%

    G 11%   **J** 36%

Name _____

The Percent Equation: Solving for the Percent

You have used division to solve for the base in the percent equation. To solve for the **rate** or **percent**, you also need to divide.

> Rate × Base = Percentage
> n% of 15 is 3

Suppose that last Monday, **3** of **15** math club members were chosen as finalists in a competition. What percent of the club were finalists?

Find: What percent of **15** is **3**?

1. Write the percent equation. $n\%$ of $15 = 3$
2. Divide each side by **15**. $\dfrac{n\% \cdot 15}{15} = \dfrac{3}{15}$
3. Simplify. $n\% = 0.2$
4. Write as a percent. $n = 20$

So **3** is **20%** of **15**.

You may have recognized that $\dfrac{3}{15} = \dfrac{1}{5}$ and $\dfrac{1}{5} = 20\%$.

When you know the fraction form of the percent, you do not need to rewrite it as a decimal.

Find: What percent of **328** is **41**?

1. Write the percent equation. $n\%$ of $328 = 41$
2. Divide each side by **328**. $\dfrac{n\% \cdot 328}{328} = \dfrac{41}{328}$
3. Simplify. $n\% = 0.125$
4. Write the decimal as a percent. $n = 12.5$

So **41** is **12.5%** of **328**.

Is the answer reasonable?

Think, **10%** of **328** = **32.8**. Since **12.5%** is close to **10%**, the answer is reasonable.

> When you solve the equation for the percent, the result is a decimal. Write the decimal as a percent.

Solve for the percent.

1. What percent of **40** is **32**? _____
2. What percent of **75** is **7.5**? _____
3. What percent of **64** is **8**? _____
4. What percent of **68** is **10.2**? _____
5. **320** is what percent of **960**? _____
6. **8.1** is what percent of **90**? _____
7. **10** is what percent of **25**? _____

What percent of **810** is **540**? _____

What percent of **24** is **16**? _____

What percent of **1,200** is **1,050**? _____

What percent of **144** is **43.2**? _____

15.5 is what percent of **124**? _____

297 is what percent of **300**? _____

128 is what percent of **1,024**? _____

Unit 5 Lesson 3   133

Recall that percents can be greater than **100%**.

For example, suppose you need to save **$380** for a new CD player, and you actually save **$456**. Then you have more than **100%** of what you need.

Think: **456** is more than **100%** of **380**.

Write: **456** is what percent of **380**?

Find: **456** is what percent of **380**?

1. Write the percent equation. $456 = n\%$ of 380

2. Divide each side by **380**. $\dfrac{456}{380} = \dfrac{n\% \cdot 380}{380}$

3. Simplify. $1.2 = n\%$

4. Write the decimal as a percent. $120 = n$

So **456** is **120%** of **380**.

Solve for the percent.

8. What percent of **200** is **400**? _____

    What percent of **44** is **55**? _____

9. What percent of **60** is **72**? _____

    What percent of **80** is **104**? _____

10. **86** is what percent of **43**? _____

    135 is what percent of **45**? _____

11. **80** is what percent of **60**? _____

    7 is what percent of **5**? _____

Problem Solving Reasoning   Solve.

12. On Friday, **27** of the **30** students attended band practice. What percent of the students were present?

    _____

13. Suppose today is day **54** out of the **180**-day school year. What percent of the school year do you have remaining?

    _____

 Quick Check

Solve for the base, rate, or percentage.

14. What is **6%** of **180**? _____

15. What is $83\tfrac{1}{3}\%$ of **108**? _____

16. What is **105%** of **70**? _____

17. **72** is **25%** of what number? _____

18. **24** is **80%** of what number? _____

19. **69** is $37\tfrac{1}{2}\%$ of what number? _____

20. What percent of **36** is **24**? _____

21. What percent of **150** is **84**? _____

Work Space.

134 Unit 5 Lesson 3

Name _____

Problem Solving Strategy: Conjecture and Verify

To solve problems, you may need to begin by making a *guess,* or **conjecture.** Then you need to *check,* or **verify,** your conjecture. Sometimes you may need to revise the conjecture and try again.

Problem

Your friend's mom offered to buy lunch for you and your friends at a baseball game. Hot dogs were $1.25 and sodas were $1.00. She spent $19.50. When you asked her how many of each she bought she would only say, "3 more hot dogs than sodas." How many of each did she buy?

① Understand   As you reread, ask yourself questions.

- How much money did she spend?
  She spent **$19.50**.

- How much did the hot dogs and sodas cost?
  Hot dogs cost **$1.25** and sodas cost **$1.00**.

- What do you need to find? _____

② Decide   Choose a method for solving.
Try the strategy Conjecture and Verify. Revise if necessary.

- Make a conjecture and verify it.

  Try **9** hot dogs and **6** sodas.
  9 × $1.25 + 6 × $1.00 = $17.25

- A conjecture of 9 hot dogs gives a total cost that is too small.

③ Solve   Revise your first conjecture.

- Make a new conjecture. Then verify it.

  Try **10** hot dogs and **7** sodas.

  10 × $1.25 + 7 × $1.00 = _____

  Were 3 more hot dogs than sodas purchased? _____

④ Look back   Ask if your answer makes sense.

- How many of each item did your friend's mom buy?

  _____

- Is your answer reasonable? Explain.

  _____

- How did the Conjecture and Verify strategy help you solve the problem?

  _____

Unit 5 Lesson 4

Use the Conjecture and Verify strategy or any other strategy you have learned.

1. You have scored **87**, **79**, and **80** on your math tests. The B-range is **84%–91%**. What is the lowest score you can earn on your fourth test and still have a B average?

   Think: If my first conjecture gives an average of **85%**, am I finished? Why or why not?

   _____

   Answer _____

2. The length of a garden is twice its width. The perimeter is **90** feet. What are the dimensions of the garden?

   Think: Could the longer dimension of the garden be more than **50** ft? Why?

   _____

   Answer _____

3. Find the digits that represent letters in the sum. Use the digits: 1, 2, 4, 5, 6, and 9.

   ```
     TWO
   + TWO
   -----
    SIX
   ```

   _____

4. Fill in the circles with **1**, **2**, **5**, and **8** so that the three numbers on all four sides add to **13**.

   _____

5. At the supermarket, canned peaches have been stacked in a pyramid shape, with **1** can on the top, **2** in the second row, **3** in the third row, and so on. There are **12** rows of cans. How many cans of peaches are displayed?

   _____

6. Find the product of the nine fractions.

   $$\frac{1}{2} \cdot \frac{2}{3} \cdot \frac{3}{4} \cdot \frac{4}{5} \cdot \frac{5}{6} \cdot \frac{6}{7} \cdot \frac{7}{8} \cdot \frac{8}{9} \cdot \frac{9}{10}$$

   _____

7. A weather balloon is launched at **10:30** A.M. It rises at a rate of **3.5** km every **30** minutes. What will be the altitude, or height, of the balloon at **2** P.M.?

   _____

8. You purchased a **$120** jacket that was on sale for **$80**. Your friend bought a **$100** jacket that was on sale for **$60**. Did you both receive the same rate of discount? If not, who received the better discount?

   _____

Percent of Increase or Decrease

Percents can be used to measure how much a quantity changes.

For example, suppose you paid **$12** for a CD two years ago. Now it sells for **$15**. The difference of **$3** is an increase of **25%**.

> The **percent of increase** or **percent of decrease** from one amount to another is the ratio of the amount of change compared to the original amount.
>
> $$\text{Percent Change} = \frac{\text{amount of change}}{\text{original amount}}$$
>
> Percent increase: new amount > original amount
>
> Percent decrease: new amount < original amount

Find the Percent of Increase:

Original price of CD: **$12**
New price of CD: **$15**

$$\text{Percent Increase} = \frac{15 - 12}{12}$$
$$= \frac{3}{12}$$
$$= \frac{1}{4} \text{ or } 25\%$$

The CD has increased **25%** in price.

Find the Percent of Decrease:

Original price of computer: **$1,250**
New price of computer: **$875**

$$\text{Percent Decrease:} = \frac{1250 - 875}{1250}$$
$$= \frac{375}{1250}$$
$$= \frac{3}{10} \text{ or } 30\%$$

The computer has decreased **30%** in price.

Find the amount of change and the percent change and write whether it is an increase or decrease.

	Original Amount	New Amount	Amount of Change	Percent Change	Increase or Decrease
1.	$72	$80			
2.	40	60			
3.	36	30			
4.	$15	$10.50			
5.	15	33			
6.	$35	$28			
7.	270	391.5			
8.	80	100			
9.	100	80			
10.	35	105			
11.	$28\frac{1}{3}$	$11\frac{1}{3}$			

Problem Solving Reasoning Solve.

12. Julia increased her reading rate from 200 words per minute to 250 words per minute. By what percent did she increase her rate?

_____

13. In September, 30 students attended special art classes on Saturday. By November this number had increased by 200%. What was the total attendance in the classes by November?

_____

14. A pet shop had 300 canaries. This number decreased $83\frac{1}{3}$% due to sales. How many canaries were sold?

_____

15. The train from Chicago to Los Angeles increased its speed from 140 to 180 kilometers per hour. By what percent was the speed increased?

_____

16. Joan sold 80 magazines last year, but only 75 magazines this year. What was the percent of decrease?

_____

17. Last year Troop No. 113 sold 100 dozen cookies. How many will they have to sell this year to have a 20% increase in sales?

_____

18. In a furniture store the price of a sofa was marked down from $225 to $200. What was the percent of decrease?

_____

19. A football was marked down from $28.00 to $24.50. By what percent was its price reduced?

_____

Test Prep ★ Mixed Review

20 What number is 7% of 86?

A 6.02

B 8.14

C 12.28

D 60.2

21 162 is 24% of what number?

F 38.9

G 188

H 675

J 3,888

Name _____   **Discount**

You can use a percent to describe the savings you will receive on items that are sale priced.

For example, a store may advertise "**25%** off all items." You save **25%** of the cost of what you purchase. If you purchase a **$40** item, you will save **$10** on the item.

> You can use the percent equation to find discounts. Become familiar with the different vocabulary used for describing discounts.
>
> **Rate:** the percent of the *list price* that the buyer **does not** pay, or the **percent of discount**
>
> **Base:** the price the store usually charges for an item; it is called the **list, marked, regular,** or **original price**
>
> **Percentage:** the part of the list price that the buyer does not pay; it is called the **amount of discount**

Find the Amount of Discount:

You want to purchase a pair of sneakers that list for **$82.00**. They are marked **15%** off. How much will you save?

You will save **15%** of the original cost of **$82**.

1. Write the percent equation.　　　　　15% of $82 = n
2. Write **15%** as a decimal.　　　　　0.15 · 82 = n
3. Simplify.　　　　　12.30 = n

The sneakers have been discounted **$12.30**, which is the amount you save.

Find the Discount Rate:

A **$38** sweatshirt is on sale. A sign on the sale rack says, "Save **$9.50**." What percent discount is this?

What percent of **$38** is **$9.50**?

1. Write the percent equation.　　$n\% \cdot 38 = 9.50$
2. Divide each side by **$38**.　　$\dfrac{n\% \cdot 38}{38} = \dfrac{9.50}{38}$
3. Simplify.　　$n\% = 0.25$
4. Write as a percent.　　$n = 25$

The discount was **25%**.

Complete the table.

	List Price	Discount Rate	Amount of Discount
1.	$45	10%	
2.	$240	15%	
3.	$250	6%	
4.	$24		$2.40
5.	$6		$.75
6.	$24.90		$4.98

	List Price	Discount Rate	Amount of Discount
7.	$69	20%	
8.	$648	$33\frac{1}{3}\%$	
9.	$840	4.5%	
10.	$19.95		$3.99
11.	$15		$4.50
12.	$6.95		$2.78

Unit 5 Lesson 6

Problem Solving Reasoning — Solve. Round to the nearest cent if necessary.

13. Holiday cards are on sale at **25%** off. What will you save on **3** boxes that have a list price of **$7.50** each?

    _____

14. Rick offers to sell his collection of baseball cards to Pete for **$112**. He originally spent **$280** for the cards. What rate of discount is he offering?

    _____

15. All books and CD's are usually $33\frac{1}{3}$% off. How much would you save on the purchase of four CD's that sell for **$15.95** each and two books that sell for **$7.95** each? _____

16. The gas station offers a **3%** discount for using cash. Your bill is **$15.50**. How much will you save?

    _____

17. The fuel oil company offers a **10%** discount for paying your bill within **10** days. Your fuel oil bill is **$124**. How much could you save by paying within **10** days?

    _____

18. Espie received a scratch card in the mail that said save **10%**, **25%**, or **40%** off any purchase. Espie finds a **$145** jacket that she likes. The cashier scratches the card to reveal the discount rate. What is the greatest amount of money Espie could save? The least?

    _____

19. If you saved **$31.98** on a **$79.95** backpack, what was the discount rate?

    _____

20. Which amount of money is greater, a **10%** discount on **$42** or a **42%** discount on **$10**? Explain.

    _____

Test Prep ★ Mixed Review

21. What percent of 4,500 is 9?

   A 0.2%   C 20%
   B 2%   D 500%

22. A store changed the price of a printer from $340 to $360. To the nearest tenth, what is the percent increase?

   F 5.6%   H 20%
   G 5.9%   J $20

List Price and Net Price

Name _____

In the last lesson you found the amount of discount on an item. Subtracting the amount of discount from the list price gives you the amount you need to pay. The amount that you pay for the item is called the **net price**.

Find the Net Price:

Carlos purchased a **$385** snowboard that is marked **15%** off. How much did he save? What was the net price?

Carlos saved **15%** of the original cost of **$385**.

1. Write the percent equation.

    15% of **$385** = n

2. Write **2%** as a decimal.   0.15 · 385 = n

3. Simplify.   57.75 = n

4. Subtract.
    $385.00 ← List price
    −$ 57.75 ← Amount of discount
    $327.25 ← Net price

When you save **15%** off the list price of an item, you pay **85%** of the cost of the item.

Find the Discount Rate:

A **$450** season ski ticket is discounted when it is purchased before December 10. Anne paid **$360** for the pass. What percent was it discounted?

What percent of the **$450** did Anne pay?

What percent of **$450** is **$360**?

1. Write the percent equation.

    $n\% \cdot \$450 = \$360$

2. Divide each side by **$450**. $\dfrac{n\% \cdot 450}{450} = \dfrac{360}{450}$

3. Simplify. $n\% = \dfrac{4}{5}$

4. Write $\dfrac{4}{5}$ as a percent.   n = 80

Anne paid **80%** of the cost and saved **20%**.

Complete the table.

	List Price	Percent Discount	Amount of Discount	Net Price
1.	$20	10%		
2.	$18	$33\frac{1}{3}\%$		
3.	$600	4%		
4.	$7.80		$1.56	
5.	$7.50		$1.50	
6.	$2,400			$1,800
7.			$6.50	$19.50
8.		40%	$12	
9.			$0.75	$9.25
10.		12.5%	$31.25	
11.	$18.95		$11.37	
12.	$210	$33\frac{1}{3}\%$		

Unit 5 Lesson 7

Problem Solving Reasoning
Solve. Round to the nearest cent if necessary.

13. You are buying a birthday gift for your friend. The original price of the gift you choose is **$18.95** and is marked **15%** off. You have **$15** with you. Do you have enough money to buy the gift? Explain.

_____

14. Mr. Lux is buying a used car marked **$1,000**. He can buy it for **$800**. What rate of discount is he getting? _____

15. Eileen paid **$31.50** for a coat marked **$36**. What percent of discount did she receive? _____

16. A sports store has reduced every item by $33\frac{1}{3}$%. What is the net price for a basketball that lists at **$42**? _____

17. A bargain store increases the discount rate the longer the item remains in the store. You save **10%** during the first **10** days, **20%** from day **11** to day **30**, and **50%** off after **30** days. A pair of pants that lists for **$48** has been at the store **28** days. What is the net price today? What would be the net price if you wait **3** days?

_____

18. Lani saved **$20** on a **$120** jacket. Andre saved **$20** on a **$80** jacket. Who saved the most? Who received the better rate of discount? Explain.

_____

✓ Quick Check

Write the percent of change. Identify whether it is a percent of increase or percent of decrease.

Work Space.

19. Originally: **$85**
Now: **$95**
_____

20. Originally: **$140**
Now: **$125**
_____

21. Originally: **$5.50**
Now: **$4.95**
_____

22. A coat regularly sells for **$95**. It is discounted **15%**. What is the sale price? _____

23. A **$599** sofa is selling for **$525**. What is the percent of discount? _____

24. A drug store buys cosmetics from its supplier at a **40%** discount from the list price. How much does the store pay for a shipment that will sell for **$1,200**? _____

25. You buy a baby grand piano that lists for **$3,600**. You pay **$3,300**. What is the rate of discount? _____

Name _____

Commission

People who work in sales often have part or all of their salary based on a **commission.** Commission is a percent of the total amount of the sale that is paid to the sales person.

For example, newspaper delivery people are paid a percentage of each newspaper they sell. They might keep **2.5¢** for each **50¢** newspaper they sell. The publisher would receive **47.5¢**.

> The **commission** on a sale is found using the percent equation.
>
> Rate: the percent of the amount of sales that is paid to the salesperson
> Base: the total cost of the product, called the *amount of sales*
> Percentage: the part of the amount of the sales that is paid to the salesperson, called the *commission*
>
> The **net proceeds** is the difference between the amount of the sale and the commission.

Find the Amount of Commission:

You work in a department store where you earn a **2%** commission on all sales. One day you have **$164** in sales. What will your commission be?

You will earn **2%** of the **$164**.

1. Write the percent equation.   **2%** of **164** = **n**
2. Write **2%** as a decimal.   **0.02 · 164 = n**
3. Simplify.   **3.28 = n**

The commission that you earn is **$3.28**. The net proceeds for the store is **$164 − $3.28** or **$160.72**.

Find the Commission Rate:

You earn a commission of **$12** on a sale of **$240**. What is the commission rate?

What percent of **$240** is **$12**?

1. Write the percent equation. $n\% \cdot 240 = 12$
2. Divide each side by **$240**. $\dfrac{n\% \cdot 240}{240} = \dfrac{12}{240}$
3. Simplify. $n\% = 0.05$
4. Write **0.05** as a percent. $n = 5$

The commission rate is **5%**.

Complete the table.

	Amount of Sales	Commission Rate	Amount of Commission	Net Proceeds
1.	$60	5%		
2.	$800	3.5%		
3.	$4,200	4.25%		
4.	$750		$150	
5.	$1,500		$75	
6.			$17.50	$857.50
7.		5%	$25,000	
8.			$2,400	$17,600
9.	$350		$24.50	

Problem Solving Reasoning — Solve. Round to the nearest cent if necessary.

10. Martha sold magazines and received a commission of $6\frac{1}{4}$%. Her sales totaled **$240**. How much did she earn in commissions? What were the net proceeds? _____

11. A real estate agent receives a **6%** commission for selling an **$8,000** piece of land. How much did she earn? How much was given to the owner of the land?

    _____

12. Find the amount of commission earned on a sale of **$200** at a rate of $6\frac{1}{2}$%. How much was given to the company?

    _____

13. Ted earned a commission of **$2.50** for each **$25** corsage he made for Mother's Day. How much commission would he receive for making **15** corsages? What is the commission rate?

    _____

14. An insurance salesperson collected **$200** commission for selling policies worth **$1,600**. What is the commission rate?

    _____

15. Mr. Finn collects rents for a real estate management company. He is paid $2\frac{1}{2}$% in commission. How much commission does he receive for collecting **$960** in rents? What are the net proceeds to the company?

    _____

16. A lumber company is purchasing **$9,000** worth of lumber through an agent whose commission is $8\frac{1}{3}$% of the sales. What are the net proceeds to the firm? _____

17. A ticket agent receives a **2.5%** commission on all concert tickets sold. The total sales were **$28,500**. How much commission did the agent earn?

    _____

Test Prep ★ Mixed Review

18 Chuck buys a $65 pair of shoes on sale at 15% off. How much money does he save?

    A $9.75   C $50

    B $15   D $55.25

19 A car battery regularly priced at $67 is on sale for 5% off. What is the sale price?

    F $3.35   H $62

    G $33.50   J $63.65

Name _____

Simple and Compound Interest

Another important application of percents is *interest*.

When you borrow money from a bank, you are charged a fee called interest. When you "invest" money in a savings account, you are paid interest.

> A person who takes out a loan at the bank is a borrower. The borrower agrees to pay **interest** (a fee) for using the bank's money.
>
> The simple interest formula is: Interest = principal × rate × time
> $$I = p \cdot r \cdot t$$
>
> p = **principal**, the amount borrowed
> r = interest **rate** per year, expressed as a decimal
> t = **time**, expressed in years
>
> The **amount due** is what you pay back to the bank ($I + p$).

Find the Interest and Amount Due:

You borrow **$2,000** at **8%** interest for **6** months. How much interest will you pay? What is the amount due to the bank?

Think: 6 mo = $\frac{1}{2}$ yr or 0.5 yr

p = $2,000, r = 8%, t = 0.5 years

1. Write the interest
   formula. $I = p \cdot r \cdot t$
2. Substitute. $I = 2,000 \cdot 0.08 \cdot 0.5$
3. Simplify. $I = 80$
4. Add. $2,000 ← Principal
           + $80 ← Interest
           ───────
           $2,080 ← Amount due

You pay **$80** interest and owe a total of **$2,080**.

Find the Interest and Amount Due:

You borrow **$12,000** at **6.5%** interest for **30** months. How much interest will you pay? What is the amount due to the bank?

Think: 30 mo = $2\frac{1}{2}$ yr or 2.5 yr

p = $12,000, r = 6.5%, t = 2.5 years

1. Write the interest
   formula. $I = p \cdot r \cdot t$
2. Substitute. $I = 12,000 \cdot 0.065 \cdot 2.5$
3. Simplify. $I = 1,950$
4. Add. $12,000 ← Principal
           + $ 1,950 ← Interest
           ────────
           $13,950 ← Amount due

You pay **$1,950** interest and owe a total of **$13,950**.

Complete the table. Round to the nearest cent if necessary.

	Principal	Rate (per year)	Time	Interest	Amount Due
1.	$400	13%	3 months		
2.	$900	12%	6 months		
3.	$6,000	8%	18 months		
4.	$2,500	6.5%	1 year		
5.	$4,500	6.25%	1 year		
6.	$8,400	9.25%	2 years		
7.	$75,000	10.95%	20 years		
8.	$37,525	17.99%	3 years		

The simple interest formula finds interest just once.

With **compound interest**, the interest earned is added to the principal at regular intervals. The amount of principal changes. You calculate the new amount of interest using the new principal.

Compounded quarterly means that interest is paid at the end of every **3** months.

Compound interest is common when money is invested in a savings account.

> You invest **$500** at **6%** interest compounded quarterly. What is your principal after **6** months?
>
> 1. Write the simple interest formula. $I = p \cdot r \cdot t$
> 2. Substitute. $I = 500 \cdot 0.06 \cdot \frac{1}{4}$
> 3. Simplify. $I = 7.50$
> 4. Add interest to principal. $500 + $7.50 = 507.50
> 5. Find the interest on the new principal. $I = 507.50 \cdot 0.06 \cdot \frac{1}{4}$
> 6. Simplify. $I = 7.61$
>
> After **6** months you have a total of **$7.61 + $507.50**, or **$515.11**.

Complete the chart for the **$1,200** investment at **6%** compounded quarterly. Round to the nearest cent if necessary.

	Principal	Rate (per year)	Time	Interest
9.	$1,200	6%	3 months	
10.		6%	3 months	
11.		6%	3 months	
12.		6%	3 months	

Problem Solving Reasoning   Solve.

13. At the end of one year, what is the total amount of principal in the bank for **$1,200** at **6%** compounded quarterly? _____

 Quick Check

Calculate the amount of commission and the net proceeds.

14. 6% commission on sales of $15,500 _____

15. 4.5% commission on sales of 565 _____

16. Calculate the rate of commission if you earn **$18** on sales of **$225**. _____

Calculate the interest on the loan

17. 8% interest on $560 for 2 years _____

18. 4.5% interest on $1,200 for 1 year _____

19. 6% interest on $450 for 6 months _____

146   Unit 5 Lesson 9

Name _____

Problem Solving Application: Use a Table

Most employed taxpayers in the United States have their income taxes withheld by their employer. The Internal Revenue Service provides employers with tables that show the amount of tax that must be withheld. A portion of the table for *not married* employees is shown.

In this lesson you will use the table to find the amount of tax to be withheld from an employee. The amount of the tax is based on the weekly salary and the number of exemptions claimed.

Federal Income Tax Withholding

Not Married			
Weekly salary		Number of exemptions	
At least	But less than	0	1
230	240	41.40	36.40
240	250	44.00	39.00
250	260	46.60	41.60
260	270	49.20	44.20
270	280	51.80	46.80
280	290	54.80	49.40
290	300	57.80	52.10

Tips to Remember:

> 1. Understand 2. Decide 3. Solve 4. Look back

- Ask yourself: What do I know? What do I need to find?
- Read the headings of the table carefully. Make sure you select the correct row and column in the table.
- Think about whether the table entry makes sense. Is it reasonable?

Use the federal income tax withholding table shown above.

1. Ms. Simoz earns **$280** a week and claims one exemption for herself. How much will be withheld from her paycheck?

   Think: Which row of the table should I use? Which column?

   Answer _____

2. Ms. Simoz also has withheld from her pay **$20.30** for Social Security Tax (FICA) and **$25.83** for health insurance. What is her weekly take-home pay?

   Think: How can you find what is left after the items have been withheld?

   Answer _____

Unit 5 Lesson 10 **147**

Use the federal income tax withholding table for married people.

Federal Income Tax Withholding

Married						
Weekly salary		Number of exemptions				
At least	But less than	0	1	2	3	4
230	240	32.30	28.30	24.60	21.20	17.70
240	250	34.40	30.40	26.40	23.00	19.50
250	260	36.50	32.50	28.50	24.80	21.30
260	270	38.60	34.60	30.60	26.60	23.10
270	280	40.70	36.70	32.70	28.60	24.90
280	290	42.80	38.80	34.80	30.70	26.70
290	300	45.10	40.90	36.90	32.80	28.80

3. Mr. Scheer earns **$291** a week. He claims **4** exemptions for himself, his wife, and their **2** children. How much will be withheld from his paycheck?

4. Mr. Scheer pays a local tax of **$17.40** per week and his social security deduction is **$19.47** per week. What is his weekly take-home pay?

5. How much more does a married person with two exemptions have withheld if they make **$270** versus **$269**?

6. How much more does a married person making **$284** have withheld if they have one exemption rather than three exemptions?

7. Brian needs to make **$220** a week after federal taxes are withheld. He is not married and has no exemptions. What weekly salary does he need?

8. Suppose a person is married and has no exemptions. About what percent of her or his salary will be withheld for federal taxes?

Extend Your Thinking

9. Who has more withheld, the married person with one exemption or the single person with one exemption? Both earn **$268**.

10. Use your answer to problem **4** to compute Mr. Scheer's take-home pay for the year.

Name _____

Unit 5 Review

Solve for the percentage, base, or rate.

1. 60% of 492 is _____.
2. $33\frac{1}{3}$% of 843 is _____.
3. 15% of $29.40 is _____.
4. 30% of what number is 27? _____
5. $66\frac{2}{3}$% of what number is 30? _____
6. What percent of 400 is 350? _____
7. 28 is what percent of 35? _____

Find the percent of change.

8. Original amount: 40
   New amount: 32

   Percent of change _____

   Increase or decrease? _____

9. Last year: 72 students tried out for the team.
   This year: 60 students tried out for the team.

   Percent of change _____

   Increase or decrease? _____

Solve.

10. The list price of a hair dryer is $28. The selling price is $19.60.

    What is the rate of discount? _____

11. The list price of a reclining chair is $210. The discount rate is 20%.

    What is the amount of the discount? _____

12. The list price of an art book is $89. The discount rate is 25%. What

    is the net price? _____

13. A broker sells $580 in goods and receives a 7% commission. What is
    the amount of the commission and the net proceeds?

    _____

14. A sales clerk sold $4,200 in clothing and received a commission of

    $126. What is the commission rate? _____

15. Calculate the interest owed when you borrow $850 at 6.5% for

    1 year. _____

16. You borrow $3,800 at 9% for 30 months. What will you pay in

    interest? What will you owe the bank? _____

17. Your aunt bought movie tickets for your family. Children's tickets
    were $4 and adult tickets were $7. She bought four more children's
    tickets than adult tickets, and the total cost was $71. How many of

    each type of ticket did she buy? _____

Unit 5 Review 149

Cumulative Review ★ Test Prep

1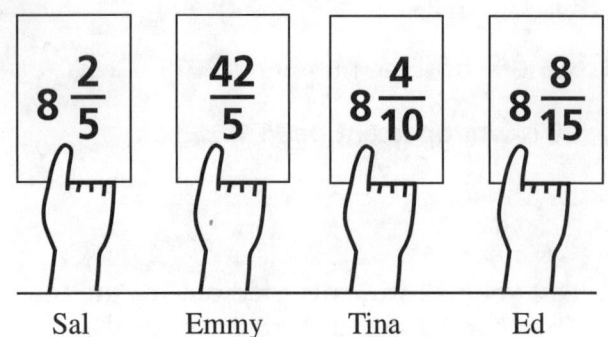

Four students were asked to write equivalent versions of the same fraction. Whose fraction is not equivalent to the others?

A Tina

B Sal

C Ed

D Emmy

2 One hundred seventy-one guests attended the class reunion at Hillside High, and the organizers said that this was a 90% attendance. How many were invited?

F 154

G 181

H 190

J 261

3 Which best represents the percent of the figure that is shaded?

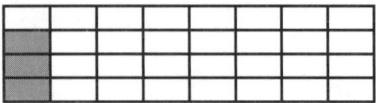

A $\frac{3}{32}$

B 0.94

C 3

D 9.4

4 A bicycle regularly priced at $165 is on sale for 5% off. What is the sale price?

F $8.25

G $82.50

H $156.75

J $160

5 What is the solution of the equation:

$x - 2\frac{4}{5} = 1\frac{2}{5}$

A $4\frac{1}{5}$

B $1\frac{2}{5}$

C $3\frac{6}{5}$

D $3\frac{8}{5}$

E Not here

6 A doctor bought a 5-foot-by-6-foot rectangular rug for her office. What is the area of the rug in square yards?

F 30

G 10

H $3\frac{1}{3}$

J $1\frac{1}{9}$

7 A pattern for a quilt is made up of 36 squares. In the pattern, 20 of the squares have shades of blue in them. If the whole quilt has 144 squares, then what simplest form ratio represents the part of the quilt that is blue?

A $\frac{1}{4}$

B $\frac{5}{9}$

C $\frac{9}{5}$

D 4

UNIT 6 • TABLE OF CONTENTS

Data, Statistics, and Probability

Lesson	Page
1 Line Plots and Histograms	153
2 Stem-and-Leaf Plots	155
3 Box-and-Whisker Plots	157
4 Scatter Plots	159
5 Misleading Graphs	161
6 **Algebra:** Making Predictions from a Graph	163
7 **Problem Solving Strategy:** Make a List	165
8 Permutations and Combinations	167
9 **Probability:** Independent Events	169
10 **Probability:** Dependent Events	171
11 **Problem Solving Application:** Use Graphs and Tables	173
• Unit 6 Review	175
• Cumulative Review ★ Test Prep	178

Dear Family,

During the next few weeks, our math class will be studying data, statistics, and probability. This includes work with reading and constructing graphs, which will help students prepare for algebra.

You can expect to see homework that provides practice with these skills. Here is a sample you may want to keep handy to give help if needed.

Finding the First, Second, and Third Quartiles, and the Range

4, 5, 5, **6**, 8, 9, 9, **10**, 11, 13, **15**, 15, 15, 18, 29

The first quartile is **6**.
The second quartile or median is **10**.
The third quartile is **15**.

The extremes are **4** and **29**.
The range is $29 - 4 = 25$.
29 is an outlier.

Determining the Probability of an Experiment

If an experiment involves two events, the probability of both of them occurring is found by multiplying their individual probabilities.

Example: You pick a letter from *a* to *j* and roll a number cube. What is the probability of picking a vowel (*a, e, i*) and rolling an even number?

$P(\text{Vowel and even number}) = P(\text{Vowel}) \cdot P(\text{even number})$

$= \dfrac{3}{10} \cdot \dfrac{3}{6} = \dfrac{9}{60}$ or $\dfrac{3}{20}$

During this unit, students will continue to learn new techniques related to problem solving and will continue to practice basic skills with fractions, decimals, and percents.

Sincerely,

We will be using this vocabulary:

mean the average of a set of data

median the middle number when a data set is arranged from least to greatest

mode the number(s) that occur(s) most often in a data set

frequency table a table that tallies the number of pieces of data in different intervals

outlier a piece of data that differs significantly from the rest of the data

quartile one of three items of data that separate the sorted data into roughly four quarters

permutation an arrangement or listing of objects in which order matters

probability a measure of how likely it is that an event will happen

independent events two or more events each of whose outcomes has no effect on the outcome of the other(s)

Name _____ **Line Plots and Histograms**

In Unit **1**, you learned to make a **line plot** and use the measures of central tendency—**mean, median,** and **mode**—to describe the data.

The data at the right shows the age at inauguration of the first 12 presidents of the United States.

President	Age	President	Age
Washington	57	Jackson	61
Adams, J.	61	Van Buren	54
Jefferson	57	Harrison	69
Madison	57	Tyler	51
Monroe	58	Polk	49
Adams, J.Q.	57	Taylor	64

This data is displayed below in a line plot.

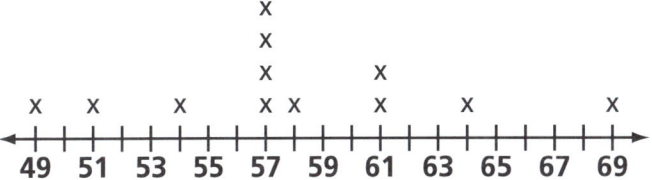

Ages of the First 12 Presidents at Inauguration

mean = $\frac{695}{12}$ or about **57.9**

median = **57**

mode = **57**

range = 69 − 49 or **20**

The mean, median, and mode are all about **57**. The typical age of a president at inauguration was **57**.

Ages of 20th-Century Presidents

President	Age	President	Age
Clinton	46	Truman	60
Bush	64	F. Roosevelt	51
Reagan	69	Hoover	54
Carter	52	Coolidge	51
Ford	61	Harding	55
Nixon	56	Wilson	56
Johnson	55	Taft	51
Kennedy	43	T. Roosevelt	42
Eisenhower	62	McKinley	54

Use the data to answer the questions.

1. Make a line plot for the data in the table.

2. From your line plot, what conclusions can you make about the age of 20th-century presidents?

_____

3. Find these measures.

Mean _____   Median _____   Mode _____   Range _____

4. Which measure best describes the data? Explain.

_____

5. Compare the graphs and measures of central tendency for both sets of data on this page.

_____

_____

A **frequency table** tallies the number of pieces of data in different intervals. The intervals used must cover the **range** of the data. The frequency table below shows that for the interval 41–45 there were two presidents inaugurated in that age group.

A **histogram** is a special bar graph that represents data from a frequency table. Each bar represents the data for one interval of the frequency table. There are no spaces between the bars because there are no gaps between intervals. Where one interval ends, the next begins.

Interval	Tally	Frequency
41–45	II	2
46–50	I	1
51–55	IIII III	8
56–60	III	3
61–65	III	3
66–70	I	1

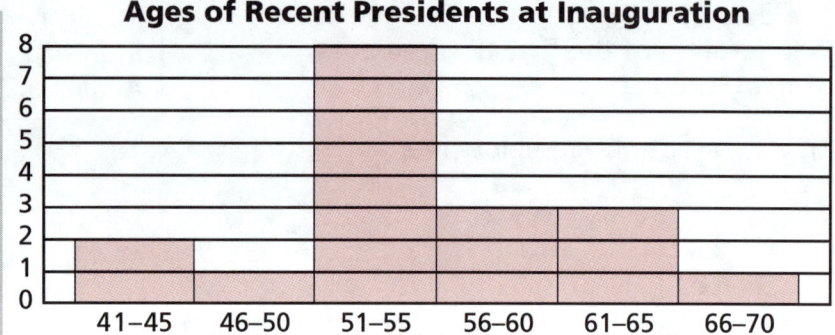

Ages of Recent Presidents at Inauguration

Solve.

6. Make a frequency table of the data. Use an interval of **10** points.

Test Scores for Period 4					
88	86	78	75	84	88
97	62	96	65	98	82
61	84	75	81	87	86
95	92	92	84	73	83
77	85	79	89	94	83

Interval	Tally	Frequency

Problem Solving Reasoning

Solve.

7. Draw a histogram of the data.

8. Write a description of the data based upon the graph. Include information about the range and comparison of number of students scoring A's (**90–100**), B's (**80–89**), C's (**70–79**), and D's (**60–69**).

Test Prep ★ Mixed Review

9 What percent of 120 is 90?

    A 100%   **C** 75%

    B 90%   **D** 7.5%

10 Jay is charged $46.75 for a pair of sneakers that had been marked down from $55. What was the discount rate?

    F 15%   **H** 85%

    G about 17%   **J** 117%

Name _____

Stem-and-Leaf Plots

A **stem-and-leaf plot** can be used to organize and display data. When the data items have **2** digits, the **stem** represents the tens digit and the **leaves** represent the ones digits.

Make a stem-and-leaf plot of the congressional data.

Congressional Representation Western States

AK 3	ID 4	OR 7
AZ 8	NE 5	UT 5
CA 54	NV 3	WA 11
CO 8	NM 5	WY 3
HI 4	MT 3	

Step 1
Make the stem. Write the tens digits for the data in order from least to greatest.

0	
1	
2	
3	
4	
5	

Step 2
Record the data for the leaves. Write the ones digit for each data item.

0	3 8 8 4 4 5 3 5 3 7 5 3
1	1
2	
3	
4	
5	4

Step 3
Sort the data for the leaves from least to greatest. Write a title and include a key.

Congressional Representation

0	3 3 3 3 4 4 5 5 5 7 8 8
1	1
2	
3	
4	
5	4

Key:
5|4 represents 54 members of Congress

You can see that the range is **54 − 3**, or **51**.
The median of the data is between the seventh and eighth number, or 5.
The mode is 3, because it occurs most often—4 times.

Use the data about the congressional representation of the southern states to answer the questions.

Congressional Representation: Southern States												
AL	AR	FL	GA	KY	LA	MS	NC	OK	SC	TN	TX	VA
9	6	25	13	8	9	7	14	8	8	11	32	13

1. Make a stem-and-leaf plot for the data.

2. a. Find the measures.

Mean _____   Median _____

Mode _____   Range _____

b. Which measure best describes the data? Explain. _____

3. Items of data that are significantly different from the rest are **outliers**. What item(s) of data might be considered outliers for this data set?

_____

4. Outliers can have a great effect on the mean. Find the mean without using the outliers. Is it more representative of the data? _____

Unit 6 Lesson 2 **155**

A **back-to-back stem-and-leaf** plot uses the same stem for two sets of data.

The example at the right shows the heights of **16** students in a fourth–grade class and **19** students in a seventh–grade class.

The plot shows that:
- most fourth graders are between **44** in. and **54** in. tall with a median of **46.5** in. and a range of **17** in.
- most seventh graders are between **54** in. and **68** in. tall with a median of **61** in. and a range of **23** in.

Seventh graders are taller than fourth graders, by about **14** or **15** inches.

Height in Inches

Fourth Grade		Seventh Grade
9 7	3	
9 7 7 6 6 6 5 4 0	4	8 9
4 3 3 1 0	5	1 4 5 5 6 8 9
	6	1 2 2 3 3 7 7 8
	7	1

Key: 0 | 4 represents 40 inches and 4 | 8 represents 48 inches

---

Problem Solving Reasoning

Use the data to answer the questions.

5. Make a back-to-back stem-and-leaf plot for the ages of first ladies and their husbands. Presidential data is found in the last lesson. Add Presidents Harrison (**56**) and Cleveland (**48**).

Ages of First Ladies

First Lady	Age	First Lady	Age
H. Clinton	45	E. Roosevelt	48
B. Bush	63	L. Hoover	54
N. Reagan	59	G. Coolidge	44
R. Carter	49	F. Harding	60
E. Ford	56	E. Wilson	52
P. Nixon	56	H. Taft	47
C. Johnson	50	E. Roosevelt	39
J. Kennedy	31	I. McKinley	49
M. Eisenhower	56	C. Harrison	56
E. Truman	60	F. Cleveland	21

6. From your plot, what conclusions can you make about the ages of first ladies compared with the ages of presidents? Include the median and range in your summary.

_____

_____

_____

Test Prep ★ Mixed Review

7. Beth saved $600 on a used car that was on sale at 15% off the list price. What was the list price of the car?

   A $9,000   C $3,400

   B $4,000   D $900

8. After 6 months, how much interest does Sam receive on his $500 investment, if his bank pays 4% simple interest annually?

   F $10   H $24

   G $20   J $250

Name _____

Box-and-Whisker Plots

A **box-and-whisker** plot shows how data are distributed. Unlike a stem-and-leaf plot, each piece of data is not displayed. Instead, the data are represented in **quartiles.**
- You know that the median separates the data set into 2 halves.
- **Quartiles** separate a data set into 4 quarters.

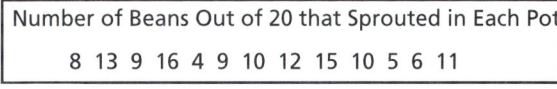

To draw a box-and-whisker plot of the data in the chart, you can use the steps below.

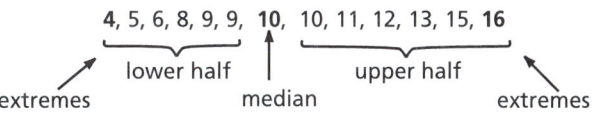

1. Arrange the data in order from least to greatest. Identify the **extremes,** or least and greatest numbers, and the median of the entire data set.

2. • Draw a number line. Below the line, draw a dot for each extreme and the median.
   - Draw a dot for the **first quartile.** It is the median of the lower half of the data set. Note that neither half of the data includes the median.
   - The **second quartile** is the median of the entire data set.
   - Draw a dot for the **third quartile.** It is the median of the upper half of the data set.

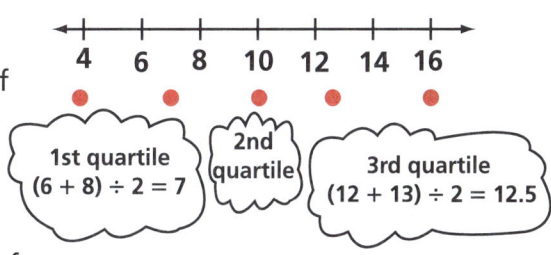

3. Draw a box-and-whisker plot. Draw a box as shown through the first and third quartiles. Draw a vertical line through the median. Show the whiskers by connecting the extremes to the first and third quartiles.

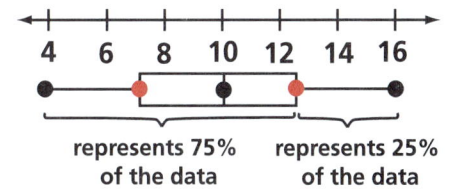

The box represents 50% of the data.

Answer the questions using the data set at the right.

Data:
33, 44, 63, 75, 52, 34, 15, 20, 68, 64, 41, 48, 67, 48

1. Sort the data from least to greatest.

   _____

2. Find the items: Least _____   1st Quartile _____

   2nd Quartile _____ 3rd Quartile _____   Greatest _____

3. Draw a box-and-whisker plot.

   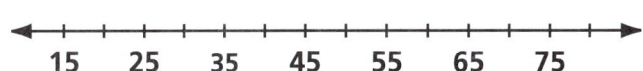

4. What percent of the data is greater than or equal to the median? _____

5. What percent of the data is less than or equal to the first quartile? _____

Unit 6 Lesson 3   157

Multiple box-and-whisker plots can be drawn using the same axes. It is easy to visually compare the **5** items of data that were used to draw the plots.

Weekly Grocery Bills for One Year

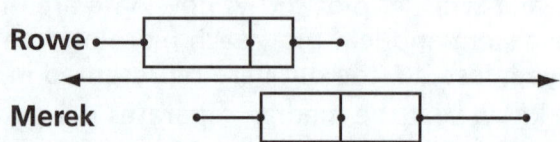

Both families bought groceries for **52** weeks. The Rowes' greatest week equals the Mereks' median, so for half the weeks, the Mereks spent more than the Rowes' greatest week. For half the weeks, the Rowes spent less than what the Mereks spent a quarter of the weeks.

Use the data to answer the questions.

6. From the plots, would you agree that the average score of the top professional basketball players is going up each year? Explain. _____

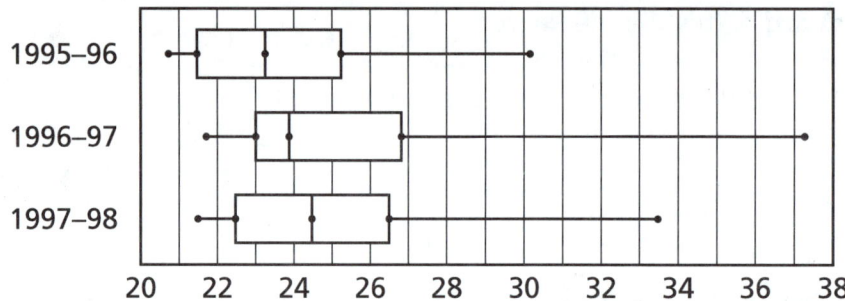

7. Compare the box-and-whisker plots for the last two seasons. Which season had the higher

a. greatest number? _____   c. third quartile? _____   e. median? _____

b. first quartile? _____   d. least number? _____

✓ Quick Check

Use the plots below for exercises 8–10. Each shows the number of times a group of sixth graders rode the bus during one month.

Bus Rides (October)

```
                              x
                              x
                            x x
         x          x       x x
      x     x       x       x x
      +--+--+--+--+--+--+--+--+--+--+→
      0     5    10    15    20
```

Bus Rides (January)

```
0 | 1 3 3
1 | 2 6 8
2 | 8
3 | 1 5 6 6 7 8 8 9
4 | 0 0 0 1 2 2 2 2
```

Work Space.

8. What are the median and mode for the first set of data?
_____

9. What are the median and mode of the second set of data?
_____

10. What are the first and third quartiles for the first set of data?
_____

Name _____

Scatter Plots

Two sets of related data can be graphed on a **scatter plot**. The chart below shows two sets of related data. Students were surveyed to find out the contents and weight of their bookbags.

Number of Books and Notebooks	2	3	2	1	4	5	4	3
Weight in Pounds	5	9	6	3	11	14	12	8

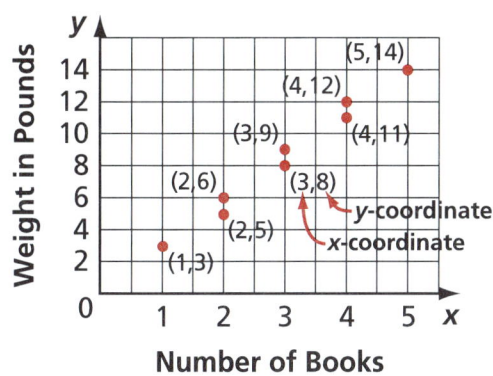

This data can be written as **ordered pairs (x, y)**; (2, 5), (3, 9), (2, 6), (1, 3), (4, 11), (5, 14), (4, 12), (3, 8).

The weight in pounds (y-coordinate) tends to increase as the number of books and notebooks (x-coordinate) increases. This is a **positive correlation**. For other data, the y-coordinate may tend to decrease as the x-coordinate increases. This is a **negative correlation**. If no pattern exists between the coordinates, then there is **no correlation**.

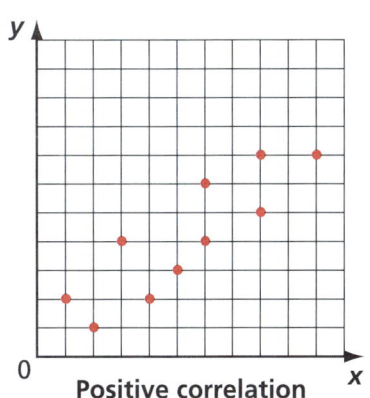
Positive correlation

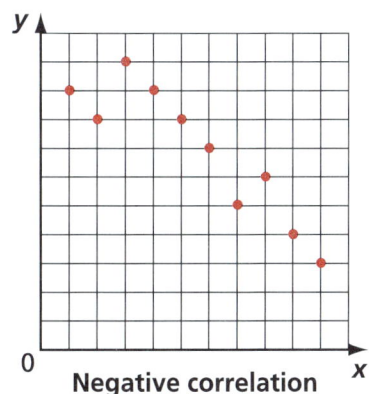
Negative correlation

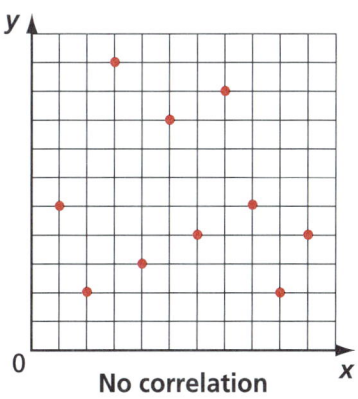
No correlation

Use the scatter plot to answer the questions.

1. Write the ordered pair represented by each letter.

A _____ B _____ C _____

D _____ E _____ F _____

2. Plot the points on the scatter plot.

G(5, 1)   H(0, 4)   I(3, 4)

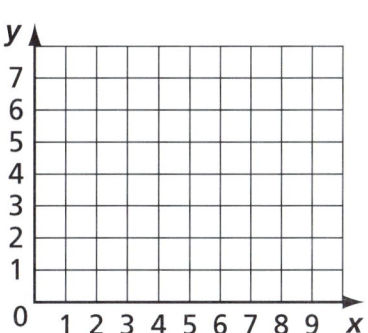

3. Draw a scatter plot for the ordered pairs below. Label each point with the correct letter.

A(8, 4.5), B(4, 2), C(6, 4), D(3, 1.5), E(7, 4)

F(2, 1), G(4, 3), H(5, 2.5), I(6, 3)

4. Describe the correlation.

_____

Unit 6 Lesson 4 **159**

5. Use the data in the table to draw a scatter plot.

Altitude (in 1,000's of feet)	0	5	10	15	20	25
Pressure (in pounds per sq in.)	14.7	12.3	10.2	8.4	6.8	5.4

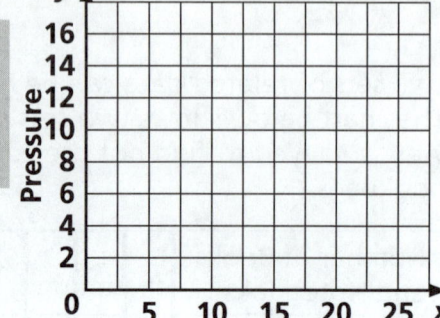

6. Describe the correlation.
_____

7. What correlation would you expect for each of the following?

a. scatter plot showing number of children in a family and number of windows in a kitchen

_____

b. scatter plot of number of hours per day you are awake and the hours you are asleep

_____

Problem Solving Reasoning Solve.

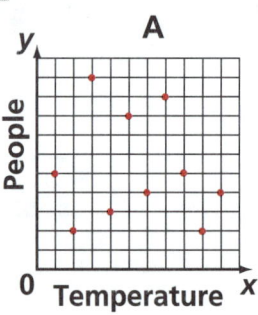

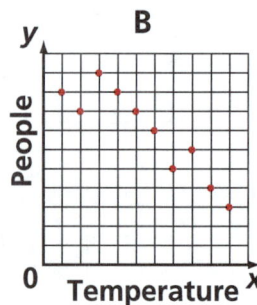

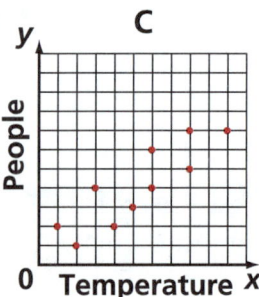

8. Which graph do you think represents daily temperature and number of people at the beach? Explain.

_____
_____

9. Which graph do you think represents daily temperature and people at the shopping mall? Explain.

_____
_____

Test Prep ★ Mixed Review

10 The data show the number of cousins that 13 students have. What is the median value?

Cousins

```
0 | 5 5 6 7
1 | 2 3 7 8
2 | 3 5 6 8 9
```
Key: 1 | 2 represents 12 cousins

A 5   **B** 7   **C** 16.2   **D** 17

11 The ages of the eleven players on a parent-student soccer team are: 12, 50, 13, 48, 14, 41, 14, 52, 15, 56, 15. Which of these values does 50 represent?

F range   **H** upper quartile

G mean   **J** median

160 Unit 6 Lesson 4

Name _____

Misleading Graphs

Look at the two graphs at the right. Both show the monthly sales for Pete's Restaurant, but they look very different.

Graph B could be misleading because the vertical scale does not start at zero. Monthly sales have tended to increase, but Graph B makes the increase look dramatic.

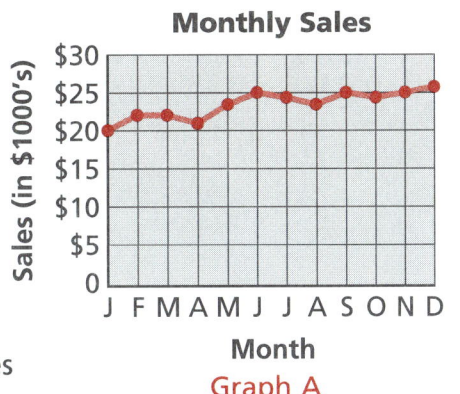

Graph A

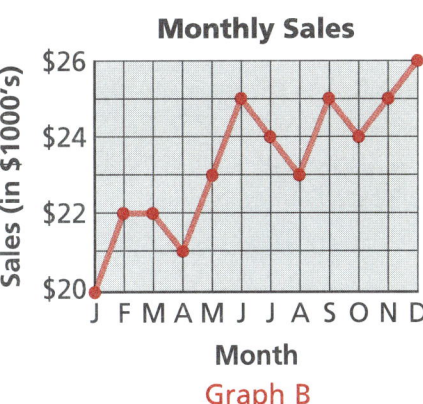

Graph B

Suppose Pete wants to attract new investors. Then, he would show Graph B. If sales had decreased, he might use a scale similar to Graph A. It would make the loss less apparent.

You may not want to include all the numbers from **0** to the top of the range in a graph's scale. Then, you can use jagged lines or a "broken scale" to show that part of the range has been omitted.

Use the graph to answer the questions.

You asked your friends to vote on their favorite ice cream flavor from the three choices shown.

1. Use just the lengths of the bars. Compare the number of people who chose vanilla with those who chose strawberry.

   _____

2. Use the horizontal scale. Compare the number of people who chose vanilla with those who chose strawberry.

   _____

3. Graph the data so it is not misleading. Use a bar graph.

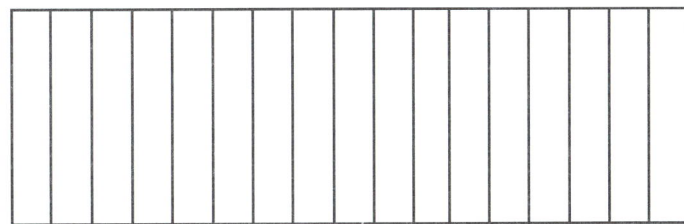

Unit 6 Lesson 5 **161**

Another way that graphs can be misleading is when the widths of the bars vary. Both graphs show the number of Internet subscribers (in thousands) for two providers, but they look very different.

Graph A is misleading because the bars are not the same width and the height of the bars do not correspond to a vertical scale. Graph B is not misleading.

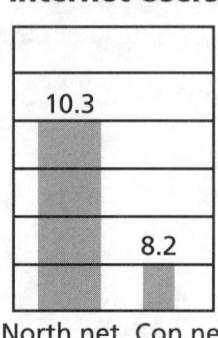
Graph A

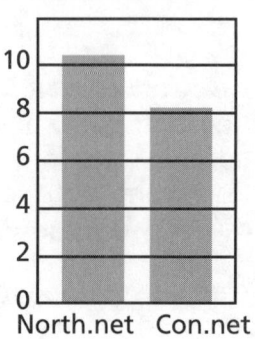
Graph B

Problem Solving Reasoning

4. Draw two bar graphs–one that is misleading and one that is not. Use the data to the right.

   Chocolate Sales for February 1–14

   Carbo's Chocolates: **328** pounds
   Mrs. Sweet's Treats: **260** pounds
   Yum Factory: **400** pounds

   Misleading Graph

   Accurate Graph
   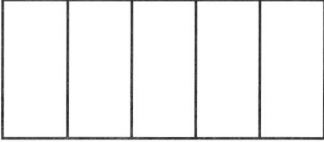

5. Draw two graphs–one that is misleading and one that is not. Use the data below.

   Monthly High
   Temperature (°F)

   Jan.: **45°**
   Feb.: **48°**
   Mar.: **51°**
   Apr.: **58°**
   May: **72°**
   June: **76°**

   Misleading Graph
   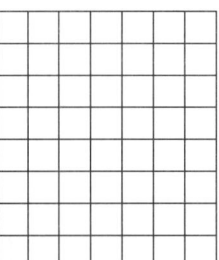

   Accurate Graph
   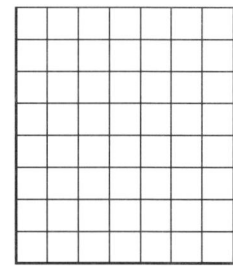

Test Prep ★ Mixed Review

6 Here are the scores in Dan's art class for last Friday's test: 83, 76, 72, 69, 54, 85, 65, 88, 79, 75, 65. Which value for these data does 75 represent?

　A range　　　　**C** median
　B upper quartile　**D** lower quartile

7 Use the data in question 9. If you wanted to make a line plot of the data, which interval would be best to show on the number line?

　F 45–100　　**H** 65–90
　G 55–100　　**J** 75–80

Name _____

Making Predictions from a Graph

A scatter plot can be used to make predictions. Study the graphs below.

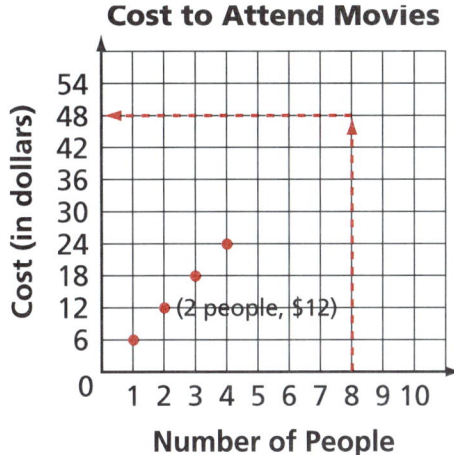

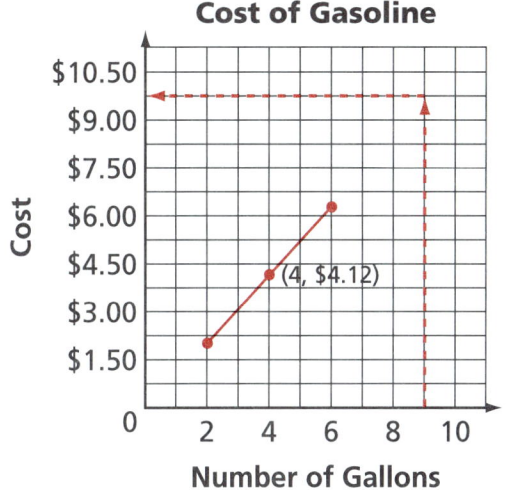

This graph shows the cost for certain numbers of people to go to the movies. The ordered pairs are (*number attending, total cost*). The ordered pairs are not connected, because you cannot have decimal parts of people.

You can use the graph to predict the cost for **8** people. Extend the pattern of points. Read up from the horizontal axis at **8**, and then read over to the left on the vertical axis. You could predict that the cost for **8** people would be a little less than **$50**.

This graph shows the cost for certain numbers of gallons of gasoline. The ordered pairs are (*gallons of gas, cost*). The ordered pairs are connected, because you can buy decimal parts of a gallon of gas.

You can use the graph to predict the cost for **9** gallons. Use a straightedge to extend the line. Read up from the horizontal axis at **9;** then, read over to the left on the vertical axis. You could predict that 9 gallons would cost about **$9**.

Use the graphs to answer the question.

1. How much money did Derek start with? _____

2. How much did Derek have after **3** weeks? _____

3. If Derek continues to save at the same rate, predict the amount he will have after:

   a. **5** weeks _____ b. **8** weeks _____

4. Estimate the cost of the following calls.

   a. **2** minutes _____ b. **3.5** minutes _____

5. Extend the graph to predict the cost.

   a. **6** minutes _____ b. **7.5** minutes _____

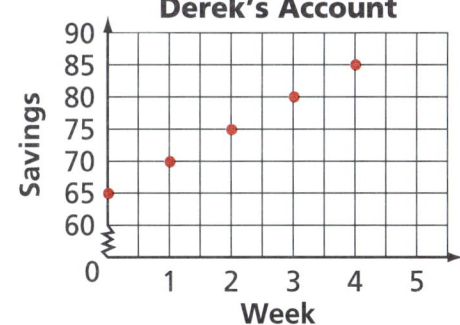

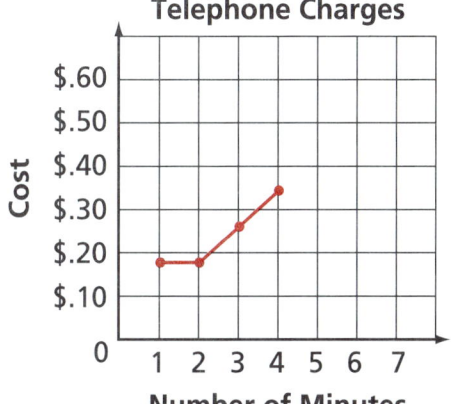

Unit 6 Lesson 6 **163**

Use the graphs to answer.

6. A fitness club began a membership drive. The graph shows the number of members at the end of each month for 6 months. How many members were there on January 1? _____

7. Estimate the number of members at the end of April. _____

8. If membership continues to increase at the same rate, predict the number of members at the end of:

   a. September _____ b. December _____

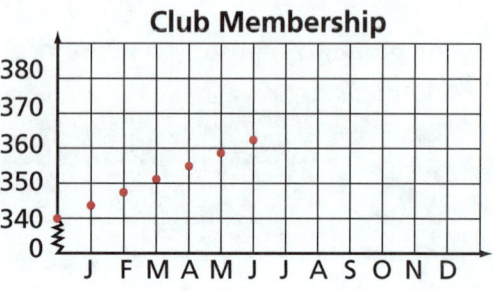

Problem Solving Reasoning — Complete.

9. Write the next three numbers.

   8, 12, 16, 20, _____, _____, _____

10. Without writing each number, predict the 20th number in the sequence. _____

11. Write the next three numbers.

    60, 57, 54, 51, _____, _____, _____

12. Without writing each number, predict the 20th number in the sequence. _____

✓ Quick Check

A scatter plot is made of the two sets of data. Tell whether you would expect to see a positive correlation, a negative correlation, or no correlation.

Work Space.

13. The number of calories in snack foods and the number of grams of fat in the same snacks

    _____

14. The number of times people brush their teeth each day and the number of cavities they have

    _____

15. Why might the broken scale make the graph appear misleading?

    _____

16. What prediction about the attendance at game 10 would be reasonable?

    _____

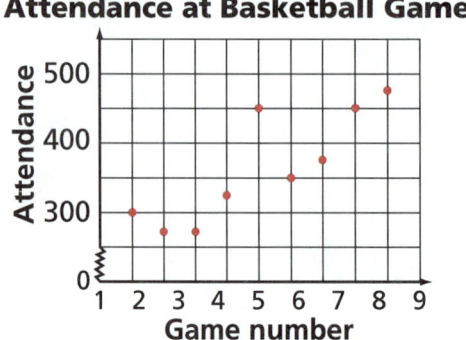

164 Unit 6 Lesson 6

Name _____

Problem Solving Strategy: Make a List

To solve some problems, making a list may help you get started. A list may be a series of numbers, words, or symbols that are written horizontally or vertically.

Problem

Your friend just dropped three coins out of his pocket and they all landed heads up. Is it unusual for all three to be heads? How many ways could they have landed?

---

1 Understand   As you reread, ask yourself questions.

- How many coins were dropped and how did they land?
  _____

- What else do you need to find? _____

---

2 Decide   Choose a method for solving.

Try the strategy Make a List. Make a tree diagram to help you to see all the ways three coins can land.

---

3 Solve   Answer the question.

- Make a list to find how many ways three coins can land.
  _____

- How often would you expect to get three heads?
  _____

---

4 Look back   Ask if your answer makes sense.

- Toss three coins at once several times. Was three heads one of the outcomes? _____

- How did making a list help you solve the problem?
  _____

Use the Make a List strategy or any other strategy you have learned.

1. In your gym locker, you have a pair of shorts, wind pants, a tank top, a white T-shirt, and a blue T-shirt. How many different outfits could you wear?

   Think: What tops can I wear with the shorts? With the pants?

   _____

   Answer _____

2. The Ice Cream Shoppe sells a sundae that has two different flavors of ice cream. The choices are vanilla, chocolate, strawberry, mocha, and mint chocolate. How many different combinations of ice cream can you have in the sundae?

   Think: Start with making a list of all the combinations that have vanilla.

   _____

   Answer _____

3. You heard an advertisement for a company selling discount tapes. The first part of the telephone number, the exchange, contained the digits **6**, **3**, and **4**, but you don't remember the order. Make a list of all the possible telephone exchanges.

   _____

4. You've forgotten your three-digit password to log onto the school computer. You remember the first digit is **4**. How many different passwords would you have to check in order to log on?

   _____

5. The area of the large square is **16** square units.
   a. What is the area of each small triangle?
   b. How many triangles of all sizes are in the figure and what is the area of each size of triangle?

   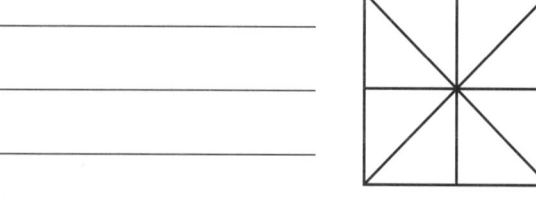

6. The area of the smallest triangle is **1** square unit.
   a. What is the area of the largest triangle?
   b. How many triangles of all sizes are in the figure and what is the area of each?

   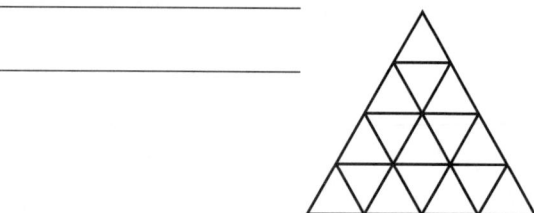

7. How many different combinations of **3** odd numbers have a sum of **15**? (Consider $3 + 3 + 9$ to be the same as $3 + 9 + 3$.)

   _____

8. During the year you must read **3** books for English class. You can choose from a list of **6** books. How many different sets of **3** books can you choose?

   _____

166 Unit 6 Lesson 7

Name _____

Permutations and Combinations

Four players are still left in a tournament. In how many different ways can the four finish in the standings?

Call the players A, B, C, and D. Make a list of the different place finishes where ABCD means A finished first, B finished second, and so on.

Possible Place Finishes

ABCD	BACD	CABD	DABC
ABDC	BADC	CADB	DACB
ACBD	BCAD	CBAD	DBAC
ACDB	BCDA	CBDA	DBCA
ADBC	BDAC	CDAB	DCAB
ADCB	BDCA	CDBA	DCBA

A **permutation** is an arrangement or listing of objects in which *order is important*.

The number of permutations of *n* objects is $n \cdot (n-1) \cdot (n-2) \cdots \cdot 1$. This number is represented by the expression *n*!. It is read as "*n* factorial."

The number of permutations of **4** players is

$$4! = 4 \cdot 3 \cdot 2 \cdot 1 \text{ or } 24$$

There are 24 ways in which they can finish in the standings. The *order* does matter.

How many ways can you arrange 6 students in the front row of the chorus?

Number of permutations of **6** students $= 6!$
$= 6 \cdot 5 \cdot 4 \cdot 3 \cdot 2 \cdot 1$
$= 720$

There are 720 arrangements. The order does matter.

Evaluate.

1. 2! _____   5! _____   3! _____

2. 7! _____   4! _____   6! _____

Solve.

3. List the permutations of the letters in the word BAN. How many of the permutations are words?

4. How many different ways can you arrange five books on a shelf?

5. How many different four-digit numbers can you make using the digits **3, 5, 1,** and **8**? No digit may repeat.

6. How many permutations are there for writing the names of the starting five players in the score book?

Unit 6 Lesson 8

A **combination** is a set of data in which order is *not* important.
Making a list is one way to find the number of combinations of a set.

You order the daily special—a two-topping pizza. You can choose from five toppings. How many different two-topping pizzas could you order?

Possible Pizza Orders				
PH	PO	PM	PG	HM
HO	HG	OM	OG	MG

To simplify the problem, label the toppings: P for pepperoni, H for hamburger, O for onions, M for mushrooms, and G for green peppers.

OM and MO are the same pizza, so order does not matter. There are **10** combinations. If order did matter, the permutations of **2** objects from a set of **5** would be **5 · 4 = 20**, or twice as many.

Solve.

7. Count the number of combinations for choosing **2** people from a group of **4** people.

8. How many ways can you select **3** pieces of fruit from a basket containing **5** pieces?

9. A buffet has **5** appetizers. How many ways can you select **2** of them?

10. A 5-person team wants to select **3** co-captains. How many different combinations are there? Make a list.

Problem Solving Reasoning **Solve.**

11. How many committees of 2 can be selected from a group of 6 students? (Hint: Label the students A, B, C, D, E, F.)

12. How many committees of 2 can be selected from a group of 6 students if one is the speaker and one is the recorder?

Test Prep ★ Mixed Review

13 The number of miles 10 people jogged was recorded in this line plot. How many people jogged *at least* 3 miles?

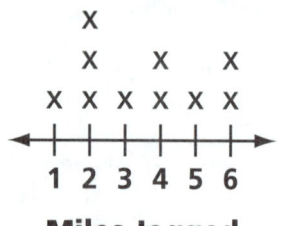

Miles Jogged

A 6   B 5   C 4   D 3

14 To find the range of a set of data from a box-and-whisker plot, what part(s) of the plot would you use?

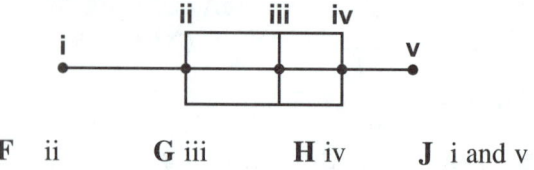

F ii   G iii   H iv   J i and v

168 Unit 6 Lesson 8

Name _____

Probability: Independent Events

The **probability of an event** tells you how likely it is that the event will happen. Probability is measured from **0** to **1**.

When the outcomes of an experiment are all equally likely, the probability (*P*) that an event (*E*) will occur is:

$P(E) = \dfrac{\text{Number of favorable events}}{\text{Number of possible events}}$

Experiment: Roll a Number Cube

Outcomes
1, 2
3, 4
5, 6

Probability of each outcome = $\dfrac{1}{6}$.

Experiment: Spin a Spinner

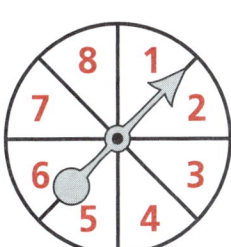

- Spin once. What is the probability of spinning a **5** or **6**?

2 *favorable* outcomes: **5** or **6**

8 possible outcomes

$P(5 \text{ or } 6) = \dfrac{2}{8}$ or $\dfrac{1}{4}$

- Spin once. What is the probability of spinning an even number greater than **3**?

3 *favorable* outcomes: **4, 6, 8**

8 possible outcomes

$P(\text{even} > 3) = \dfrac{3}{8}$

Spin once. Write the probability of the event.

1. Probability of an odd number? _____

2. Probability of an even number? _____

3. Probability of an odd number or a number greater than 9? _____

4. Probability of a multiple of 3? _____

5. Probability of a factor of 36? _____

Write the probability of the event.

6. You toss two coins at the same time. What is the probability that

    a. both land heads? _____ b. both land tails? _____ c. both coins are different? _____

7. You write the letters of the word "coins" on **5** separate pieces of paper. You will select one piece of paper at random. What is the probability that you draw

    a. a vowel? _____ b. a consonant? _____

Unit 6 Lesson 9 **169**

$P(\text{Red and } 4) = \frac{1}{16}$

You spin the two spinners shown. What is the probability of spinning Red and 4?

Method 1: List all of the outcomes.

1 *favorable* outcome: Red, 4
16 possible outcomes

$P(\text{Red and } 4) = \frac{1}{16}$

Method 2: Multiply the probabilities of each event.

$P(\text{Red}) = \frac{1}{4}$, $P(4) = \frac{1}{4}$; $P(\text{Red and } 4) = \frac{1}{4} \cdot \frac{1}{4}$ or $\frac{1}{16}$

The result of the second spinner does not depend on the result of the first spinner. These events are **independent events.** The results for each spinner are independent of one another.

Experiment: Spin Two Spinners

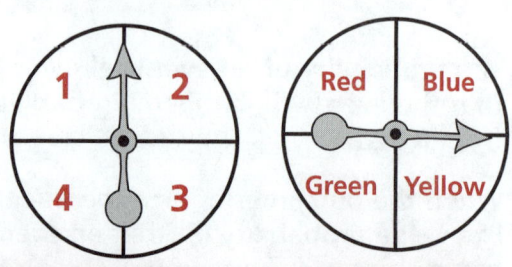

Outcomes			
Red, 1	Blue, 1	Green, 1	Yellow, 1
Red, 2	Blue, 2	Green, 2	Yellow, 2
Red, 3	Blue, 3	Green, 3	Yellow, 3
Red, 4	Blue, 4	Green, 4	Yellow, 4

Spin each spinner once. Write the probability.

8. $P(\text{red and } 2) = $ _____

9. $P(\text{red and even}) = $ _____

10. $P(\text{not red and } 3) = $ _____

11. $P(\text{blue and not } 2) = $ _____

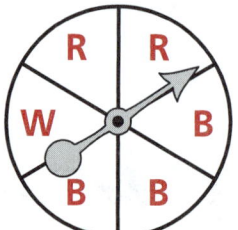
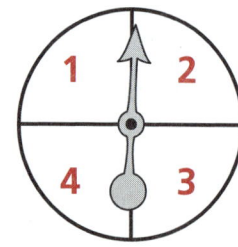

Problem Solving Reasoning Write the probability of the event.

12. You toss a coin and roll a number cube.

    $P(\text{heads and } 4) = $ _____ $P(\text{heads and even}) = $ _____ $P(\text{tails and factor of } 6) = $ _____

13. You select a letter at random from "ice" and a letter at random from "warm."

    $P(\text{both are vowels}) = $ _____ $P(\text{E and R}) = $ _____ $P(\text{both are consonants}) = $ _____

Test Prep ★ Mixed Review

14 To complete her basketball team, in how many ways can Fiona choose four other players from among her six friends?

    A 4   C 15

    B 6   D 24

15 What number represents the median of the box-and-whisker plot?

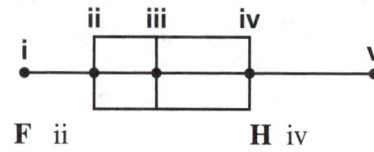

    F ii   H iv

    G iii   J i and v

Name _____

Probability: Dependent Events

When two or more events are combined, the result is a **compound event.** The probability of a compound event is related to the probabilities of the events that make it up.

Two events are independent if the outcome of one event has no effect on the outcome of the other. Two events are **dependent** if the outcome of the first event affects the outcome of a second event.

Probability of Independent Events (A and B)	Probability of Dependent Events (A and B)
$P(A \text{ and } B) = P(A) \cdot P(B)$	$P(A, \text{ then } B) = P(A) \cdot P(B \text{ after } A)$

Independent Events

Draw a marble. Note the color. Replace it. Draw again. What is the probability that both marbles you draw are red?

$P(\text{red and red}) = P(\text{red}) \cdot P(\text{red})$
$= \dfrac{4 \cdot 4}{10 \cdot 10}$
$= \dfrac{16}{100}$ or **0.16**

Because the first red marble was replaced, the probability of drawing the second red marble was not affected.

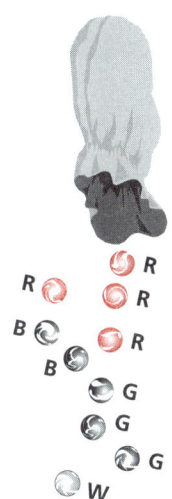

Dependent Events

Draw a marble. Note the color. Do not replace it. Draw again. What is the probability that both the marbles you draw are red?

$P(\text{red, then red}) = P(\text{red}) \cdot P(\text{red after red})$
$= \dfrac{4}{10} \cdot \dfrac{3}{9}$
$= \dfrac{12}{90}$ or about **0.133**

Without replacing the first red marble, the probability of drawing the second red marble was affected.

Write the probability of the compound event. Use the bag of marbles shown above. (R is red, G is green, B is blue, and W is white.)

1. With replacement, *P*(blue and green) = _____

2. Without replacement, *P*(blue and green) = _____

3. With replacement, *P*(blue and red) = _____

4. Without replacement, *P*(blue and red) = _____

5. With replacement, *P*(white and white) = _____

6. Without replacement, *P*(white and white) = _____

You write the letters P-R-O-B-A-B-I-L-I-T-Y on separate pieces of paper and put them in a bag. You draw two letters without replacement. What is the probability of drawing two B's?

$P(B, \text{ then } B) = P(B) \cdot P(B \text{ after } B)$

$= \dfrac{2}{11} \cdot \dfrac{1}{10}$

$= \dfrac{2}{110} \approx 0.018$

This experiment is a dependent event. The result of the first event affected the probability of the second event.

Problem Solving Reasoning Write the probability of the compound event. Round to the nearest thousandth.

7. The letters M-I-S-S-I-S-S-I-P-P-I are placed in a bag. Without replacement, two letters are drawn.

$P(\text{both are S's}) \approx$ _____ $P(\text{both are I's}) \approx$ _____ $P(\text{both are P's}) \approx$ _____

Quick Check

Solve. The Shutterbug Club has 7 members.

Work Space.

8. In how many ways can they stand in a line for a group photo? _____

9. How many combinations of 2 club officers are possible?

_____

10. In how many ways can they elect one president and one vice president? _____

Find the probability. You either toss a coin (H or T) or roll a number cube (1, 2, 3, 4, 5, 6) or both.

11. $P(4 \text{ or } 5)$ **12.** $P(T \text{ and not } 4)$ **13.** $P(\text{number} > 4 \text{ and } H)$

_____   _____   _____

A bag contains 16 cards, each with one of the letters M-A-T-H-E-M-A-T-I-C-S-I-S-A-O-K on it. Two draws are made without replacing the first card. Find the probability.

14. $P(M, \text{ then } M)$ **15.** $P(M, \text{ then } S)$ **16.** $P(A, \text{ then } K)$

_____   _____   _____

172   Unit 6 Lesson 10

Name _____

Problem Solving Application: Use Graphs and Tables

This bar graph does not show numbers on the vertical scale. It is still useful for making comparisons.

In this lesson, you will use graphs and tables to compare, make estimates, or draw conclusions about the data in the graph.

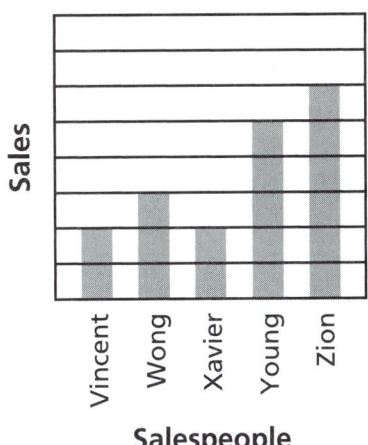
Sales for Week 1 — XYZ Company

Tips to Remember:

| 1. Understand | 2. Decide | 3. Solve | 4. Look back |

- Ask yourself: What do I know? What do I need to find?
- When you can, make a prediction about the answer. Then, compare your answer and your prediction.
- Think about strategies you have learned and use them to help you solve a problem.

Use the bar graph shown above.

1. Who had sales that were three times what Vincent or Xavier had?

   Think: If you triple the height of Vincent's bar, it would be the same height as whose bar?

   _____

   Answer _____

2. Who had sales that were the closest to the average for the company?

   Think: What is the average for the company? Add the heights of all the bars. Each bar's height is the number of units or spaces tall it is. Divide that height by 5.

   _____

   Answer _____

3. About how many times Xavier's sales is Young's sales?

   _____

4. About what part of Zion's sales is Young's sales?

   _____

Unit 6 Lesson 11 **173**

Use the table and graphs to answer problems 5–10.

Sales for Week 2 — XYZ Company

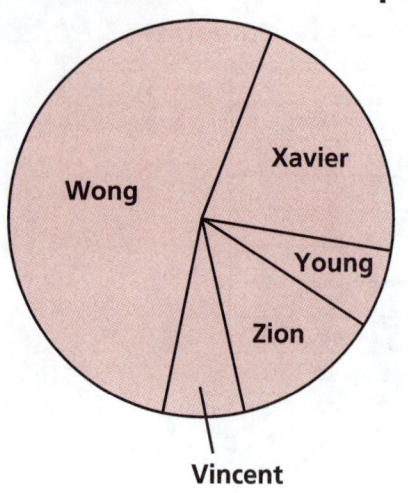

Sales ABC Company

Week	Sales
1	$1,799
2	$ 988
3	$3,040
4	$5,806
5	$4,109
6	$7,750
7	$9,032
8	$5,498

Sales ABC Company

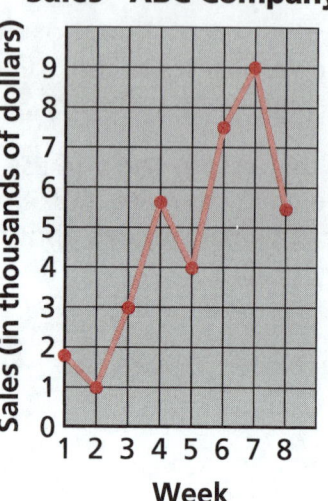

5. The circle graph shows the relationship of five parts (individual sales) to the whole (total company sales). Tell three things that the graph shows.

6. In the XYZ Company sales for Week 2, about what percent of the total company sales were by Vincent, Zion, and Young together? Explain your reasoning.

7. To find the difference in sales between the fifth and sixth weeks, would you use the table or the line graph? Explain why. What was the difference?

8. To find the two weeks during which sales increased the most, would you use the table or the line graph? Explain why. Between which two weeks did the sales increase most?

Extend Your Thinking

9. Determine the mean, median, and range of sales for the ABC Company for the 8 weeks.

10. In the XYZ Company sales for Week 2, about what was the ratio of Wong's sales to Young's sales? Explain.

Name _____

Unit 6 Review

Use the line plot to complete exercises 1–3.

Student Heights

```
            x x
      x     x x     x
    x x x x x x x x x x
    ┼─┼─┼─┼─┼─┼─┼─┼─┼─→
    48 49 50 51 52 53 54 55 56
```

1. How many student heights are represented?

   _____

2. Range _____ Median _____

   Mode _____

3. Suppose a new piece of data was plotted at **56**. Would the range, median, or mode change? Explain.

   _____

   _____

Use the histogram to complete exercises 4–6.

4. How many test scores are represented?

   _____

5. How many students scored above 70?

   _____

6. Write a description of the class results.

   _____

   _____

   _____

Test Scores

(histogram with bars: 41–50: 2, 51–60: 1, 61–70: 5, 71–80: 6, 81–90: 10, 91–100: 4)

Use the data below for exercises 7–10. It lists the ages of 18 moviegoers.

12, 15, 22, 36, 28, 18, 24, 32, 41, 18, 16, 25, 22, 34, 16, 26, 30, 18

7. Complete the stem-and-leaf plot of the data.

8. Range _____ Median _____

   Mode _____

9. First quartile _____

   Third quartile _____

10. Make a box-and-whisker plot for the data.

Ages of Moviegoers

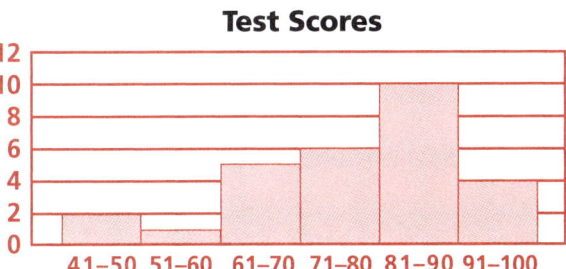

Key: 4 | 1 represents a moviegoer who is 41 years old.

Unit 6 Review **175**

Use the graphs to complete.

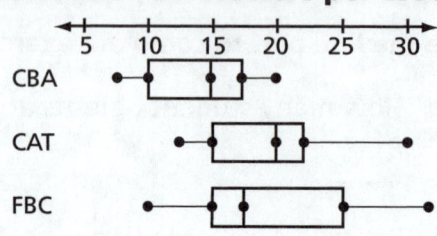

Millions of TV Viewers per Week

11. What was the median number of viewers (in millions) for each station?

    CBA _____   CAT _____   FBC _____

12. What percent of the weekly averages are represented within the box? _____

13. Which station do you believe had the best weekly averages? Explain. _____

---

14. Did Laurel do twice as well on the test as Megan? Explain. _____

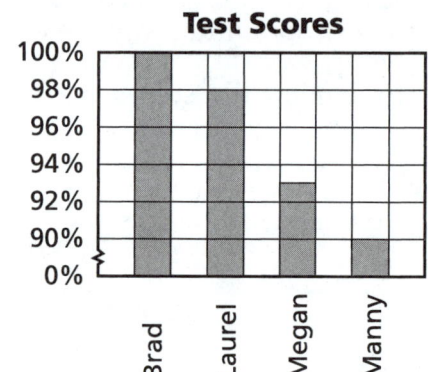

15. Is this a misleading graph? Explain. _____

---

16. Complete the scatter plot for the ordered pairs below.

    (3, 5), (1, 2), (4, 9), (3, 6.5), (2, 4)
    (5, 9), (3, 5.5), (4, 8), (2, 4.5), (1, 2.5)

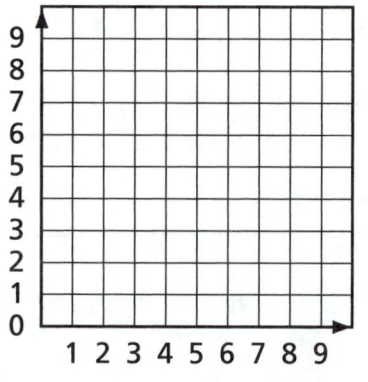

17. What type of correlation does the scatter plot show? _____

---

18. How much snow fell after **1** hour? _____

19. How much snow fell after **2.5** hours? _____

20. The snow kept falling at the same rate. How much snow do you predict had fallen after **5** hours? _____

Name _____

Complete.

21. Calculate 5! _____

22. How many permutations of the letters A, B, and C are there? _____

23. In how many ways could you arrange 5 people in a line for a photograph? _____

24. In how many ways could you select 2 people from a group of 5 people where order does not matter? _____

25. List the different two-topping pizzas that you could order. The topping choices are onion, sausage, extra cheese, and green peppers. _____

26. What is the probability that a pizza selected at random from your list in exercise **25** contains onion? _____

27. You spin once. Write the probability.

a. $P(1)$ = _____

b. $P(prime)$ = _____

c. $P(even)$ = _____

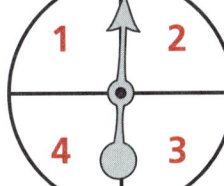

28. You select a card at random from a deck of 52 pattern block cards. The deck contains 4 hexagons, 6 trapezoids, 6 squares, 14 rhombuses, and 22 triangles. Write the probability.

a. $P(triangle)$ = _____

b. $P(hexagon)$ = _____

c. $P(rhombus)$ = _____

29. You toss a coin and roll a number cube numbered **1–6**. What is the probability that the outcome will be a head and a four?

_____

30. Without replacement, you draw two number cards from the numbers 0–20 inclusive. What is the probability that you draw a prime number followed by a multiple of 4?

_____

Unit 6 Review

Name _____

Cumulative Review
★ Test Prep

1 Which scatter plot of the following sets of ordered pairs would tend to show a negative correlation?

A Linda's time spent studying and her test scores

B An athlete's age and her time for the 400 meters

C Pete's age and his height

D The age and resale value of a car

2 Yumi needs to divide 0.5 L of liquid into laboratory samples that contain 0.02 L each. How many samples can she make?

F 2.5   H 250

G 25   J 2,500

3 A class turned in pictures for an art exhibit. Only 36 pictures, or 75% of them, could be displayed. How many pictures were turned in?

A 40

B 48

C 54

D 60

4 In a sample, 13 out of 25 seventh grade students said that they planned to go to the school play on Saturday. What percent of the students are going to the school play on Saturday?

F 52%

G 48%

H 45%

J 26%

5 Sixteen students out of a sample of 50 seventh graders claimed they would vote for Jeff for class president. About how many students out of 135 students would you predict might vote for Jeff?

A 58   C 43

B 53   D 16

6 Suppose it costs $41 in credit card interest to finance a $400 purchase over a year. How much could be saved by borrowing the money at a bank at 8.9% interest for a year?

F $6.40

G $5.40

H $.54

J $.06

7 What value for n is the solution of the equation?

$$\frac{1}{2} + \frac{3}{4} + \frac{5}{8} = \frac{3}{4} + n + \frac{1}{2}$$

A $\frac{1}{2}$ C $\frac{5}{4}$

B $\frac{3}{4}$ D $\frac{5}{8}$

8 Chris has 5 pounds of pennies. How many ounces is this?

F 16

G 80

H 160

J 530

K Not here

Unit 6 Cumulative Review

UNIT 7 • TABLE OF CONTENTS

Geometry

Lesson	Page
1 Points, Lines, and Angles	181
2 Planes	183
3 Measuring Angles	185
4 Angle Relationships	187
5 Angle Relationships of Parallel Lines	189
6 Triangles	191
7 **Problem Solving Strategy:** Find a Pattern	193
8 Constructing Congruent Segments and Angles	195
9 Constructing Bisectors	197
10 Polygons and Congruent Figures	199
11 Circles and Central Angles	202
12 Making and Interpreting Circle Graphs	204
13 Polyhedrons	207
14 **Problem Solving Application:** Use a Diagram	209
• Unit 7 Review	211
• Cumulative Review ★ Test Prep	214

Dear Family,

During the next few weeks, our math class will be studying topics from geometry. We will work with plane figures such as parallel lines, triangles, polygons, and circle graphs and space figures such as prisms and pyramids.

You can expect to see homework that provides practice with these skills. Here is a sample you may want to keep handy to give help if needed.

We will be using this vocabulary:

segment part of a line that has two endpoints

ray part of a line that has one endpoint and continues indefinitely in the other direction

acute angle an angle whose measure is between 0° and 90°

right angle an angle whose measure is 90°

obtuse angle an angle whose measure is between 90° and 180°

complementary two angles whose measures total 90°

supplementary two angles whose measures total 180°

congruent same size and shape

isosceles triangle one with at least two sides congruent

polyhedron a closed figure in space whose faces are all polygons

circle graph a graph that represents data as part of a circle; the parts are often labeled using percents

Finding Measures of Angles

When two lines are parallel and crossed by a third line, called a transversal, corresponding angles are congruent. In the diagram, ∠1 and ∠2 are corresponding angles. If ∠1 measures 40°, ∠2 would also measure 40°.

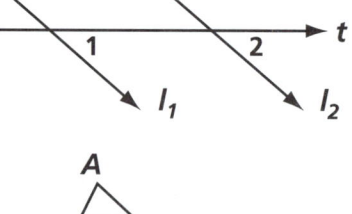

The sum of the angles of a triangle is 180°. In the diagram, the measure of ∠C would be 180° − (42° + 75°) = 63°.

Reading Information from Circle Graphs

Region A in the circle graph represents 40% of the 280 students surveyed. The number of students represented in this region is 40% of 280 = 0.4 · 280 or 112 students.

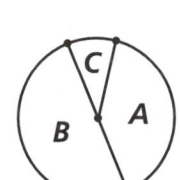

During this unit, students will continue to learn new techniques for problem solving and will continue to practice basic skills with fractions, decimals, and percents.

Sincerely,

Name _____

Points, Lines, and Angles

Concept

A **point** locates a position in space. It has no length, width, or height.

A **line** is a series of points that form a straight path. It has one dimension, length, although it can't be measured.

A **line segment** or **segment** is a part of a line. It has two endpoints. Its length can be measured.

A **ray** is a part of a line with one endpoint that continues indefinitely in the other direction.

A line that is level with the horizon, left to right, is **horizontal**. A line that is straight up and down is **vertical**. Three or more points that lie on the same line, such as **J, K,** and **L,** are **collinear**.

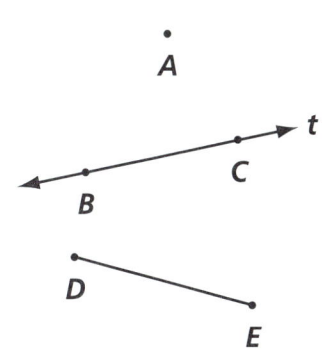

How to Name It

Use a capital letter.

Use any two points on the line or a single letter.
$\overleftrightarrow{BC}$ or $\overleftrightarrow{CB}$ or t

Use the two endpoints.
$\overline{DE}$ or $\overline{ED}$

Use the endpoint and any other point.
$\overrightarrow{FG}$ or $\overrightarrow{FH}$

Use a straightedge when needed.

1. Draw a line. Label three points **D, M, T** on it. Write three different names for the line.

   _____, _____, _____

2. Draw a segment. Label the endpoints **C** and **W**. Write two different names for the segment.

   _____, _____

3. Draw a ray. Label the endpoint **P**. Label two other points **A** and **N** on the ray. Write two different names for the ray.

   _____, _____

Answer the question.

4. How many lines can you draw through two points? _____

5. How many lines can you draw through one point? _____

6. On $\overline{AB}$, what are points **A** and **B** called? _____

7. Which points are used to name a line? _____

8. In exercises **1–3**, which set of points is collinear? _____

Unit 7 Lesson 1   **181**

An **angle** is formed by two rays that have the same endpoint.

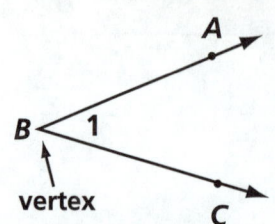

It is named using three points of the angle. The **vertex** is the middle point.

∠ABC or ∠CBA

The angle could also be named ∠B or ∠1.

You do not use ∠P to refer to any of the angles at the right. It would not be clear which angle you were referring to. You may locate points on each ray. Then, use three points to name each angle.

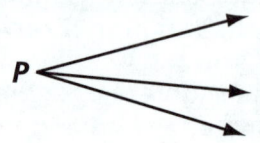

Name each angle in four ways.

9.

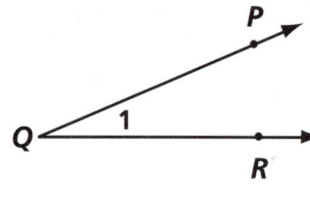 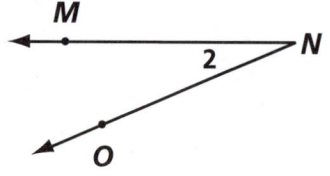 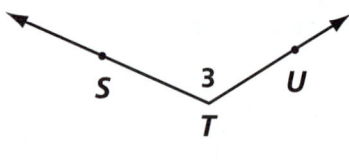

_____ _____   _____ _____   _____ _____

_____ _____   _____ _____   _____ _____

Problem Solving Reasoning Solve.

10. How many different segments are shown? Name each one.

11. How many different angles are shown? Name each one.

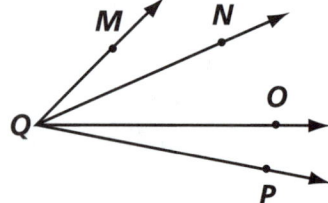

_____   _____

Test Prep ★ Mixed Review

12 What number is 9% of 360?

　A 32.4　　　C 67.5

　B 40　　　　D 324

13 Judy's bank gives her 4% interest on her $600 investment. The interest is compounded every quarter. Which amount best shows the value of her investment after one year?

　F $624.00　　H $701.91

　G $624.36　　J $6,243.60

Name _____   **Planes**

A **plane** is a flat surface that extends indefinitely in all directions. It has two dimensions, length and width, although neither can be measured.

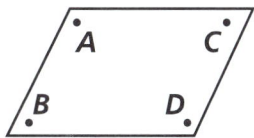

The plane indicated by the parallelogram is named using at least three points, such as *ABC, BCD,* or *ABCD.*

A plane is usually represented by a parallelogram.

Points, segments, or lines that are in the same plane are **coplanar.**
For example, in the plane at the right, $\overline{AB}$ and $\overrightarrow{CD}$ are coplanar.

$\overline{AB}$ and $\overleftrightarrow{EF}$ are not coplanar.

$\overrightarrow{CD}$ and $\overleftrightarrow{EF}$ are not coplanar.

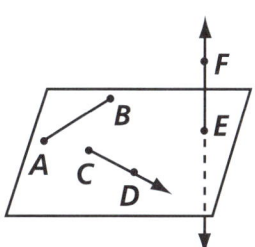

Planes are sketched by using parallelograms. A dashed line shows that a portion of a line is hidden by a plane.

Sketches of two planes: Sketches of three planes:

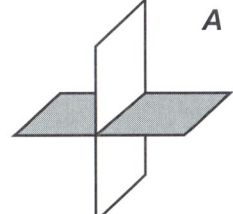   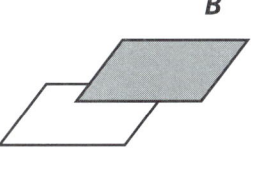   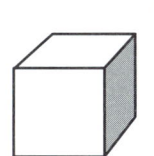   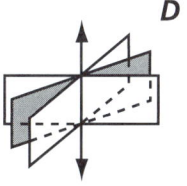

Use the sketches A–D above. Answer the question.
Explain your reasoning.

1. Will any two planes always intersect? _____

2. Can the intersection of two planes be a single point? _____

3. Can the intersection of two planes be a line? _____

4. Will any three planes intersect? _____

5. Could the intersection of three planes be a single point? _____

6. Could the intersection of three planes be a line? _____

Use the diagram of a cube. Answer the question.

7. Name the intersection of planes *ABCD* and *ABFE.* _____

8. Name the intersection of planes *ABCD* and *DCGH.* _____

9. Name the planes that point *B* lies on. _____

10. Are $\overline{AB}$ and $\overline{EF}$ coplanar? _____

11. Are $\overline{AB}$ and $\overline{CG}$ coplanar? _____

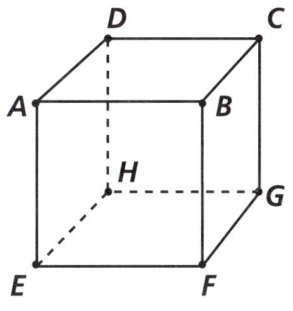

Unit 7 Lesson 2   **183**

You can sketch intersecting planes as shown below. Notice how the parallelograms help to give the sketch a three-dimensional look.

1. Sketch a horizontal plane.

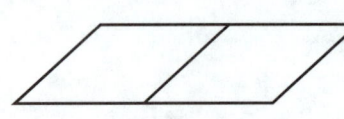

2. Sketch the vertical plane.

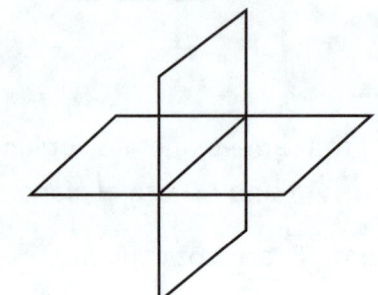

3. Erase hidden lines. Shade.

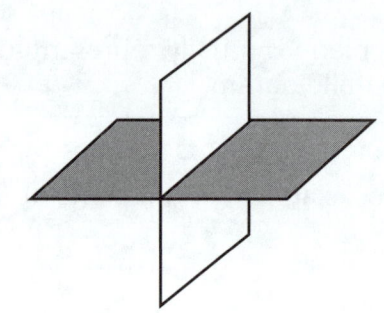

Sketch.

12. Two intersecting planes

13. Three intersecting planes

14. Two planes that do not intersect

Problem Solving / Reasoning — Solve.

15. How many planes are used to form the faces of this hat box?

_____

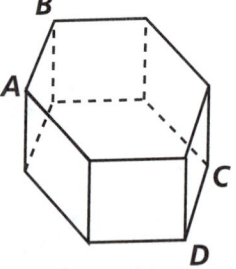

16. Sketch and shade the plane that $\overline{AB}$ and $\overline{CD}$ lie in.

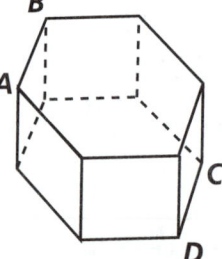

Test Prep ★ Mixed Review

17. In the data represented in the stem-and-leaf plot, what is the mode?

```
0 | 2 5 6 7 8 9
1 | 2 4 4 7 9
2 | 1 2 3 6 8 9
```
Key: 2 | 9 represents 29

A 14   C 7
B 9   D 4

18. The ages of the eleven players in Horseville's all-age soccer team were: 13, 51, 14, 47, 15, 42, 14, 53, 16, 57, 15. Which typical value does 16 represent?

F mean   H range
G lower quartile   J median

184 Unit 7 Lesson 2

Name _____   **Measuring Angles**

A **protractor** can be used to approximate the measure of an angle. An angle is measured in units called **degrees**. Two angles are **congruent** if they have the same measure.

How to measure an angle:

1. Place the center of the protractor at the vertex of the angle.

2. Line up **0°** on the protractor with one ray of the angle.

3. Read the measure where the other ray crosses the protractor.

Be sure to read the correct scale (inside or outside). Ask yourself which scale starts at **0°** for your angle. Use that scale to read the angle measure.

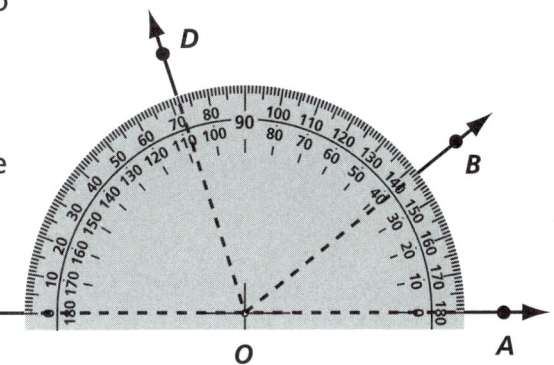

∠AOB = 38°   ∠COD = 72°   ∠AOD = 108°

Use a protractor to measure the angle. Write your answer on the answer line.

1.

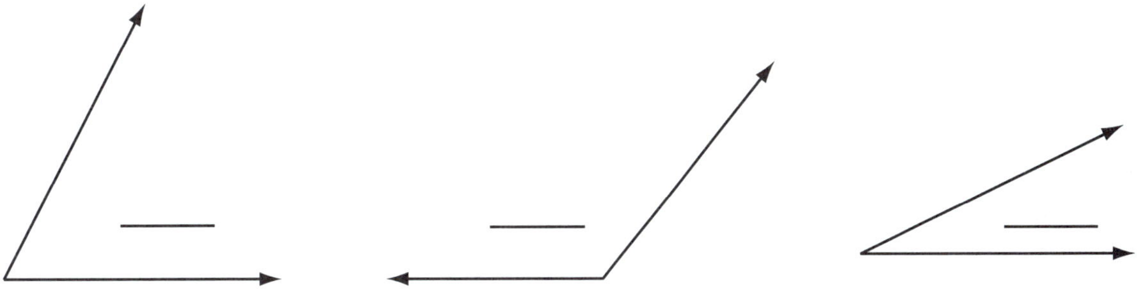

2.

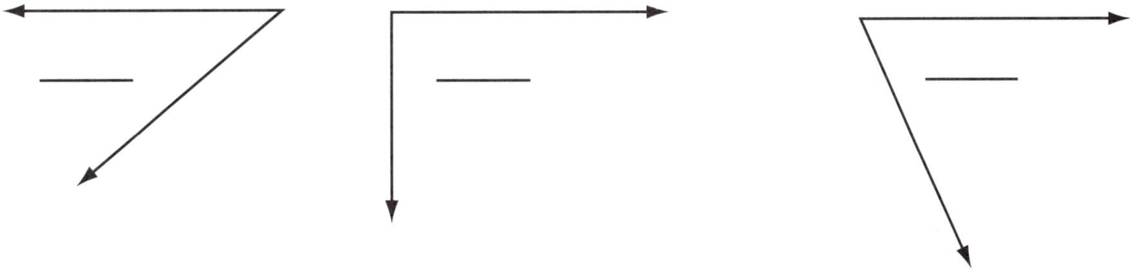

3.

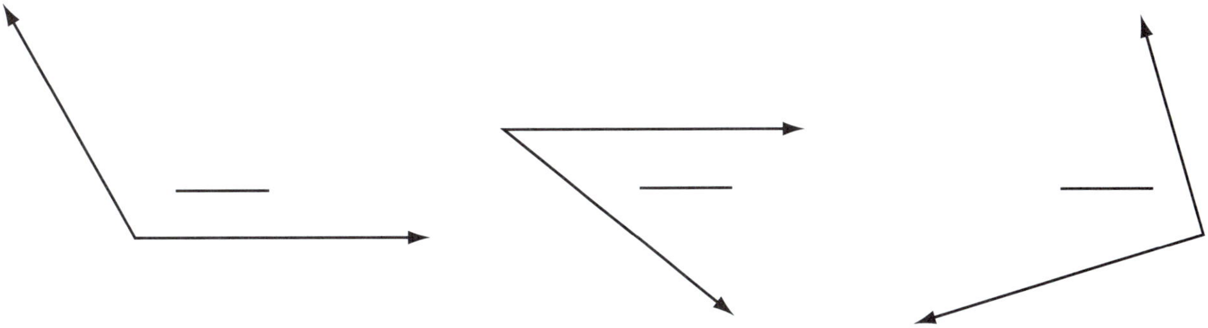

Unit 7 Lesson 3 **185**

Angles are classified by their measures.

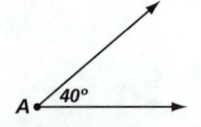
Acute angle
Its measure is between 0° and 90°.

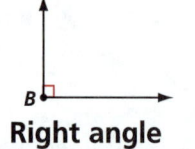
Right angle
Its measure is 90°.

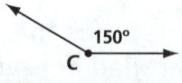
Obtuse angle
Its measure is between 90° and 180°.

Straight angle
Its measure is 180°.

Classify the angle as acute, right, obtuse, or straight.

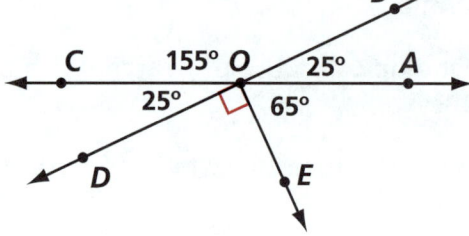

4. ∠AOB _____   ∠BOC _____

5. ∠COD _____   ∠DOE _____

6. ∠EOB _____   ∠AOC _____

7. Name two pairs of congruent angles.

   _____ and _____   _____ and _____ or _____ and _____

Problem Solving / Reasoning — Solve.

8. How many acute angles? Obtuse angles? _____

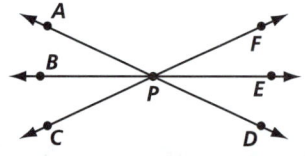

9. How many right angles? Straight angles? _____

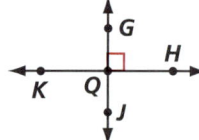

✓ Quick Check

10. A line contains the points *P*, *Q*, and *R*. Write four ways to name this line. _____

Work Space.

Use the angle below for exercises 11–13.

11. Write three ways to name the angle. _____

12. Is the angle acute, obtuse, right, or straight? _____

13. Use your protractor. What is the measure of the angle? _____

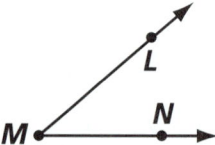

Use the cube at the right for exercises 14–15.

14. Name two lines that are coplanar with $\overleftrightarrow{AE}$. _____

15. Name a line that is not coplanar with $\overleftrightarrow{AE}$. _____

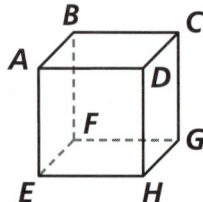

Name _____   **Angle Relationships**

Pairs of angles may be related in several ways.

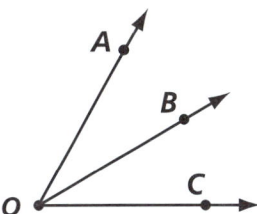
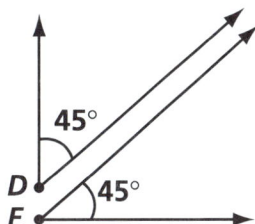
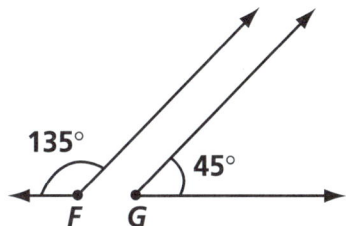

Adjacent angles
Two angles that share a common vertex and common side, but their interiors have no points in common

∠AOB is adjacent to ∠BOC.

Complementary angles
Two angles whose measures total **90°**

Complementary angles may or may not be adjacent.

∠D is complementary to ∠E.

Supplementary angles
Two angles whose measures total **180°**

Supplementary angles may or may not be adjacent.

∠F is supplementary to ∠G.

Suppose ∠XYZ = 32°. An angle complementary to ∠XYZ would measure **90° − 32°**, or **58°**.
An angle supplementary to ∠XYZ would measure **180° − 32°**, or **148°**.

Use the diagram to answer.

1. Name the adjacent angles in the diagram.

   _____ and _____, _____ and _____

   _____ and _____, _____ and _____

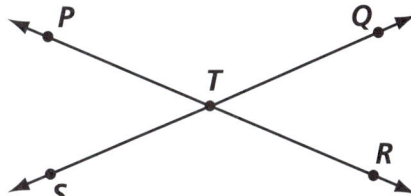

2. Measure the angles with a protractor. Write the measures on the diagram.

3. Name a pair of congruent angles. _____ and _____

4. How many of the pairs of angles in exercise **1** are supplementary? _____

Write the complement and supplement of the angle.

	Complement	Supplement			Complement	Supplement
5. ∠COB = 30°	_____	_____		6. ∠COB = 72°	_____	_____
7. ∠COB = 18°	_____			8. ∠COB = 90°		_____
9. ∠COB = 120°		_____		10. ∠COB = 81°	_____	_____
11. ∠COB = 2°	_____			12. ∠COB = 148°		_____

Unit 7 Lesson 4 **187**

Vertical angles are "opposite" angles that are formed when two lines intersect.

In the diagram, if ∠AOC = 40°, then ∠AOB = 140° because the two angles are adjacent, and ∠COB is a straight angle.

Using the same reasoning, ∠BOD = 40°. So vertical angles AOC and BOD have the same measure. They are congruent. By using the same reasoning, any two vertical angles are congruent.

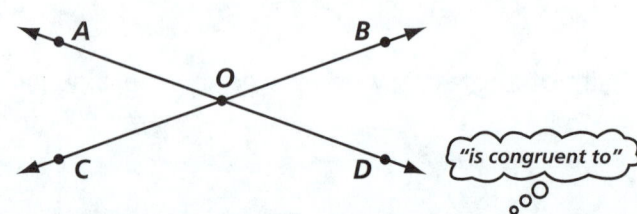

∠AOB and ∠COD are vertical angles. ∠AOB ≅ ∠COD

∠AOC and ∠BOD are vertical angles. ∠AOC ≅ ∠BOD

"is congruent to"

Find the missing measures of the angles. Use vertical, complementary, and supplementary angles.

13.

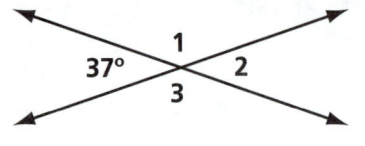

∠1 = _____, ∠2 = _____

∠3 = _____

14.

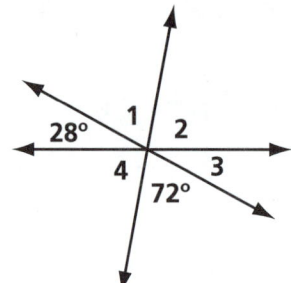

∠1 = _____, ∠2 = _____

∠3 = _____, ∠4 = _____

15.

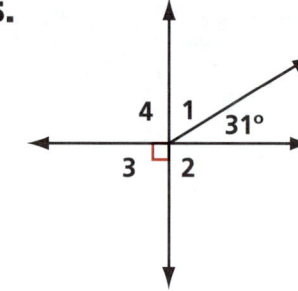

∠1 = _____, ∠2 = _____

∠3 = _____, ∠4 = _____

Problem Solving Reasoning Tell whether the statement is true or false. Explain your reasoning.

16. Every acute angle has a complement and supplement. _____

17. Every obtuse angle has a complement and a supplement. _____

18. Vertical angles can be acute, obtuse, or right. _____

19. Vertical angles can be adjacent angles. _____

Test Prep ★ Mixed Review

20 Which of the statements is false?

A A and C are collinear with B.

B AB + BC = AC

C $\overline{AC}$ represents a ray.

D $\overline{AC}$ represents the distance from A to C.

21 Which of the statements is false?

F Two planes are shown intersecting at the line through points A and B.

G Points A, B, C, and D, are coplanar.

H Points A, B, and C are coplanar.

J Points A, B, and D are coplanar.

188 Unit 7 Lesson 4

Name _____

Angle Relationships of Parallel Lines

A **transversal** is a line that intersects two other lines at two distinct points.

In the diagram, l_1 is a transversal to l_2 and l_3. If the lines are extended, you see that each line is a transversal of the other two.

When a transversal intersects two lines, pairs of angles are formed that have special names.

Corresponding angles are on the same side of the transversal (*t*) and in a corresponding position with the lines, either both above or both below. The corresponding angles in the diagram at the right are:

∠1 and ∠5, ∠2 and ∠6, ∠3 and ∠7, ∠4 and ∠8.

Lines in the same plane that do not intersect are **parallel**. Lines l_4 and l_5 are parallel.

Whenever lines l_4 and l_5 are parallel, corresponding angles will be congruent.

∠1 ≅ ∠5, ∠2 ≅ ∠6, ∠3 ≅ ∠7, ∠4 ≅ ∠8

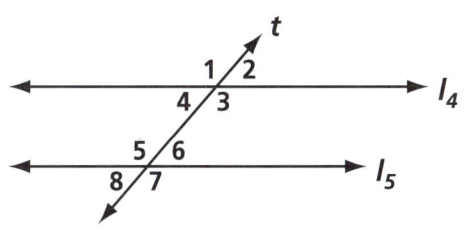

Identify pairs of angles as vertical, supplementary, or corresponding.

1. ∠1 and ∠4 _____   ∠2 and ∠4 _____

2. ∠1 and ∠5 _____   ∠5 and ∠7 _____

3. ∠6 and ∠7 _____   ∠2 and ∠6 _____

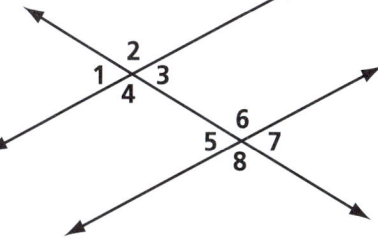

Find the measure of the missing angles. Lines l_1 and l_2 are parallel.

4. ∠1 = _____   ∠2 = _____   ∠3 = _____

   ∠4 = _____   ∠5 = _____   ∠6 = _____

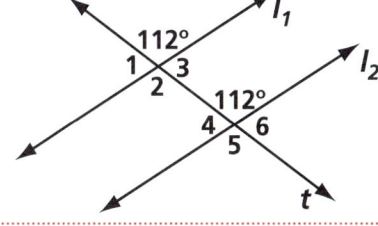

5. ∠1 = _____   ∠2 = _____   ∠3 = _____

   ∠4 = _____   ∠5 = _____   ∠6 = _____

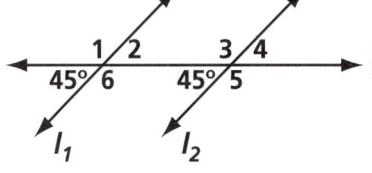

6. ∠1 = _____   ∠2 = _____   ∠3 = _____

   ∠4 = _____   ∠5 = _____   ∠6 = _____

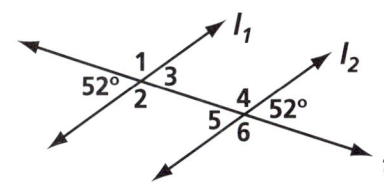

Unit 7 Lesson 5   **189**

Alternate interior angles are on opposite sides of the transversal (**t**) and interior (inside) to the two lines. In the diagram at the right, the alternate interior angles are:

∠3 and ∠6, ∠4 and ∠5

For this figure there are:
  4 pairs of vertical angles
  8 pairs of supplementary angles
  4 pairs of corresponding angles
  2 pairs of alternate interior angles

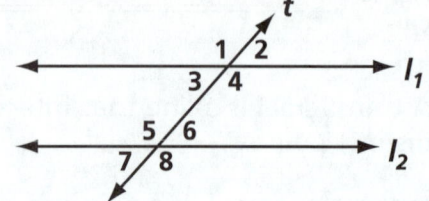

Whenever lines l_1 and l_2 are parallel, alternate interior angles will be congruent.

∠3 ≅ ∠6, ∠4 ≅ ∠5

Find the measure of the angle. Justify your reasoning.

7. ∠2 = _____° because _____

8. ∠3 = _____° because _____

9. ∠4 = _____° because _____

10. ∠5 = _____° because _____

11. ∠6 = _____° because _____

12. ∠7 = _____° because _____

13. ∠8 = _____° because _____

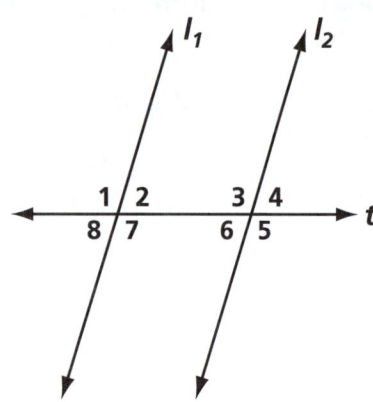

Given: l_1 and l_2 are parallel; ∠1 = 107°

Problem Solving / Reasoning   Write true or false.

14. Corresponding angles are always congruent. _____

15. Vertical angles are always congruent. _____

16. Supplementary angles are always congruent. _____

17. Alternate interior angles are always congruent. _____

Test Prep ★ Mixed Review

18. When the hands of a clock show exactly two o'clock, what is the angle between the hands?

  A 10°
  B 20°
  C 30°
  D 60°

19. What other angle measures 40°?

  F ∠AOB
  G ∠BOC
  H ∠DOE
  J ∠DOC

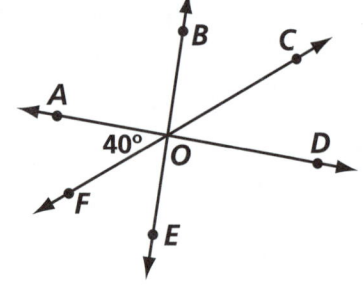

190 Unit 7 Lesson 5

Name _____   **Triangles**

You already know many things about triangles. In this lesson you will learn to classify them by their angles and by their sides. Note how two segments of equal length, **congruent segments,** are marked on the diagrams.

Classifying Triangles by their Angles

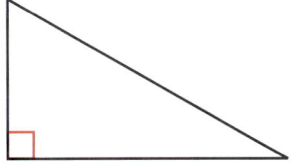 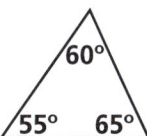 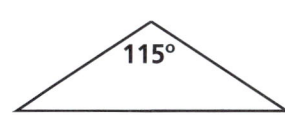

Right Triangle
A triangle with one right angle

Acute Triangle
A triangle with three acute angles

Obtuse Triangle
A triangle with one obtuse angle

Classifying Triangles by their Sides

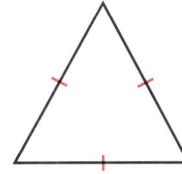 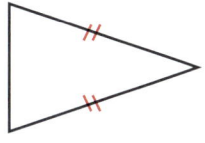 

The marks show congruent sides.

Equilateral Triangle
A triangle with all sides equal in measure, or congruent

Isosceles Triangle
A triangle with at least two sides equal in measure, or congruent

Scalene Triangle
A triangle with no sides equal in measure, or congruent

Classify the triangle by its sides and by its angles.

1. Sides _____
   Angles _____

2. Sides _____
   Angles _____

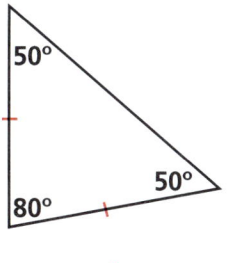

3. Sides _____
   Angles _____

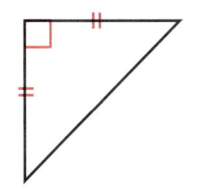

4. Sides _____
   Angles _____

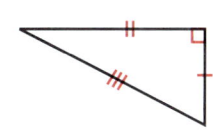

Make a sketch of the triangle, if possible.

5. An acute, isosceles triangle

6. An obtuse, scalene triangle

7. An equilateral, obtuse triangle

8. A right, isosceles triangle

Recall: The sum of the angle measures of a triangle is **180°**.

Example 1: Find ∠B = ___?___

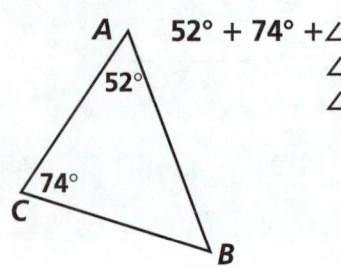

$52° + 74° + ∠B = 180°$
$∠B = 180° − (52° + 74°)$
$∠B = 54°$

Example 2: Find the measure of ∠D.

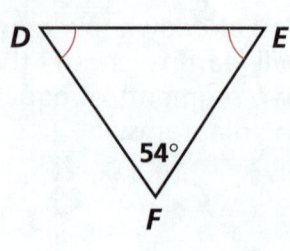

∠D ≅ ∠E

Let $x = ∠D = ∠E$.

$x + x + 54° = 180°$
$2x + 54° = 180°$
$2x = 126°$
$x = 63°$

So ∠D = 63°.

Find the measure of the angle.

9.

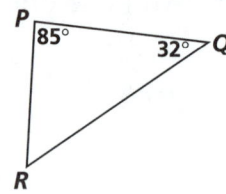

∠R = _____

∠N = _____

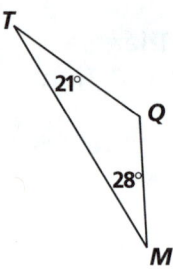

∠Q = _____

10.

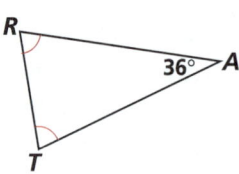

∠R = _____

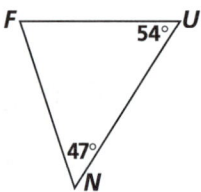

∠F = _____

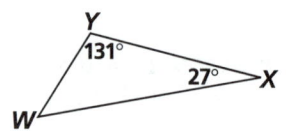

∠W = _____

✓ Quick Check

Use the diagram for exercises 11–14.

11. Name a pair of vertical angles.

_____

12. Name a pair of supplementary angles.

_____

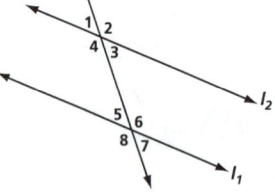

Work Space.

13. Name a pair of corresponding angles. _____

14. Name a pair of alternate interior angles. _____

Find the measure of the third angle of triangle ABC.

15. ∠A = 18°, ∠B = 36°, ∠C = _____

192 Unit 7 Lesson 6

Name _____

Problem Solving Strategy: Find a Pattern

To solve some problems, finding a pattern can help. The pattern may become clear by making a list, solving a simpler problem, or drawing a diagram. Once the pattern is observed, a generalization can be made.

Problem
Five friends have all met at a restaurant for a bit of a reunion. It has been two years since they've seen one another. If all friends shake hands with one another, how many handshakes are there?

---

1 Understand — As you reread, ask yourself questions.

- How many people are there? _____
- Can a person shake his or her own hand? _____
- How many hands does each person shake? _____

---

2 Decide — Choose a method for solving.

- What if there were only one friend? Two friends? Three friends? Four friends?

1 person	2 people	3 people	4 people
•	•—•	△	⊠
0 handshakes	1 handshake	3 handshakes	6 handshakes

Number of people	1	2	3	4	5
Number of handshakes	0	1	3	6	?

(+1) (+2) (+3)

---

3 Solve — Describe the pattern. Solve the problem.

- What is the pattern you found? _____
  _____

- Use your pattern to complete the chart.

---

4 Look back — Check your answer. Write your answer as a complete sentence.

Answer: _____

Is there another pattern you could have used? _____

Unit 7 Lesson 7 193

Use the Find a Pattern or any other strategy you have learned to solve these problems.

1. If ten people all greet one another with a handshake, how many handshakes will there be?

Think: How can you use the pattern from the previous page?

_____

Answer: _____

2. Remember you can use exponents to show repeated factors. For example:

$10^3 = 10 \cdot 10 \cdot 10$, or **1,000**.

What is the ones digit of the number 3^{20} written in standard form?

Think: Is there a pattern in the ones digits of 3^1, 3^2, 3^3, 3^4, and so on?

_____

Answer: _____

3. The circle below represents a pizza. Show how you could cut the pizza into eleven pieces using exactly four straight cuts.

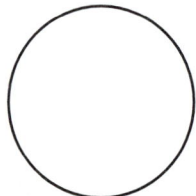

4. To mark her property line along a **50**-foot road, a rancher needs to set down fence posts at the beginning and end and every **5** feet in between. If it takes **12** minutes to dig and set each post, how many hours will it take her to set the posts along the road?

_____

5. The first three *pentagonal numbers* are shown. What is the fifth pentagonal number?

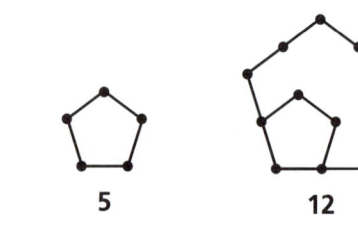

1   5   12

_____

6. What is the sum of the first twenty odd numbers?

_____

7. A segment that connects two vertices of a polygon and is not a side is called a **diagonal**. The diagonals of a rectangle are shown. How many diagonals does an 8-sided polygon have?

_____

8. The first three figures in a pattern are shown. What will the area and the perimeter of the tenth figure be?

 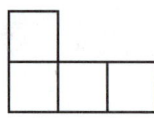

Figure 1   Figure 2   Figure 3

_____

194 Unit 7 Lesson 7

Name _____

Constructing Congruent Segments and Angles

The compass and straightedge are "construction tools." You can use them to make copies of geometric figures that are congruent to the original figure. You can construct congruent segments.

Constructing a Segment Congruent to $\overline{AB}$

1. Use a straightedge. Draw a segment that is longer than $\overline{AB}$. Label one endpoint **C**.

2. Set your compass to the length of $\overline{AB}$. Place the compass point at **C** and draw an arc. Label point **D**.

By construction, $\overline{AB} \cong \overline{CD}$.

You can also construct a segment that is twice as long as $\overline{AB}$. You simply repeat the construction again from endpoint **D**.

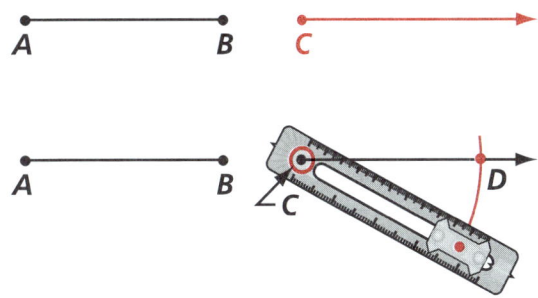

Use a straightedge and compass. Construct a line segment congruent to the given one.

1. •————————•

2. •——————————————•

3. •——————————————————————•

Use a straightedge, compass, and the lengths of $\overline{AB}$ and $\overline{CD}$ below. Construct a line segment of the given length.

•——•   •————•
A   B   C   D

4. twice $\overline{AB}$

5. three times $\overline{AB}$

6. $\overline{AB} + \overline{CD}$

7. $\overline{CD} - \overline{AB}$

8. twice $(\overline{AB} + \overline{CD})$

Unit 7 Lesson 8   195

Constructing an Angle Congruent to ∠A.

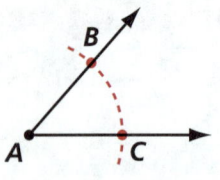

1. Draw a ray with endpoint **D**. Place the compass point at **A** and draw an arc. Label points **B** and **C**.

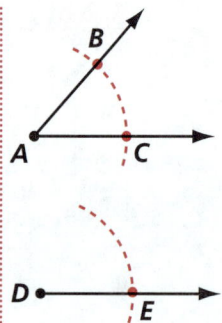

2. Use the same compass setting. Draw an arc, placing the compass point at **D**. Label point **E**.

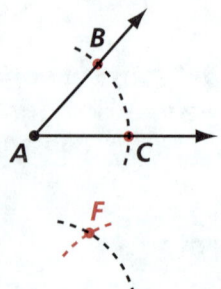

3. Set your compass to the length of $\overline{BC}$. Place the compass point at **E**. Mark point **F**.

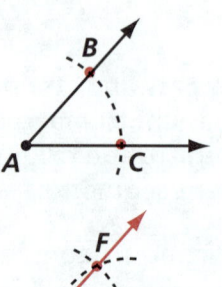

4. Draw a ray from **D** through **F**.

By construction, ∠BAC ≅ ∠FDE.

Use a straightedge and compass. Construct a congruent angle below the angle.

9.

Test Prep ★ Mixed Review

10 If lines *AB* and *CD* are parallel, how many angles altogether have a measure of 55°?

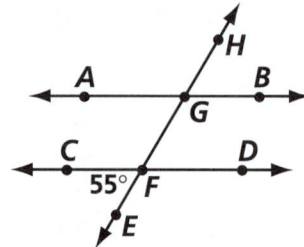

- **A** one
- **B** two
- **C** three
- **D** four

11 How many triangles, of all sizes, are in the diagram?

- **F** 25
- **G** 40
- **H** 48
- **J** 56

196 Unit 7 Lesson 8

Name _____ **Constructing Bisectors**

A **bisector** divides a figure into two parts of equal measure. An angle bisector is a ray that divides the angle into two adjacent angles of equal measure. A segment bisector is a point, called a **midpoint,** that divides the segment into two segments of equal length.

Constructing an Angle Bisector

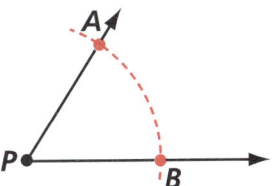 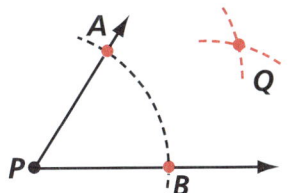 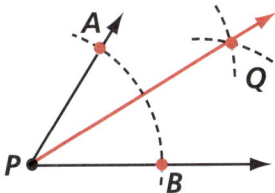

1. From point *P,* draw an arc that intersects both rays. Label the two points *A* and *B.*

2. From point *A* and from point *B,* draw intersecting arcs. Label the point *Q.*

3. Draw ray *PQ.* Then, ∠*APQ* ≅ ∠*BPQ* by construction.

Constructing a Segment Bisector.

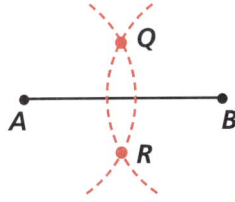 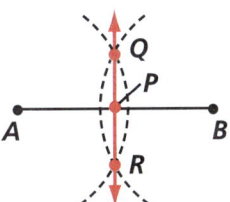

1. From point *A* and from point *B,* draw intersecting arcs above and below $\overline{AB}$. Label the points of intersection *Q* and *R.* Note: $\overline{AQ} \cong \overline{BQ}$ and $\overline{AR} \cong \overline{BR}$.

2. Draw a line through points *R* and *Q.* Label the point of intersection *P.*

   By construction, $\overline{AP} \cong \overline{BP}$.

Use a straightedge and compass. Bisect the angle or segment.

1.

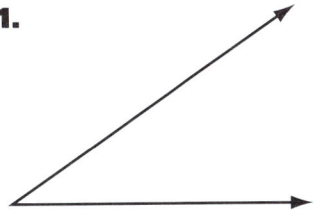 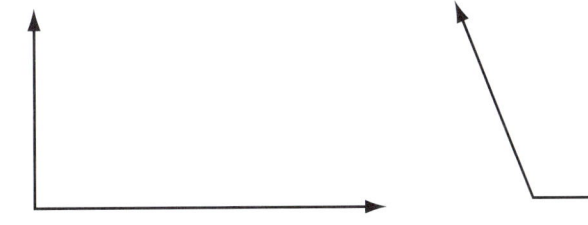

2.

Unit 7 Lesson 9 197

Two lines that intersect to form four right angles are **perpendicular**.

Notice that in the second construction on page 197, $\overleftrightarrow{QR}$ is perpendicular to $\overline{AB}$. You can use similar steps to construct perpendicular lines.

Constructing Perpendicular lines.

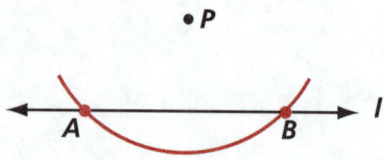

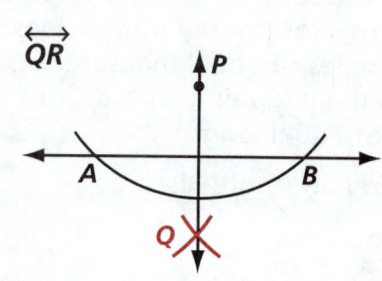

1. Draw an arc from **P** intersecting line **l** at two points. Label the points **A** and **B**.

2. From **A** and from **B**, draw intersecting arcs. Label the point of intersection **Q**. Draw $\overleftrightarrow{PQ}$. By construction, $\overleftrightarrow{PQ}$ is perpendicular to $\overline{AB}$.

Use a straightedge and compass. Construct a line through P perpendicular to l.

3.

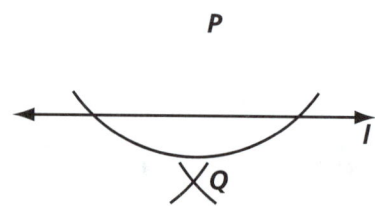

4.

Problem Solving Reasoning Solve.

5. Suppose **P** is a point on line **l**. Describe a method of constructing a line perpendicular to **l**. (Hint: Start by finding two points on **l** that are the same distance from **P**.)

6. Describe a method for constructing a right triangle.

Test Prep ★ Mixed Review

7. At what hour, on the hour, will the hands of a clock form a 150° angle?

   A 5 o'clock only
   C 7 o'clock only
   B 5 and 7 o'clock
   D 11 and 1 o'clock

8. How many times, on the hour, will the hands of a clock form an acute angle during a 24-hour period?

   F 2
   H 6
   G 4
   J 8

198 Unit 7 Lesson 9

Name _____

Polygons and Congruent Figures

You have studied triangles and their properties. In this lesson you will learn about other polygons. **Polygons** are all closed figures made up of line segments joined at their endpoints.

A **quadrilateral** is a polygon that has four sides and four angles. It has two pairs of **opposite sides,** and two pairs of **opposite angles.** You use four letters to name quadrilaterals. Possible names for the figure at right are: quadrilateral **ABCD**, quadrilateral **CBAD**.

Four quadrilaterals are shown. The arrowheads (< and <<) on the figures indicate parallel sides.

Opposite sides: $\overline{AB}$ and $\overline{CD}$
$\overline{AD}$ and $\overline{BC}$

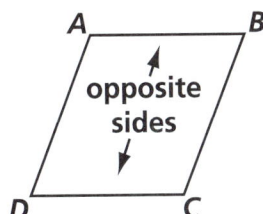

Opposite angles: $\angle A$ and $\angle C$
$\angle B$ and $\angle D$

Parallelogram
A quadrilateral with both pairs of opposite sides parallel

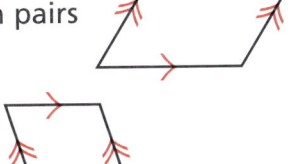

Rectangle
A parallelogram with four right angles

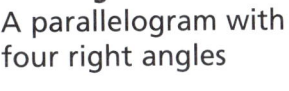

Rhombus
A parallelogram with four congruent sides

Square
A rectangle with four congruent sides

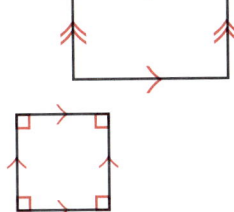

From the definitions, all four quadrilaterals are parallelograms. A square is both a rectangle and a rhombus.

Use the diagram to answer the following.

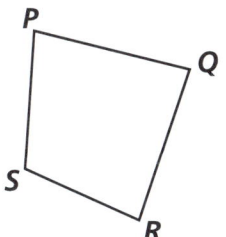

1. 3 different names for the quadrilateral _____

2. Name the opposite sides _____ and _____, _____ and _____

3. Name the opposite angles _____ and _____, _____ and _____

Classify the figure. Use parallelogram (P), rectangle (R), rhombus (Rh), square (S), or none of these (N). Use all names that apply.

4. 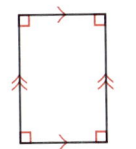 _____   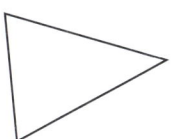 _____   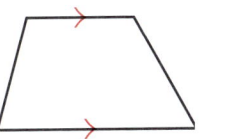 _____

5. 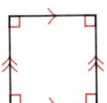 _____   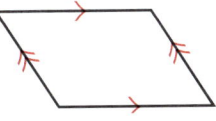 _____    _____

6.  _____    _____   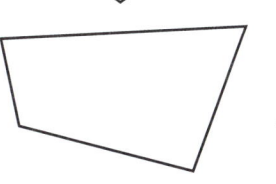 _____

Unit 7 Lesson 10 **199**

Recall this list that names some other polygons and the number of sides and angles they have.

pentagon: **5** angles and sides   hexagon: **6** angles and sides   heptagon: **7** angles and sides

octagon: **8** angles and sides   nonagon: **9** angles and sides   decagon: **10** angles and sides

---

Two polygons are **congruent** if they are the same size and shape. This means that corresponding sides are congruent and their corresponding angles are congruent.

The two triangles at the right are congruent, so their corresponding sides are congruent and their corresponding angles are congruent.

Notice that the order in which the triangles are written does matter. Corresponding vertices are written in the same order. For example, if you know that △ABC ≅ △DEF, then ∠A ≅ ∠D and AB ≅ DE.

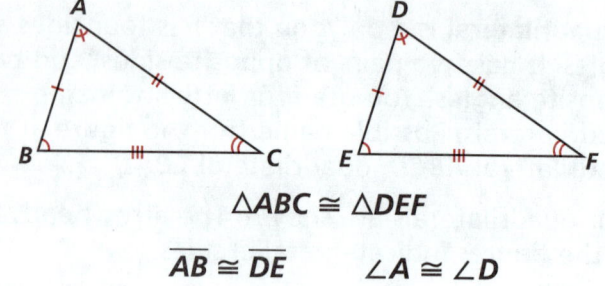

△ABC ≅ △DEF

$\overline{AB} \cong \overline{DE}$ ∠A ≅ ∠D
$\overline{BC} \cong \overline{EF}$ ∠B ≅ ∠E
$\overline{AC} \cong \overline{DF}$ ∠C ≅ ∠F

Complete.

7. If △DGE ≅ △LMN, then $\overline{DG} \cong$ _____, $\overline{GE} \cong$ _____, $\overline{DE} \cong$ _____, ∠D ≅ _____,

   ∠G ≅ _____, ∠E ≅ _____.

8. If △TIL ≅ △ACP, then $\overline{TI} \cong$ _____, $\overline{IL} \cong$ _____, $\overline{TL} \cong$ _____, ∠T ≅ _____,

   ∠I ≅ _____, ∠L ≅ _____.

9. If △XYZ ≅ △RST, then $\overline{RS} \cong$ _____, $\overline{ST} \cong$ _____, $\overline{RT} \cong$ _____, ∠R ≅ _____,

   ∠S ≅ _____, ∠T ≅ _____.

10. If quadrilateral **CARD** ≅ quadrilateral **MINE**, then

    $\overline{CA} \cong$ _____, $\overline{AR} \cong$ _____, $\overline{RD} \cong$ _____, $\overline{CD} \cong$ _____,

    ∠C ≅ _____, ∠A ≅ _____, ∠R ≅ _____, ∠D ≅ _____.

---

11. **Complete to show that the triangles are congruent.**

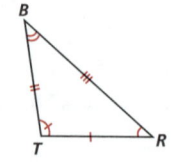 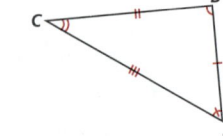  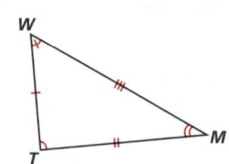

Corresponding Sides	Corresponding Angles	Corresponding Sides	Corresponding Angles
_____ ≅ _____	_____ ≅ _____	_____ ≅ _____	_____ ≅ _____
_____ ≅ _____	_____ ≅ _____	_____ ≅ _____	_____ ≅ _____
_____ ≅ _____	_____ ≅ _____	_____ ≅ _____	_____ ≅ _____

△_____ ≅ △_____   △_____ ≅ △_____

Name _____

Complete the sentence. Use the vocabulary and concepts from this lesson.

12. A parallelogram with four sides congruent and four right angles is a(n) _____.

13. In quadrilateral TERM, sides $\overline{TE}$ and $\overline{RM}$ are called _____ sides.

14. A quadrilateral with both pairs of opposite sides parallel is called a(n) _____.

15. A polygon with eight sides is called a(n) _____.

16. A decagon is a polygon with _____ sides and _____ angles.

17. If $\triangle TPQ \cong \triangle WIN$, then $\overline{TQ}$ corresponds to _____ and $\angle Q$ corresponds to _____.

Problem Solving Reasoning Solve.

18. Sketch two polygons whose corresponding sides are congruent, but corresponding angles are not congruent.

19. Sketch two polygons whose corresponding angles are congruent, but corresponding sides are not congruent.

✓ Quick Check

Construct a segment of the given length. Use the lengths below.

W———X   Y————————Z

Work Space.

20. Twice WX

21. WX + YZ

Complete.

22. A ray that divides an angle into two congruent, adjacent angles is a(n) _____.

23. Two lines that meet at right angles are _____.

$\triangle DEF \cong \triangle JKL$. **Name the corresponding parts.**

24. $\angle D$ and _____   **25.** $\overline{EF}$ and _____   **26.** $\overline{LJ}$ and _____

Unit 7 Lesson 10 **201**

Circles and Central Angles

A **circle** is the set of all points in a plane at a fixed distance, called the **radius**, from a fixed point called the **center**. A circle has no line segments for its sides, so it is not a polygon.

Circle Vocabulary

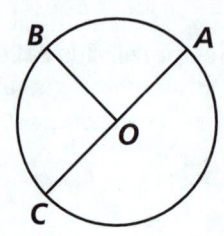

chord: a segment with its endpoints on a circle

diameter: a chord that passes through the center; $\overline{CA}$ is a diameter on this circle.
$$\text{diameter} = 2 \cdot \text{radius}$$

central angle: an angle whose vertex is at the center of the circle; $\angle BOA$ is a central angle.

arc: a part of a circle; there are three types:
- semicircle, or half circle; $\overparen{CBA}$ is a semicircle
- minor arc; shorter than half a circle; $\overparen{AB}$ is a minor arc
- major arc; longer than half a circle; $\overparen{ACB}$ is a major arc

The measure of an arc equals the measure of the central angle that intersects its endpoints. You indicate an arc with this symbol: ⌢.

Central Angles and Arcs

Remember, there are **360°** in a circle.

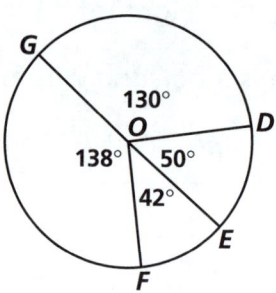

Center at O

$\angle DOE = 50°$, so $\overparen{DE} = 50°$

$\angle DOF = 92°$, so $\overparen{DF} = 92°$

$\angle GOE = 180°$, so $\overparen{GE} = 180°$

$\overparen{DE} = 50°$, so $\overparen{DGE} = 310°$

Identify the part of circle O. Use the vocabulary above.

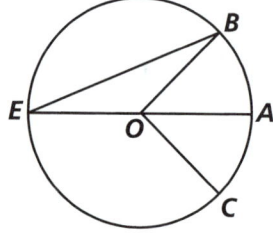

1. $\overline{AE}$: _____
2. $\overline{OB}$: _____
3. $\overline{BE}$: _____
4. $\angle BOA$: _____
5. $\overparen{EBA}$: _____   O: _____
6. $\overparen{BC}$: _____ $\overparen{CEB}$: _____

Write the measure of the arc or the angle.

7.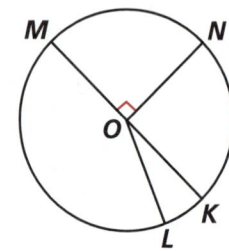

center at O
diameter $\overline{MK}$
$\angle LOK = 23°$
$\angle MON = 90°$

$\angle LOM =$ _____ $\overparen{LK} =$ _____

$\overparen{LNM} =$ _____ $\overparen{MNK} =$ _____

$\angle KON =$ _____ $\overparen{LM} =$ _____

202 Unit 7 Lesson 11

Name _____

You know that a circle has **360°**. You can use this to find what fraction or percent of the whole circle each section represents when you know its central angle.

- What fraction of the circle does section *AOB* represent if ∠*AOB* = 60°?

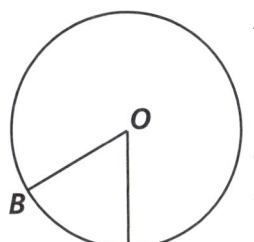

∠*AOB* = 60°

$\frac{60}{360} = \frac{1}{6}$

So section *AOB* is $\frac{1}{6}$ of the circle.

- Find the measure of the central angle for the section that is $\frac{2}{5}$ of the circle.

$\frac{2}{5}$ of 360 = $\frac{2}{5} \cdot \frac{360}{1}$

= 144°

- Find the measure of the central angle for the section that is **30%** of the circle.

30% of 360 = 0.30 · 360

= 108°

What part of a circle is the section with the given central angle?

8. 45° _____   135° _____   90° _____

9. 20° _____   225° _____   15° _____

10. 80° _____   200° _____   5° _____

Write the measure of the central angle for the section that is the fractional part of a circle.

11. $\frac{1}{5}$ _____ $\frac{1}{12}$ _____ $\frac{3}{8}$ _____

12. 25% _____   10% _____   40% _____

13. $\frac{2}{3}$ _____   60% _____   75% _____

Test Prep ★ Mixed Review

14 How many diagonals are there in an octagon?

  A 15   C 30
  B 20   D 40

15 Which description best refers to a pair of congruent polygons?

  F They have three or more sides.
  G Corresponding angles are congruent.
  H Corresponding angles are congruent and corresponding sides are congruent.
  J Corresponding sides are congruent.

Unit 7 Lesson 11 **203**

Name _____

Circle Graphs

The graph at the right is a **circle graph**. A circle graph can be used to represent parts of a whole. The parts of the circle graph are labeled as fractions, decimals, or percents. The entire circle represents **1** whole or **100%**.

Tran received **$300** for his birthday. The graph shows how he used his birthday money.

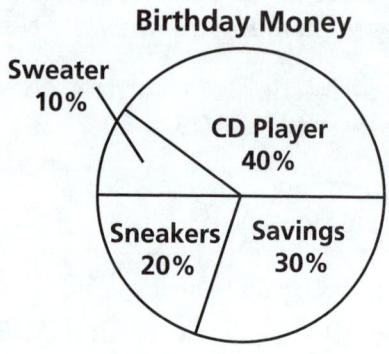

CD player: 40% of $300 = 0.40 · $300, or $120
Savings: 30% of $300 = 0.30 · $300, or $ 90
Sneakers: 20% of $300 = 0.20 · $300, or $ 60
Sweater: 10% of $300 = 0.10 · $300, or $ 30

Totals: 100% $300

Use the circle graphs to answer the questions.

1. What percent of the money was raised by donations?

   _____ By the magazine drive? _____

   By the school dance? _____

2. If the total money raised was **$900**, how much was raised by

   donations? _____ Magazine Drive? _____

   _____ Dance? _____

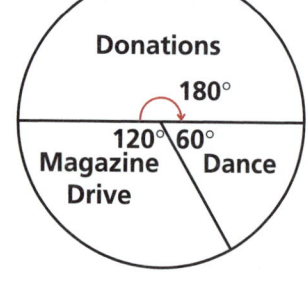

3. What category provided the least amount of money?

   _____

4. What category accounts for the greatest amount of time?

   _____

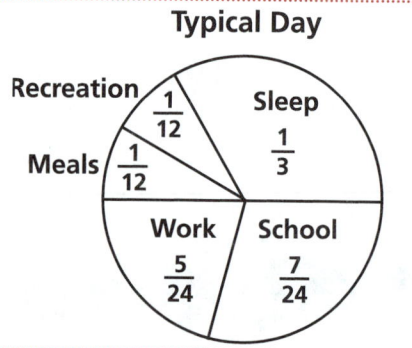

5. How many hours does each activity take?

   Sleep _____ School _____ Work _____

   Recreation _____ Meals _____

6. Which eye color is the most common? _____

7. How many students were surveyed? _____

8. What percent have blue eyes? _____

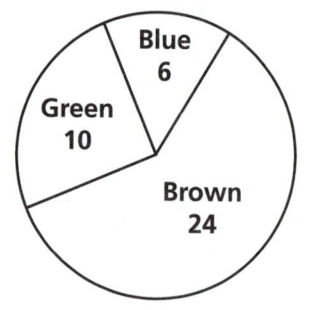

204 Unit 7 Lesson 12

Name _____

To construct a circle graph, use what you know about central angles. You will need a protractor to draw angles accurately.

Complete the table and the circle graph. Use the central angle measures to construct each angle in the graph. Label each part with the correct category.

9. The family's income is **$48,000** a year. How much is spent in each category? What is the central angle for each category? Complete the circle graph.

Category	Percent	Expense	Central Angle
Food	25%	25% of $48,000 is $12,000.	25% of 360° is 90°.
Housing	25%		
Insurance	15%		
Recreation	10%		
Savings	5%		
Clothing	15%		
Miscellaneous	5%		

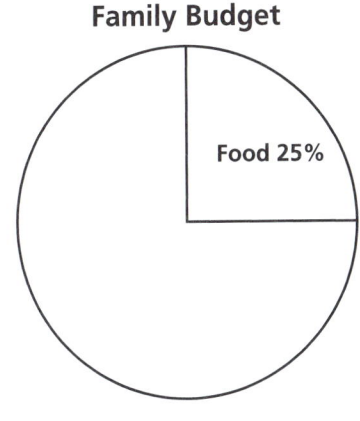

Family Budget

Food 25%

10. Find the sum of the following columns.

    Percent _____ Expense _____ Central Angle _____

11. The town of Middlefield has a budget of **$3,000,000**. It spends the money as shown in the table. What fraction of the budget was each category? What is the central angle for each category? Complete the circle graph.

Category	Amount	Fraction	Central Angle
Education	$1,000,000	$\frac{1,000,000}{3,000,000} = \frac{1}{3}$	$\frac{1}{3}$ of 360° = 120°
Highways	$750,000		
Health	$500,000		
Library Renovations	$375,000		
Miscellaneous	$375,000		

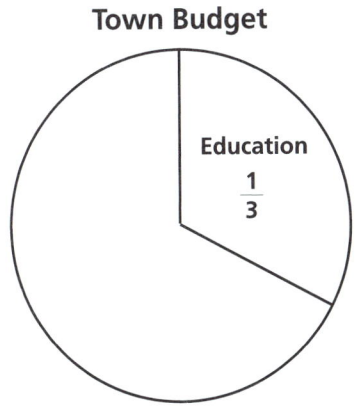

Town Budget

Education $\frac{1}{3}$

Unit 7 Lesson 12

Use the circle graphs to answer the questions.

Favorite Meal of 200 Students

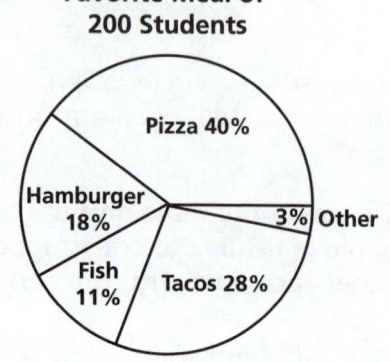

12. How many students selected pizza as their favorite meal? _____

13. How many students selected fish or hamburgers as their favorite meal? _____

14. What is the measure of the central angle for tacos? _____

15. Approximate the number of students for each category.

    no television _____   0.5–2 hours _____

    2.5–4 hours _____   more than 4 hours _____

Daily Television Time Survey of 50 Students

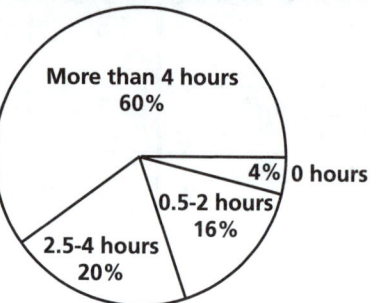

16. What is the central angle for each category?

    no television _____   0.5–2 hours _____

    2.5–4 hours _____   more than 4 hours _____

Problem Solving Reasoning Solve.

17. Which part of the circle corresponds to the results of 50 responses?

    _____

300 people are surveyed.

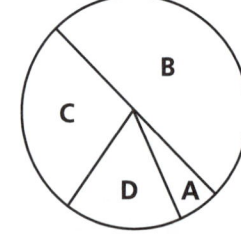

18. Part B represents approximately how many responses?

    _____

Test Prep ★ Mixed Review

19. What is the measure of ∠AOB?

    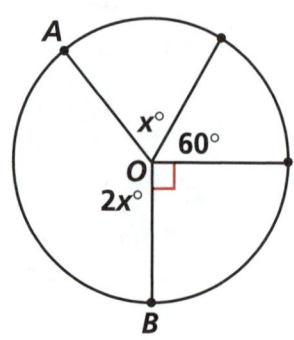

    A 140°
    B 120°
    C 100°
    D 70°

20. Enid wants to represent 52% on her circle graph. Which number best represents the measure of the central angle she should make?

    F 52°
    G 104°
    H 187°
    J 308°

206 Unit 7 Lesson 12

Polyhedrons

The space figures shown have polygonal regions as sides. They are called **polyhedrons**. **Prisms** and **pyramids** are two types of polyhedrons.

- A prism has two parallel faces, called **bases**. The other faces are parallelograms.

- A pyramid has one base. The other faces are triangles. Prisms and pyramids are named for the shape of their bases.

The polygonal regions that are the sides of a polyhedron are its **faces**. The line segments where the faces meet are its **edges**. Each point where the edges meet is a **vertex**.

Prisms
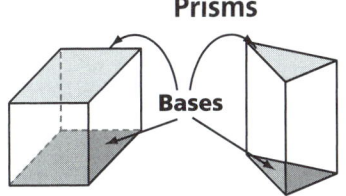

Pyramids
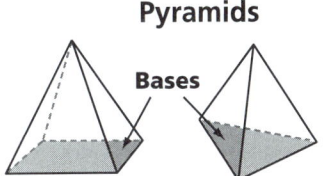

Other Polyhedrons
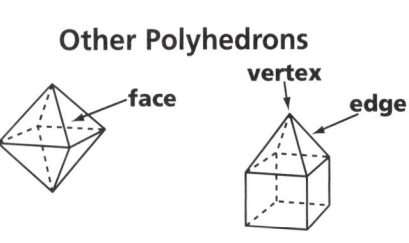

Complete the table. Count the number of faces, vertices, and edges.

1.

	Prism 1	Prism 2	Prism 3	Prism 4
				A prism whose base is an n-gon
Faces				
Vertices				
Edges				
Name	Rectangular Prism	Triangular Prism	Hexagonal Prism	

2.

	Pyramid 1	Pyramid 2	Pyramid 3	Pyramid 4
				A pyramid whose base is an n-gon
Faces				
Vertices				
Edges				
Name	Rectangular Pyramid	Triangular Pyramid	Pentagonal Pyramid	

A cube is a prism that has six faces that are all congruent squares. You can use the lines formed by the edges of a cube to investigate relationships between two lines in space.

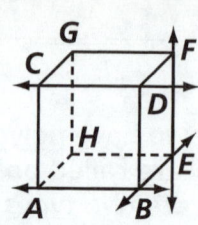

Skew lines are non-coplanar lines, which means they do not intersect.

You know that a polygon has diagonals. Some polyhedrons also have diagonals. It is a segment between two vertices that are not in the same face. For example, a cube has four diagonals.

Lines in space	Diagonals
$\overleftrightarrow{AB}$ and $\overleftrightarrow{CD}$ are parallel.	$\overline{AF}$ $\overline{CE}$
$\overleftrightarrow{AB}$ and $\overleftrightarrow{BE}$ are perpendicular.	$\overline{BG}$ $\overline{DH}$
$\overleftrightarrow{AB}$ and $\overleftrightarrow{FE}$ are skew.	

Identify the relationship between the pair of lines.

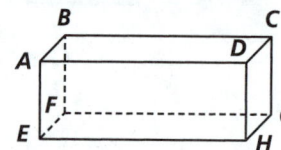   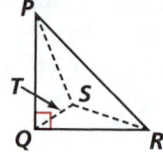

3. $\overleftrightarrow{BC}$ and $\overleftrightarrow{AB}$ _____ $\overleftrightarrow{BC}$ and $\overleftrightarrow{EH}$ _____ $\overleftrightarrow{BC}$ and $\overleftrightarrow{GH}$ _____

4. $\overleftrightarrow{PQ}$ and $\overleftrightarrow{OR}$ _____ $\overleftrightarrow{PQ}$ and $\overleftrightarrow{SR}$ _____ $\overleftrightarrow{PQ}$ and $\overleftrightarrow{QS}$ _____

5. Name two diagonals in the rectangular prism. _____ and _____

Problem Solving Reasoning   Solve.

6. Compare the number of faces plus the number of vertices to the number of edges for each polyhedron in the tables for exercises 1 and 2. What pattern can you find?

7. Show that the relationship you found in exercise 6 is true for any pyramid. (Hint: Use an *n*-gon as the base of the pyramid.)

 Quick Check

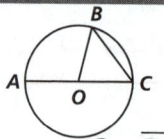

Use Circle O at the right. O is the center of the circle.

Work Space.

8. $\overline{OC}$ is a _____.   9. $\overline{BC}$ is a _____.
10. $\overparen{BC}$ is a _____.   11. ∠BOC is a _____.

You need to make a circle graph to show how people spend their time each day. You know that sleeping is 8 hours, school is 6 hours, and other activities is 10 hours. What is the measure of the central angle for each category?

12. Sleeping _____   13. School _____   14. Other _____

Suppose you have a pentagonal prism. Find how many of each item it has.

15. Edges _____   16. Bases _____   17. Diagonals _____

Name _____

Problem Solving Application: Use a Diagram

You already know how to use proportions and measuring tools like rulers and protractors to interpret diagrams. You also know how to use construction tools to copy figures.

Sometimes you need to decide what kind of tool to use in drawing diagrams for problems.

Tips to Remember:

| 1. Understand | 2. Decide | 3. Solve | 4. Look back |

- Ask yourself: What do I know? What do I need to find?
- What kind of diagram can you use? Do you need to use a construction to solve a problem, or would an accurate drawing or rough sketch be sufficient?
- Think about strategies you have learned, and use them to help you solve a problem.

The scale drawing at the right shows a hexagonal frame and **3** pieces of cord.

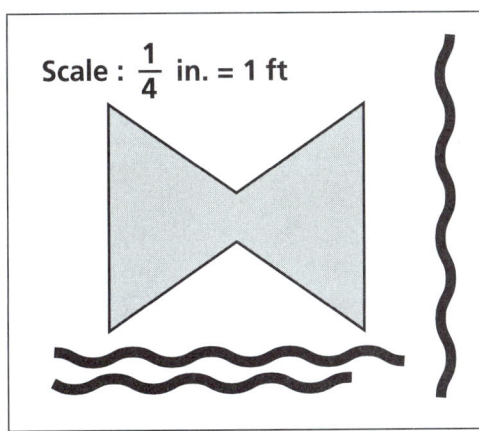

Scale: $\frac{1}{4}$ in. = 1 ft

1. Does measuring the lengths answer the question "Is there enough cord to go around the outside of the frame?"

   Think: What is the length of the perimeter? Of the cord?

   _____

   Answer: _____

2. Draw two lines. Mark off lengths, end to end, of the sides of the polygon on one. Mark off lengths of the cord, end to end, on the other. Is there enough cord to go around the frame?

   Think: What do the lengths of constructed segments represent?

   _____

   Answer: _____

Unit 7 Lesson 14 **209**

Use a diagram to help you solve each problem.

3. Sarah hiked 3 miles north, 5 miles east, 3 miles south, and 2 miles west. How far is she from her starting point? (Do you need to use measuring or construction tools? Is a sketch enough?)

4. Matthew walked 2 miles north, turned right, walked 2 miles, turned right, walked 1 mile, turned right, walked 3 miles, turned right, walked 3 miles, turned right, and walked 1 mile. How far and in what direction is he from his starting point?

5. You want to tile a 4 foot by 6 foot region with one foot square tiles. How many tiles will you need?

6. You want to tile a 4 foot by 6 foot region with six inch square tiles. How many tiles will you need?

7. A transversal intersects three parallel lines. How many pairs of corresponding angles are formed?

8. Two streets meet at point *P*. One of the streets is shown. The streets meet at an angle of 135°. How can you use just a compass and straightedge to draw the other street? Try it.

Extend Your Thinking

9. If you used two foot square tiles to cover a 4 foot by 6 foot rectangular region, how many tiles would you need? How is this answer related to the answer for problem 5? Explain.

10. Explain your method for solving problem 6. Did you need to draw all of the tiles, or could you use some other method?

11. For which exercises did a sketch make a reasonably accurate diagram?

12. Would the construction in problem 8 look the same for everyone in the class?

210 Unit 7 Lesson 14

Name _____

Unit 7 Review

Use the figure to complete the statement or answer the question.

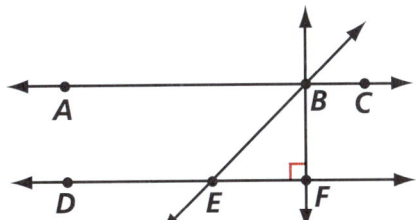

1. Two lines that contain *E* are _____, _____

2. A pair of parallel lines are _____ and _____

3. A pair of perpendicular lines are _____, _____

4. Name an acute angle. _____

5. Name an obtuse angle. _____

6. Name a right angle. _____

7. Name two rays with endpoint *F*. _____, _____

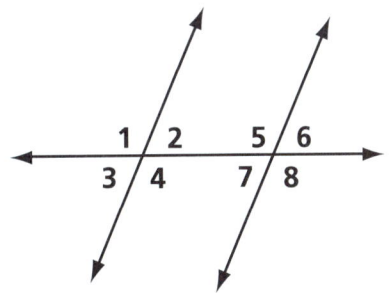

8. An angle vertical to ∠1 is _____.

9. An angle corresponding to ∠1 is _____.

10. An angle supplementary to ∠1 is _____.

11. If ∠1 = 108°, what other angle(s) measure 108°?
    _____

Write the measure of the angle if ∠1 = 108°.

12. ∠3 = _____ 13. ∠4 = _____ 14. ∠5 = _____

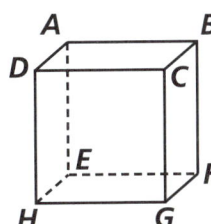

15. Name a line parallel to $\overleftrightarrow{AB}$. _____

16. Name a plane that contains $\overleftrightarrow{AB}$. _____

17. Name a line perpendicular to $\overleftrightarrow{AB}$. _____

18. Name a line skew to $\overleftrightarrow{AB}$. _____

19. This polyhedron has _____ faces, _____ vertices, and _____ edges.

20. Name the four diagonals of the polyhedron.
    _____

Unit 7 Review **211**

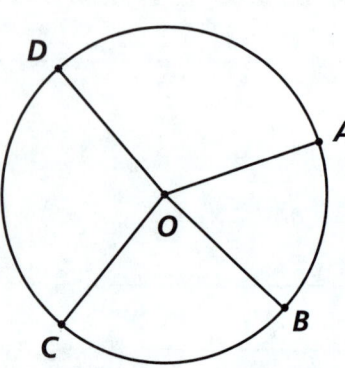

O is the center of the circle.

21. Name a radius. _____

22. Name a minor arc. _____

23. Name a major arc. _____

24. Write the measure of the arc if ∠AOB = 75°.

$\widehat{AB}$ = _____ $\widehat{AD}$ = _____

25. What fractional part of the circle does ∠AOB represent?

_____

What percent is this? _____

Education of Teachers

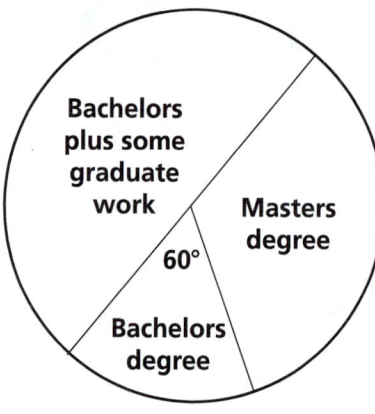

The circle graph shows the amount of education that the 300 teachers in one school district have.

26. How many teachers have a masters degree?

_____

27. What percent of the teachers is this? _____

28. The number of teachers that have a bachelors degree plus some graduate work is 150. What percent is this?

_____

29. What is the measure of the angle for the section "Bachelors degree plus some graduate work"?

_____

Write another name for the figure.

30. A parallelogram with four right angles _____

31. A quadrilateral with both pairs of opposite sides parallel _____

32. A rectangular prism whose faces are congruent squares _____

Measure the angle to the nearest degree. Use a protractor.

33. 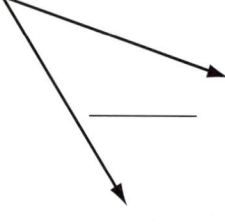   **34.** 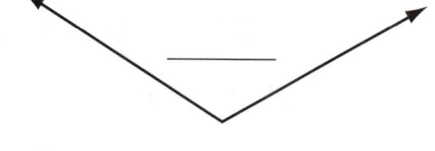   **35.**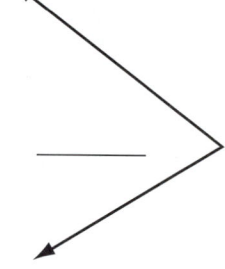

212   Unit 7 Review

Name _____

Answer the question. △ABC ≅ △PQR.

36. Name the congruent sides and angles. _____

Sketch the figure.

37. A right isosceles triangle   **38.** An obtuse scalene triangle   **39.** Two intersecting planes

Write the measure of the angle.

40.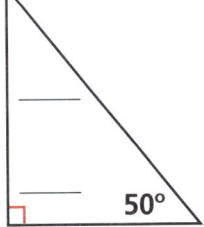

41.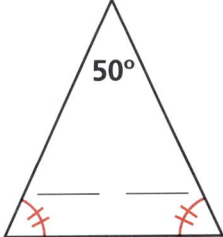

42.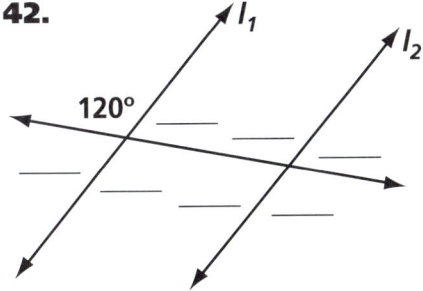

Construct the figure. Use a straightedge and compass.

43. An angle congruent to ∠ABC

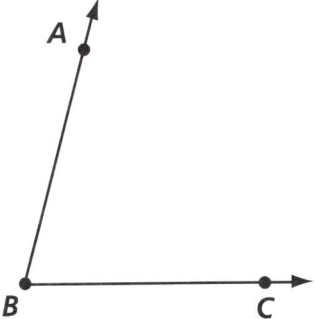

44. The midpoint of $\overline{DE}$

Solve.

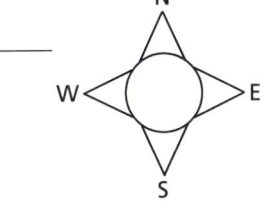

45. What is the ones digit of 4^{15} when it is written in standard form? _____

46. From school, Rosita walks two blocks north, then **1** block west to her friend's house. Next, she walks with her friend **3** blocks east and **2** blocks north to the mall. They both walk back to her house, **4** blocks south and **2** blocks east of the mall. How many blocks and in which direction does Rosita walk each morning from her home to school? _____

Cumulative Review
★ Test Prep

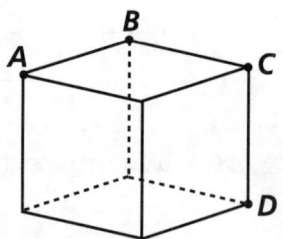

1 Which of the statements is true?

A A and C are collinear with B.

B AB + BC = AC

C A, B, C, and D are coplanar.

D CD represents the distance from C to D.

2 What other angle measures 30°?

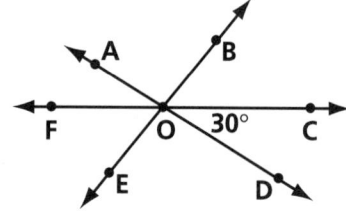

F ∠BOC   H ∠AOF

G ∠EOF   J ∠EOD

3 Mark's bank gives him 3% interest on his $700 investment. The interest is compounded every quarter. After one year, what will be the value of his investment?

A $703.00   C $721.24

B $721.00   D $787.86

4 A compact car uses 2.5 gallons of gas to go 90 miles. At that rate, about how many gallons of gas will be needed for a trip of 300 miles?

F less than 6   H between 8 and 9

G exactly 8   J more than 10

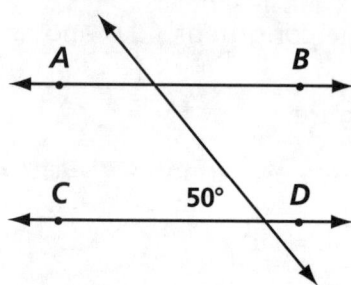

5 If lines AB and CD are parallel, how many angles altogether in the diagram have a measure of 50°?

A four   C two

B three   D one

6 If Annie buys a $73 pair of shoes that have been marked down 15%, how much cash does she save?

F $10.95   H $27

G $15   J $62.05

7 Which speed is equivalent to 60 miles per hour?

A 5,280 feet per minute

B 1,760 feet per minute

C 88 feet per minute

D 30 feet per minute

8 Of the 120 Grade 7 students in Wilson Middle School, 45% are boys. How many boys are in Grade 7?

F 45

G 54

H 55

J 66

214 Unit 7 Cumulative Review

UNIT 8 • TABLE OF CONTENTS

Integers and Rational Numbers

Lesson	Page
1 Integers	217
2 Adding Integers	221
3 Subtracting Integers	223
4 **Problem Solving Strategy:** Draw a Diagram	225
5 Multiplying Integers	227
6 Dividing Integers	229
7 Rational Numbers on the Number Line	231
8 Adding and Subtracting Rational Numbers	233
9 Multiplying and Dividing Rational Numbers	235
10 **Problem Solving Application:** Use a Graph	237
• **Unit 8 Review**	239
• **Cumulative Review ★ Test Prep**	240

> We will be using this vocabulary:
>
> **integer** any number in the set . . . , ⁻3, ⁻2, ⁻1, 0, 1, 2, 3, . . .
>
> **positive integer** an integer that is greater than 0; for example 1, 2, 3, . . .
>
> **negative integer** an integer that is less than 0; for example . . . , ⁻3, ⁻2, ⁻1
>
> **opposites** two numbers whose sum is 0; for example, ⁻2 and 2 are opposites since ⁻2 + 2 = 0
>
> **absolute value** the distance of a number from 0 on the number line, regardless of direction; for example |3| = 3 and |⁻5| = 5
>
> **rational number** a number that can be expressed as the quotient of two integers; for example, ⁻1.6 = $\frac{-16}{10}$ and 3 = $\frac{-3}{-1}$

Dear Family,

During the next few weeks, our math class will be using addition, subtraction, multiplication, and division of positive and negative numbers to solve problems. This includes using the number line to locate, add, and subtract positive and negative numbers. You can expect to see homework that provides practice with these skills. Here is a sample you may want to keep handy to give help if needed.

Locating Integers and Rational Numbers

This number line shows some integers and rational numbers. Negative numbers are less than 0. Positive numbers are greater than 0. The number 0 is neither positive nor negative.

Negative Direction: numbers decrease

Positive Direction: numbers increase

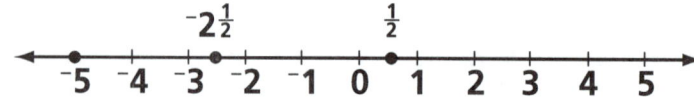

Read ⁻5 as negative 5.   Read $\frac{1}{2}$ as positive one half.

Notice that as you move right, you move in the positive direction. As you move left, you move in the negative direction.

During this unit, students will continue to learn new techniques related to problem solving and will continue to practice basic skills with fractions, decimals, and integers.

Sincerely,

Name _____   **Integers**

Integers are the set of numbers including positive whole numbers, negative whole numbers, and zero. The integers greater than **0** are called **positive integers.** They are sometimes written using a positive sign. For example, the number positive **5** is written as ⁺**5** or **5.**

The integers less than **0** are called **negative integers.** They are always written with a negative sign. For example, the number negative **4** is written ⁻**4.**

The integer **0** is neither positive nor negative. The number line below is labeled with integers.

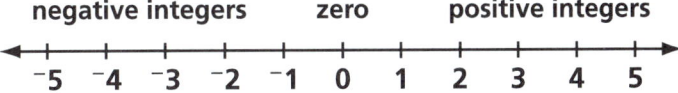

Pairs of integers that are the same distance from **0** on the number line are called **opposites.** The numbers ⁻**3** and **3** are opposites because each integer is **3** units from **0.** The opposite of **6** is ⁻**6.** The opposite of ⁻**10** is **10.** The integer **0** is its own opposite.

Write the number in the set that is not an integer.

1. ⁻5, $\frac{1}{2}$, 8, ⁻2 _____   9, ⁻1, 0.25, 30 _____

2. 0.175, ⁻12, 15, ⁻3, 0 _____   ⁻4, 0, 17, $\frac{5}{8}$, ⁻12 _____

Write the opposite of the integer.

3. 7 _____   ⁻8 _____   ⁻2 _____   12 _____

4. 0 _____   23 _____   ⁻67 _____   45 _____

Complete each statement by writing *positive* or *negative*.

5. The opposite of a negative number is _____.

6. The opposite of the opposite of a negative number is _____.

7. Two units to the right of ⁻3 is _____ and **2** units to the

left of the opposite of ⁻3 is _____.

Unit 8 Lesson 1   **217**

The **absolute value** of an integer is the distance it is from zero on the number line, regardless of whether the integer is to the left or to the right of **0**.

The absolute value of **4** (written as |**4**|) is **4**, since **4** is **4** units to the right of **0**.

The absolute value of **-3** (written as |**-3**|) is **3**, since **-3** is **3** units to the left of **0**.

Opposite integers have the same absolute value, since both integers are the same distance from **0** but in opposite directions. For example, **-5** and **+5** both have an absolute value of **5**.

Write the absolute value of the integer.

8. 8 _____   -11 _____   -27 _____   36 _____

9. -52 _____   0 _____   73 _____   -49 _____

Evaluate.

10. |-5| _____ |12| _____ |-86| _____ |94| _____

11. |33| _____ |-75| _____ |-67| _____ |58| _____

The number line shows how integers are ordered and helps you compare them.

Notice that in a pair of numbers, the number that is farther to the left is the lesser number. The number that is farther to the right is the greater number.

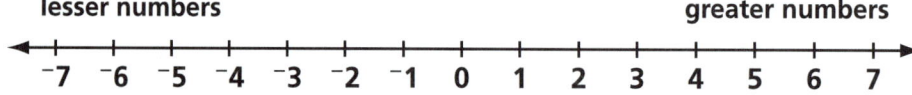

-7 < -2   5 > 2

Compare. Write <, >, or =.

12. -2 ◯ 2 |-3| ◯ 3   7 ◯ 5   4 ◯ 6

13. |-3| ◯ |2| -14 ◯ -12   8 ◯ 7   -12 ◯ 12

14. 3 ◯ 5   -2 ◯ -3   1 ◯ 0 |-4| ◯ |-5|

15. |-5| ◯ |5| 0 ◯ -5   0 ◯ 5 |0| ◯ |5|

218 Unit 8 Lesson 1

Name _____

On each number line, place a point for the integer or integers described.

16. the integers that have an absolute value of 4

17. the integer that is 2 units to the right of ⁻2

18. the integer that is the opposite of ⁺3

19. the integer that is 2 less than ⁺1

20. the integers that have an absolute value of 2

21. the integer that is 3 greater than ⁻4

Look back at your answers to exercises 16 and 20.

There are two integers that have an absolute value of 4. Both ⁻4 and 4 are 4 units from 0.

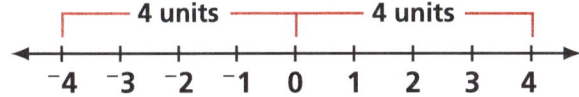

There are two integers that have an absolute value of 2. Both ⁻2 and 2 are 2 units from 0.

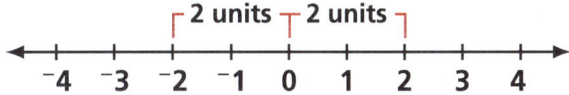

Another way to write these exercises is to use an equation.

| $|n| = 4$ | $|n| = 2$ |

Think: What two integers are 4 units from 0?

$n = {}^-4, n = 4$ (or $n = {}^+4$)

Think: What two integers are 2 units from 0?

$n = {}^-2, n = 2$

Complete.

22. What integers are 7 units from 0 on the number line? _____

23. What integers are 18 units from 0 on the number line? _____

24. What integers are 25 units from 0 on the number line? _____

Solve for *n*.

25. $|n| = 6$ _____ $|n| = 81$ _____ $|n| = 42$ _____

Integers have many applications.

Prices increase and decrease.	During the winter, temperatures can fall below zero.	Elevations can be described as above or below sea level.
A **5** point increase in a stock price can be written as **⁺$5**.	In January, the temperature was **10** degrees below **0°F**. The temperature was **⁻10°F**.	A scuba diver is **20** m below sea level. The diver's position is **⁻20** m.

Write an integer that represents the statement. Label the integer.

26. A running back for a football team lost **8** yards. ⁻8 yards

27. The Dow Jones average rose **2** points. +2 points

28. The temperature on a cold winter's day is **10** degrees below **0°C**. ⁻10 degrees

29. A person deposited **$50** into a bank account. +50

Problem Solving / Reasoning Solve.

30. Uri took an elevator from the first floor up **5** floors to the cafeteria, down **2** floors to the mailroom, up **1** floor to visit a friend, and then down **2** floors to his workspace. Use integers to describe each activity. What floor did he end up on?
    3 floor +5, -2, +1, -2

31. Mount Everest is about **29,000** feet above sea level. The Marianas Trench in the ocean is about **36,200** feet below sea level. Mount McKinley is **20,320** feet above sea level. Death Valley is **282** feet below sea level. Use integers to describe each location. Then write the elevations in greatest to least order.

Test Prep ★ Mixed Review

32 A person bought a used sound system for $160, then quickly sold it for $224. What is the percent of increase from $160 to $224?

  A 4%
  B 28%
  C 40%
  D 64%

33 A money-market fund offers its customers $6\frac{1}{2}$% simple interest per year. What is the interest on a $300 investment for 2 years?

  F $13
  G $19.50
  H $36
  J $39

Name _____

Problem Solving Strategy: Draw a Diagram

You have used the Draw a Diagram strategy before. In this lesson you will find how it can help you solve problems with integers.

Number lines are diagrams that help to show the relationship of positive and negative numbers to each other.

Problem

A particle is in a magnetic field. It moves along a number line as the field changes. It starts at 0, and after each second, it moves to these locations: 1, −2, 3, −4. What is the total distance that the particle travels?

❶ Understand   As you reread the problem, ask yourself questions.

- What do you know about the position of the particle? It moves from **0** to **1** to **−2** to **3** to **−4** during the **4** seconds.

- What do you need to find? _____

❷ Decide   Choose a method for solving.

Try the Draw a Diagram strategy.

- How can you show the particle's positions on a number line?

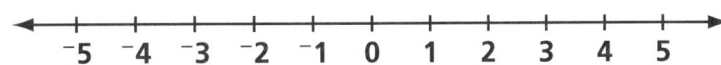

- How can you find the distance it moves during each second?

_____

❸ Solve   Answer the question.

- List the distances that you need to total. _____

- What is the total? _____

❹ Look back   Check your answer. Write the answer as a full sentence.

Answer _____

How did your diagram help you to answer the question?

_____

Unit 8 Lesson 4   225

Use the Draw a Diagram strategy or any other strategy you have learned.

1. Sue walked from her house 2 blocks east to Tammy's house. Together they walked 7 blocks west to the mall. After shopping they walked 6 blocks east to a restaurant. Then they walked back to Tammy's house for the evening. How many blocks did Sue walk?

   Think: How can you use a number line to help you? Where will you place 0?

   Answer _____

2. In the midwest, some days can have great temperature variations. One day in Detroit, the temperature was 45°F at 6 A.M. At 9 A.M. it was 7° warmer. From 9 A.M. until noon, the temperature fell 12°. During the next three hours, the temperature increased by 16°. What was the temperature at 3 P.M.?

   Think: What would be a good way to organize this information?

   Answer _____

3. Ramon has $15 in his wallet. He spends $8 for a CD. He earns $5 for doing a chore. He spends $3 for lunch. How much money does Ramon have left?

4. The elevation of a level plot of land is 15 feet below sea level. A 32-foot television antenna is erected on this site. How far above sea level is the antenna?

5. A particle starts at ⁻3 on a number line. After 1 second it moves 5 units to the right; after 2 seconds it moves 10 units to the left; after 3 seconds it moves 15 units to the right. If this pattern continues, where is the particle after 5 seconds?

6. Four towns are located along a 24-mile railroad line that runs from Northville to Southville. The town of Centerville is in the middle of the route. The town of Rockville is located 3 miles north of Centerville. How far is Rockville from Northville? How far is Rockville from Southville?

7. According to the newspapers in Jane's town, the temperature there during the last 24 hours had plunged from 7°C to ⁻31°C. What is the difference between these two temperatures?

8. On Joe's football team's next possession, they gained 10 yards on the first play, then lost 13 yards on the second play, and then managed to gain 7 yards on the third play. What was the team's total gain on these three plays?

Name _____

Rational Numbers on the Number Line

You know that positive integers (or whole numbers) have fractions and decimals between them on the number line. Negative integers also have numbers between them, such as $^-1\frac{1}{2}$ and $^-2.3$.

These numbers can be located on a number line. For example, $^-1\frac{1}{2}$ is between $^-1$ and $^-2$, and $^-2.3$ is between $^-2$ and $^-3$.

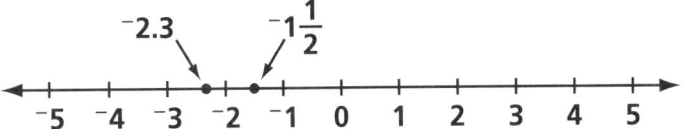

These numbers are called **rational numbers**, because they can be written as the *ratio* of two integers.

A negative rational number can be written in several ways. These represent the same number:

$\frac{^-3}{4}$ $\frac{3}{^-4}$ $^-\frac{3}{4}$

$^-1\frac{1}{2}$ can be written as $\frac{^-3}{2}$

$^-2.3$ can be written as $^-\frac{23}{10}$

0 can be written as $\frac{0}{1}$

A rational expression may contain more than one positive or negative sign. Follow these rules for simplifying negative rational numbers.

Rule	Rational Number	Simplify
The quotient of a negative integer and a positive integer is negative.	$\frac{^-4}{8}$	$^-\frac{1}{2}$
The quotient of a positive integer and a negative integer is negative.	$\frac{3}{^-9}$	$^-\frac{1}{3}$
If there is a negative integer in parentheses and there is a negative sign outside the parentheses, write the number's opposite.	$^-(^-\frac{2}{3})$ $^-(^-\frac{5}{7})$	$\frac{2}{3}$ $\frac{5}{7}$

Write the rational number as a ratio of two integers.

1. $^-7$ _____ $2\frac{1}{2}$ _____ $^-3.03$ _____ 0.1708 _____ $^-6\frac{5}{6}$ _____ $^-0.9$ _____

2. 4.444 _____ $3\frac{7}{12}$ _____ $^-1\frac{5}{8}$ _____ $^-12.5$ _____ 0.1011 _____ $^-15$ _____

3. $^-2\frac{3}{12}$ _____ $^-4.7$ _____ $^-3\frac{1}{4}$ _____ 1.03 _____ 0.301 _____ $^-0.79$ _____

Place the rational numbers on the number line next to them.

4. $\frac{3}{4}$ $^-\frac{1}{2}$ $^-1\frac{1}{4}$ $2\frac{1}{2}$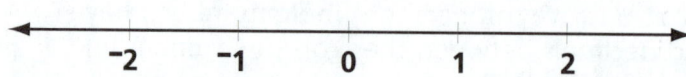

5. $^-1\frac{5}{8}$ $\frac{13}{8}$ $^-2\frac{7}{8}$ $2\frac{1}{8}$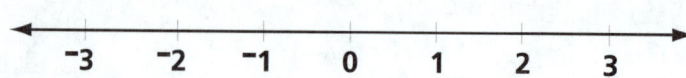

Simplify the expression.

6. $\frac{4}{-8} = $ _____ $\frac{6}{12} = $ _____ $^-(\frac{-3}{6}) = $ _____ $\frac{-3}{-6} = $ _____

7. $^-(\frac{4}{-16}) = $ _____ $^-(\frac{-2}{4}) = $ _____ $^-(\frac{3}{-6}) = $ _____ $\frac{-8}{18} = $ _____

Problem Solving Reasoning Solve.

8. The *density property* of rational numbers says that between two rational numbers is another rational number. Does the set of integers have the density property? Explain.

_____

_____

✓ Quick Check

Write the product or quotient.

9. $7 \times (^-8) = $ _____

10. $^-12 \times 11 = $ _____

11. $^-14 \times {}^-25 = $ _____

12. $156 \div {}^-12 = $ _____

13. $^-144 \div 16 = $ _____

14. $^-275 \div {}^-25 = $ _____

Write the rational number as a ratio of two integers.

15. $^-17$ _____

16. $^-11\frac{3}{4}$ _____

17. $^-2.04$ _____

Work Space.

232 Unit 8 Lesson 7

Name _____

Adding and Subtracting Rational Numbers

To add or subtract rational numbers, use the same rules you used for integers.

Addition

- Both addends are positive or both are negative.

  $-\frac{3}{4} + -\frac{1}{2}$ Add the absolute values. $\frac{3}{4} + \frac{1}{2} = \frac{5}{4}$ or $1\frac{1}{4}$

              Use the same sign as the original addends (−). $-1\frac{1}{4}$

- One addend is positive and one is negative.

  $-\frac{5}{6} + \frac{3}{4}$ Compare the absolute values. $\frac{5}{6} > \frac{3}{4}$

              Find the difference of the absolute values. $\frac{5}{6} - \frac{3}{4} = \frac{10}{12} - \frac{9}{12}$ or $\frac{1}{12}$

              Use the same sign as the greater value. $-\frac{1}{12}$

Subtraction

$-\frac{4}{5} - -\frac{2}{3}$ Rewrite as an addition expression. $-\frac{4}{5} + \frac{2}{3}$

           Compare the absolute values. $\frac{4}{5} > \frac{2}{3}$

           Find the difference of the absolute values. $\frac{4}{5} - \frac{2}{3} = \frac{12}{15} - \frac{10}{15}$ or $\frac{2}{15}$

           Use the same sign as the greater value. $-\frac{2}{15}$

$4.3 - 6.55$ Rewrite as an addition expression. $4.3 - 6.55 = 4.3 + {}^-6.55$

           Compare the absolute values. $6.55 > 4.3$

           Find the difference of the absolute values. $6.55 - 4.3 = 2.25$

           Use the same sign as ${}^-6.55$. -2.25

Write the sum or difference. Write fractions in simplest form.

1. $\frac{2}{3}$ $-\frac{7}{20}$ $\frac{2}{3}$ -4

     $+ -\frac{5}{6}$ $+ \frac{1}{5}$ $- -\frac{1}{3}$ $- 1\frac{2}{3}$

Find each sum or difference. Write fractions in simplest form.

2. $-\frac{9}{10} - -\frac{3}{5}$ $-1\frac{1}{5} - -\frac{1}{5}$ $-\frac{7}{12} + -\frac{3}{4}$ $2\frac{5}{6} + -\frac{5}{6}$

3. $19.6 + {}^-12.8$ $22.3 - {}^-57.1$ $-14.7 - {}^-4.3$ $-6.009 + 4.62$

4. -6.82
    7.09
    $+ {}^-3.75$

    $\frac{2}{3}$
    $\frac{7}{8}$
    $+ -\frac{5}{6}$

    $-\frac{1}{7}$
    $-\frac{3}{4}$
    $+ \frac{19}{28}$

    9.343
    -10.47
    $+ 5.72$

Problem Solving / Reasoning Complete. Let $a = 8$ and $b = -\frac{1}{2}$.

5. Find each sum or difference.

   $a + b$ _____ $|a + b|$ _____

   $|a| - |b|$ _____ $|b| - |a|$ _____

6. Find each sum or difference.

   $a - b$ _____ $b - a$ _____

   $|a - b|$ _____ $|a| + |b|$ _____

7. Write true or false. If $a > b$, then $|a + b| = |a| - |b|$. Explain.

_____

8. Write true or false. If a is positive and b is negative, then $|a - b| = |a| + |b|$. Explain.

_____

Test Prep ★ Mixed Review

9 Which expression is equivalent to $(^-18 \times 5) \div {}^-(3^2)$?

   A $\frac{^-18 \times 5}{9}$ C $\frac{^-18}{5 \times 9}$

   B $\frac{^-18 \times 5}{^-9}$ D $\frac{^-18}{5 \times 9}$

10 What is the value of $\frac{^-294 \div 7}{^-6}$?

   F 252   H $^-7$

   G 7   J $^-252$

234   Unit 8 Lesson 8

Multiplying and Dividing Rational Numbers

You can multiply and divide rational numbers using the same rules that you used for integers.

Multiplication

$\frac{-3}{4} \times \frac{-2}{5} = \frac{6}{20}$, or $\frac{3}{10}$ — Both factors are negative, so the product is positive.

$\frac{-4}{9} \times \frac{3}{8} = \frac{-12}{72}$, or $\frac{-1}{6}$ — One factor is positive and the other negative, so the product is negative.

Division

$\frac{-1}{3} \div \frac{7}{8} = \frac{-1}{3} \times \frac{8}{7}$, or $\frac{-8}{21}$ — The dividend is negative and the divisor is positive, so the quotient is negative.

$2.49 \div {}^-0.3 = {}^-24.9 \div 3$, or $^-8.3$ — The dividend is positive and the divisor is negative, so the quotient is negative.

Write the product or quotient in simplest form.

1. $\frac{3}{4} \times \frac{-7}{9} =$ _____ $^-45 \times \frac{5}{12} =$ _____ $2\frac{4}{5} \times \frac{-5}{8} =$ _____

2. $36 \div \frac{-3}{5} =$ _____ $\frac{15}{16} \times \frac{-2}{3} =$ _____ $\frac{-4}{9} \times \frac{-9}{10} =$ _____

3. $\frac{-7}{8} \div \frac{4}{5} =$ _____ $0.32 \times {}^-0.08 =$ _____ $\frac{1}{5} \times {}^-2\frac{5}{7} =$ _____

4. $^-1\frac{1}{2} \times {}^-1\frac{1}{5} =$ _____ $^-72 \div \frac{8}{9} =$ _____ $1.44 \div {}^-12 =$ _____

5. $\frac{4}{5} \times \frac{-6}{7} =$ _____ $1\frac{1}{3} \div {}^-2\frac{1}{6} =$ _____ $^-36 \times \frac{-7}{9} =$ _____

6. $\frac{-2}{5} \div \frac{-11}{2} =$ _____ $^-0.72 \times {}^-5 =$ _____ $15 \div \frac{-5}{9} =$ _____

When working with positive and negative variables, you must pay close attention to the signs.

When a negative sign is before a grouping symbol, distribute the negative sign to each addend in the group.

Evaluate $^-(a - b)$ for $a = \frac{1}{2}$ and $b = {}^-5$.

$^-(a - b) = {}^-a - ({}^-b)$
$= {}^-a + b$
$= {}^-\frac{1}{2} + ({}^-5)$
$= {}^-5\frac{1}{2}$

When a power has a negative sign, evaluate the power first, then find its opposite.

Evaluate $^-x^2$ and $({}^-x)^2$ for $x = \frac{1}{6}$.

$^-x^2 = {}^-(\frac{1}{6})^2$ $({}^-x)^2 = ({}^-\frac{1}{6})^2$
$= {}^-\frac{1}{36}$ $= \frac{1}{36}$

Evaluate the expression when $x = {}^-\frac{1}{2}$, $y = \frac{2}{3}$, and $z = {}^-2$.

7. $x + y + z$ _____ $-(x + y + z)$ _____ $-(2x - y) + 3z$ _____ $3x - (3y - z)$ _____

8. $-z^2$ _____ $-(x^2 + y)$ _____ $x^3 + 9y^3$ _____ $x^3 - z^3$ _____

9. $-(x + 3y - z)$ _____ $z + y - 4x^2$ _____ $2xy$ _____ $3yz$ _____

Problem Solving / Reasoning

10. Use the relationship between multiplication and division to explain why you cannot divide an integer by 0.

    _____
    _____
    _____

11. For each of the equations below, use reasoning to deduce the value(s) of n.

    $n = |10|$ $|n| = 10$ $|{}^-n| = 10$

    _____   _____   _____

 Quick Check

Write the sum or difference.   Work Space.

12. $\frac{3}{4} + ({}^-\frac{3}{8}) = $ _____   13. $^-\frac{5}{6} + {}^-1\frac{1}{3} = $ _____

14. $^-2.4 - 2 = $ _____

Write the product or quotient.

15. $2.3 \times {}^-4.5 = $ _____   16. $^-2\frac{4}{5} \div \frac{1}{10} = $ _____

17. $^-\frac{7}{8} \times {}^-1\frac{3}{5} = $ _____

Name _____

Problem Solving Application: Use a Graph

The bar graph shows the favorite food of students at Lincoln Middle School.

You can use the graph to compare, make estimates, or draw conclusions about the data.

> **Tips to Remember**
>
> 1. Understand   2. Decide   3. Solve   4. Look back
>
> - Ask yourself whether you have solved other problems like this before.
> - Try to estimate or predict your answer before solving. Use your estimate to check that your answer was reasonable.
> - Think about strategies you have learned and use them to help you to solve the problem.

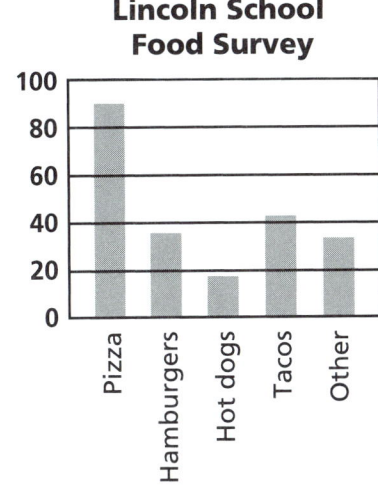

Solve.

1. Is it true that about $\frac{1}{5}$ of the students in the school listed pizza as their favorite food?

   Think: Since "Pizza" represents $\frac{1}{5}$ of the bars, does this mean it represents $\frac{1}{5}$ of the responses?

   Answer _____

2. How many times as many students chose pizza as hot dogs?

   Think: Should you think about subtraction or division to compare the two numbers?

   _____

   Answer _____

3. About how many of the students did not choose pizza?

   _____

4. About what percent of the students chose tacos or hot dogs?

   _____

Unit 8 Lesson 10 **237**

Use the line graph. It shows the average monthly 10 A.M. temperature at Lincoln School.

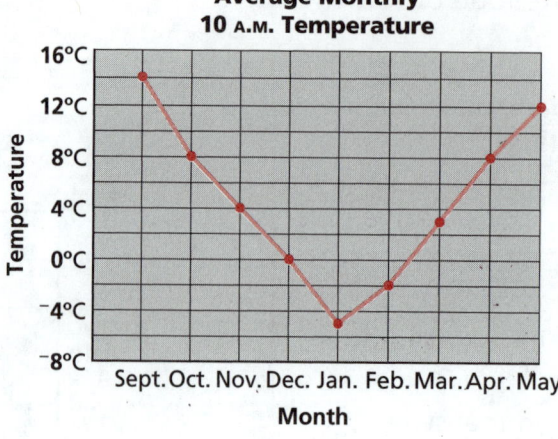

5. Is it reasonable to talk about the temperature in October being so many times greater than the January temperature? Explain your reasoning.

_____

_____

6. Suppose the temperature was recorded on 20 school days in November and 16 days in December. Would the average temperature for the two months be halfway between 4°C and 0°C? Explain your reasoning.

_____

_____

7. Between which two months did the average temperature increase the least? Explain how you can tell from the graph.

_____

8. Between which two months did the average temperature increase the most?

_____

_____

Extend Your Thinking

9. During one month of the following year, students collected the following data. Without calculating the monthly average, to which month in the graph will the average be closest? Then, calculate the average and write the answer below.

Temperatures in Degrees Celsius

⁻8   ⁻4   1   0   3   ⁻5   2   0   1   ⁻1
4   6   3   0   ⁻4 ⁻6   ⁻3 ⁻1 1   ⁻3

Answer _____

10. Look back at problem 8. Explain the method you used to solve the problem. Tell what data you used from the graph. What operations did you use to find the answer?

_____

_____

238 Unit 8 Lesson 10

Name Dante Collins

Unit 8 Review

Write the absolute value of the number.

1. $|{-6}| =$ __6__
2. $|22| =$ ____
3. $|{-4}| =$ __4__
4. $|2| =$ ____
5. $|0| =$ __0__
6. $\left|\dfrac{-5}{8}\right| =$ ____

Write the sum or difference.

7. $-15 + 16 =$ __1__
8. $18 + {-32} =$ ____
9. $-15 + {-8} =$ __23__
10. $-15 - {-27} =$ ____
11. $27 - 32 =$ __-5__
12. $8 - {-15} =$ ____
13. $-5.8 + 9.03 =$ __3.23__
14. $7.42 + {-4.66} =$ ____
15. $\dfrac{-4}{5} + \dfrac{3}{4} =$ __-1/20__
16. $\dfrac{2}{3} - \dfrac{-1}{4} =$ ____
17. $-1\dfrac{5}{8} - 3\dfrac{1}{3} =$ __-2 4/5__
18. $-1.6 - {-2.9} =$ ____

Write the product or quotient.

19. $-6 \times 3 =$ __-18__
20. $-12 \times {-7} =$ ____
21. $-(8)^3 =$ __512__
22. $-15 \div 3 =$ ____
23. $-65 \div {-5} =$ __13__
24. $18 \div {-3} =$ ____
25. $\dfrac{3}{5} \times \dfrac{-5}{9} =$ __-15/45 = -1/3__
26. $\dfrac{-4}{7} \times \dfrac{-3}{2} =$ ____
27. $-4.62 \times 3.4 =$ __-15.708__

Solve.

28. A weight suspended from a string swings from left to right and back again. Each left-to-right or right-to-left swing is half as long as the previous one. The first swing was 4 m long. How far has the weight moved after 6 swings? ____

29. What is the average high temperature for the week if the daily high temperatures are 7°F, −4°F, −8°F, −10°F, −1°F, 5°F, and 4°F?

____

The formula $t = g - 5.6k$ gives the temperature (t) in °C at a point in Earth's troposphere if you know the ground temperature (g) and the altitude of the point in kilometers (k). Use the formula to complete the table.

	Ground level temperature	Temperature at 4 km	Temperature at 6 km	Temperature at 8 km	Temperature at 10 km
30.	20°C				
31.	−5°C				

Unit 8 Review 239

Cumulative Review
★ Test Prep

This week's cold spell!
(Daily lows in °F)
Monday .... −2
Tuesday 3
Wednesday.. −5
Thursday 15

1 How would you order the temperatures from coldest to warmest?

A 2, 3, 5, 15
B −5, −2, 3, 15
C −2, −5, 3, 15
D −2, 3, −5, 15

2 A storage building with an area of 2,000 ft² is to be partly converted at one end into an office with an area of 375 ft². By what percent will the storage area have been decreased?

F 81.2%
G 77%
H 23%
J 18.8%

Petty Cash Account 1/5/99
Lunch −$2.85
Babysitting $18.50
CD −$12.35

3 What is the final balance of the cash account?

A $28.00
B $9.00
C $3.30
D −$3.30

4 During a 24-hour period starting at 1 o'clock, how many times, on the hour, will the hands of a clock form an angle that is neither acute nor obtuse.

F 8
G 6
H 4
J 2

5 Which equation has a solution that is equivalent to the equation $n - 12 = 18$?

A $2n = 27$
B $n - 5 = 25$
C $2n + 3 = 18$
D $\frac{45}{n} = 9$

6 The formula for finding the temperature in degrees Fahrenheit (°F) given the temperature in degrees Celsius (°C) is $F = \frac{9}{5}C + 32$. The temperature on a spring day is 59°F. What is the equivalent temperature in degrees Celsius?

F 91°C
G 46°C
H 31°C
J 15°C

7 Which operation do you perform first in simplifying the expression $3 \div 4.5 \times 1.8 + (1.2 + 3.8)^2$?

A $3 \div 45$
B 4.5×1.8
C $1.2 + 3.8$
D $(1.2 + 3.8)^2$

8 How many diagonals are there in a heptagon?

F 7
G 10
H 14
J 28

UNIT 9 • TABLE OF CONTENTS

Algebra: Expressions and Equations

Lesson	Page
1 Exponents and Roots	243
2 Operations with Monomial Expressions	246
3 Operations with Polynomial Expressions	248
4 Evaluating Polynomial Expressions	250
5 **Problem Solving Application:** Choose an Equation	252
6 Scientific Notation	254
7 Solving Equations with Rational Numbers	257
8 Solving Two-Step Equations	260
9 Equations and Inequalities	263
10 **Problem Solving Strategy:** Write an Equation	266
11 Solving Inequalities	268
• Unit 9 Review	271
• Cumulative Review ★ Test Prep	274

Dear Family,

During the next few weeks, our math class will be learning and practicing how to solve one-step and two-step equations involving whole numbers and rational numbers. Several new ideas leading up to this will also be included.

You can expect to see homework that provides practice with these skills. Here is a sample you may want to keep handy if help is needed.

We will be using this vocabulary:

exponent a number that tells how many times a base is to be used as a factor

power a number than can be expressed using a single base and exponent; 2^3 is 2 to the third power

square root a number such that its square is a given number. **5** and **⁻5** are square roots of **25**

irrational number a number that is not rational. The square root of **10** ($\sqrt{10}$) is an irrational number

monomial an expression consisting of a number, a variable, or the product of a number and one or more variables

polynomial an expression that is itself a monomial or is the sum or product of monomials

coefficient the numerical factor in a variable expression

constant the numerical term in a polynomial

scientific notation a notation for writing a number as a product of a number from **1** to **10** and a power of **10**

Solving Two-Step Equations

$3x + 5 = 29$	
$3x + (5 + {}^-5) = 29 + {}^-5$	Add the opposite (⁻5) to each side of the equation.
$3x + 0 = 24$	Simplify.
$\dfrac{3x}{3} = \dfrac{24}{3}$	Divide each side by 3.
$x = 8$	Simplify.

Check by substitution.

$3x + 5 = 29$	Original equation
$3(8) + 5 = 29$	Substitute 8 for the variable.
$24 + 5 = 29$	Add.

During this unit, students will need to continue practicing with opposites of numbers and all operations with rational numbers and decimals.

Sincerely,

Name _____

Expressions and Roots

You have used powers with positive exponents to show repeated multiplication when you write, simplify, and evaluate expressions.

In the following examples you will see how the exponents in factors, products, and quotients are related to each other.

$5 \cdot 5 \cdot 5 = 5^3$

factors — base, exponent

Read 5^3 as "5 cubed" or "5 to the third power."

Simplify: $5^2 \cdot 5^3$

Multiplying Powers When you multiply powers with the same base, add the exponents.

$5^2 \cdot 5^3 = \underbrace{(5 \cdot 5)}_{\text{2 factors}} \cdot \underbrace{(5 \cdot 5 \cdot 5)}_{\text{3 factors}} = \underbrace{(5 \cdot 5 \cdot 5 \cdot 5 \cdot 5)}_{\text{2 factors + 3 factors}}$
$= 5^5 \rightarrow 3{,}125$

Simplify: $\dfrac{5^5}{5^3}$

Dividing Powers When you divide powers with the same base, subtract the exponents.

$\dfrac{5^5}{5^3} = \dfrac{\overbrace{5 \cdot 5 \cdot 5 \cdot 5 \cdot 5}^{\text{5 factors}}}{\underbrace{5 \cdot 5 \cdot 5}_{\text{3 factors}}} = 5 \cdot 5 \rightarrow 5^2 \rightarrow 25$ (5 factors − 3 factors)

Simplify: $\dfrac{5^3}{5^3}$

- You can simplify the expression using fractions.

$\dfrac{5^3}{5^3} = \dfrac{5 \cdot 5 \cdot 5}{5 \cdot 5 \cdot 5} \rightarrow 1$

- You can simplify the expression using exponents.

$\dfrac{5^3}{5^3} = 5^{3-3} = 5^0 \rightarrow 1$

You read 5^0 as "5 to the zero power."

Zero Exponents
If b is a nonzero number, then $b^0 = 1$.

Simplify: $\dfrac{5^3}{5^5}$

- You can simplify the expression using fractions.

$\dfrac{5^3}{5^5} = \dfrac{5 \cdot 5 \cdot 5}{5 \cdot 5 \cdot 5 \cdot 5 \cdot 5} \rightarrow \dfrac{1}{5 \cdot 5} \rightarrow \dfrac{1}{25}$

- You can simplify the expression using exponents.

$\dfrac{5^3}{5^5} = 5^{3-5} \rightarrow 5^{-2} \rightarrow \dfrac{1}{5 \cdot 5} \rightarrow \dfrac{1}{5^2} \rightarrow \dfrac{1}{25}$

You read 5^{-2} as "5 to the negative 2 power."

Negative Exponents
If b is a nonzero number and n is a positive integer, then $b^{-n} = \dfrac{1}{b^n}$.

Write the expressions using negative exponents.

1. $\dfrac{1}{4} = $ _____ $\dfrac{1}{y} = $ _____ $\dfrac{1}{5 \cdot 5} = $ _____ $\dfrac{1}{x \cdot x \cdot x \cdot x} = $ _____

2. $\dfrac{1}{2 \cdot 2 \cdot 2} = $ _____ $\dfrac{1}{a^5} = $ _____ $\dfrac{1}{\left(\frac{1}{7}\right)^6} = $ _____ $\dfrac{1}{\frac{b}{6}} = $ _____

Unit 9 Lesson 1 243

Here are some other examples that show how to simplify both rational and variable expressions with negative exponents.

Simplify: $\left(\dfrac{3}{4}\right)^{-2}$ | Simplify: $\left(\dfrac{a}{4}\right)^{-2}$

1. Use the definition of negative exponents.

$$\left(\dfrac{3}{4}\right)^{-2} = \dfrac{1}{\left(\dfrac{3}{4}\right)^2}$$

$$\left(\dfrac{a}{4}\right)^{-2} = \dfrac{1}{\left(\dfrac{a}{4}\right)^2}$$

2. Multiply.

$$= \dfrac{1}{\dfrac{3}{4} \cdot \dfrac{3}{4}}$$

$$= \dfrac{1}{\left(\dfrac{a}{4}\right)\left(\dfrac{a}{4}\right)}$$

3. Write the reciprocal. Simplify.

$$= \dfrac{1}{\dfrac{9}{16}} \rightarrow \dfrac{16}{9} \rightarrow 1\dfrac{7}{9}$$

$$= \dfrac{1}{\dfrac{a^2}{16}} \rightarrow \dfrac{16}{a^2}$$

Sometimes you need to use number properties to rewrite expressions before you can simplify them.

Use the associative and commutative properties to group numbers with the same base together.

Simplify: $(2^3 \cdot 3^5) \cdot (2^{-8} \cdot 3^2)$.
Write the result using positive exponents.

$(2^3 \cdot 3^5) \cdot (2^{-8} \cdot 3^2) = (2^3 \cdot 2^{-8}) \cdot (3^5 \cdot 3^2)$
$\qquad = 2^{-5} \cdot 3^7$
$\qquad = \dfrac{3^7}{2^5}$

⁻5 is a negative exponent.

Simplify.

3. $(^-2)^{-5} =$ _____ $(^-x)^{-3} =$ _____ $(^-5)^{-4} =$ _____

4. $\left(\dfrac{3}{5}\right)^{-2} =$ _____ $\left(\dfrac{1}{3}\right)^{-3} =$ _____ $\left(\dfrac{3}{7}\right)^{-2} =$ _____

5. $\left(\dfrac{4}{c}\right)^{-2} =$ _____ $\left(\dfrac{1}{5}\right)^{-4} =$ _____ $\left(\dfrac{2}{11}\right)^{-2} =$ _____

6. $\left(\dfrac{^-2}{b}\right)^{-1} =$ _____ $\left(\dfrac{^-1}{3}\right)^3 =$ _____ $\left(\dfrac{a}{7}\right)^{-3} =$ _____

Simplify. Write your result using positive exponents.

7. $5^{-9} \cdot 5^{-1} \cdot 5^6 =$ _____ $x^{-3} \cdot x^6 =$ _____ $a^{-5} \cdot a^3 \cdot a^{-8} =$ _____

8. $7^{-8} \div 7^{-3} =$ _____ $y^{-4} \div y^5 =$ _____ $2^6 \div 2^6 =$ _____

9. $9^6 \div 9^{-9} =$ _____ $c^{-2} \div c =$ _____ $(ab)^8 \div (ab)^{-2} =$ _____

10. $(3^4 \cdot 5^5) \cdot (3^{-7} \cdot 5^3)$ _____ $(x^6 \cdot y^9) \cdot (x^{-6} \cdot y^{-5})$ _____ $(2^8 \cdot a^3) \cdot (2^{-3} \cdot a^{-2})$ _____

11. $(5^2 \cdot 7^3) \div (5^{-3} \cdot 7^2)$ _____ $(a^{-1} \cdot 4^2) \div (a^{-3} \cdot 4^7)$ _____ $(6^3 \cdot x^2) \div (6^{-4} \cdot x^{-2})$ _____

Name _____

You know that inverse operations "undo" each other. Raising a base to a power and finding a **root** or base are inverse operations, so they undo each other.

$(^-5)^2 = (^-5)(^-5) \rightarrow 25$

$5^2 = (5)(5) \rightarrow 25$

The square of any base is that number multiplied by itself. Since $(^-5)^2$ and $(5)^2$ equal **25**, both $^-5$ and **5** are called **square roots** of **25**.

The symbol for square root ($\sqrt{\ }$) is called a *radical sign*. The $\sqrt{\ }$ symbol represents the *principal*, or positive square root.

$\sqrt{25} = 5$ — Think: $5 \times 5 = 25$ So $\sqrt{25}$ is **5**.

$\sqrt{49} = 7$ — Think: $7 \times 7 = 49$ So $\sqrt{49}$ is **7**.

$\sqrt{\frac{36}{121}} = \frac{6}{11}$ — Think: $\frac{6}{11} \times \frac{6}{11} = \frac{36}{121}$ So $\sqrt{\frac{36}{121}}$ is $\frac{6}{11}$.

When the square root of a number cannot be written as a fraction with integer terms, it is an **irrational number**.

You can estimate the square root of an irrational number between integer values.

Estimate. $\sqrt{17}$.
- $\sqrt{16} = 4$ and $\sqrt{25} = 5$, so $\sqrt{17}$ must be *between* **4** and **5**.
- $\sqrt{17}$ is closer to $\sqrt{16}$ than to $\sqrt{25}$, so $\sqrt{17}$ is closer to **4** than to **5**.

Find the square root.

12. $\sqrt{64}$ _____ $\sqrt{100}$ _____ $\sqrt{400}$ _____ $\sqrt{625}$ _____

13. $\sqrt{\frac{144}{169}}$ _____ $\sqrt{\frac{4}{49}}$ _____ $\sqrt{\frac{289}{676}}$ _____ $\sqrt{\frac{1225}{529}}$ _____

Tell whether the square root is rational or irrational. If it is rational, write the square root. If it is irrational, write which two integers the square root falls between.

14. $\sqrt{21}$ _____ $\sqrt{31}$ _____ $\sqrt{144}$ _____

15. $\sqrt{120}$ _____ $\sqrt{225}$ _____ $\sqrt{150}$ _____

Problem Solving Reasoning

You can find square roots of algebraic expressions with even powers. For example, $\sqrt{25x^2}$ is the same as $\sqrt{5x \cdot 5x}$ or $5x$, when x is postive. Find the square root. Assume $x > 0$.

16. $\sqrt{81x^4y^6}$ _____

17. $\sqrt{\frac{x^2 \cdot 2^4}{y^6}}$ _____

Test Prep ★ Mixed Review

18 If two cubes, each numbered 1–6, are rolled, what is the probability that two fours appear?

A $\frac{1}{3}$ **B** $\frac{1}{6}$ **C** $\frac{1}{18}$ **D** $\frac{1}{36}$

19 Which of the following types of quadrilaterals has just one pair of parallel sides?

F trapezoid   **H** rectangle

G parallelogram   **J** square

Unit 9 Lesson 1

Name _____

Operations with Monomial Expressions

Algebraic expressions can be **monomials** or **polynomials**. A monomial is an expression that has a number, a variable, or has a product of a number and one or more variables. In a monomial, a numerical factor is called a **coefficient**.

A polynomial is an expression that is itself a monomial or is the sum or difference of monomials. In a polynomial, a numerical term is called a **constant**.

Monomials

8 is coefficient of x

2, **8**x, and **4**a^2b^2

4 is a coefficient of a^2b^2

Polynomials

constants

8 + x, **8**x + **5**, and 4x − 3x^2 + 7y

Monomials with the same variable base (or bases) and exponents have **like terms**.

- These monomials have like terms.

  $-2x^2$ and $9x^2$ } same base, same exponent

  $16ab^3$ and $8ab^3$

- These monomials have unlike terms.

  $-2a^3$ and $11b^3$ } different base, same exponents

  $3x^2y$ and $-4xy^2$

When you multiply or divide monomials with like bases, you can use the rules of exponents to simplify factors.

Simplify: $3xy^7 \cdot 4x^2y^9$

To multiply powers, you add exponents.

$3xy^7 \cdot 4x^2y^9 = (3 \cdot 4) \cdot (x \cdot x^2)(y^7 \cdot y^9)$

$= 12\,(x^{1+2})\,(y^{7+9}) \rightarrow 12x^3y^{16}$

Simplify: $\dfrac{6y^{14}}{2y^8}$

To divide powers, you subtract exponents.

$\dfrac{6y^{14}}{2y^8} = \left(\dfrac{6}{2}\right)y^{14-8} \rightarrow 3y^6$

State whether the expression is a monomial or a polynomial.

1. $3x + 5y$ _____ $4x^2y^2$ _____ 3 _____

2. $u^2 + 3u + 2$ _____ $y^2 + (9 - 2)z^2$ _____ $\frac{1}{2}z$ _____

Write the coefficient of the variables.

3. $3x$ ____ $5y$ ____ $4x^2y^2$ ____ y^2 ____ $(9-2)z^2$ ____ $\frac{1}{2}z$ ____

Simplify.

4. $a^4b^9c^2 \cdot a^2b^5c^3$ _____ $x^7 \cdot x^5$ _____ $3g^4 \cdot 5g^6 \cdot 6g^2$ _____

5. $\dfrac{y^{13}}{y^8}$ _____ $\dfrac{12b^{10}}{4b^2}$ _____ $4z^5 \cdot \left(\dfrac{-2z^7}{8z^3}\right)$ _____

246 Unit 9 Lesson 2

Name _____

When you add or subtract monomials, you can use number properties to combine like terms.

Simplify: $^-5a^2b - 2a^2b$.

1. Rewrite it as an addition expression. $^-5a^2b - 2a^2b = {}^-5a^2b + {}^-2a^2b$

2. Use the distributive property. $= (^-5 + {}^-2)a^2b$

3. Combine (add) the coefficients. $= {}^-7a^2b$

Simplify the expression.

6. $5x - 2x$ _____ $7a - {}^-4a$ _____ $2rs + {}^-8rs$ _____

7. $8a^2b^3 - {}^-4a^2b^3$ _____ $^-7x - {}^-4x$ _____ $^-9x + 5x - {}^-12x + 2x$ _____

8. $8m^2 - 2m^2 + 4m^2$ _____ $3e - 7e + 6e + {}^-2e$ _____ $5a^5c^4 + 2a^5c^4 - 9a^5c^4$ _____

9. $^-6x^2 + 10x^2$ _____ $a^3b^6c^9 - 5a^3b^6c^9$ _____ $4x - {}^-3x + 8x + {}^-6x - 5x$ _____

Problem Solving Reasoning   Write and simplify an expression for the area of the figure.

10. 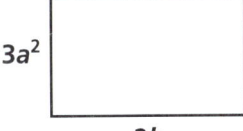   A: _____   11. 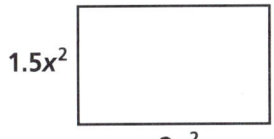   A: _____

Test Prep ★ Mixed Review

12 Which expression has the value $^-19$?

A $9 + |^-5| + |^-33|$

B $9 - |^-5| - |^-33|$

C $9 + |^-5| - |^-33|$

D $^-9 + |^-5| - |^-33|$

13 What is the value of $^-9 \cdot {}^-12 \div {}^-6 \cdot 2$?

F $^-1296$

G $^-36$

H 36

J $1{,}296$

Unit 9 Lesson 2   247

Name _____

Operations with Polynomial Expressions

You can also use the number properties to simplify polynomials.

Simplify: $8x - 7y - 6x + 4y$.

To subtract integers, add the opposites.

1. Rewrite the subtractions as additions.
2. Use the commutative and associative properties.
3. Use the distributive property to combine like terms.
4. Simplify.

$$8x - 7y - 6x + 4y = 8x + {}^-7y + {}^-6x + 4y$$
$$= 8x + {}^-6x + {}^-7y + 4y$$
$$= (8 + {}^-6)x + ({}^-7 + 4)y$$
$$= 2x + {}^-3y \text{ or } 2x - 3y$$

Simplify by adding or subtracting like terms.

1. $2n + 3m + {}^-4n + 2m$ _____ $3x^2 + 2x + 4x^2 + {}^-3x$ _____

2. $4c + 5d + {}^-2c + {}^-3d$ _____ $a^2 + b^2 + 2a^2 + 2b^2$ _____

3. $6r + 5s + 7t + 5r + 2t$ _____ $3m + 4n + 2 + 2m + {}^-3n + 5$ _____

4. $5x^2 + 2x + 4 + 2x^2 + {}^-2x$ _____ $18y^2 + 8y + 5 + 9y^2 + 6y + {}^-7$ _____

5. $(4x^2 + 3) - (x^2 + 2)$ _____ $(6r + 5) - (2r + 4)$ _____

6. $(6a^2 + 5b) - (2a^2 + 3b)$ _____ $(6m + 2n) - (3m + n)$ _____

7. $(7t^2 + 2y) - (6t^2 + 2y)$ _____ $(8d + 6e) - (5d + 3e)$ _____

You also use the distributive property when you multiply or divide a polynomial by a monomial.

Simplify: $3x(x^2 + {}^-4x + 5)$.

Simplify: $\dfrac{6x^2 - 4x}{2x}$.

To multiply, use the distributive property to *multiply* each term.

To divide, use the distributive property to *rewrite* the polynomial first.

$3x(x^2 + {}^-4x + 5) = 3x \cdot x^2 + (3x) \cdot ({}^-4x) + 3x \cdot 5$

$\quad = 3x^3 + {}^-12x^2 + 15x$ or

$\quad 3x^3 - 12x^2 + 15x$

$\dfrac{6x^2 - 4x}{2x} = \dfrac{2x(3x - 2)}{2x}$

$\quad = 3x - 2$

Multiply.

8. $3a(a + {}^-2)$ _____ $3a(a + 1)$ _____

9. $c(4c + d)$ _____ $2t(r + s)$ _____

248 Unit 9 Lesson 3

Name _____

Simplify by multiplying.

10. $5x(3x + {}^-2)$ _____ $x({}^-3x + y)$ _____

11. $4(x^2 + 2x + {}^-2)$ _____ $6(y^2 + 3y + 2)$ _____

12. $2a(3a + 4b + c)$ _____ $2r(3r + 4s + {}^-3)$ _____

13. ${}^-2a(3a + 4b + c)$ _____ ${}^-4x(2x + {}^-3y + 2z)$ _____

Simplify by dividing.

14. $\dfrac{9ab^2 + 3b}{3b}$ _____ $\dfrac{6a^2b + {}^-4b}{2b}$ _____

15. $\dfrac{12n^2 + 10n + 6}{2}$ _____ $\dfrac{16y^2 + {}^-8y + 12}{4}$ _____

16. $\dfrac{20x^3 + 15x^2 + 10x}{5x}$ _____ $\dfrac{12n^3 + 16n^2 + {}^-20n}{4n}$ _____

Problem Solving / Reasoning — Write an expression for the perimeter and area of the shaded figure.

17. 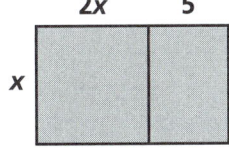   P: _____   A: _____

18. 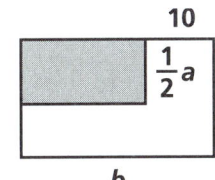   P: _____   A: _____

 Quick Check

Simplify.   Work Space.

19. 4^{-3} _____   **20.** $x^{-6} \div x^5$ _____

21. $(2^3 \cdot y) \cdot (3^2 \cdot y^5)$ _____   **22.** $\sqrt{64}$ _____

23. $8y^2 - {}^-2y^2$ _____   **24.** $8y^2 \cdot {}^-2y^2$ _____

25. $\dfrac{8y^2}{{}^-2y^2}$ _____   **26.** $3x(3x^2 + 7)$ _____

27. $6b^2 + 8b - (2b + 8b^2)$ _____

Name _____

Evaluating Polynomial Expressions

Remember, to **evaluate** or find the value of a variable expression, you substitute numbers for the variables. Then, find the value of the numerical expression. The value of the expression depends on the values for the variable.

Evaluate **3x + 4** for **x = 2** and **x = ⁻2**.

- Substitute **2** for *x*. Then evaluate.

  $3x + 4$
  $3(2) + 4$
  $6 + 4$
  10

- Substitute **⁻2** for *x*. Then evaluate.

  $3x + 4$
  $3(⁻2) + 4$
  $⁻6 + 4$
  $⁻2$

When you evaluate polynomials, you evaluate them in the same way.

Evaluate $3x^2 - x - 4$ for $x = 2$ and $x = ⁻2$.

- Substitute **2** for *x* in each term. Then evaluate.

  $3x^2 - x - 4$
  $3(2)^2 - (2) - 4$
  $3(4) - 2 - 4$
  $12 - 2 - 4$
  6

- Substitute **⁻2** for *x* in each term. Then evaluate.

  $3x^2 - x - 4$
  $3(⁻2)^2 - (⁻2) - 4$
  $3(4) + 2 - 4$
  $12 + 2 - 4$
  10

Evaluate the expressions.

1. $2x^2 - 3x + 1$ for $x = 2$

   _____

2. $3x^5 + 4x - 7$ for $x = 1$

   _____

3. $7x^3 - 2x^2 + 1x$ for $x = ⁻1$

   _____

4. $⁻2x^2 - x + 3$ for $x = ⁻2$

   _____

5. $⁻4x^2 + 5x - 2$ for $x = 3$

   _____

6. $6x^4 + 5x^2 + 12$ for $x = 0$

   _____

Evaluate the expressions to complete the tables below.

7.

x	⁻x²	2	⁻x² + 2
⁻1			
0			
1			
2			
3			

8.

y	2y²	y	⁻3	2y² + y − 3
⁻1				
0				
1				
2				
3				

Name _____

One way to evaluate polynomial expressions is to use an **electronic spreadsheet,** a computer program that organizes, uses, and stores numerical data. A spreadsheet looks like a table. As you change a value in one **cell** (box), the program automatically changes the values in all the other cells.

> On a computer X^2 means X^2.

Study the spreadsheet below and determine the missing data.

	Evaluating a Polynomial Expression				
	X	X^2	5X	−2	X^2 + 5X − 2
9.	0	0	0	−2	
10.	1	1		−2	4
11.	2		10	−2	12
12.	3			−2	22
13.	4	16	20		
14.	5	25		−2	48
15.	6		30	−2	64
16.	7	49		−2	
17.	8	64	40		102

Problem Solving Reasoning

If you toss a ball up in the air at a rate of 20 meters per second, then the formula $h = {}^-5t^2 + 20t$ gives the height of the ball above the ground at time t seconds. Complete the spreadsheet. Then, answer the questions.

18.

T	−5T^2	20T	−5T^2 + 20T
1			
2			
3			
4			

19. How long is the ball in the air before it hits the ground?

_____

20. After how many seconds does the ball reach its highest height? What is its highest height?

_____

Test Prep ★ Mixed Review

Circle the letter of your choice.

21. What is the simplest form of the expression $m^{-2} \cdot m^5 \cdot m^{-3}$?

A m^{30} **C** $3m^{-30}$

B m^{-30} **D** 1

22. Which polynomial can be simplified to the expression $2xy + 3$?

F $\dfrac{14x^3y^3 + 21x^2y^2}{7xy}$ **G** $\dfrac{14x^3y^3 + 21x^2y^2}{7}$

H $\dfrac{14x^3y^3 + 21x^2y^2}{7x^2y^2}$ **J** $\dfrac{14x^3y^3 + 21x^2y^2}{7x^3y^3}$

Name _____

Problem Solving Application: Choose an Equation

In this lesson, equations are used to model problem situations. Clues in a problem can help you decide whether to choose an addition, subtraction, multiplication, or division equation. The following information is known.

- The yearly cost is **$1,800**
- There are **12** months in a year.

Understanding the relationship between the units in a problem will help you decide on the correct operation.

> The yearly cost for renting a car from a dealer is **$1,800**. If n = *the cost per month*, then which equation below could be used to find the cost per month?
>
> A $n + 12 = 1{,}800$ C $n \cdot 12 = 1{,}800$
>
> B $n - 12 = 1{,}800$ D $\dfrac{n}{12} = 1{,}800$

Tips to Remember:

1. Understand   2. Decide   3. Solve   4. Look back

- Ask yourself whether you have solved a problem like this before.
- Think about the relationships between the units. Which operation do you use to relate the units or data in the problem? What unit will the solution have?
- Think about the strategies you have learned, and use them to help you solve a problem.

Solve.

1. In the problem above, which equation (A, B, C, or D) models the situation correctly?

   Think: What operation do you use to write years as months? What expression do you use to write the monthly cost given the yearly cost?

   _____

   _____

   Answer _____

2. The quotient of **twice** a number x and **three** is **4**. Which equation, $\dfrac{2x}{3} = 4$ or $\dfrac{x + 2}{3} = 4$, models the situation correctly?

   Think: Which operation do you use for "twice" a number? Which operation do you use to find a quotient?

   _____

   _____

   Answer _____

252 Unit 9 Lesson 5

Choose the appropriate equation. Do not solve. Explain why you choose the equation.

3. If you divide Mara's age by **4**, then take away **2** more years, you get **10**. How old is Mara?

A $\frac{n}{4} + 2 = 10$ C $4n + 2 = 10$

B $\frac{n}{4} - 2 = 10$ D $4n - 2 = 10$

_____

4. Mara takes **4** piano lessons per month. The total cost per month is **$60**. How much does each piano lesson cost?

F $n + 4 = 60$ H $4n = 60$

G $n - 4 = 60$ J $\frac{n}{4} = 60$

_____

5. The rent for a basement apartment is **$20** less per month than for a first floor apartment. The rental fee for a basement apartment is **$750**. What is the rental fee for the first floor apartment?

A $n + 20 = 750$ C $20n = 750$

B $n - 20 = 750$ D $\frac{n}{20} = 750$

_____

6. Dante wants to buy some used furniture for **$875**. He has saved **$650** toward the total cost. How much more does he need?

F $650 + n = 875$ H $650n = 875$

G $650 - n = 875$ J $\frac{n}{650} = 875$

_____

7. A used typewriter costs about $\frac{1}{2}$ the price of a new one. If a used typewriter costs **$90**, how much did it cost new?

A $n + \frac{1}{2} = 90$ C $2n = 90$

B $n - \frac{1}{2} = 90$ D $\frac{n}{2} = 90$

_____

8. The product of two and the sum of a number increased by three is the same as the number decreased by **4**.

F $2(n + 3) = n - 4$ H $2n + 3 = n - 4$

G $(2 + n) \cdot 3 = 4 - n$ J $n^2 + 3 = n - 4$

_____

Extend Your Thinking

9. Choose a problem. Then, use the equation you picked to solve the problem. Check your answer in the original problem. Did you pick the correct equation?

_____

10. Explain your method for choosing the correct equation in problem **8**. Which words or phrases helped you choose the operation?

_____

Unit 9 Lesson 5

Name _____ **Scientific Notation**

A fast and accurate way to express numbers such as those to the right is to use **scientific notation**. In scientific notation, a number is written as the product of a factor between **1** and **10** and a power of ten.

> A light year is about **9,460,000,000,000** kilometers.
>
> The diameter of an electron is about **0.0000000000010** centimeters.

For example:

- **4,000** can be written as: 4×1000 or 4×10^3.
- **0.004** can be written as: 4×0.001 or 4×10^{-3}.

Use these steps to write greater or lesser numbers in scientific notation.

Greater Numbers

Write in scientific notation:
9,460,000,000,000

1. Move the decimal point to the left to get a number between **1** and **10**. Count the number of places you moved the decimal point. That number is the exponent of the power of **10**.

   9.460,000,000,000.

   12 places, so the exponent is 12. Exponents for greater numbers are positive.

2. Write the number in scientific notation.

   9.46×10^{12}

   a number between 1 and 10   *a positive power of 10*

Lesser Numbers

Write in scientific notation:
0.0000000000010

1. Move the decimal point to the right to get a number between **1** and **10**. Count the number of places you moved the decimal point. That number is the exponent of the power of **10**.

   0.0000000000010

   12 places, so the exponent is 12. Exponents for lesser numbers are negative.

2. Write the number in scientific notation.

   1.0×10^{-12}

   a number between 1 and 10   *a negative power of 10*

Express the number in scientific notation.

1. 300 _____   40,000 _____   700,000 _____

2. 264 _____   92,400 _____   58 _____

3. 6,100 _____   8,400,000 _____   6,429,500 _____

Express the decimal in scientific notation.

4. 0.05 _____   0.095 _____   0.00000000001 _____

5. 0.862 _____   0.0000567 _____   0.006 _____

6. 0.00937 _____   0.0695 _____   0.01684 _____

Name _____

You can write a number that is in scientific notation in standard form.

Write in standard form: 7.2×10^4

A positive power of **10** represents a number greater than **1**.

*Move the decimal point **4** places to the right. Write zeros as needed.*

7.2×10^4

Write zeros to the right as needed.

7.2000.

$7.2 \times 10^4 = 72{,}000$

Write in standard form: 8.4×10^{-7}

A negative power of **10** represents a number between **0** and **1**.

*Move the decimal point **7** places to the left. Write zeros as needed.*

8.4×10^{-7}

Write zeros to the left as needed.

0.0000008.4

$8.4 \times 10^{-7} = 0.00000084$

Write these numbers in standard form.

7. 5.683×10^{-2} _____ 2.345×10^{-8} _____

8. 1.834×10^4 _____ 4.1012×10^{-6} _____

9. 9.36×10^{-5} _____ 8.4368×10^6 _____

10. 7.7519×10^{-9} _____ 7.73192×10^7 _____

11. 9.3×10^{12} _____ 3.9768×10^{-7} _____

Choose the standard form of the number given in scientific notation.

12. 7.3×10^4	0.00073	7.3	7,300	73,000
13. 9.1×10^{-2}	0.0091	0.091	0.00091	910
14. 8.65×10^2	865	8.65	0.0865	0.865
15. 6×10^{-3}	0.006	0.00006	0.6	6
16. 3.52×10^{-4}	352	0.0352	0.352	0.000352
17. 9.9×10^5	9,900	99,900	99,000	990,000
18. 1.92×10^{-1}	0.000192	0.192	192	0.0192

Unit 9 Lesson 6 **255**

Sometimes a number may look as if it is written in scientific notation, but the first factor is not between **1** and **10**. In this case, to be in scientific notation, it must be rewritten in correct form.

$98 \times 10^4 = 9.8 \times 10^5$ $0.04 \times 10^{-5} = 4 \times 10^{-7}$ $0.53 \times 10^{-2} = 5.3 \times 10^{-3}$

Write these numbers in scientific notation.

19. 95×10^4 _____ 0.001×10^{-10} _____

20. 75.7×10^{10} _____ 56.29×10^{-4} _____

21. 960×10^5 _____ 0.058×10^{-3} _____

22. 855×10^7 _____ 75×10^{-8} _____

23. 87.4×10^9 _____ 984.3×10^{-9} _____

24. Lightning strikes Earth about 864×10^4 times a year. _____

Problem Solving Reasoning — Solve.

25. Write in standard form: An average size thundercloud holds about 610×10^{10} raindrops.

_____

26. Write in standard form: The diameter of an atom is about 106×10^{-10} centimeters.

_____

27. Is 2.36×10^8 closer to **200** million or **1** billion? Explain.

_____

28. Is 0.03×10^2 greater than **1** or between **0** and **1**?

_____

 ## Quick Check

Evaluate the expressions.

29. $x^2 - 3x + 2$ for $x = 2$ _____   **30.** $8 + 5x - 2x^3$ for $x = {}^-2$ _____

Work Space.

Write in scientific notation.

31. 0.00000678   **32.** 3,050,000,000   **33.** 17.9×10^{-2}

_____   _____   _____

Write in standard form.

34. 2.3×10^{-4} _____   **35.** 1.98×10^5 _____

Name _____

Solving Equations with Rational Numbers

You know how to solve equations using positive numbers. In this unit you will apply those same rules to solve equations with integers and rational numbers. Remember, addition and subtraction are inverse operations.

> **Solving Addition and Subtraction Equations**
> - To solve an addition equation, you subtract the same number from each side of the equation.
> - To solve a subtraction equation, you add the same number to each side of the equation.

Solve: $x + 5 = 2$

1. Original equation $\qquad x + 5 = 2$
2. Subtract 5 from each side. $\qquad x + 5 - 5 = 2 - 5$
3. Simplify each side. $\qquad x = {}^-3$

√ Check: $x + 5 = 2$

$\quad {}^-3 + 5 = 2$

Solve: $x - \frac{3}{4} = 2$

1. Original equation $\qquad x - \frac{3}{4} = 2$
2. Add $\frac{3}{4}$ to each side. $\qquad x - \frac{3}{4} + \frac{3}{4} = 2 + \frac{3}{4}$
3. Simplify each side. $\qquad x = 2 + \frac{3}{4}$
4. Write 2 as a fraction. $\qquad x = \frac{8}{4} + \frac{3}{4}$

$\qquad\qquad\qquad\qquad\qquad x = \frac{11}{4}$ or $2\frac{3}{4}$

√ Check: $x - \frac{3}{4} = 2$

$\quad 2\frac{3}{4} - \frac{3}{4} = 2$

Solve these addition and subtraction equations. Check your answer by substitution.

1. $c + {}^-15 = 7$ _____ $12 = b + 32$ _____ $16 + x = 25$ _____

2. $b + 5.2 = 8.9$ _____ $18 + x = {}^-15$ _____ $8.4 + x = 6.2$ _____

3. $12 - b = 17$ _____ $15 - x = 9$ _____ $y - 9 = 12$ _____

4. ${}^-17 - a = 20$ _____ $x - 11 = {}^-4$ _____ $a - 6 = {}^-12$ _____

Unit 9 Lesson 7 257

Solve these addition and subtraction equations. Check your answer by substitution.

5. $a + 23 = 19$ _____ $104 = 92 + a$ _____ $b + 47 = {}^-15$ _____

6. ${}^-86 + n = 100$ _____ $b + 3.6 = 5.2$ _____ $x + {}^-78 = 33$ _____

7. $\frac{3}{4} + y = \frac{5}{4}$ _____ $\frac{5}{8} + x = 1\frac{1}{8}$ _____ $\frac{9}{11} - n = \frac{3}{11}$ _____

8. $b - \frac{4}{7} = 1\frac{2}{7}$ _____ $x + \frac{5}{9} = \frac{-7}{9}$ _____ $z + \frac{2}{3} = \frac{1}{12}$ _____

Remember, multiplication and division are inverse operations too.

> **Solving Multiplication and Division Equations**
> - To solve a multiplication equation, you divide each side of the equation by the same nonzero number.
> - To solve a division equation, you multiply each side of the equation by the same nonzero number.

Solve: $6n = {}^-30$

1. Original equation $\qquad 6n = {}^-30$
2. Divide each side by 6. $\qquad \frac{6n}{6} = \frac{-30}{6}$
3. Simplify each side. $\qquad 1 \cdot n = {}^-5$
$\qquad\qquad\qquad\qquad\quad n = {}^-5$

√ Check: $6n = {}^-30$
$\qquad\quad 6({}^-5) = {}^-30$

Solve: $\frac{x}{3} = \frac{-5}{6}$

1. Original equation $\qquad \frac{x}{3} = \frac{-5}{6}$
2. Multiply each side by 3. $\qquad 3\left(\frac{x}{3}\right) = 3\left(\frac{-5}{6}\right)$
3. Simplify each side. $\qquad x = \frac{-5}{2}$

√ Check: $\frac{x}{3} = \frac{-5}{6}$
$\qquad\quad \frac{\frac{-5}{2}}{3} = \left(\frac{-5}{2}\right)\left(\frac{1}{3}\right)$
$\qquad\qquad = \frac{-5}{6}$

Name _____

Solve the multiplication or division equation. Check your answer by substitution.

9. $7x = 28$ _____ $4c = {}^-36$ _____ $2a = {}^-144$ _____ $9n = {}^-81$ _____

10. $\frac{8}{9}x = 64$ _____ $2.3x = 12.88$ _____ $2a = {}^-28$ _____ $3b = 57$ _____

11. $2\frac{1}{4} = 7c$ _____ ${}^-228 = 4d$ _____ $3\frac{5}{6}y = 46$ _____ $\frac{2}{5} = \frac{3}{4}z$ _____

12. $7 = \frac{n}{9}$ _____ $\frac{-12}{x} = 3$ _____ $\frac{x}{2} = {}^-32$ _____ $\frac{1}{4} = \frac{4}{z}$ _____

Problem Solving Reasoning

You can use what you know about solving equations to rewrite formulas. For example, $A = lw$ can be rewritten as $l = \frac{A}{w}$ and $w = \frac{A}{l}$. So $l = \frac{A}{w}$ means that you can find the length by dividing the area by the width.

13. Rewrite the formula for the circumference of a circle $C = \pi d$ for d.

_____

14. Rewrite the formula for the perimeter of a triangle $P = a + b + c$ for b.

_____

Test Prep ★ Mixed Review

15. If $a = {}^-3$, what is the value of the polynomial $2a^2 + 3a - 4$?

   A ${}^-31$ C 5
   B ${}^-5$ D 23

16. A man said that he had 4.735×10^4 pennies. How much money does he have?

   F $4.735   H $473.50
   G $47.35   J $4,735

Name _____   **Solving Two-Step Equations**

A two-step equation is an equation that has two operations. When solving a two-step equation, you must follow the order of operations.

Solve: $5x + 33 = 63$ | $\sqrt{}$ Check by substitution.

1. Original equation. $5x + 33 = 63$
2. Add $^-33$ to each side. $5x + (33 + {^-33}) = 63 + {^-33}$

$5x = 30$

3. Divide each side by 5. $\dfrac{5x}{5} = \dfrac{30}{5}$
4. Simplify. $1x = 6$

$x = 6$

Check:
$5x + 33 = 63$
$(5 \cdot 6) + 33 = 63$
$30 + 33 = 63$
$63 = 63$

Sometimes you need to simplify the equation before you solve for the variable.

Solve: $3 \cdot 4 + x = 17$ | $\sqrt{}$ Check by substitution.

1. Original equation. $3 \cdot 4 + x = 17$
2. Multiply. $12 + x = 17$
3. Add $^-12$ to each side. $(12 + {^-12}) + x = 17 + {^-12}$
4. Simplify. $0 + x = 5$

$x = 5$

Check:
$3 \cdot 4 + x = 17$
$3 \cdot 4 + 5 = 17$
$12 + 5 = 17$
$17 = 17$

Solve the equation. Remember to perform all possible calculations before solving for the variable.

1. $7 \cdot 6 + x = 45$ _____ $4 \cdot 4 + n = 25$ _____ $5 \cdot 7 + y = 39$ _____

2. $3 \cdot 6 + c = 50$ _____ $10 \cdot 8 + a = 92$ _____ $9 \cdot 8 + b = 80$ _____

Name _____

Solve the equation. Show all your work. The first one is done for you.

3. $3x + 5 = 23$ $\qquad$ $4a + 8 = 32$ $\qquad$ $8c + 6 = 62$

$3x + (5 + {}^-5) = 23 + {}^-5$

$\qquad 3x = 18$

$\qquad \dfrac{3x}{3} = \dfrac{18}{3}$

$\qquad x = 6$

4. $21 + 7x = 105$ $\qquad$ $7.6 + 4x = 10.4$ $\qquad$ $8x + 15 = {}^-89$

5. $2.3y + 1.2 = 10.4$ $\qquad$ $5n + {}^-11 = 24$ $\qquad$ $6y + 12 = 99$

When you solve an equation with subtraction, you need to write it as addition before you solve for the variable.

	Solve: $6x - 8 = 34$	Check by substitution.
1. Original equation.	$6x - 8 = 34$	$6x - 8 = 34$
2. Rewrite the subtraction as an addition.	$6x + {}^-8 = 34$	$6(7) - 8 = 34$
3. Add 8 to each side.	$6x + ({}^-8 + 8) = 34 + 8$	$42 - 8 = 34$
4. Simplify each side.	$6x + 0 = 42$	
	$6x = 42$	
5. Divide each side by 6.	$\dfrac{6x}{6} = \dfrac{42}{6}$	
6. Simplify each side.	$1x = 7$	
	$x = 7$	

Solve the equation. Show your work.

6. $9x - 8 = 55$ $\qquad$ $65 = 8 \cdot 9 - y$ $\qquad$ $12x - 6 = 90$

Solve the two-step equation. Show your work.

7. $23 = 13 - 2a$ $7c - 14 = 49$ $6m - 4 = 3.2$

8. $^-16x - {^-7} = {^-121}$ $4.5b - {^-1.8} = 12.15$ $\frac{3}{4}x - \frac{1}{8} = \frac{1}{4}$

Problem Solving / Reasoning — Choose an equation that could be used to solve the problem. Then, solve the equation.

9. The difference of **4** and twice a number is **50**. What is the number?

   Choose $4 - 2x = 50$ or $2x - 4 = 50$

10. The sum of $^-6$ and twice a number is **24**. What is the number?

    Choose $^-6 + 24 = 2x$ or $^-6 + 2x = 24$

Quick Check

Solve these equations. Show your work.

Work Space.

11. $^-8x = 24$ _____

12. $z + 4 = {^-12}$ _____

13. $4 = x - 1.5$ _____

14. $\frac{x}{7} = {^-9.2}$ _____

15. $\frac{3}{4}n - 3 = 5$ _____

16. $\frac{3x - 4}{3} = 5$ _____

Name _____

Equations and Inequalities

The word phrase "the sum of four and seven" can be written as the numerical expression "4 + 7." In order to understand and solve problems, it is important to be able to write word phrases as numerical or algebraic expressions and to write expressions using words.

Word Phrase	Expression
The sum of **12** and **x**	$12 + x$
The product of **6** and **y**	$6y$
The product of **20** and the difference of **8** and **3**	$20(8 - 3)$
The quotient of **18** and **5**	$\frac{18}{5}$ or $18 \div 5$
The difference between the opposite of **7** and **6**	$^-7 - 6$

Write as word phrases.

1. $9 + 19$ _____

2. $58 \div x$ _____

3. $16 \div 4$ _____

4. $\frac{y}{32}$ _____

5. $11(7 - x)$ _____

6. $^-14 - 36$ _____

7. $36 - 11$ _____

8. $(3 + a)9$ _____

Write an expression.

9. Six more than eleven _____   The sum of **a** and thirteen _____

10. Three increased by nine _____   The product of five and nine _____

11. Two times **x** _____   The quotient of thirty-two divided by **y** _____

12. Eight less than fifty _____   Ten percent of eighty-five _____

Just as the verb in a word sentence tells you what kind of sentence you have, a symbol such as =, <, >, or ≠ tells you what kind of number sentence you have. You know that a number sentence that has an = sign in it is an equation. In an equation, the expressions on each side of the = have the same value.

Symbols
= is equal to
\> is greater than
< is less than
≥ is greater than or equal to, or is at least
≤ is less than or equal to, or is at most
≠ is not equal to

Word Equation   **Equation**

Ten is three less than *x*. $10 = x - 3$

The product of **6** and *y* is **30**. $6y = 30$

A number sentence that has an <, >, ≤, ≥, or ≠ sign in it is an **inequality**. In an inequality, the expressions on each side of the symbol do not have the same value.

Word Inequality   **Inequality**

The sum of two and *z* is greater than seven. $2 + z > 7$

The product of one half and *x* times the sum of negative five and three is less than or equal to **4**. $\frac{1}{2}x(^-5 + 3) \leq 4$

Write an equation or an inequality.

13. Seventeen is greater than fifteen. _____

14. The sum of one and three is equal to *y*. _____

15. The difference of *x* subtracted from six is less than two. _____

16. The product of nine times the sum of *a* and two equals twenty. _____

17. Negative seven is less than the sum of *n* and four. _____

18. The quotient of *z* divided by three is less than or equal to twelve. _____

19. One fourth of a number *y* is two more than one fifth of the number. _____

20. Three times the quotient of *m* divided by 4 is at least five. _____

21. Two thirds of a number *x* is at most five less than ten. _____

22. A number *z* decreased by two is equal to the product of three and *z*. _____

23. The quotient of three times a number *c* divided by nine is four. _____

24. A number *x* increased by the product of two and *y* is not equal to one. _____

Name _____

Write in words.

25. $17 > x$ _____

26. $y + 2 = 5$ _____

27. $14 - 2 = t$ _____

28. $x + y = 9$ _____

29. $b + 3 \leq 4$ _____

30. $7 - n > 1$ _____

31. $5x + 3 \neq 6x - 2$ _____
_____

32. $\frac{(1 + x)}{2} < 5$ _____

Problem Solving Reasoning — Write the expression using symbols and units of measure.

Examples:

The number of minutes in *x* hours   60*x* minutes
The number of days in *y* weeks   7*y* days

33. The number of feet in *x* yards _____

34. The number of ounces in *p* pounds _____

35. The number of millimeters in *m* meters _____

36. The number of inches in *x* feet increased by 5 _____

Test Prep ★ Mixed Review

37 If $x - 6.52 = {}^-4.01$, what is the value of *x*?

    A $^-10.53$ C   2.51
    B $^-2.51$ D   10.53

38 If $\frac{1}{3}n - \frac{5}{6} = \frac{1}{6}$, what is the value of *n*?

    F   3   H $\frac{1}{3}$
    G   2   J $\frac{2}{9}$

Unit 9 Lesson 9

Name _____

Problem Solving Strategy: Write an Equation

To solve problems, sometimes you can write an equation.

You need to read the problem to look for the facts and what you are trying to find. You can represent what you are trying to find with a variable.

Problem
Two students are comparing their stamp collections. Ron has 109 fewer stamps than Tara. Together they have 725 stamps. How many stamps does Ron have?

1 Understand

As you reread, ask yourself questions.

- What do you already know?

    Ron has **109** fewer stamps than Tara.

    Tara has **109** more stamps than Ron.

    Together Ron and Tara have **725** stamps.

- What do you need to find? _____

2 Decide

Choose a method for solving.

Try the strategy Write an Equation.

- Let s = the number of stamps Ron has.

    Ron's number and Tara's number = 725

    $$s + (s + 109) = 725$$

- Write the simplified equation. _____

3 Solve

Solve the addition equation.

Equation:

Be neat in your solution. Remember that whatever you do to one side of an equation, you must do the same to the other.

4 Look back

Check your answer.

Substitute your solution into the equation.

Write your answer as a full sentence.

Answer _____

What steps did you use to solve the problem?

_____

Use the Write an Equation strategy or any other strategy you have learned.

1. A student has **13** coins, all nickels and dimes, worth **$.95**. There is **1** dime less than there are nickels. How many nickels are there?

   Think: If there are *n* nickels, then how many dimes are there?

   _____

   _____

2. Carlo has **$3** more than twice as many dollars as Jake. If Carlo has **$15**, then how much does Jake have?

   Think: Carlo has $15 and Carlo has $3 more than twice as many dollars as Jake. What equation can you write?

   _____

   _____

3. The sum of three consecutive integers is **93**. What are the integers?

   _____

4. I am thinking of a number. If I add **63** to it the result is **13**. What number am I thinking of?

   _____

5. The towns of Dory, Elba, and Faro are all in a line on the same route. The town of Dory is **52** kilometers from Elba. Dory is **3.7** kilometers closer to Elba than Faro is. How far is Faro from Elba?

   _____

6. Manuel scored **8** fewer points than Will scored. Together they scored **44** points. How many points did Will score?

   _____

7. A student has **12** coins, all dimes and quarters. The value of the coins is **$1.95**. How many dimes are there?

   _____

8. It took **8** students **3** hours to clean up after a school play. How long would it have taken **6** students?

   _____

9. A submarine exploring the ocean floor is **300** meters below the surface. It takes **5** minutes to ascend to a depth of **100** meters. If the submarine is traveling at a constant rate, in how many more minutes will the submarine ascend to the surface?

   _____

10. It is **13°F** now. If the temperature is dropping at a constant rate of **4°F** per hour, what was the temperature $1\frac{1}{2}$ hours ago?

    _____

Name _____   **Solving Inequalities**

You know how to write an inequality to represent a verbal sentence. Now you will learn how to solve an inequality. Any number that makes the inequality true is a **solution of the inequality.**

What are the possible solutions for the inequality $x > 4$?

- Is **4** a solution?

  No, 4 is not greater than 4.

- Is $4\frac{1}{2}$ a solution?

  Yes, $4\frac{1}{2}$ is greater than 4.

- Is **4.0001** a solution?

  Yes, **4.0001** is greater than **4**.

If $x > 4$, then any rational or irrational number greater than 4 is a solution of the inequality.

To solve inequalities such as $x + 3 < 5$ or $x - 6 > 4$, you use inverse operations.

Solve: $x + 3 < 5$

1. Original inequality $x + 3 < 5$
2. Subtract 3 from each side. $x + 3 - 3 < 5 - 3$
3. Simplify each side. $x + 0 < 2$
                                 $x < 2$

Solve: $x - 6 \geq 4$

1. Original inequality $x - 6 \geq 4$
2. Add 6 to each side. $x - 6 + 6 \geq 4 + 6$
3. Simplify each side. $x + 0 \geq 10$
                                 $x \geq 10$

Check. Is the given value a solution of the inequality? Write *yes* or *no*.

1. $x + 20 > 25$ _____
   Given value: **10**

   $a - 8 < 18$ _____
   Given value: **⁻4**

   $y + 68 \neq 101$ _____
   Given value: **0**

2. $b + 2 > 3$ _____
   Given value: $\frac{1}{2}$

   $x - 2 < {}^-15$ _____
   Given value: **10**

   $(w - 5) + 7 < 18$ _____
   Given value: **6**

Solve.

3. $x - 3 < 9$ _____

   $x + 10 > {}^-5$ _____

   $x + 4 < {}^-10$ _____

4. $x + 8 > 3$ _____

   $x - 7 < {}^-5$ _____

   $x - 13 < {}^-7$ _____

5. $x - 9 < 3$ _____

   $x + 15 < {}^-3$ _____

   $x + 5 > {}^-16$ _____

Name _____

Multiply and divide each side of these inequalities by 2.
Decide whether the resulting inequality is still true.

6. $6 < 8$ $6 > {}^-8$ ${}^-6 > {}^-8$

_____   _____   _____

Multiply and divide each side of these inequalities by ${}^-2$.
Decide whether the resulting inequality is still true.

7. $6 < 8$ $6 > {}^-8$ ${}^-6 > {}^-8$

_____   _____   _____

From your computations in the last few exercises, you can see that:

> When both sides of an inequality are multiplied or divided by a **negative number,** the inequality sign must be reversed.

To solve inequalities such as $5x < 25$ or ${}^-8x < 4$, you use inverse operations, but when you multiply or divide by a negative number, you need to reverse the inequality sign.

Solve: $\dfrac{x}{3} < 5$

1. Original inequality $\qquad\qquad \dfrac{x}{3} < 5$

2. Multiply each side by 3. $\qquad 3 \cdot \dfrac{x}{3} < 3 \cdot 5$

3. Simplify each side. $\qquad\qquad 1x < 15$

$\qquad\qquad\qquad\qquad\qquad\qquad x < 15$

Solve: ${}^-8x < 4$

1. Original inequality $\qquad\qquad {}^-8x < 4$

2. Divide each side by ${}^-8$, $\qquad \dfrac{{}^-8x}{{}^-8} > \dfrac{4}{{}^-8}$
   and reverse the inequality.

3. Simplify each side. $\qquad\qquad 1x > \dfrac{1}{{}^-2}$

$\qquad\qquad\qquad\qquad\qquad\qquad x > {}^-\dfrac{1}{2}$

Solve.

8. $7x < 21$ _____ $\dfrac{1}{5}x < 11$ _____ $\dfrac{3}{7}x > 5$ _____

9. $3x > 20$ _____ ${}^-2x < 10$ _____ $\dfrac{2}{9}x < {}^-30$ _____

10. $\dfrac{3}{4}x > 24$ _____ ${}^-3x > {}^-16$ _____ $\dfrac{-1}{4}x > {}^-15$ _____

Unit 9 Lesson 11 **269**

To solve a two-step inequality, remember to always perform the operations in the correct order.

Solve: $3x + 2 \leq 3$

1. Original inequality $3x + 2 \leq 3$
2. Subtract 2 from each side. $3x + 2 - 2 < 3 - 2$
3. Simplify. $3x < 1$
4. Divide each side by 3. $\frac{3x}{3} < \frac{1}{3}$
5. Simplify. $x < \frac{1}{3}$

Solve: $^-x + 6 < 3$

1. Original inequality $^-x - 6 < 3$
2. Add 6 to each side. $^-x - 6 + 6 < 3 + 6$
3. Simplify. $^-x < 9$
4. Multiply each side by $^-1$. Reverse the inequality. $^-1 \cdot {^-x} > {^-1} \cdot 9$
5. Simplify. $1x > {^-9}$
   $x > {^-9}$

Solve these inequalities.

11. $3x + 1 > 10$ _____ $15x - 3 < 6$ _____ $\frac{x+1}{5} < 2$ _____

12. $4x + 3 > 9$ _____ $^-5x + 4 > 12$ _____ $^-3x - 7 > 8$ _____

Problem Solving Reasoning   For each problem, choose a variable. Then, write and solve an inequality.

13. A number is increased by ten. The result is at least 15. What is the number?

_____

14. Negative 8 is added to 5 times a number. The result is less than 2. What is the number?

_____

✓ Quick Check

Write the expression, equation, or inequality.   Work Space.

15. One third of a number n and seven _____

16. The product of a number y and three is greater than or equal to four. _____

17. The difference of negative eight from a number z is equal to negative one. _____

Solve the inequality.

18. $^-9x \geq {^-18}$ _____   **19.** $\frac{x+3}{2} \geq 3$ _____

Name _____

Unit 9 Review

Simplify.

1. 3^{-2} _____
2. $\left(\dfrac{-4}{5}\right)^2$ _____
3. $\left(\dfrac{-1}{2}\right)^{-3}$ _____
4. $\left(\dfrac{7}{11}\right)^0$ _____
5. $2^4 \cdot 2^{-7}$ _____
6. $3^{-5} \cdot 3^9$ _____
7. $x^3 \div x^{-2}$ _____
8. $(2^5 \cdot 5^3) \div (2^2 \cdot 5^4)$ _____

Write true or false.

9. $\sqrt{16} = 4$ _____
10. $\sqrt{44}$ is between 5 and 6. _____
11. $\sqrt{3}$ is a rational number. _____
12. $\sqrt{\dfrac{36}{49}} = \dfrac{6}{7}$ _____
13. In the monomial $3x^2$, 2 is a constant. _____
14. In the monomial $3x^2$, 3 is a coefficient. _____

Simplify.

15. $9x - {}^-3x$ _____
16. $b^5 \cdot b^7$ _____
17. $x^6 \div x^{10}$ _____
18. $5a - 3b + 6a + {}^-7b - {}^-8a$ _____
19. $(6x^2 - 4x) - ({}^-2x^2 - {}^-5x)$ _____
20. $8a^2 + 6a - 2 + 3a^2 - 5a - 7$ _____

Multiply or divide.

21. $4x(3x + 5)$
22. ${}^-2y(5 - 4y)$
23. $\dfrac{15a^2 - 5a + 10}{5}$
24. $\dfrac{8b^3 + 4b^2 - 12b}{4b}$

Evaluate the expression.

25. $x^2 - 5x + 7$ for $x = 2$
26. ${}^-3x^2 + 2x - 1$ for $x = {}^-1$
27. $x^3 - 4x + 2$ for $x = 3$

Express in scientific notation.

28. 7,000,000
29. 31,408,000
30. 9,460,000,000
31. $1,260 \times 10^4$
32. 0.00825
33. 0.0000068
34. 0.0000519
35. 0.015×10^{-2}

Express in standard form.

36. 4.267×10^{-8} _____

37. 8.228×10^{7} _____

Solve the equation. Use addition or subtraction.

38. $35 + y = 51$

39. $^{-}7 + d = 15$

40. $\frac{1}{6} + n = \frac{11}{18}$

41. $x + 15.6 = {^-}4.2$

42. $y - {^-}6 = {^-}13$

43. $^{-}9 - n = {^-}19$

Solve the equation. Use multiplication or division.

44. $\frac{x}{10} = {^-}20$

45. $9 = \frac{108}{y}$

46. $\frac{c}{^-2} = {^-}6$

47. $\frac{b}{8} = 9$

48. $\frac{13 \cdot 8}{d} = 2$

49. $\frac{156}{y} = 3$

Solve the two-step equation.

50. $8x + 4 = 60$

51. $9b - 10 = 26$

52. $\frac{2}{3}y - \frac{1}{6} = 7\frac{5}{6}$

53. $^{-}15x - {^-}8 = 233$

54. $2.7 + 6a = {^-}6.3$

55. $9.6n - {^-}2.6 = 6.44$

Name _____

Write an expression, an equation, or an inequality.

56. Four times the sum of six and *c* _____

57. The difference when six is subtracted from *c* is fifteen. _____

58. The quotient of *x* plus seven divided by three is less than ten. _____

Write in words. Word phrases or sentences may vary.

59. $^-6 + 4$ _____

60. $^-x < 15$ _____

61. $7 + \frac{5}{c} > 4$ _____

Solve these inequalities.

62. $3x + 4 < 7$

63. $^-2x - 5 > 8$

64. $\frac{3}{5}x - 4 \leq \frac{1}{2}$

_____   _____   _____

Choose an equation to solve the problem. Then solve.

65. The quotient of twice a number divided by three is four. What is the number?

$\frac{2x}{3} = 4$ or $\frac{x+2}{3} = 4$

_____

66. In December the new recreation center added **16** more videos to its collection. The new videos represent $\frac{1}{4}$ of the total number of videos. How many videos do they have in all?

$x \cdot \frac{1}{4} = 16$ or $16 = \frac{1}{4}x$

_____

Write an equation to solve this problem.

67. The average of two numbers is **14.6**. One of the numbers is **18**. What is the other number?

_____

Unit 9 Review **273**

Name _____

Cumulative Review
★ Test Prep

1 What is the missing measurement?

15.7 in.
?
Area = 144.44 in.²

A 128.74 in.   C 9.2 in.

B 15.7 in.   D 7.85 in.

2 This spreadsheet is using the formula $M = 0.037t^2 + 10$ to calculate figures for the number of movie theaters in the U.S. during certain years. What is the missing number?

t	t²	0.037t²	10	M
3	9	0.333	10	10.333
2	4	0.148	10	10.148
1	1	0.037	10	10.037
0	0	0	10	?

F 0   H 10.037

G 10   J 10.10

3 Which expression is equivalent to $24r^3s^2$?

A $4 \cdot r \cdot s \cdot 6 \cdot r \cdot s$

B $4 \cdot r \cdot r \cdot s \cdot 9 \cdot r \cdot s$

C $7 \cdot r \cdot s \cdot r \cdot 3 \cdot s \cdot r$

D $r \cdot 8 \cdot s \cdot r \cdot 3 \cdot s \cdot r$

4 It takes 20 workers about 2.5 days to prepare a building site. How many workers would you need to complete the job in just about 1.5 days?

F 12   H 33

G 18   J 50

5 Which describes a scalene triangle?

A no congruent sides

B 2 or 3 congruent sides

C all angles less than 90°

D one angle greater than 90°

6 $\frac{-2}{3}$ and $\frac{5}{6}$ are factors of what product?

F $-\frac{5}{9}$

G $-\frac{9}{5}$

H $\frac{5}{9}$

J $\frac{7}{18}$

7 At a grand opening of the arts and crafts store, every 3rd person who enters the store gets a drawing pen. Every 5th person gets a pad of paper. Every 20th person gets a gift certificate for $5. Which person is the first person to get all three gifts?

A the 28th person

B the 50th person

C the 60th person

D the 300th person

8 If $a + b = 4$, and $a - b = 38$, what are the values of a and b?

F $a = {}^-21, b = 17$

G $a = 21, b = {}^-17$

H $a = 21, b = 17$

J $a = {}^-21, b = {}^-17$

K Not here

UNIT 10 • TABLE OF CONTENTS

Using Formulas in Geometry

Lesson	Page
1 Circumference and Area of Circles	277
2 Complex Plane Figures	280
3 Area of a Trapezoid	283
4 **Algebra** • Area of Regular Polygons	285
5 Estimating the Area of Irregular Plane Figures on a Grid	287
6 **Problem Solving Strategy:** Solve a Simpler Problem	289
7 Spatial Visualization with Nets	291
8 Surface Area of Prisms	293
9 Surface Area of Cylinders	296
10 Volume of Prisms	298
11 Volume of Composite Space Figures	300
12 **Algebra** • Relating Length, Area, and Volume	302
13 Volume of Cylinders	304
14 **Problem Solving Application:** Use a Diagram	306
15 **Algebra** • Pythagorean Property of Right Triangles	308
• Unit 10 Review	311

Dear Family,

During the next few weeks, our math class will be reviewing how to find area, finding surface area, and volume.

You can expect to see homework that provides practice with these skills. Here is a sample you may want to keep handy to give help when needed.

Finding the surface area of a rectangular prism

A rectangular prism has three dimensions: length, width, and height. You can use these dimensions to find its surface area.

To find the surface area, add the areas of all six faces. The area of a rectangle is found by multiplying the length times the width.

SA = lw + lw + lh + lh + wh + wh
= 2(8 · 12) + 2(12 · 4) + 2(8 · 4)
= 192 + 96 + 64
= 352

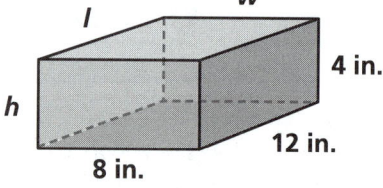

The surface area of the prism is **352** square inches.

To find the volume of the prism, multiply the length times the width times the height. This is written as the formula **V = lwh**. For this prism, the volume is **4 in. · 8 in. · 12 in. = 384** cubic inches.

During this unit, students will continue to learn new techniques related to problem solving and will continue to practice basic skills with fractions and decimals.

Sincerely,

We will be using this vocabulary:

area the measure of a region within a closed curve

circumference the distance around a circle

cone a space figure with a circular base and another surface that is curved

cube a rectangular prism whose faces are congruent squares

cylinder a space figure with two congruent circular bases that are joined by a curved surface

diameter of a circle a chord that goes through the center of the circle

prism a space figure with two faces that are congruent and parallel and whose other faces are parallelograms

pyramid a space figure with a polygonal base and whose other sides are triangles

rectangular prism a space figure all of whose faces are rectangles

Name _____

Circumference and Area of Circles

A **circle** is a plane figure with points all the same distance from a given point called the **center**.

A segment from any point on a circle to the center is a **radius (r)**.

A segment that joins any two points on a circle is a **chord**.

Any chord that contains the center of a circle is a **diameter (d)**. A diameter is twice as long as a radius ($d = 2r$).

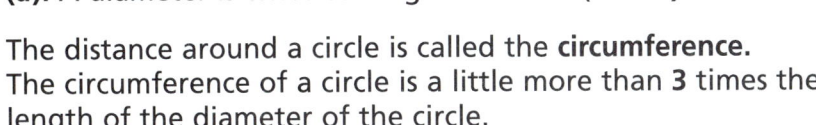

The distance around a circle is called the **circumference**. The circumference of a circle is a little more than **3** times the length of the diameter of the circle.

The ratio $\frac{\text{circumference}}{\text{diameter}}$ was named by the Greeks as π **(pi)**.

The value of pi cannot be written as an exact decimal. It is an **irrational number**, that is, its decimal form never repeats or terminates.

Use $\frac{22}{7}$ or **3.14** as close approximations for π.

You can review the formulas for finding the circumference of a circle.

$$C = \pi d \text{ or } C = 2\pi r$$

Find the circumference of the circle to the nearest tenth. Use **3.14** for π.

$C = \pi d$

≈ 3.14 · 4.9 cm

≈ 15.386 cm ➡ **15.4** cm

(4.9 cm)

Find the circumference of the circle. Use $\frac{22}{7}$ for π.

$C = 2\pi r$

≈ $2 \cdot \frac{22}{7} \cdot 3\frac{1}{2}$ in.

≈ $2 \cdot \frac{22}{7} \cdot \frac{7}{2}$ in.

≈ **22** in.

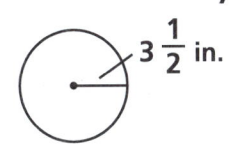
$3\frac{1}{2}$ in.

Find the circumference of the circle. Use $\frac{22}{7}$ for π.

	Diameter	14 m	15.4 mm	$3\frac{1}{2}$ ft	$7\frac{2}{3}$ in.	42.07 cm	$3\frac{1}{3}$ yd
1.	Circumference						

Find the diameter and circumference to the nearest tenth. Use 3.14 for π.

	Radius	63 cm	32 m	6 dm	5 cm	9 km	3 m
2.	Diameter						
3.	Circumference						

Unit 10 Lesson 1 277

Here is a way to think about the area of a circle. The circle to the right has been divided into **20** sections. Half of the circle has been shaded. Separate the sections and arrange them as shown.

This arrangement resembles a parallelogram whose base is half the circumference of the circle and whose height is the radius.

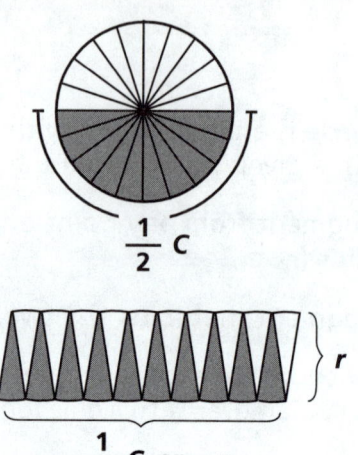

Area of a parallelogram: $A = bh$

Area of a circle: $A = \frac{1}{2} C \cdot r$
$= \frac{1}{2}(2\pi r) \cdot r$
$= \pi r^2$

Find the area to the nearest tenth. Use **3.14** for π.

$A = \pi r^2$
$= 3.14 \cdot 15 \text{ cm}^2$
$= 3.14 \cdot 225 \text{ cm}^2$
$= 706.5 \text{ cm}^2$

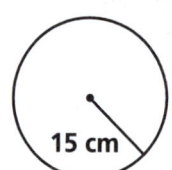

Find the area of the circle. Use $\frac{22}{7}$ for π.

$A = \pi r^2$
$= \frac{22}{7}(42 \div 2)^2 \text{ in.}^2$
$= \frac{22}{7} \times \overset{3}{\cancel{21}} \times 21 \text{ in.}^2$
$= 1{,}386 \text{ in.}^2$

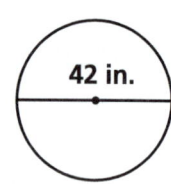

Complete the table. Use either 3.14 or $\frac{22}{7}$ as an approximation for π.

4. Radius	14 m	10.5 cm			$1\frac{3}{4}$ in.		63 ft	
5. Diameter			52 ft	$3\frac{1}{2}$ yd		56 in.		$4\frac{2}{3}$ yd
6. Area								

Find the area of the shaded region.

7.

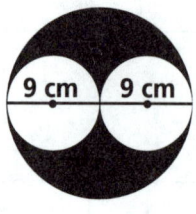

8.

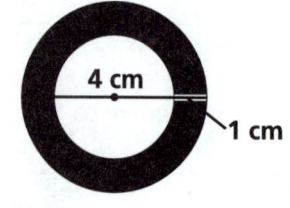

278 Unit 10 Lesson 1

Name _____

If you know the circumference of a circle, you can find its diameter or radius.

What is the diameter of a circular mirror whose circumference is **44** in.?

1. Use the formula.

$C = \pi d$, so $\dfrac{C}{\pi} = d$

2. Substitute.

$\dfrac{44}{\frac{22}{7}} \approx d$

3. Evaluate.

$d \approx \overset{2}{\cancel{44}} \cdot \dfrac{7}{\underset{1}{\cancel{22}}} \rightarrow 14$ in.

Find the missing measures.

9.	Radius						
10.	Diameter						
	Circumference	77 in.	198 ft	176 yd	66 in.	88 mi	76 yd

11. the area of a circular lamp base that is **20** cm in diameter _____

12. the total television viewing area for a **51**-mile radius _____

13. the distance a tire that is **70** cm in diameter travels in one revolution

_____

14. the area of the largest circle that can be cut out from a

9 in. by **12** in. piece of construction paper _____

Problem Solving Reasoning

The decimal form of irrational numbers, such as π, are non-terminating and non-repeating. Choose the irrational number in each pair and explain your choice.

15. a. 0.010101...
b. 0.010010001...

16. a. 0.525522555222...
b. 0.5255255255...

Test Prep ★ Mixed Review

17. What is the simplest form of the expression $m^3 \cdot m^8 \cdot m^{-5}$?

A m^{120}

B m^6

C m^{-6}

D m^{-120}

18. If $a = {}^-4$, what is the value of the polynomial $2a^2 - 3a + 4$?

F 48

G 24

H ${}^-24$

J ${}^-48$

Unit 10 Lesson 1 **279**

Name _____

Complex Plane Figures

Area is the measure of how much surface a figure covers. To find the area of a figure like the one shown at the right, you may need to use more than one formula. This figure is called a **complex figure** because it is made up of different geometric figures.

Find the area of the figure.

1. Divide the figure into different geometric figures. Draw $\overline{AB}$. Label vertices of all the figures you see. Find any missing lengths.

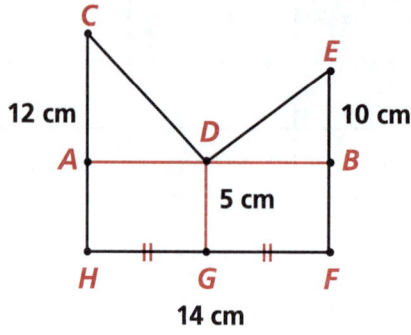

- Rectangle *ABFH* is **14** cm long and **5** cm wide.

- $\overline{DG}$ divides the base into **2** congruent segments **7** cm long.

- Since $\overline{AB}$ is congruent to $\overline{HF}$, $\overline{AD}$ = **7** cm and $\overline{DB}$ = **7** cm.

- △ *ADC* has a base of **7** cm and a height of (12 cm − 5 cm), or **7** cm.

- △ *BDE* has a base of **7** cm and a height of (10 cm − 5 cm), or **5** cm.

2. Find the area of each different figure.

• Triangle *ACD*

$A = \frac{1}{2}bh$ or $\frac{b \cdot h}{2}$

$= \frac{7 \cdot 7}{2} \rightarrow \frac{49}{2}$ or **24.5** cm²

• Triangle *BED*

$A = \frac{b \cdot h}{2}$

$= \frac{7 \cdot 5}{2} \rightarrow \frac{35}{2}$ or **17.5** cm²

• Rectangle *ABFH*

$A = lw$

$= 14 \cdot 5 \rightarrow$ **70** cm²

3. Find the sum of the areas.

A = 24.5 cm² + 17.5 cm² + 70 cm² → **112** cm²

The total area of the complex figure above is **112** cm².

Find the area. Draw segments where needed.

1.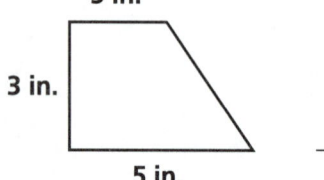

   _____

2.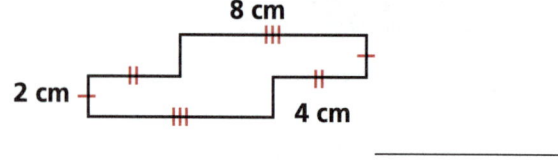

   _____

280 Unit 10 Lesson 2

Name _____

Find the area of the complex figures. Draw segments when you need to.

3.
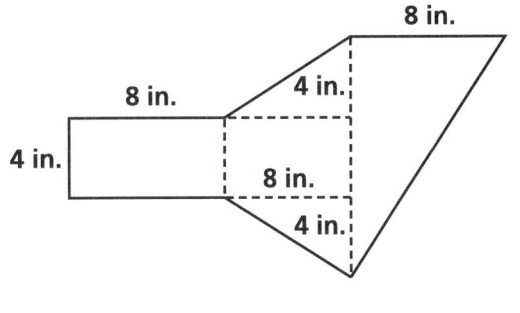
_____

4.
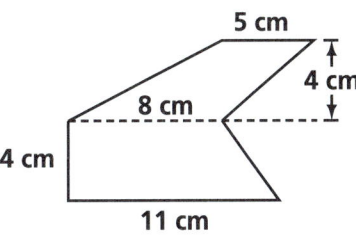
_____

5.
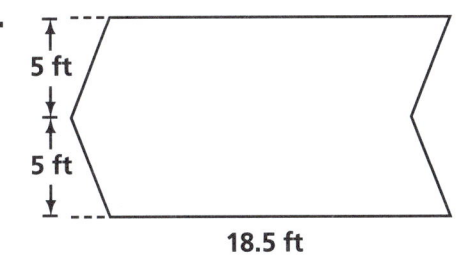
_____

6.
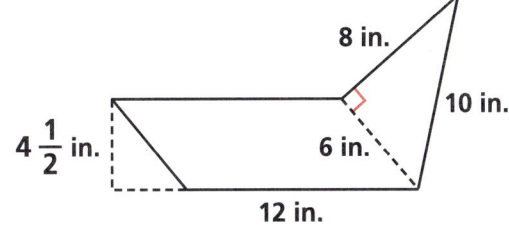
_____

7.
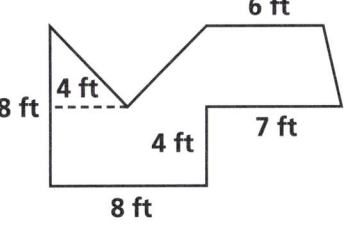
_____

8.
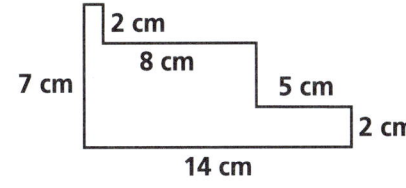
_____

9.
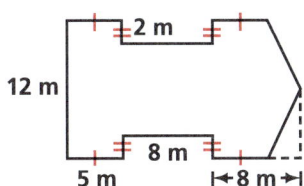
_____

10.
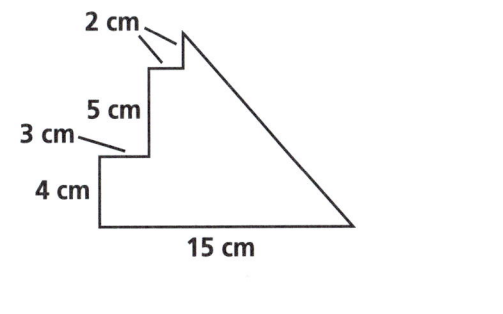
_____

Unit 10 Lesson 2 281

Problem Solving Reasoning — Solve. Find the area of the complex figure to the nearest tenth.

11. Architects and house designers use complex figures in their work. An arched door or a *lassway* mirror looks like this.

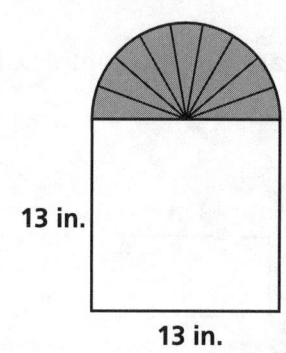

- The shaded part of the mirror is a semicircle or half a circle. The diameter of the semicircle is the same as the length of the rectangle, or **13 in.**

- The radius of the semicircle is $\frac{13}{2}$ in., or **6.5 in.**

What is the total area of the mirror to the nearest tenth? _____

12. What is the area of this plate?

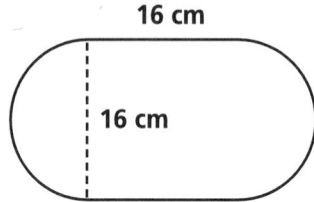

13. The circular parts of this mirror will be covered in tiles. What is the area of the part that will be covered in tiles?

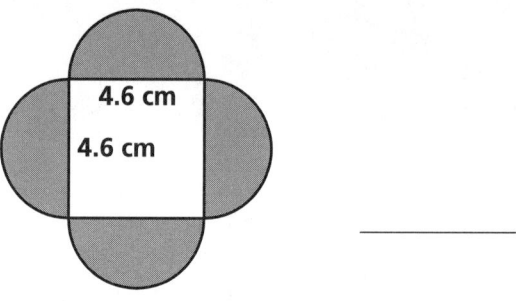

14. In order to complete a design, you need to cut paper circles from construction paper. About what percent of the paper is wasted?

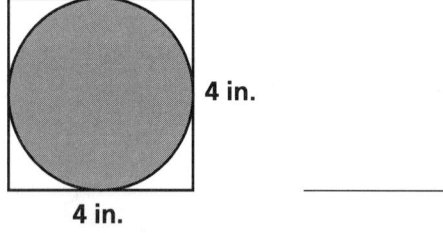

15. A homeowner is designing paths through her flower garden. If the shaded regions represent flower beds, then what is the area of the pathways?

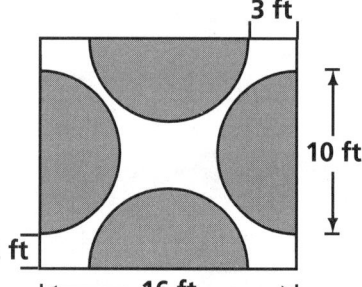

Test Prep ★ Mixed Review

16. If $a + 4.12 = {}^-3.01$, what is the value of a?

A $^-7.13$
B $^-1.11$
C 1.11
D 7.13

17. If $\frac{1}{5}n - \frac{4}{5} = 1\frac{2}{5}$, what is the value of n?

F 11
G 3
H $2\frac{1}{5}$
J $\frac{3}{5}$

282 Unit 10 Lesson 2

Name _____ **Area of a Trapezoid**

A trapezoid is a quadrilateral that has one pair of parallel sides called **bases**. The bases, b_1 and b_2, are of unequal length.

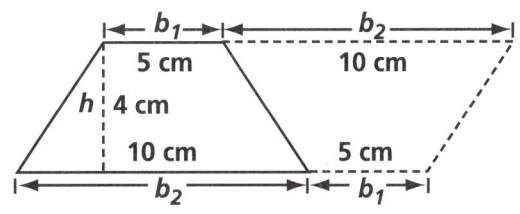

One way to find a formula for the area of a trapezoid is to arrange two congruent trapezoids to form a parallelogram.

- The parallelogram has a base of $(b_1 + b_2)$. Its height is h. The area of the parallelogram is:

$$A = bh \rightarrow A = (b_1 + b_2)h \rightarrow A = h(b_1 + b_2)$$

- The area of the trapezoid is half the area of the parallelogram.

$$A = \tfrac{1}{2}h(b_1 + b_2)$$

You can use the formula to find the area of the trapezoid.

1. Write the formula.

$$A = \tfrac{1}{2}h(b_1 + b_2)$$

2. Substitute.

$$A = \tfrac{1}{2} \cdot 4 \text{ cm} \cdot (10 \text{ cm} + 5 \text{ cm})$$

3. Evaluate.

$$A = \tfrac{1}{2} \cdot 4 \text{ cm} \cdot (15 \text{ cm})$$

$$= 30 \text{ cm}^2$$

↑ area of the trapezoid

Find the area of the trapezoid.

	b_1	b_2	h	Area		b_1	b_2	h	Area
1.	12 m	16 m	10 m	_____	**2.**	9 in.	8 in.	6 in.	_____
3.	54 mm	45 mm	20 mm	_____	**4.**	18 mm	28 mm	15 mm	_____
5.	65 ft	32 ft	24 ft	_____	**6.**	4 cm	8 cm	7 cm	_____
7.	12 km	13 km	10 km	_____	**8.**	$1\tfrac{1}{4}$ yd	$2\tfrac{3}{4}$ yd	$1\tfrac{1}{2}$ yd	_____

9. What is the area of a trapezoidal sign that has bases **12 ft** and **18 ft** and a height of **6 ft**?

_____

10. An open field is trapezoidal in shape. The bases are **21 m** and **40 m**. The height is **18 m**. What is the area?

_____

Find the area of the complex figure.

11.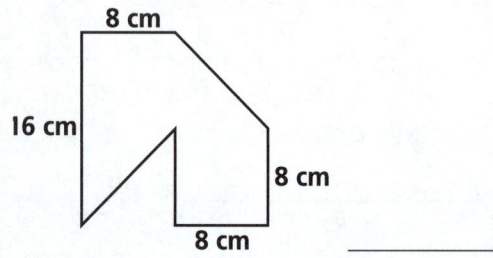

12.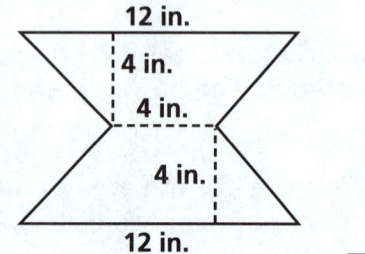

13.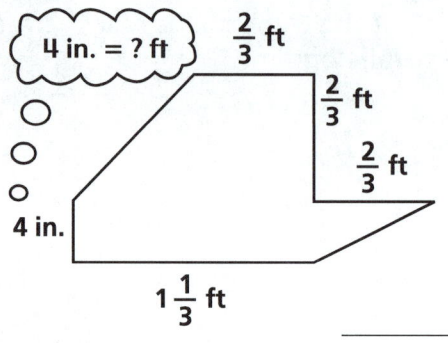

14.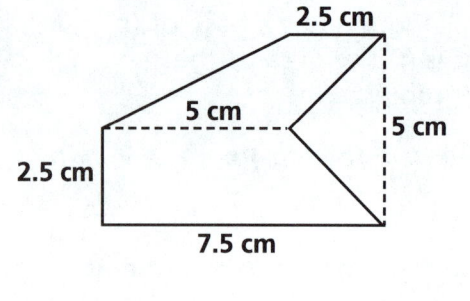

Problem Solving	Solve.
Reasoning	

A flag maker is making a square flag that will have a black trapezoid and a red triangle as shown. The rest of the flag will be white.

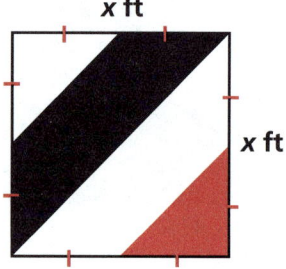

15. What is the area of the black section of the flag? _____

16. What is the area of the red section? _____

17. What percent of the flag is white? _____

✓ Quick Check

Find the circumference and area to the nearest tenth. Use 3.14 for π.   **Work Space.**

18. a circle with diameter **20 m** _____ _____

19. a circle with radius **7 in.** _____ _____

Find the area.

20.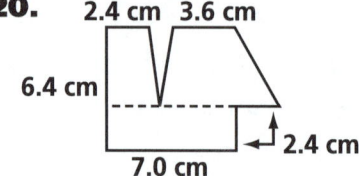

21.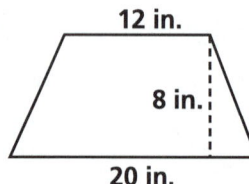

Name _____

Area of Regular Polygons

A **regular polygon** has all congruent sides and all congruent angles. You can use what you know about finding the area of complex figures to find the area of regular polygons. Each polygon has been divided into congruent triangles with base *b* and height *h* as shown. The number of triangles is the same as the number of sides in the figure.

Regular pentagon

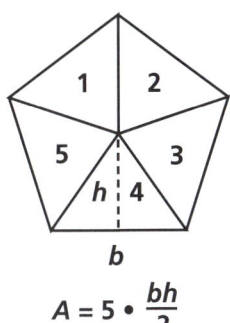

$A = 5 \cdot \dfrac{bh}{2}$

Regular hexagon

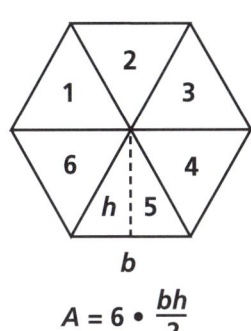

$A = 6 \cdot \dfrac{bh}{2}$

Regular octagon

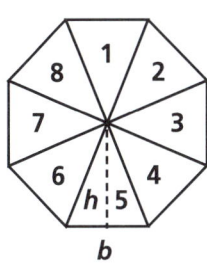

$A = 8 \cdot \dfrac{bh}{2}$

> The area of a regular polygon of *n* sides is *n* times the area of 1 congruent triangle, or
>
> $A = n \cdot \dfrac{bh}{2}$

Find the area of the regular polygon.

Regular Polygon	Base *b*	Height *h*	Area *A*
1. Hexagon	11.7 in.	8 in.	_____
2. Decagon (10 sides)	3.4 cm	5.3 cm	_____
3. Octagon	4.5 ft	$5\frac{1}{2}$ ft	_____
4. Heptagon (7 sides)	8.6 m	8.8 m	_____
5. Nonagon (9 sides)	3.7 cm	5.2 cm	_____
6. Pentagon	9.5 yd	$6\frac{1}{2}$ yd	_____

Solve.

7. How much surface area is in a regular hexagonal flower bed in which each triangle has a base of **10.4** ft and a height of **9** ft? How many tons of topsoil are needed if each ton covers **4** yd²?

   _____

8. One regular hexagonal table mat measures **4.6** in. on a side and has a height of **4** in. How many mats can be cut from a piece of felt that is **2** ft by **4** ft?

   _____

To find the perimeter of a regular polygon with *n* sides, use the formula:

$$P = nb$$
Perimeter = number of sides × base

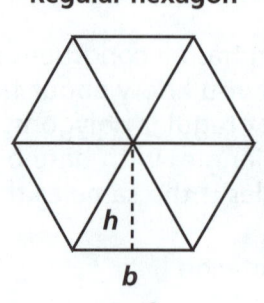

Regular hexagon   Regular octagon

$n = 6$ $n = 8$
$P = 6b$ $P = 8b$

If you know the perimeter of a regular polygon, you can find its area. A regular polygon with *n* sides is made up of *n* triangles.

Its area is *n* times the area of one triangle:

$$A = n \cdot \frac{bh}{2} \rightarrow \frac{1}{2}n \cdot b \cdot h \rightarrow \frac{1}{2}Ph$$

Substitute *P* for *n • b*.

$$A = \frac{1}{2}Ph$$

Find the area of the regular polygon.

	Regular Polygon	Height *h*	Perimeter *P*	Area *A*
9.	Hexagon	9 in.	63 in.	_____
10.	Decagon	6.8 cm	43.5 cm	_____
11.	Octagon	$5\frac{2}{3}$ ft	37.4 ft	_____
12.	Heptagon	10 m	68.6 m	_____
13.	Nonagon	7.2 cm	46.7 cm	_____
14.	Pentagon	$3\frac{1}{2}$ yd	25.6 yd	_____

Problem Solving Reasoning Solve.

15. A quilted design, in the shape of a regular hexagon, is made up of triangles that are 6 cm high. If the area of the design is 125 cm², then what is the length of each side of the design? How much ribbon would you use to border the design?

_____

16. A sign, in the shape of a regular octagon, has an area in square inches that is three times the numerical value of its perimeter. What is the height (*h*) in inches of the octagon? _____

Test Prep ★ Mixed Review

17 What is the area of a circle whose radius is 8 cm? (Use π ≈ 3.14.)

  A 25.12 cm²   **C** 200.96 cm²
  B 50.24 cm²   **D** 803.84 cm²

18 A trapezoid has a height of 6.5 in., and the lengths of the bases are 4.8 in. and 10 in. What is the area of the trapezoid?

  F 48.1 in.²   **H** 96.3 in.²
  G 65 in.²   **J** 113 in.²

Name _____

Estimating the Area of Irregular Plane Figures on a Grid

Sometimes you may not be able to find the area of an irregular figure using a formula. To estimate the area of an irregular figure, you can use a grid.

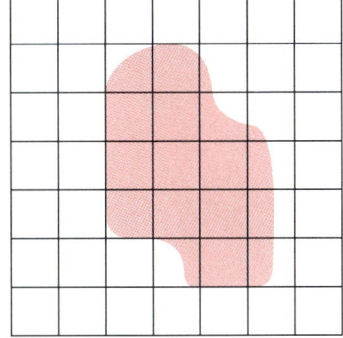

Estimate the area of the irregular figure shown.

1. Count the number of whole squares.

2. Put together parts of other squares to approximate whole squares.

3. Add the area of the whole squares to the area of the partial squares.

This figure has an estimated area of about **14** square units.

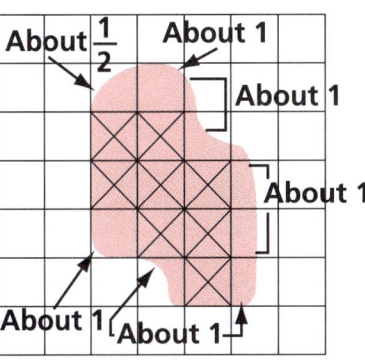

Estimate the area in square units.

1.

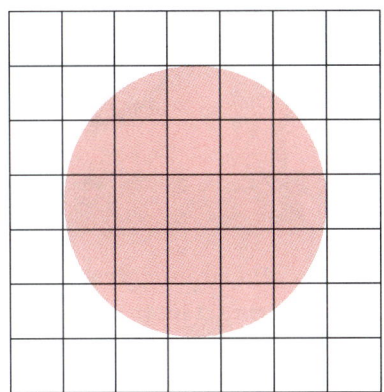

_____

2.

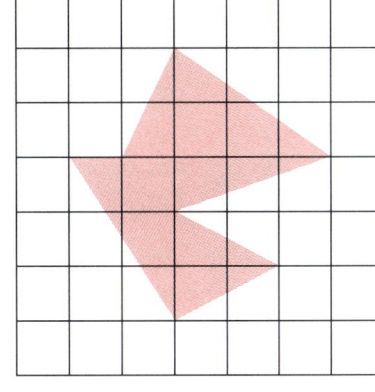

_____

Unit 10 Lesson 5 **287**

Estimate the area in square units.

3.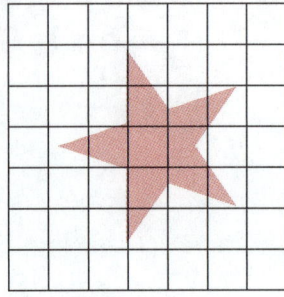

   $A \approx$ _____

4.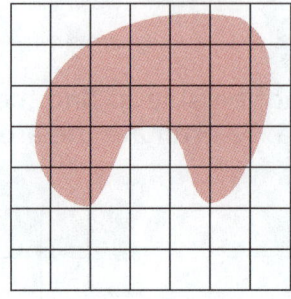

   $A \approx$ _____

5.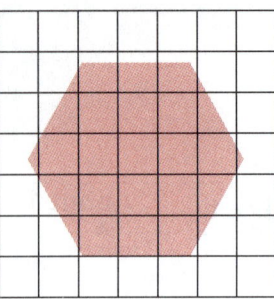

   $A \approx$ _____

6.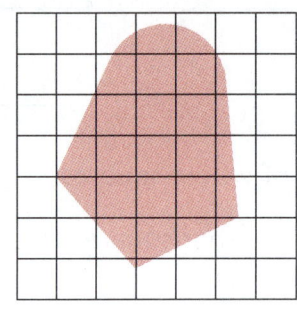

   $A \approx$ _____

Problem Solving / Reasoning — Use what you know about area to complete.

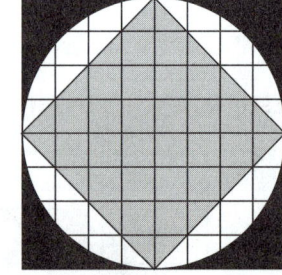

7. Find the area of the inner shaded square. _____

8. Estimate the area of the circle that is outside the square. _____

9. Estimate the area of the shaded corners. _____

Test Prep ★ Mixed Review

10. A regular pentagon is divided into 5 congruent isosceles triangles. △ABC is one of the triangles. It has a base BC that is 6 cm and a height of 4.1 cm. What is the area of the pentagon?

  A 12.3 cm²   **C** 129 cm²
  B 61.5 cm²   **D** 615 cm²

11. A scale drawing of a running track consists of a rectangle measuring 3 in. by 12 in., with a semicircle at each of the shorter sides. What is the area of the scale drawing to the nearest square inch? (Use $\pi \approx 3.14$)

  F 36 in.²   **H** 43 in.²
  G 40 in.²   **J** 64 in.²

Name _____

Problem Solving Strategy: Solve a Simpler Problem

To solve some problems, you can work an easier problem like it and find a pattern.

When you solve a simpler problem, think about how the problem you have to solve relates to the simpler problem.

Problem

You want to enlarge a photo so that its length and width are each $3\frac{1}{2}$ times their original size. How many times greater is the area of the enlargement?

---

1 Understand   **As you reread the problem, ask yourself questions.**

- The length and the width of the photo will increase to $3\frac{1}{2}$ times their original size.

- Do you know what the original size is? _____

- What do you need to find? _____

---

2 Decide   **Choose a method for solving.**

Try the Solve a Simpler Problem strategy.

- Pick any rectangle, perhaps 2 in. by 3 in. How does its area increase when the sides increase 2, 3, and 4 times?

Rectangle	Length	Width	Area	Number of Times Larger
Original	2	3	6	
2 times	4	6	24	4 times
3 times	___	___	___	___ times
4 times	___	___	___	___ times

---

3 Solve   **Answer the question.**

- Complete the table.

- If the dimensions increase *n* times, then how many times does the area increase? _____

- How many times as great will the area of the enlargement be? _____

---

4 Look back   **Ask if your answers make sense.**

- Write the answer as a complete sentence.

_____

Use the Solve a Simpler Problem strategy or any other strategy you have learned.

1. What is the total number of squares of all sizes in the checkerboard below?

Think: What simpler problem can you use? How does the total number of squares increase as the size of the board increases?

_____

_____

Answer _____

2. What is the total number of triangles of all sizes in the figure below?

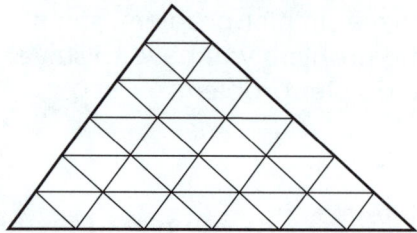

Think: What simpler problem can you use? How does the total number of triangles increase as the size of the large triangle increases?

_____

_____

Answer _____

3. The sides of a square increase from **4** cm to **10** cm. How many times as large is the area of the new square?

_____

4. The sides of a triangle are enlarged to **3.3** times their original length. How many times as large is the area of the new triangle?

_____

5. The dot patterns below represent triangle numbers. How many dots are in the 8th triangle number?

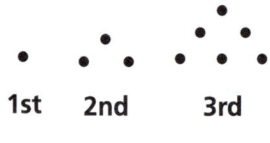

1st   2nd   3rd

_____

6. With one straight cut, you can cut a pizza into **2** pieces. With two straight cuts, you can cut it into **4** pieces. What is the greatest number of pieces you can cut with **5** straight cuts? (Hint: Not all the pieces will have a curved side.)

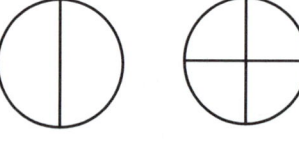

_____

7. Two numbers have a sum of **8.125** and a product of **1**. What are the two numbers?

_____

8. You spend half your money on gloves. Then, you spend $\frac{1}{3}$ of what you have left on a book. You spend **$4** on lunch and have **$6** left. How much money did you start with? _____

Name _____

Spatial Visualization with Nets

Any figure that is not entirely in one plane is a space figure. For example, the figure at the right is a rectangular prism. A rectangular prism unfolded might look like this:

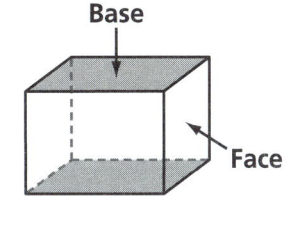

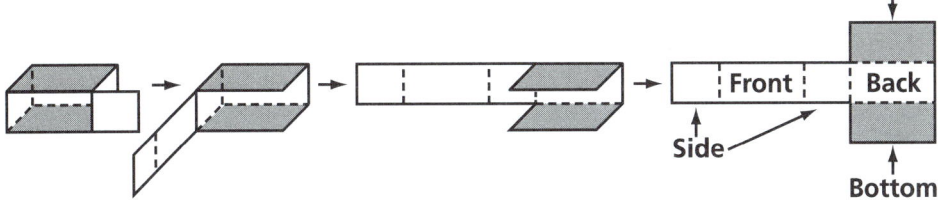

Any flat pattern that can be folded to form a space figure is a **net**. These are nets for a cube.

Space figures are named by the shape of their bases. A prism has two bases. A pyramid has only one base. Here are nets for a prism and a pyramid.

Rectangular prism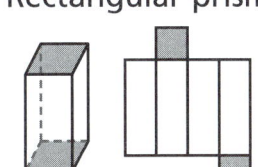

Triangular pyramid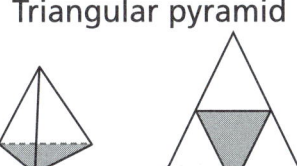

Circle the figure that can be made from the net.

1.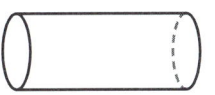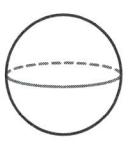

Cylinder   Sphere   Cone

2.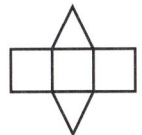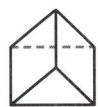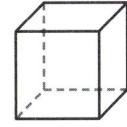

Triangular prism   Cube   Square pyramid

3.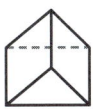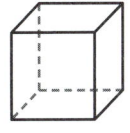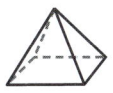

Triangular prism   Cube   Square pyramid

Unit 10 Lesson 7

Sketch a net for the space figure.

4. Pentagonal prism

5. Pentagonal pyramid

6. There are **11** different nets that can be made for a cube. Four are shown at the beginning of the lesson. How many can you find? Hint: This net **cannot** be folded to form a cube.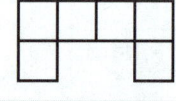

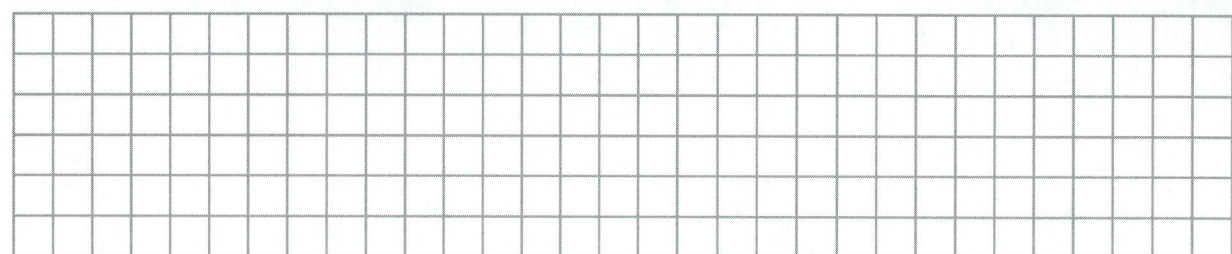

Problem Solving / Reasoning

Architects use technical drawings of front, side, and top views to visualize space figures. Match the drawing to the correct figure on page 291. Explain your choice.

7.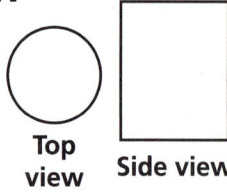

Top view Side view

Figure: _____

_____

_____

_____

8.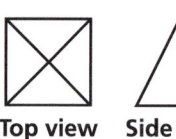

Top view Side view

Figure: _____

_____

_____

_____

✓ Quick Check

9. Find the perimeter and area of this regular figure.

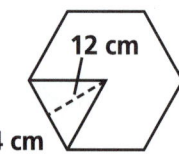

_____

10. Each ☐ is **1** square unit. Find the area.

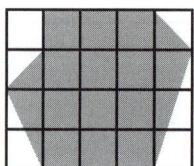

_____

Work Space.

11. What space figure can be made with this net?

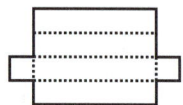

_____

292 Unit 10 Lesson 7

Name _____

Surface Area of Prisms

The **surface area (SA)** of a space figure is the sum of the areas of all its surfaces. To find the surface area of a rectangular prism, find the area of each pair of opposite faces.

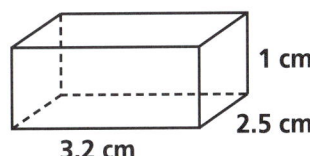

Find the surface area of the regular prism

Sides

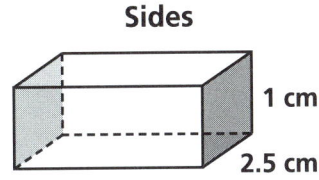

$A = 2(2.5 \text{ cm} \cdot 1 \text{ cm})$

$= 2(2.5 \text{ cm}^2)$

$= 5 \text{ cm}^2$

Front and Back

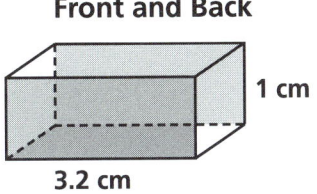

$A = 2(3.2 \text{ cm} \cdot 1 \text{ cm})$

$= 2(3.2 \text{ cm}^2)$

$= 6.4 \text{ cm}^2$

Top and Bottom

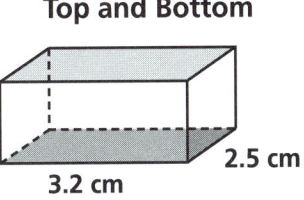

$A = 2(3.2 \text{ cm} \cdot 2.5 \text{ cm})$

$= 2(8 \text{ cm}^2)$

$= 16 \text{ cm}^2$

Total surface area $SA = 5 \text{ cm}^2 + 6.4 \text{ m}^2 + 16 \text{ m}^2$

$= 27.4 \text{ cm}^2$

The general formula for the surface area of any rectangular prism with length *l*, width *w*, and height *h* can be given as:

Surface area of a rectangular prism: $SA = 2(lw + lh + wh)$

Other examples:

If a prism has a square base, the formula becomes simpler.

Square prism

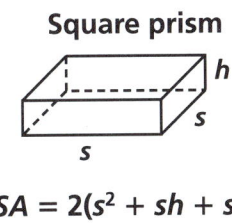

$SA = 2(s^2 + sh + sh)$

$= 2(s^2 + 2sh)$

A cube is a special kind of square prism in which $h = s$.

$SA = 2(s^2 + 2sh)$

$= 2(s^2 + 2s \cdot s)$

$= 2(s^2 + 2s^2)$

$= 2(3s^2)$

$= 6s^2$

Cube

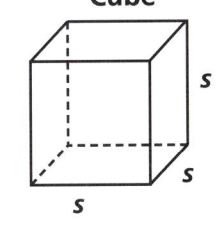

Unit 10 Lesson 8

Find the surface area of the rectangular prism.

	Length *l*	Width *w*	Height *h*	SA
1.	3 m	2 m	2 m	_____
2.	15 cm	4 cm	11 cm	_____
3.	7.2 dm	6 dm	4.6 dm	_____
4.	8.2 cm	9.1 cm	6.3 cm	_____
5.	$4\frac{1}{2}$ ft	$7\frac{3}{4}$ ft	$8\frac{1}{2}$ ft	_____
6.	$2\frac{1}{4}$ in.	$3\frac{1}{2}$ in.	4 in.	_____
7.	*l* m	*w* m	*h* m	_____

Find the surface area of the square prism.

	Length *l*	Width *w*	Height *h*	SA
8.	7 cm	7 cm	10 cm	_____
9.	16 m	16 m	12 m	_____
10.	$3\frac{1}{2}$ ft	$3\frac{1}{2}$ ft	5 ft	_____
11.	$8\frac{1}{4}$ in.	$8\frac{1}{4}$ in.	$10\frac{3}{4}$ in.	_____
12.	3.5 m	3.5 m	5 m	_____
13.	*s* in.	*w* in.	*s* in.	_____

Find the surface area of the cube.

	Side *s*	SA	Side *s*	SA	Side *s*	SA
14.	5 mm	_____	$\frac{1}{2}$ yd	_____	12 cm	_____
15.	8.5 m	_____	$\frac{2}{3}$ ft	_____	10.6 dm	_____

Compare the surface areas of the rectangular prisms. Write >, <, or =.

16. Prism *A*: *l* = 6 in., *w* = 6 in., *h* = 6 in. _____ Prism *B*: *l* = 6 in., *w* = 10 in., *h* = 4 in.

17. Prism *C*: *l* = 2 cm, *w* = 2 cm, *h* = 2 cm _____ Prism *D*: *l* = 2 cm, *w* = 4 cm, *h* = 1 cm

18. Prism *E*: *l* = 3 ft, *w* = 3 ft, *h* = 2 ft _____ Prism *F*: *l* = 10 ft, *w* = 1 ft, *h* = 1 ft

Name _____

To find the surface area of a triangular prism, use a net as a complex model of the figure.

Area of faces **A** and **B:**

$$2(8 \cdot 5.4) \text{ cm}^2 = 86.4 \text{ cm}^2$$

Area of face **C:**

$$(8 \cdot 4) \text{ cm}^2 = 32 \text{ cm}^2$$

Total area of faces: 118.4 cm²

Area of bases **D** and **E:**

$$2(\tfrac{1}{2} \cdot 4 \cdot 5) \text{ cm}^2 = 20 \text{ cm}^2$$

Total surface area: 118.4 cm² + 20 cm² = 138.4 cm²

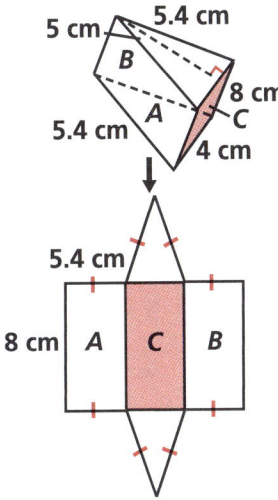

Faces **A** and **B** are congruent. So are the triangular bases.

Find the surface area of the triangular prism.

19.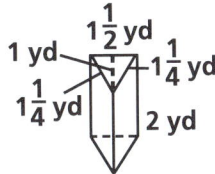

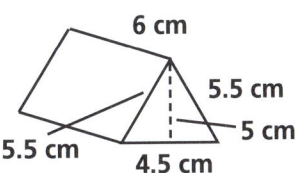

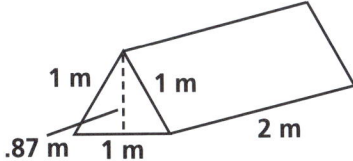

_____   _____   _____

Problem Solving / Reasoning   Solve.

20. What is the surface area of a cube that is twice as long, twice as wide, and twice as high as this cube? What is the ratio of the surface area of the new cube to that of the original cube?

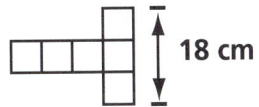

_____

Test Prep ★ Mixed Review

21 A regular hexagon has a side of 6 ft, and the distance from the center of the hexagon to the midpoint of each side is 5.2 ft. What is the area of the hexagon?

  A 93.6 ft   C 87.2 ft²

  B 93.6 ft²   D 15.6 ft²

22 Laurie's lawn is in the shape of a rectangle measuring 18 ft by 8 ft., with a semicircle at one of the short sides. Which solution best represents the area of the lawn? (Use π ≈ 3.14.)

  F 169 ft   H 199 ft

  G 169 ft²   J 199 ft²

Unit 10 Lesson 8   **295**

Name _____

Surface Area of Cylinders

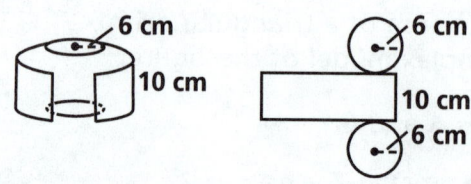

As you can see from its net, a cylinder is a space figure that is made up of two circular bases and a rectangle.

To find the surface area of a cylinder, you find the area of its parts.

The width of the rectangle is equal to the height of the cylinder. The length of the rectangle is equal to the circumference of the circular base.

Think: $A = \pi r^2$

Area of the circular bases: $2 \cdot 3.14 \cdot 36$ cm² = 226.08 cm²

Think: $A = l \cdot w$

Area of the rectangle: $2 \cdot (3.14 \cdot 6 \text{ cm}) \cdot 10 \text{ cm} = 376.80$ cm²

Total surface area of the cylinder: 226.08 cm² + 376.80 cm² = 602.88 cm²

Find the surface area of the cylinder. Use 3.14 for π.

	Radius r	Diameter d	Height h	SA
1.	_____	7 m	11 m	_____
2.	_____	$3\frac{1}{2}$ ft	15 ft	_____
3.	_____	8 cm	12 cm	_____
4.	$1\frac{1}{2}$ in.	_____	4 in.	_____

Find the surface area of the cylinder. Use 3.14 for π.

5. 2.5 cm, 8 cm

6. $3\frac{3}{4}$ in., 30 in.

7. 2 m, 4.2 m

Name _____

The surface of a cylinder with radius *r* and height *h* is given by the formula **SA = 2πr(r + h)**.

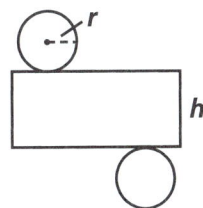

Use the formula to complete the table. Use 3.14 for π.

	h	r	2πr	r + h	SA
	5 in.	2 in.	12.56 in.	7 in.	87.92 in.²
8.	2 cm	5 cm			
9.	3 ft			7 ft	
10.		4 m		9 m	

Find the surface area.

11.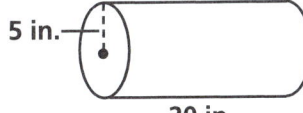
5 in.
20 in.

_____

12.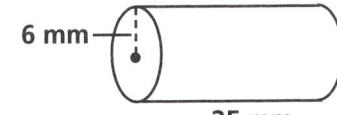
6 mm
25 mm

_____

13.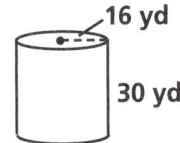
16 yd
30 yd

_____

Problem Solving Reasoning Solve.

A cylinder has a radius of **5 cm** and a height of **10 cm**.

14. What is the surface area of a cylinder whose radius is double the given cylinder? What is the ratio of the surface area of the new figure to the original one?

_____

15. What is the surface area of a cylinder whose height is double the given cylinder? What is the ratio of the surface area of the new figure to the original one?

_____

Test Prep ★ Mixed Review

16 Leon wants to wrap a box that measures 18 in. by 12 in. by 5 in. What is the minimum area of wrapping paper he needs?

A 732 in.²   C 366 in.²
B 732 in.   D 366 in.

17 The base of a prism is an equilateral triangle with 4-inch sides and a height of about 3.5 in. If the height of the prism is 10 in., which best represents the surface area of the prism?

F 120 in.²   H 134 in.²
G 127 in.²   J 148 in.²

Unit 10 Lesson 9 **297**

Name _____

Volume of Prisms

The volume of a space figure is the number of cubic units it contains. Remember, volume is expressed in cubic units, for example, cm³, m³, or in.³.

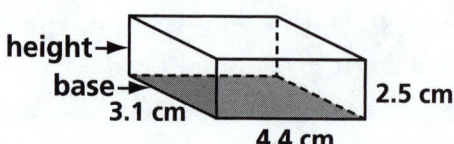

To find the volume of any prism, multiply the area of the base *B* by the height *h*.

   V = Bh

The volume (*V*) of the prism above is:

   $V = (3.1 \cdot 4.4)$ cm² $\cdot$ 2.5 cm

   $= 34.1$ cm³

The volume (*V*) of any rectangular prism with length *l*, width *w*, and height *h* is:
   V = lwh

A cube is a rectangular prism in which the length, width, and height are all equal.

Find the volume of the cube.

   $V = 4.3$ cm $\cdot$ 4.3 cm $\cdot$ 4.3 cm

   $= 4.3^3$ cm³

   $= 79.5$ cm³

The volume (*V*) of any cube with side *s* is:
   $V = s^3$

Find the volume of the rectangular prism.

	Length *l*	Width *w*	Height *h*	Volume *V*
1.	5.2 cm	8.1 cm	4.5 cm	_____
2.	16 in.	16 in.	16 in.	_____
3.	7.2 m	3.4 m	4.5 m	_____

Use the formula *V = Bh* to find the volume.

	Area of rectangular base *B*	Height *h*	Volume *V*
4.	16 cm²	6.5 cm	_____
5.	42 in.²	$8\frac{1}{2}$ in.	_____
6.	26 ft²	$5\frac{3}{4}$ ft	_____

Name _____

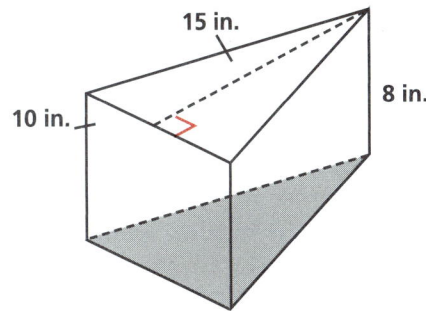

You can find the volume of a triangular prism by multiplying the area of the triangular base by the height. To find the volume of the prism at right you need two formulas.

1. First, find the area of the base.

   $A = \frac{1}{2}bh$

   $= \frac{1}{2} \cdot 10 \text{ in.} \cdot 15 \text{ in.}$

   $= 75 \text{ in.}^2$

2. Then, find the volume.

   $V = Bh$

   $= 75 \text{ in.}^2 \cdot 8 \text{ in.}$

   $= 600 \text{ in.}^3$ — Volume of the triangular prism

Find the volume of the triangular prism.

7.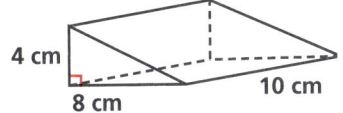
   _____

8.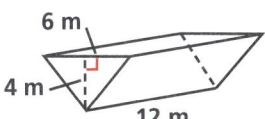
   _____

9.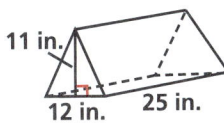
   _____

Solve. Draw the figure if you need to.

10. The base of a prism is a regular hexagon. The height of the prism is **10 cm**. The hexagonal base can be divided into **6** triangles, each with base **8 cm** and height **7 cm**. Find the volume of the prism.

    _____

11. The base of a prism is a regular pentagon. The height of the prism is **5 cm**. The pentagonal base can be divided into **5** triangles, each with base **6.5 cm** and height **4.5 cm**. Find the volume of the prism.

    _____

✓ Quick Check

Find the surface area.   Work Space

12. 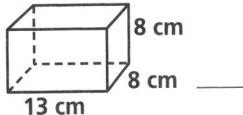 _____

13. 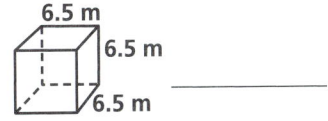 _____

14. 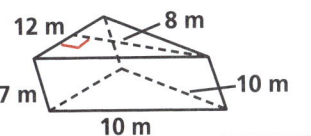 _____

15.  _____

Find the volume of the figures in exercises 12–14.

16. Exercise 12 _____

17. Exercise 13 _____

18. Exercise 14 _____

Name _____

Volume of Composite Space Figures

Many space figures are combinations of different types of prisms. For example, the figure at the right is made up of centimeter cubes. To find its volume, you can count the number of cubes. Make sure you count any cubes that are hidden from view.

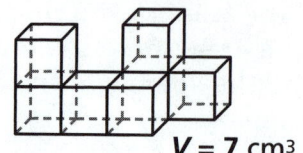

V = 7 cm³

To find the volume of **composite space** figures that are made up of different space figures, you may need to use more than one formula.

Find the volume of the figure at right.

1. Divide the figure into space figures you know. Then, find any missing lengths.

Rectangular prism: *l* = **8** ft   *w* = **5** ft   *h* = **4** ft

Triangular prism: You need the dimensions of the triangular bases.

- The *base* of the triangle is equal to the width of the rectangular prism, or **5** ft.

- The height of the triangle is **3** ft.

- The height of the triangular prism is equal to the length of the rectangular prism, or **8** ft.

This figure is made up of a triangular prism and a rectangular prism.

2. Find the volume of each figure.

Volume of rectangular prism: *V = lwh*

or   *V* = **8** ft · **5** ft · **4** ft or **160** ft³

Volume of triangular prism: *V = Bh*

or   *V* = ($\frac{1}{2}$ · **5** ft · **3** ft) · **8** ft or **60** ft³

3. Find the sum of the volumes.

V = **160** ft³ + **60** ft³

= **220** ft³

The total volume of the composite figure is **220** ft³.

Count cubes to find the volume. Write the answer in cm³. Remember to count cubes that are hidden from view.

1.

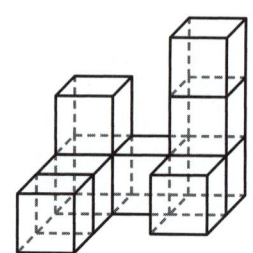   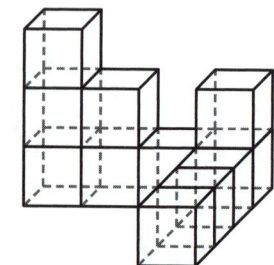

_____   _____

300 Unit 10 Lesson 11

Find the volume of the composite figure.

2.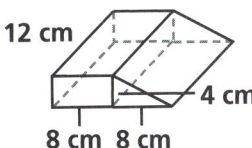

_____   _____   _____

3.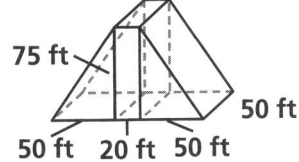

_____   _____   _____

Problem Solving Reasoning   Complete. You may need to use cubes to model the figure.

4. This figure is made up of centimeter cubes. You are painting the outside faces of the figure, including the bottom.

   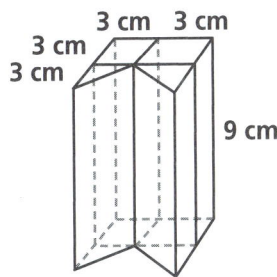

   a. How many centimeter cubes make up the figure? _____

   b. How many painted faces are there? _____

Test Prep ★ Mixed Review

5. The height of a cylindrical can of paint is 7.5 in. and the diameter of its base is 6 in. Which number best represents the surface area of the can? (Use $\pi \approx 3.14$.)

   A 45 in.^{2}

   B 170 in.^{2}

   C 198 in.^{2}

   D 508 in.^{2}

6. The volume of a cube-shaped box is 729 in.^{3}. What is the area of one of its faces?

   F 9 in.^{2}

   G 81 in.^{2}

   H 121.5 in.^{2}

   J 243 in.^{2}

Unit 10 Lesson 11 301

Name _____

Relating Length, Area, and Volume

Throughout this unit, you have measured geometric figures in one, two, and three dimensions. You have found perimeters, areas, and volumes. In this lesson, you will investigate relationships among length, area, and volume. You have already studied some of these relationships.

How does the area of a face, surface area, and volume of Figure A change when the length of a side is increased **2** times, **3** times, **4** times, and **5** times?

Figure A

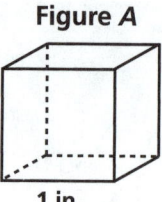

1 in.

1. Record what you know about the figure.
   • The area of a face is **1 × 1**, or **1 in.²**
   • The surface area is **6 × 1**, or **6 in.²**
   • The volume is **1 × 1 × 1**, or **1 in.³**

2. To look for relationships, find the area, surface area, and volume. Record the results in a table. Then, look for patterns.

When the side is increased **2** times:
   • the area of a face increases **4** times.
   • the surface area increases **4** times.
   • the volume increases **8** times.

Figure	Side (s)	Area of a Face	Surface Area	Volume
A	1 in.	1 in.²	6 in.²	1 in.³
B	2 in.	4 in.²	24 in.²	8 in.³
C	3 in.	9 in.²	54 in.²	27 in.³
D	4 in.	16 in.²	96 in.²	64 in.³
E	5 in.	25 in.²	150 in.²	125 in.³

Complete.

1. When the side of Figure A is increased 3 times, how does the area of a face, surface area, and volume change?

   _____
   _____
   _____

2. When the side of Figure A is increased 4 times, how does the area of a face, surface area, and volume change?

   _____
   _____
   _____

The change in the length of a side from an original figure to a new figure is called the *scale factor*. In this lesson the scale factor (*k*) is the ratio of the length of a new side to that of the previous figure. Find the scale factors.

> The scale factor for a side of Figure C to Figure B is $\frac{3}{2}$.

Original Figure	New Figure	Scale Factor (*k*)		Original Figure	New Figure	Scale Factor (*k*)
3. 3 cm	6 cm	_____		**4.** 5 in.	15 in.	_____
5. $2\frac{1}{2}$ in.	$7\frac{1}{2}$ ft	_____		**6.** 23 mm	92 mm	_____

302 Unit 10 Lesson 12

Use the scale factor (k) of the sides to find the surface area and volume of the new figure. The first one has been done for you.

7. k = 6   Original Surface Area: **1** in.²   (k^2)   Original Volume: **1** in.³   (k^3)

New Surface Area: $6^2 \cdot 1$ in.² = **36** in.²   New Volume: $6^3 \cdot 1$ in.³ = **216** in.³

8. k = 2   Original Surface Area: **54** cm²   Original Volume: **27** cm³

New Surface Area: _____   New Volume: _____

9. k = $\frac{1}{4}$ Original Surface Area: **96** ft²   Original Volume: **64** ft³

New Surface Area: _____   New Volume: _____

10. k = 3   Original Surface Area: **30.25** cm²   Original Volume: **166.375** cm³

New Surface Area: _____   New Volume: _____

11. k = $\frac{2}{3}$ Original Surface Area: **54** cm²   Original Volume: **27** cm³

New Surface Area: _____   New Volume: _____

Problem Solving Reasoning Figures A and B are two different space figures. Complete the tables for the figures.

	k (A:B)	Length A	Surface Area A	Volume A	Length B	Surface Area B	Volume B
12.	$\frac{1}{16}$	4 in.		64 in.³		24,576 in.²	
13.	7.5		11,137.5 cm²		3 cm		162 cm³

Quick Check

Find the volume.

14. Each block is 1 cm³.

15. 5 m, 5 m, 4 m, 4 m

Work Space

Complete the table for scale factor k = 2.

16.

	Side Length	Surface Area	Volume
New Figure		1,536 in.²	
Original Figure	4 in.		64 in.³

Volume of Cylinders

Remember that a cylinder is a space figure with two circular bases. You find the volume of a cylinder by multiplying the number of square units of area in the circular base by the number of units of height.

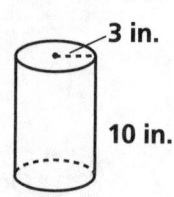

Area of base: $B = \pi \cdot 3^2$ in.^{2}

$\approx 3.14 \cdot 9$ in.^{2}

≈ 28.26 in.^{2}

Volume of cylinder: $V = 28.26$ in.$^2 \cdot 10$ in.

$= 282.60$ in.^{3}

$$V = Bh = \pi r^2 h$$

You can use what you know about volume and scale factors to investigate how the volumes of different cylinders are related.

- **Volume and Height**

Cylinders *A* and *B* have the same radius. The height of Cylinder *A* is twice the height of Cylinder *B*. What is the ratio of the volume of Cylinder *A* to Cylinder *B*?

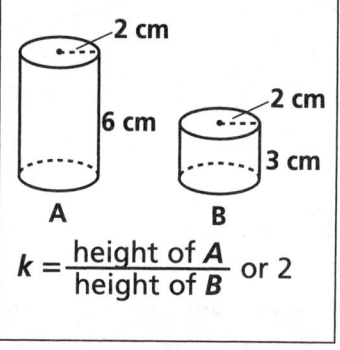

$k = \dfrac{\text{height of } A}{\text{height of } B}$ or 2

Volume of *A*: $V_A = \pi r^2 h$
$= \pi \cdot 2^2 \cdot 6$
≈ 75.36 cm^3

Volume of *B*: $V_B = \pi r^2 h$
$= \pi \cdot 2^2 \cdot 3$
≈ 37.68 cm^3

Ratio of Volumes
$\dfrac{V_A}{V_B} = \dfrac{\pi \cdot 2^2 \cdot 6}{\pi \cdot 2^2 \cdot 3}$
$\approx \dfrac{75.36 \text{ cm}^3}{37.68 \text{ cm}^3}$ or $\dfrac{2}{1}$

The ratio of volumes equals *k*. The ratio of volumes remains the same as the ratio of heights: **2 to 1**.

- **Volume and Radius**

Cylinders *C* and *D* have the same height. The radius of Cylinder *C* is twice the radius of Cylinder *D*. What is the ratio of the volume of Cylinder *C* to Cylinder *D*?

$V_C = \pi r^2 h$
$= \pi \cdot 4^2 \cdot 6$
≈ 301.44 in.^{3}

$V_D = \pi r^2 h$
$= \pi \cdot 2^2 \cdot 6$
≈ 75.36 in.^{3}

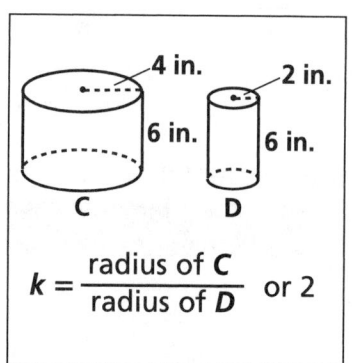

$k = \dfrac{\text{radius of } C}{\text{radius of } D}$ or 2

Ratio of Volumes $\dfrac{\pi \cdot 4^2 \cdot 6}{\pi \cdot 2^2 \cdot 6} = \dfrac{301.44 \text{ in.}^3}{75.36 \text{ in.}^3}$ or 4 (k^2)

The ratio of radii is **2 to 1**, but the ratio of volumes is **4 to 1**.

Name _____

Find the volume of the cylinder. Remember that d = 2r.

1.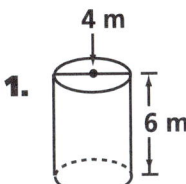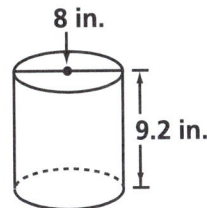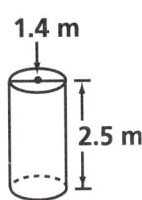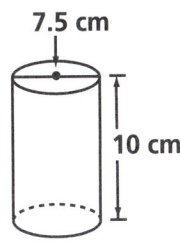

_____ _____ _____ _____

Find the missing values.

	radius	height	volume		radius	height	volume
2. Cylinder P	2.5 cm	10 cm	_____	Cylinder Q	5 cm	10 cm	_____
3. Cylinder R	2.5 cm	_____	98.125 cm³	Cylinder S	5 cm	_____	392.5 cm³
4. Cylinder T	2.5 cm	20 cm	_____	Cylinder U	10 cm	_____	3,140 cm³

Use the values from exercises 2–4 to compare the cylinders.

	ratio of radii	ratio of heights	ratio of volumes		ratio of radii	ratio of heights	ratio of volumes
5. Q and P	___	___	___	P and R	___	___	___
6. U and S	___	___	___	T and R	___	___	___

Problem Solving Reasoning   Solve.

7. Remember that **1** cubic decimeter is **1** liter. About how many liters will a cylinder hold if it has a radius of **2** meters and a height of **0.5** meters?

_____

8. A cylinder has a height of **8** ft and a volume of **226.08** ft³. What is its radius?

_____

Test Prep ★ Mixed Review

9. A cylindrical can of paint has a diameter of **6** in. and a height of **8** in. To the nearest cubic inch, how many cubic inches of paint does it hold? (Use π ≈ 3.14.)

     A 72   C 204

     B 75   D 226

10. If a cylindrical container can hold 452 in.³ of water, how much water could it hold if the height remained the same but the radius were doubled?

     F 2,712 in.³   H 904 in.³

     G 1,808 in.³   J 452 in.³

Unit 10 Lesson 13 **305**

Name _____

Problem Solving Application: Use a Diagram

Sometimes you can use a coordinate grid to find an area.

Remember: To find the point (**4, 5**) on the coordinate plane, start at (**0, 0**). Go right **4** and up **5**.

Problem

What is the area of the outer circle in the diagram?

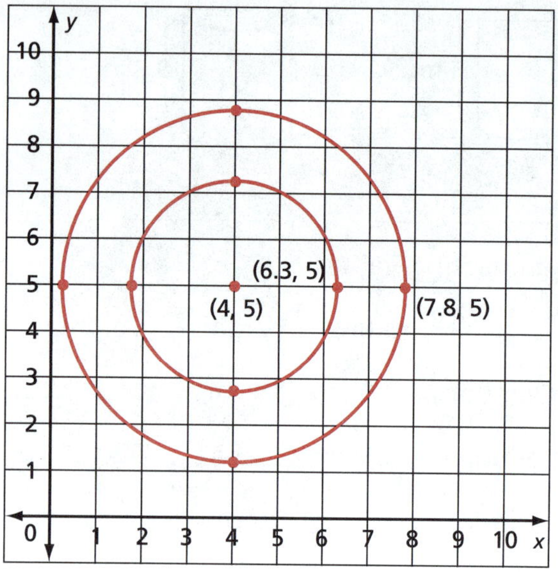

(Diagram shows two concentric circles on a coordinate grid with center (4, 5), inner circle passing through (6.3, 5), and outer circle passing through (7.8, 5).)

Tips to Remember:

| 1. Understand | 2. Decide | 3. Solve | 4. Look back |

- Ask yourself: What do I know? What do I need to find?
- How can I find the length of a horizontal line segment? Of a vertical line segment?
- Think about whether the area makes sense. Is it reasonable?

1. What is the area of the inner circle?

Think: How long is its radius? How can I use this length to find the area?

Answer _____

2. What is the area of the region between the two circles?

Think: I know the area of both circles. How can I use these areas to find the area of the region between them?

Answer _____

306 Unit 10 Lesson 14

Name _____

Use the diagrams or any other strategy you have learned.

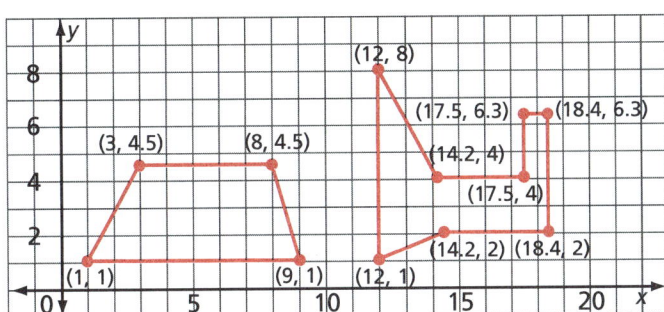

3. What is the height of the trapezoid? What is the area of the trapezoid?

   _____

4. What is the approximate area of the figure to the right of the trapezoid?

   _____

5. You want to frame a picture that is **10** in. by **14** in. The width of the wooden molding you want to use is **3** in. How many inches of molding do you need? Hint: Use diagonal cuts at the corners.

   _____

6. For a math fair, tables with displays are placed around three sides of a gymnasium that is **40** feet wide and **60** feet long. Each **2**-foot by **4**-foot table is placed lengthwise **2** feet from a wall and **2** feet from each other. What is the greatest number of tables that can be set up in the gym?

   _____

7. A **20** ft × **40** ft in-ground swimming pool is **8** ft deep. If the concrete on the bottom and sides of the pool is **12** in. thick, how many cubic feet of concrete were used to make the pool?

   _____

8. In Mr. Keyes's math class, **14** students have one or more sisters, **15** have one or more brothers, **6** have one or more brothers and sisters, and **5** have no brothers or sisters. How many students are in the class?

   _____

Extend Your Thinking

9. The two endpoints of a radius are (**5.4, 6**) and (**5.4, 3.8**). What is the area of the circle? How did you find your answer?

   _____
   _____

10. How did using the coordinate grid help you to find the answer to problem **4** above?

    _____
    _____

Unit 10 Lesson 14

Name _____

Pythagorean Property of Right Triangles

Over 2,500 years ago, the Greek mathematician Pythagoras made an important discovery:

In a right triangle, the square of the hypotenuse equals the sum of the squares of the legs. The **Pythagorean Property** can also be written as a formula.

$$a^2 + b^2 = c^2$$

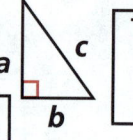

The **hypotenuse** is opposite the right angle.

The **legs** form the right angle.

Look at the model.

- The square on side *a* has an area of 16 square units.
- The square on side *b* has an area of 9 square units.
- The square on side *c* has an area of 25 square units.

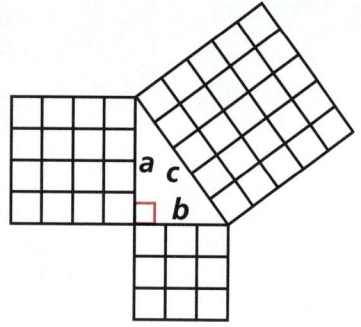

If you know the lengths of the sides of a triangle, you can use the Pythagorean Property to decide whether it is a right triangle.

$a^2 + b^2 = c^2$

$(5 \text{ cm})^2 + (12 \text{ cm})^2 \stackrel{?}{=} (13 \text{ cm})^2$

$25 \text{ cm}^2 + 144 \text{ cm}^2 \stackrel{?}{=} 169 \text{ cm}^2$ True.

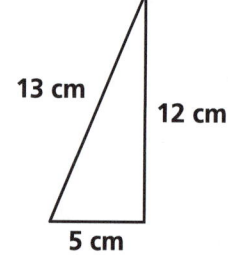

A set of three whole numbers *a, b, c* that satisfies the Pythagorean Property, such as **5, 12, 13,** is called a **Pythagorean triple.**

Use the Pythagorean Property to decide whether the triangle is a right triangle.

1.

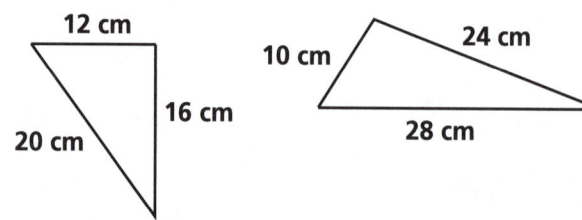

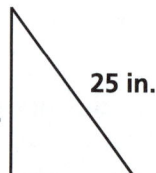

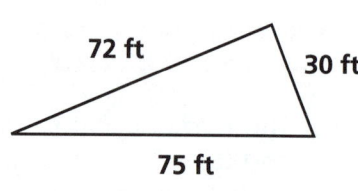

_____   _____   _____   _____

308   Unit 10 Lesson 15

Name _____

If you know the length of two sides of a right triangle, you can use the Pythagorean Property to find the length of the third side.

1. Write the formula and substitute.

   $a^2 + b^2 = c^2$

   $a^2 + 16^2 = 20^2$

   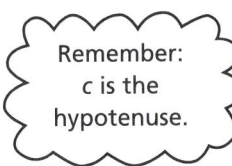
   Remember: c is the hypotenuse.

2. Simplify.

   $a^2 + 16^2 = 20^2$

   $a^2 + 256 = 400$

   $a^2 = 144$

3. Find the square root.

   $\sqrt{144} = 12 \rightarrow a = 12$

   So, the third side is 12 cm.

Sometimes the square root you need is an irrational number. It cannot be written as an exact decimal.

$2^2 + 3^2 = c^2$

$4 + 9 = c^2$

$13 = c^2 \rightarrow c = \sqrt{13}$

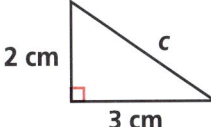

To estimate this value, you can use a calculator:

Press   [1][3] [√]

$\sqrt{13} \approx 3.6055513$

Or, you can use a table.

$\sqrt{13} \approx 3.6$

N	√N	N	√N
2	1.141	225	15
13	3.606	289	17
121	11	676	26
162	12.728	1,156	34
169	13	3,025	55

Find the missing lengths to the nearest tenth.

	Side a	Side b	Side c
2.	4 in.		6 in.
3.	3 cm	3 cm	
4.	1 m	3 m	

	Side a	Side b	Side c
5.	4 ft	2 ft	
6.		6 m	10 m
7.		15 in.	17 in.

△XYZ is an isosceles triangle. If we draw a line segment from point Z to the opposite base at point P, we form two right triangles.

8. Name the two right triangles. _____ and _____

9. What is the measure of the hypotenuse of each triangle?

   _____

10. What is the measure of each side? _____ and _____

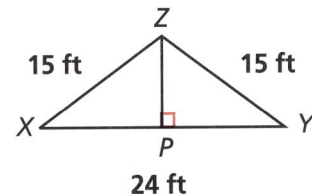

Unit 10 Lesson 15   **309**

Find the measure of the diagonal.

11.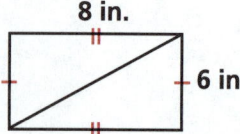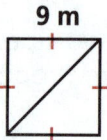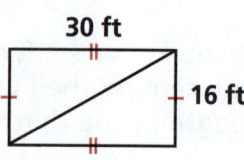

Problem Solving Reasoning Draw a right triangle and label the sides as indicated in the problem. Use the Pythagorean Property to compute the missing measurement.

12. A wire cable is attached to the top of a pole that is **4** meters high. How long must the cable be if it is fastened to the ground **3** meters from the base of the pole?

13. A ladder reaches to the top of a sign **8** feet from the ground. How long is the ladder if the bottom of it is placed **6** feet from the base of the sign?

14. Ken swims diagonally across a swimming pool that is **25** feet wide and **60** feet long. Dick swims the length of the pool. Who swims the longer distance and by how much? (A diagonal cuts a rectangle into two congruent right triangles.)

✓ Quick Check

Find the volume. Use $\pi = 3.14$.

15.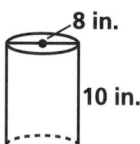

16.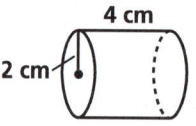

Work Space.

Find the missing measure.

17.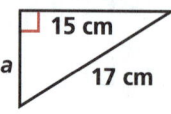

18.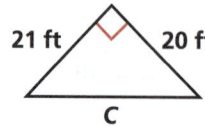

Name _____

Unit 10 Review

Write the formula for the area of the figure. Then, find the area.
Use 3.14 for π.

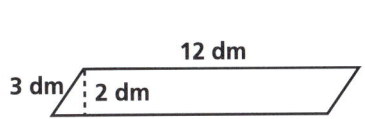
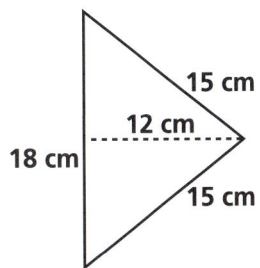
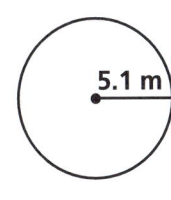

1. Formula: A = _____

Area is _____.

2. Formula: A = _____

Area is _____.

3. Formula: A = _____

Area is about _____.

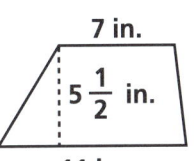
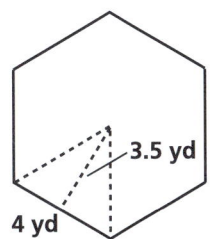
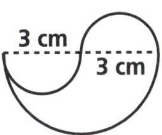

4. Formula: A = _____

Area is _____.

5. Formula: A = _____

Area is _____.

6. Area is about _____.

Use the nets below for exercises 7–10.

Net A

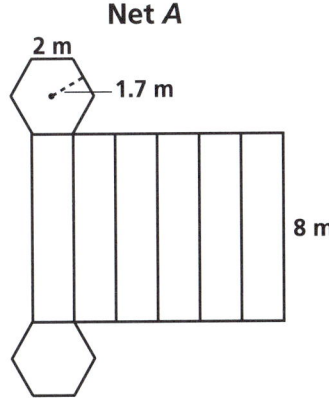

Net B

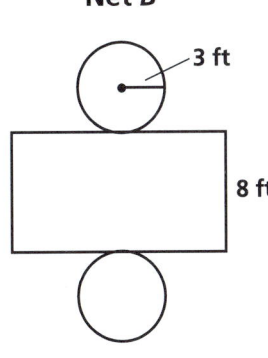

7. Net A will form a _____.

8. Net B will form a _____.

9. The surface area of the figure Net A forms is _____.

10. The surface area of the figure Net B forms is about _____.

Write the formula for the volume of the space figure. Then, compute the volume.

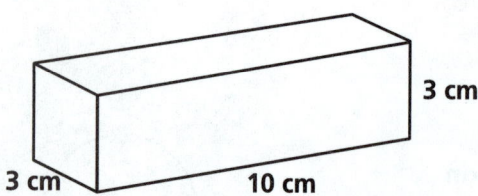
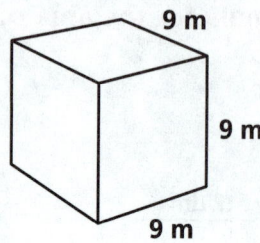

11. Formula: V = _____

The volume is _____.

12. Formula: V = _____

The volume is _____.

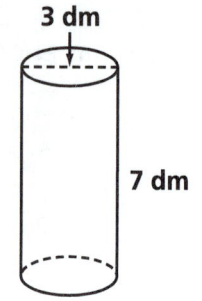
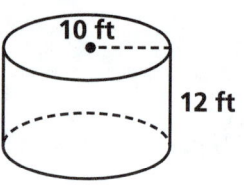

13. Formula: V = _____

The volume is about _____.

14. Formula: V = _____

The volume is about _____.

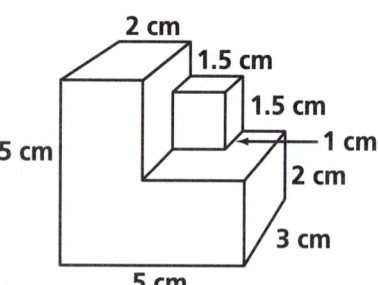
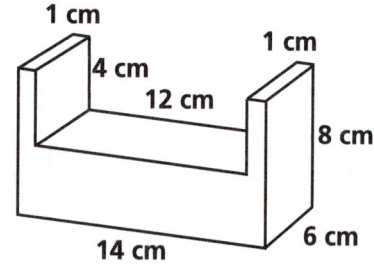

15. The volume is _____.

16. The volume is _____.

Answer the question.

17. A rectangle is enlarged so that its sides are $1\frac{1}{3}$ times their original length. How many times as great is the area of the new rectangle? _____

18. A prism is enlarged so that its edges are **3** times as long as before. How many times greater is the new surface area? _____

19. How many times as great is the volume of the new prism in exercise **18**?

_____

312 Unit 10 Review

Name _____

Find the missing length of the triangle. Use the table on page 309.

20. c = _____

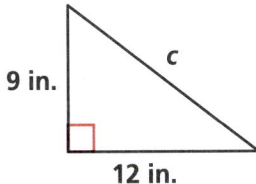

21. c ≈ _____

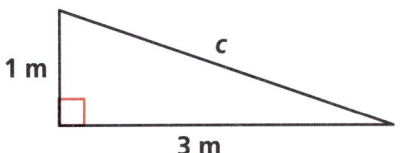

22. a ≈ _____

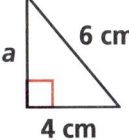

23. h = _____   x ≈ _____

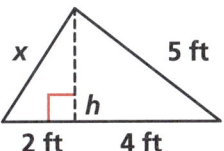

Solve. Use the figure on the coordinate grid below.

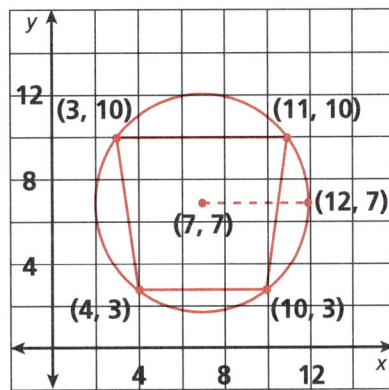

24. What are the lengths of the bases of the trapezoid? How did you find these lengths?

_____

_____

25. What is the area of the region between the circle and the trapezoid?

_____

Unit 10 Review **313**

Cumulative Review ★ Test Prep

Name _____

1 What is the area of the regular octagon?

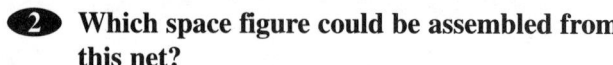

A 360 cm²   **C** 180 cm²

B 180 cm   **D** 90 cm²

2 Which space figure could be assembled from this net?

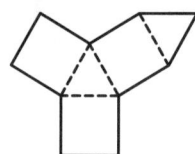

F square pyramid

G triangular prism

H tetrahedron

J pentagonal prism

3 Which of the numbers is irrational?

A $\sqrt{36}$

B $\sqrt{4 \cdot 5^3}$

C $\sqrt{11}$

D $\sqrt{100}$

4 What is the quotient when $^-535.5$ is divided by 8.5?

F 63

G 6.3

H $^-63$

J $^-6.3$

K Not here

5 A school pennant is in the shape of a triangle. The base of the pennant is 12 inches, while the height is 30 inches. Which formula would you use to find the area of the pennant?

A $A = bh$

B $A = 2(b + h)$

C $A = \frac{1}{2}bh$

D $A = \frac{h}{2}(b_1 + b_2)$

6 How many pieces of wood, each $1\frac{2}{3}$ feet long, can be cut from a board that is $16\frac{1}{2}$ feet long?

F 16

G 14

H 12

J 10

K Not here

7 What is the simplified form of the polynomial: $^-2p(3p + 2q + r)$?

A $^-6p^2 + 4pq + 2pr$

B $^-6p^2 + {}^-4pq + {}^-2pr$

C $^-6p^2 + 2pq + pr$

D $^-6p + {}^-4q + {}^-2r$

8 Jill is cutting strips of colored material, all of equal width, for a quilt pattern. To fit the pattern, the minimum width of each strip in inches (w) is given by the formula $5w - 2 > 7$. What values can w have?

F $w > 1$

G $w > 1\frac{4}{5}$

H $w > 25$

J $w > 45$

314 Unit 10 Cumulative Review

UNIT 11 • TABLE OF CONTENTS

The Coordinate Plane: Graphs and Transformations

Lesson	Page
1 **Algebra** • Graphing Polynomials	317
2 Symmetry in the Coordinate Plane	320
3 Congruence and Similarity	323
4 Translations and Reflections	326
5 **Algebra** • Equations with Two Variables	329
6 **Algebra** • **Problem Solving Application:** Choose an Equation	332
7 **Algebra** • Graphing Linear Functions	334
8 **Algebra** • Slope of a Line	336
9 **Algebra** • Direct Variation	338
10 **Algebra** • **Problem Solving Strategy:** Write an Equation	340
11 **Algebra** • Non-Linear Functions	342
• **Unit 11 Review**	345
• **Cumulative Review ★ Test Prep**	348

Dear Family,

During the next few weeks, our math class will be learning about and practicing how to graph geometric figures and equations in two variables in the coordinate plane. This includes solving algebraic equations to find ordered pairs as well as finding matching points for ordered pairs in symmetric, congruent, and similar polygons.

You can expect to see homework that provides practice with these skills. Here is a sample you may want to keep handy to give help if needed.

We will be using this vocabulary:

congruent figures figures that have the same size and shape

symmetry a property of figures such that each point has a matching point on the opposite line

similar figures figures that have the same shape but not necessarily the same size

geometric transformation a procedure for moving figures in a plane

reflection a transformation that changes the position of a figure by flipping it about a line

translation a transformation that changes the position of a figure by sliding it in the same plane

solution of an equation in two variables an ordered pair of values that satisfy an equation

slope the ratio of the difference in y-coordinates (the rise) to the difference in x-coordinates (the run)

Graphing Ordered Pairs in the Coordinate Plane

The table of values at the right shows some x- and y-values for the equation $y = 2x - 1$. The table values can be also written as ordered pairs and graphed in the coordinate plane.

x	$y = 2x - 1$
0	$^-1$
1	1
2	3
$^-1$	$^-3$
$^-2$	$^-5$

(0, $^-$1), (1, 1), (2, 3), ($^-$1, $^-$3), ($^-$2, $^-$5)

When the points are plotted on the grid, and then connected, the result is a straight line.

You can find the slope of the line by finding a ratio of the changes in y-values to the changes in x-values for any two points on the line:

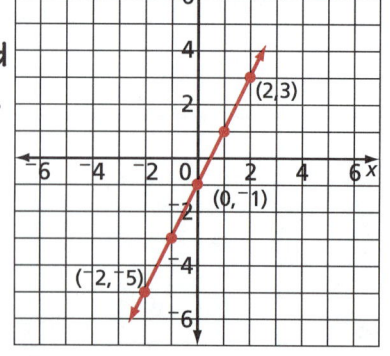

$$\text{slope} = \frac{\text{change in } y\text{-values}}{\text{change in } x\text{-values}} \rightarrow \frac{3 - {}^-1}{2 - 0} \rightarrow \frac{4}{2} \rightarrow 2$$

Sincerely,

Name _____   # Graphing Polynomials

You have used tables to evaluate polynomials such as **2x + 3** and **x² − 5x + 1** for certain values of **x**. In the tables below, the *x* and *y* columns are related to each other by rules.

Rule: $x + 1 = y$

x	y
2	3
1	2
0	1
-1	0
-2	-1
-3	-2

Think: $2 + 1 = 3$

Rule: $x^2 - 2 = y$

x	y
2	2
1	-1
0	-2
-1	-1
-2	2
-3	7

Think: $2^2 - 2 = 4 - 2 = 2$

For each table, you can write ordered pairs of numbers. You can then graph the set of ordered pairs for a table in the coordinate plane.

The solutions for the first table are shown on the graph at the right.

(2, 3), (1, 2), (0, 1), (⁻1, 0), (⁻2, ⁻1), and (⁻3, ⁻2)

You make a coordinate plane using two number lines called **axes**. The **x-axis** and **y-axis** divide the coordinate plane into four parts called **quadrants**.

- Both coordinates of the point **(2, 3)** are positive, so the point is in the first quadrant.

- Both coordinates of the point **(⁻3, ⁻2)** are negative, so the point is in the third quadrant.

In the graph, the ordered pairs appear to be in a straight line when they are plotted. Take a straightedge, line it up with the points, and draw the line. This line is called the **graph of the polynomial**.

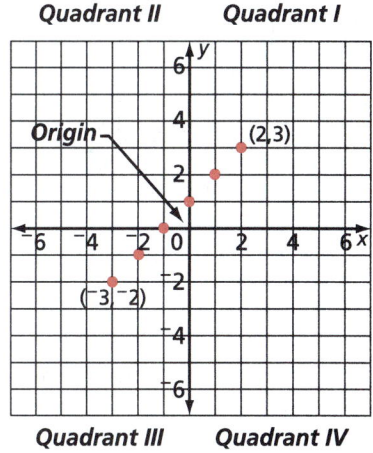

Complete the table of values for each rule.

1.

Rule: $-x = y$

x	y
3	
-2	
-1	

Rule: $x - 2 = y$

x	y
-2	
-1	
0	
1	
2	

Rule: $2x = y$

x	y
-2	
-1	
0	
1	
2	

Rule: $-2x = y$

x	y
-2	
-1	
0	
1	
2	

Unit 11 Lesson 1 **317**

Some ordered pair solutions for the rule $x^2 - 2 = y$ are shown on the graph.

(3, 7), (2, 2), (1, ⁻1), (0, ⁻2), (⁻1, ⁻1), (⁻2, 2), and (⁻3, 7)

The ordered pairs from the second table form a curved figure when they are plotted.

Notice that when the *x*-coordinates are opposites, they have the same *y*-coordinates. When this happens, the points form a curved figure called a **parabola**.

Connect the points.

The turning point of the parabola, point **(0, ⁻2)**, is called the **vertex** of the parabola.

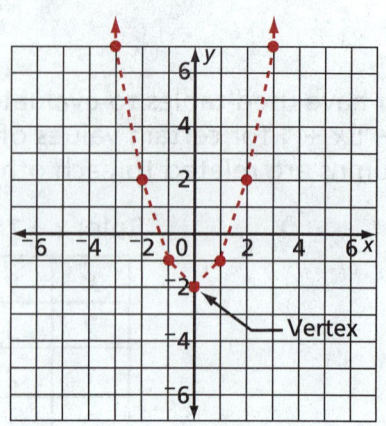

Find ordered pairs for $x = ⁻2, ⁻1, 0, 1,$ and 2 for each rule.

2. Rule: $x + 2 = y$

x	y

Rule: $x^2 - 1 = y$

x	y

Rule: $-x^2 = y$

x	y

Rule: $2x^2 + 1 = y$

x	y

Find solutions for $x = ⁻2, ⁻1, 0, 1,$ and 2 for each rule. Then draw and label the graph of the pair of figures on the coordinate grid. What do you notice about the graphs?

3. Rule: $x = y$

x	y

Rule: $\frac{1}{2}x = y$

x	y

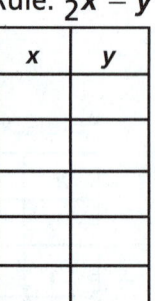

Describe the figures. Where do they intersect?

_____

318 Unit 11 Lesson 1

Name _____

Find solutions for $x = {}^-2, {}^-1, 0, 1,$ and 2 for each rule. Then draw and label the graph of the pair of figures on a coordinate grid. What do you notice about the graphs?

4. Rule: $3x + 1 = y$ Rule: $-3x + 1 = y$

x	y

x	y

5. Rule: $\frac{1}{2}x^2 = y$ Rule: $2x^2 = y$

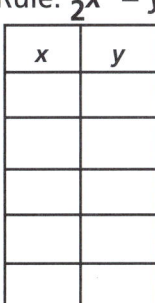 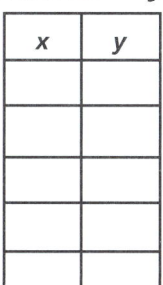

Problem Solving / Reasoning

Find some ordered pairs for these rules. Then graph them. Describe how the graphs are alike and how they are different.

6. Rule: $x^3 = y$ Rule: $-x^3 = y$

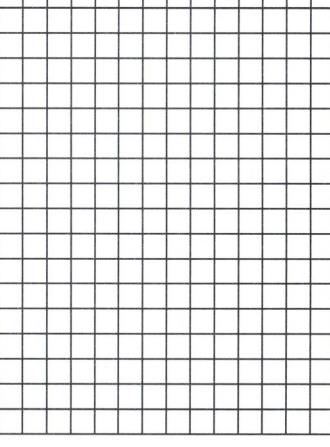

Test Prep ★ Mixed Review

7 Which is the standard form of the number 3.8×10^{-5}?

A 0.0000038

B 0.000038

C 380,000

D 3,800,000

8 If $a = {}^-3$, what is the value of the polynomial $4a^2 + 2a - 10$?

F 40

G 26

H 20

J ${}^-20$

Unit 11 Lesson 1 **319**

Name _____

Symmetry in the Coordinate Plane

In the trapezoid shown at the right, the *y*-axis, or fold line, is a **line of symmetry**. Look at the relationship between pairs of points on the trapezoid.

Point *A*, (⁻2, 4), is 2 units to the left of the *y*-axis.
Point *B*, (2, 4), is 2 units to the right of the *y*-axis.

The *x*-coordinate for Point *A* is the opposite of the *x*-coordinate for Point *B*, but the *y*-coordinates are the same.

Line of symmetry A line that divides a figure into two parts that are the same size and shape and are mirror images of one another

If the *y*-axis is a line of symmetry for a figure, then every point on the figure has a matching point.
 • The *x*-coordinate for one point is the opposite of the *x*-coordinate of the other point.
 • The *y*-coordinates are the same for both points.

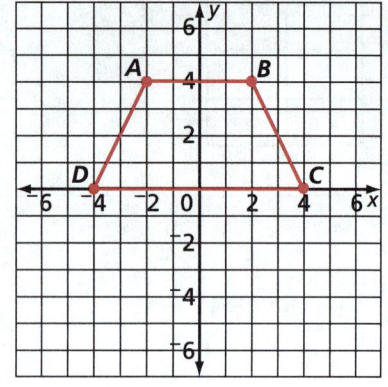

Now look at the coordinates for point *C* and point *D*.
 (4, 0) and (⁻4, 0)
 • The *x*-coordinates are opposites.
 • The *y*-coordinates are the same.
D is the matching point of *C*.

The point (0, 4) is on the line of symmetry. The opposite of 0 is 0, so its matching point is itself, (0, 4).

Complete the table below by finding matching points for other points on the trapezoid.

1.

Point	(2,0)	(⁻1,4)	(⁻3,0)	($\frac{5}{2}$,3)
Matching Point				

Complete the figure so that the *y*-axis is the line of symmetry. Write the coordinates of the matching points for *A* and *B*.

2.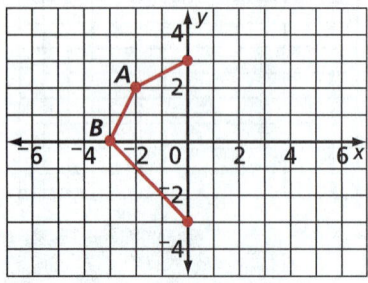

Matching point for *A*
_____

Matching point for *B*
_____

Matching point for *A*
_____

Matching point for *B*
_____

Matching point for *A*
_____

Matching point for *B*
_____

Name _____

**In some figures, the x-axis is the line of symmetry.
Study the figure on the graph at the right to answer the questions.**

3. Point A has coordinates (0, 3). Its matching point is Point D, with coordinates (0, ⁻3).

   How far is Point A from the x-axis? _____

   How far is Point D from the x-axis? _____

4. Another point on the figure is B (5, 2).

   What is its matching point? _____

   Is each of these points the same distance from the x-axis?

   _____

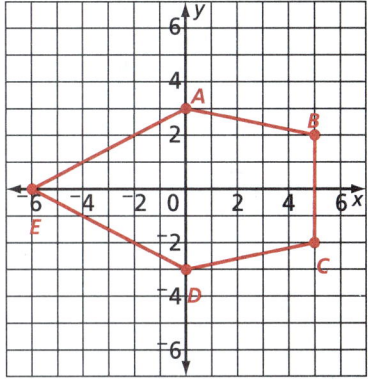

Complete the table by finding matching points for other points on the figure. Then use the table to complete the statements.

5.
Point	(⁻2,⁻2)	(⁻4,⁻1)	(5,0)	(4, $\frac{11}{5}$)
Matching Point				

6. If the x-axis is a line of symmetry for a figure, then every point with coordinates x and y on the figure has a "matching point" whose x-coordinate is the

   _____ and whose y-coordinate is the

   _____.

**Complete the figures so that the x-axis is the line of symmetry.
Write the coordinates of the matching points for A and B.**

7.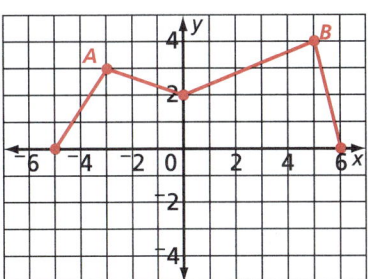

Matching point for A

_____

Matching point for B

_____

Matching point for A

_____

Matching point for B

_____

Matching point for A

_____

Matching point for B

_____

Unit 11 Lesson 2   321

Plot the points and then connect them in order. Find the matching points to complete the symmetric figure.

8. (⁻4, 0), (⁻2, 4), (1, 1), (3, 3), (4, 1), (4, 0)   (⁻3, 0), (⁻1, ⁻2), (1, ⁻1), (1, ⁻3), (3, ⁻3), (3, 0)

Line of symmetry: *x*-axis   Line of symmetry: *x*-axis

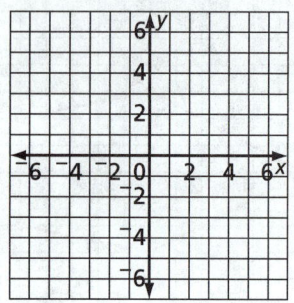   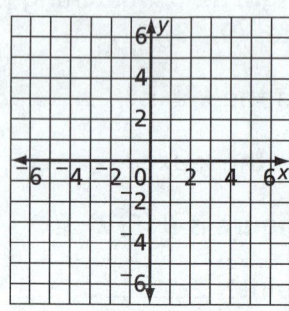

9. (0, ⁻5), (4, ⁻4), (1, ⁻3), (3, 0), (0, ⁻3)   (0, ⁻4), (⁻1, ⁻4), (⁻1, ⁻3), (⁻4, ⁻1), (⁻1, 2), (0, 4)

Line of symmetry: *y*-axis   Line of symmetry: *y*-axis

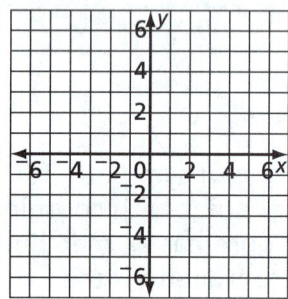   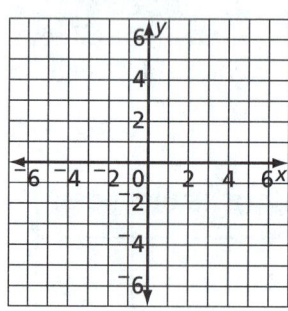

Problem Solving Reasoning

Use the coordinate grid to graph the quadrilaterals.

10. Graph a quadrilateral *ABCD* that is only symmetric about the *x*-axis.

11. Graph a quadrilateral *EFGH* that is only symmetric about the *y*-axis.

12. Graph a quadrilateral *WXYZ* that is symmetric about both axes.

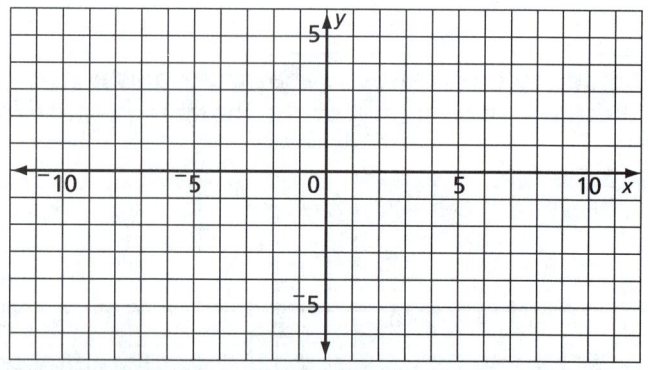

Test Prep ★ Mixed Review

13 If the sides of a right triangle measure 7.5 cm and 9.2 cm, what is the length of the hypotenuse?

　A 11.9 cm　　　C 141 cm

　B 16.7 cm　　　D 119 cm

14 The height of a can is 5.7 in. and the radius of its base is 2.5 in. Which represents the surface area? (Use π = 3.14.)

　F 109.1 in.²　　H 83.9 in.²

　G 128.7 in.²　　J 105.2 in.²

Name _____

Congruence and Similarity

The quadrilaterals *ABCD* and *EFGH* shown in the coordinate grids are **congruent**.

ABCD ≅ EFGH

Read ≅ as "is congruent to"

Congruent figures have the same size and the same shape.

If two figures are congruent, corresponding sides and angles in the figures are also congruent. For example:

- Side $\overline{BC}$ in quadrilateral *ABCD* corresponds to side $\overline{FG}$ in quadrilateral *EFGH*. So $\overline{BC} \cong \overline{FG}$.

- ∠*A* in quadrilateral *ABCD* corresponds to ∠*E* in quadrilateral *EFGH*, so ∠*A* ≅ ∠*E*.

All of this information lets us state a more complete definition for congruent polygons.

Two polygons are **congruent** if corresponding angles are congruent and corresponding sides are congruent.

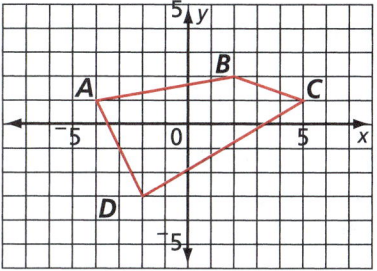

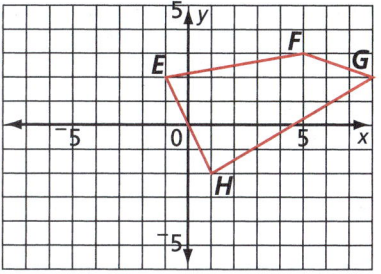

Draw a polygon congruent to the polygon shown. One side has been given for you to start.

1.

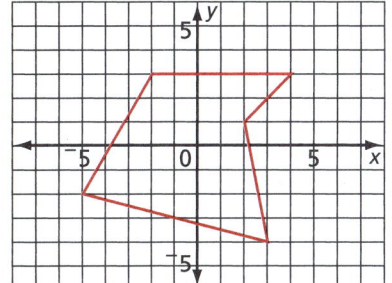

2.

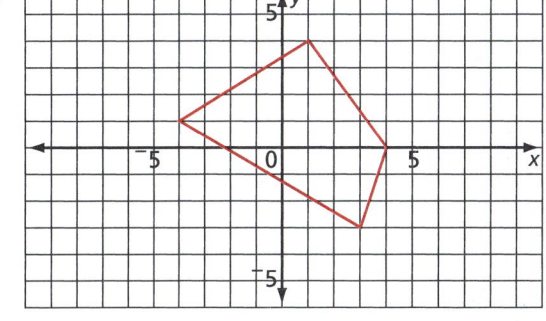

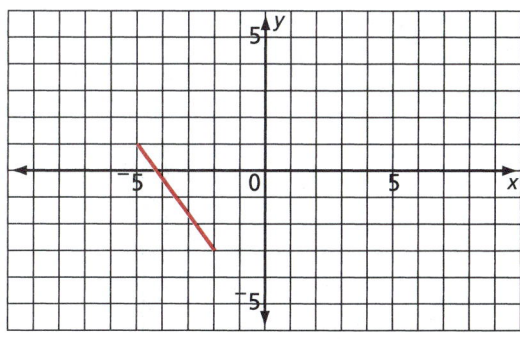

Unit 11 Lesson 3 **323**

The triangles *ABC* and *EFG* shown below are not congruent triangles, but they are **similar** triangles.

Triangle *ABC* ~ Triangle *EFG*   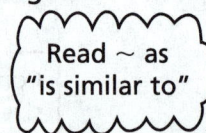 Read ~ as "is similar to"

Similar figures have the same shape but not necessarily the same size.

Are the corresponding sides and angles of similar figures congruent?

- Corresponding angles of similar figures are congruent. For example,

  ∠*A* in triangle *ABC* corresponds to ∠*E* in triangle *EFG*. ∠*A* ≅ ∠*E*

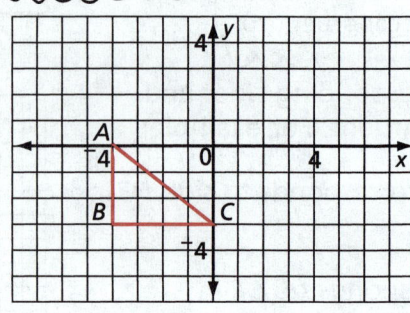 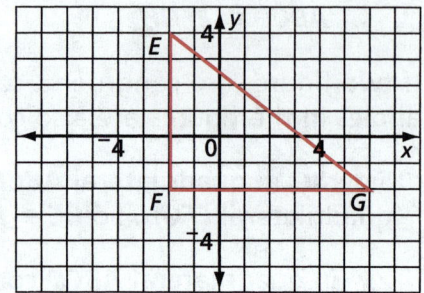

- Corresponding sides of similar figures may not be congruent, but the scale factor of the ratio of corresponding sides is the same.

Side $\overline{AB}$ is **3** units.   Side $\overline{BC}$ is **4** units.   Side $\overline{CA}$ is **5** units.
Side $\overline{EF}$ is **6** units.   Side $\overline{FG}$ is **8** units.   Side $\overline{GE}$ is **10** units.

$$\frac{6}{3} = 2 \qquad \frac{8}{4} = 2 \qquad \frac{10}{5} = 2$$

Triangle *EFG* is similar to triangle *ABC* by a scale factor of **2**.

All of this information lets us state a more complete definition for similar polygons.

Two polygons are **similar** if corresponding angles are congruent and corresponding sides are proportional.

A polygon is shown on the first grid below. Suppose that the scale factor is 2. Draw the enlargement of the polygon, using the origin as one vertex.

3.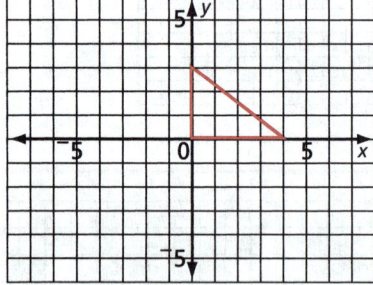

4.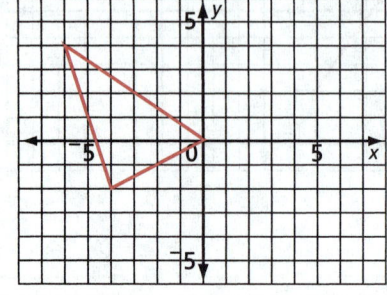

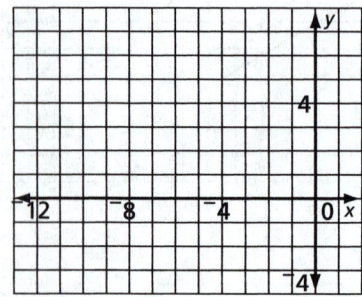

324 Unit 11 Lesson 3

Name _____

You can use similar triangles to find the heights of objects that are difficult to measure directly.

You know that a parking meter that is **3.5** feet tall casts a shadow that is **2** feet long at the same time that a telephone pole that is *h* feet tall casts a shadow that is **12** feet long. How tall is the telephone pole?

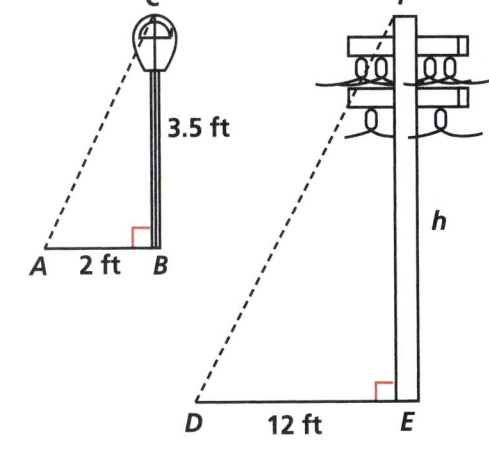

Since you know the sides of similar figures are proportional, you can write and solve a proportion to find *h*.

$$\frac{3.5}{2} = \frac{h}{12}$$
$$2h = 42$$
$$h = 21$$

The telephone pole is **21** feet tall.

---

5. Find the missing measure.

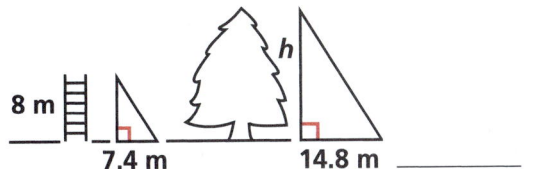

6. Some boys noticed that the flagpole cast a shadow of **28** feet. The boys asked Alan, a **4**-foot first grader, to stand beside the pole. He cast a **7**-foot shadow. How high is the flagpole?

_____

✓ Quick Check

Find three ordered pairs that satisfy the rule.

Work Space.

7. Rule: $x^2 - 3 = y$

8. Rule: $2x + 5 = y$

_____ _____

9. Tell whether the graphs of the rules in exercises **7** and **8** will be lines or parabolas. _____

10. Point *A* **(2, 4)** in trapezoid *ABCD* is symmetric about the *x*-axis. What are the coordinates of its matching point?

_____

11. Segment *AB* in one triangle has endpoints **(0,0)** and **(0,3)**. Its corresponding segment in another triangle has endpoints **(4,4)** and **(4,10)**. Could the triangles be congruent or similar? Explain. _____

Translations and Reflections

Some **geometric transformations** change only the position of a figure, not its size or shape. For example, imagine flipping Triangle *ABC* over the *y*-axis.

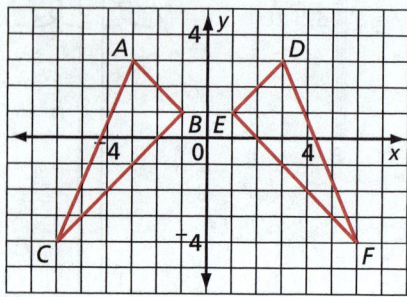

The resulting triangle, Triangle *DEF*, is the **line reflection image** of Triangle *ABC* over the *y*-axis.

Vertex *A* has coordinates (⁻3,3). Its image, Point *D*, has coordinates (3,3). Vertex *B* has coordinates (⁻1,1), and its image, Point *E*, has coordinates (1,1). Finally, Vertex *C*, with coordinates (⁻6,⁻4), has Point *F* as its image, with coordinates (6,⁻4).

For each vertex in Triangle *ABC*, its image has an *x*-coordinate that is just the opposite and a *y*-coordinate that is exactly the same.

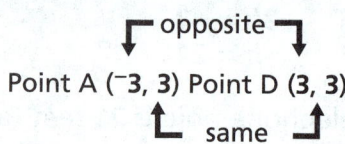

On the coordinate grid at the right, Quadrilateral *ABCD* has been flipped over the *x*-axis. Look at the coordinates of corresponding points.

Point A: (⁻4,4)   Point E: (⁻4,⁻4)
Point B: (2,3)   Point F: (2,⁻3)
Point C: (3,1)   Point G: (3,⁻1)
Point D: (⁻6,2)   Point H: (⁻6,⁻2)

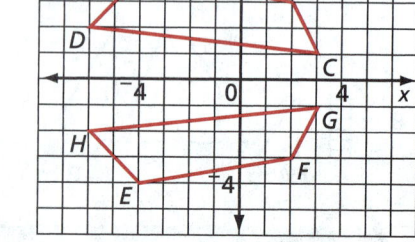

What do you notice about the coordinates of corresponding points?

_____

Reflect the figure over the *y*-axis. Write the coordinates of each image point.

1.

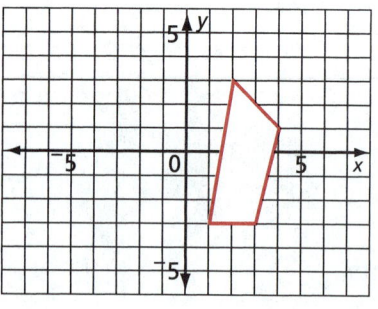   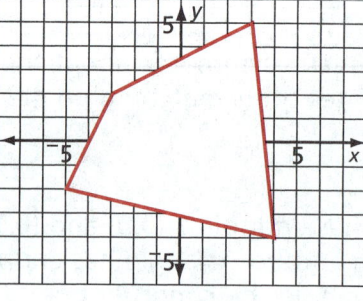   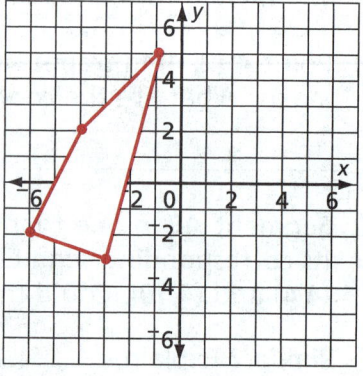

326 Unit 11 Lesson 4

Name _____

Reflect each figure over the x-axis. Write the coordinates for each image point.

2.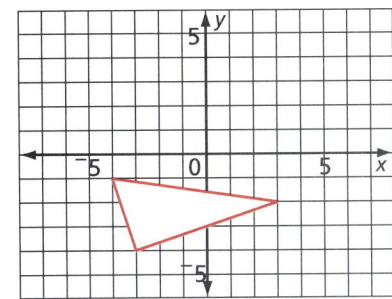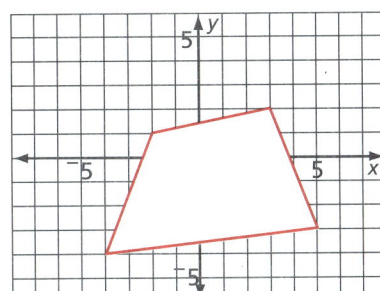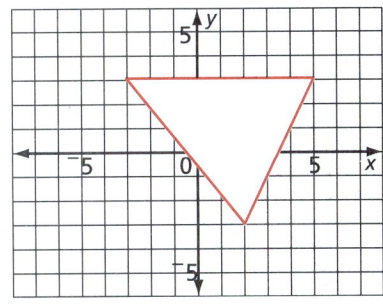

_____   _____   _____

Another geometric transformation is called a **translation** or **slide**. In a translation, the figure slides to a new position on the coordinate grid.

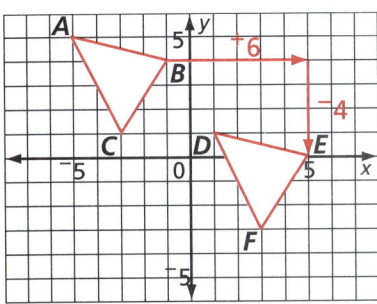

The corresponding pairs of vertices for the translation are *A* and *D*, *B* and *E*, and *C* and *F*. The coordinates for Vertex *B* are (⁻1,4). To find the image Point *F*, move 6 units to the right and 4 units down. Point *F* has coordinates (5,0).

⁻1 + 6 = 5 and 4 − 4 = 0; (5,0) is the image.

Adding 6 to the *x*-coordinate and subtracting 4 from the *y*-coordinate of Points *A* and *C* will give the image Points *D* and *F*.

Here is another example. To slide from Vertex *D* to Vertex *H*, move 6 units to the left and then 3 units up. Point *D* has coordinates (⁻1,⁻4). Point *H* has coordinates (⁻7,⁻1).

⁻1 − 6 = ⁻7 and ⁻4 + 3 = ⁻1.

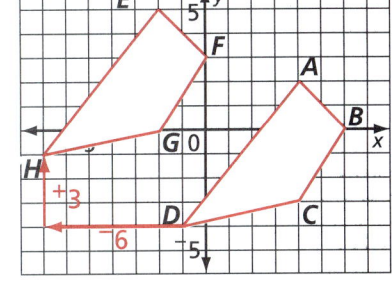

Find the coordinates of the image point if the given point is translated according to the directions.

3. (4,5); translated 3 units right and 4 units up _____

4. (⁻3,1); translated 2 units right and 2 units down _____

5. (3,⁻6); translated 5 units left and 7 units up _____

6. (⁻2,⁻4); translated 3 units left and 10 units up _____

7. A triangle has the following vertices: (⁻1,3), (⁻5,1), and (⁻2,0). It is translated 5 units right and 3 units down. What are the coordinates of the image triangle?

_____

Translate the figures below, following the rules given.

8. Right 3 units   Left 5 units   Right 1 unit
   Up 4 units   Down 3 units   Up 5 units

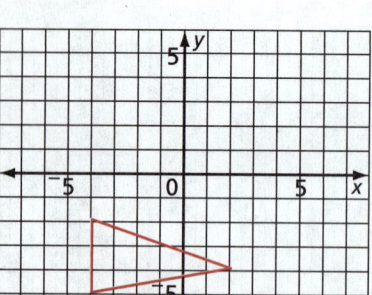 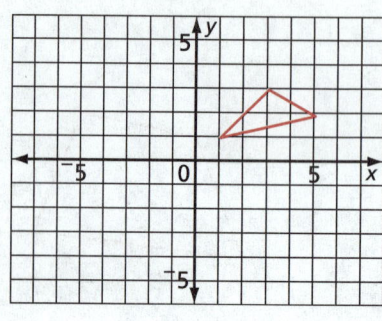 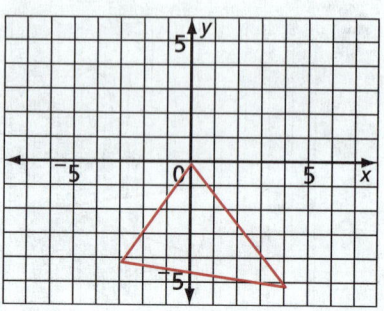

Each Triangle ABC shown below has been translated. The image is Triangle DEF.
State the directions for the slide (Right or Left __ units, Up or Down __ units).

9.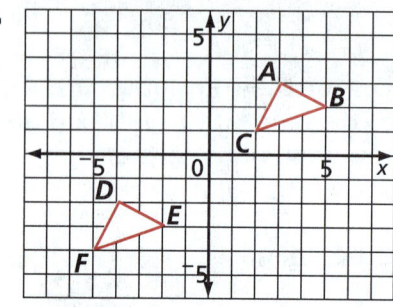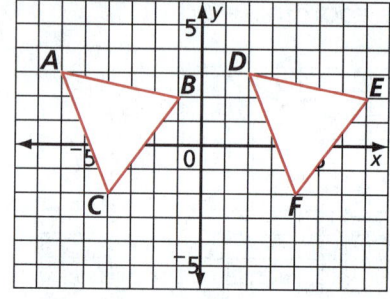

Problem Solving
Reasoning

10. The point (6,⁻2) is flipped over the y-axis first. This result is then flipped over the x-axis. What are the coordinates of this final result?

11. A triangle with vertices (1,⁻1), (5,1), and (3,4) is flipped over the x-axis first. This result is then flipped over the y-axis. What are the coordinates of this final result?

Test Prep ★ Mixed Review

12. In right △ABC, A is the point (0, 5), B is (0, 0), and C (7, 0). Hal wants to draw a right △DEF congruent to △ABC. He puts point E at (3, 5) and point F at (10, 5). Where could he place point D?

    A (10, 10)   C (3, 0)
    B (3, 10)   D (3, 10) or (3, 0)

13. In right △ABC, A is the point (0, 6), B is (0, 0), and C (10, 0). Maya wants to draw a right △DEF similar to △ABC. She puts point D at (5, 9) and point E at (5, 6). Where could she place point F?

    F (10, 9)   H (0, 6)
    G (10, 6)   J (10, 6) or (0, 6)

328 Unit 11 Lesson 4

Equations with Two Variables

Throughout this text you have been using equations with one variable such as $n + 2 = 3$ or $\frac{2}{3} = \frac{n}{6}$ to solve problems. What happens when an equation has two variables?

$$y = 2x + 3$$

Notice that if you substitute **1** for *x* and **5** for *y*, the resulting number sentence is true.

$$5 = 2(1) + 3$$

The ordered pair **(1, 5)** is called a **solution** of the equation. Similarly, when $x = {}^-2$ and $y = {}^-1$, the resulting number sentence, $^-1 = 2(^-2) + 3$, is true. The ordered pairs **(⁻2, ⁻1)**, **(0, 3)**, **(100, 203)** are other solutions of the equation.

> In an ordered pair, the first number represents the value of *x* and the second number represents the value of *y*.

$$y = 2x + 3 \qquad\qquad y = 2x + 3$$
$$3 = 2(0) + 3 \qquad\qquad 203 = 2(100) + 3$$

In fact, the equation $y = 2x + 3$ and equations like it have an infinite number of ordered pair solutions. (Equally, there are an infinite number of ordered pairs that are not solutions. Try the ordered pair **(0, 0)**. What do you notice?)

Here is another example.
Find three solutions for the equation $y = 3x - 4$.

Choose a value for *x*. Then find a value for *y*.

Try $x = 2$	Try $x = (^-3)$	Try $x = \frac{2}{3}$
$y = 3(2) - 4$	$y = 3(^-3) - 4$	$y = 3(\frac{2}{3}) - 4$
$= 2$	$= {}^-13$	$= {}^-2$
So **(2, 2)** is a solution.	So **(⁻3, ⁻13)** is a solution.	So $(\frac{2}{3}, {}^-2)$ is a solution.

Complete each table of values.

1.

$y = 2x$	
x	y
⁻2	
⁻1	
0	
1	
2	

$y = {}^-3x$	
x	y
⁻3	
⁻2	
⁻1	
0	
1	

$y = 5x + 1$	
x	y
⁻1	
0	
1	
2	
3	

$y = \frac{1}{2}x - 1$	
x	y
⁻2	
0	
2	
4	
6	

Make a table of values showing four solutions for each equation.

2.

$y = 5x + 2$	
x	y

$y = {}^-3x - 8$	
x	y

$y = \frac{1}{3}x + 4$	
x	y

$y = \frac{-5}{6}x - 2$	
x	y

Write two ordered pairs that are not solutions for the equation.

3. $y = 2x + 1$ _____ $y = \frac{-4}{5}x - 2$ _____

4. $y = {}^-3x$ _____ $y = 4x - 7$ _____

You can use equations with two variables to express relationships between two values. Consider these equations:

$$y = 3x$$

If **x** = number of yards, then **y** = number of feet.

If **x** = number of 3-point baskets in a basketball game, then **y** = number of points scored.

The value of **y** depends on the value of **x**.

$$y = 12x$$

If **x** = number of feet, then **y** = number of inches.

If **x** = number of years, then **y** = number of months.

Again, the value of **y** depends on the value of **x**.

Even some of the formulas you use in geometry express a relationship between two numbers.

$P = 4s$ or $y = 4x$ If **s** is the length of a side of a square, then **P** is the perimeter. The value of **P** depends on the value of **s**.

$C = 2\pi r$ or $y = 2\pi x$ If **r** is the radius of a circle, then **C** is the circumference of the circle. The value of **C** depends on the value of **r**.

Throughout these examples, the value of **y** depends on the value of **x**. So in an **x, y** equation, **y** is the **dependent variable**, while **x** is the **independent variable**.

Name _____

Use the equation $y = 12x$ or the formula $C = \frac{5}{9}(F - 32)$ to find the value.

5. How many inches are in **5** feet? _____

6. How many months are in **15** years? _____

7. If the temperature is **32°F**, what is the temperature in degrees Celsius? _____

8. If the temperature is **212°F**, what is the temperature in degrees Celsius? _____

9. If the temperature is **84°F**, what is the temperature in degrees Celsius? _____

Problem Solving Reasoning — Solve.

10. The length of a rectangle is twice as long as the width. Write an equation to find the perimeter of the rectangle. Find five solutions. Graph them in the coordinate plane. What do you notice about the graph?

    _____

11. Think of another real-life example of a relationship between two quantities, write an equation to express that relationship, and identify the independent variable and the dependent variable in your equation.

    _____

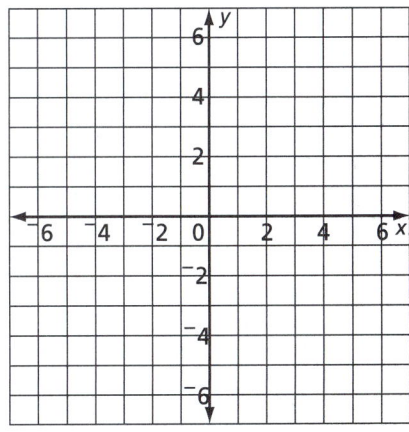

Test Prep ★ Mixed Review

This spreadsheet computes the volumes of cylinders with height 5 in. and variable radius r. Use it for exercises 12 and 13.

r (in.)	r^2	$\pi = 3.14$	πr^2	$h = 5$ (in.)	$V = \pi r^2 h$ (in.^{3})
1	1	3.14	3.14	5	15.7
2	4	3.14	12.56	5	62.8
3	9	3.14	?	5	141.3
4	16	3.14	50.24	5	?

12 What is the missing value in the fourth column?

    A 12.56   C 3.14

    B 28.26   D 9.42

13 What is the missing value in the sixth column?

    F 141.3   H 251.2

    G 15.7   J 314.0

Name _____

Problem Solving Application: Choose an Equation

In this lesson, you will be asked to choose an equation that models a problem situation. Clues in a table of values can help you choose an equation.

For example, you know

- The value of l depends on the value of w
- When $w = 0$, $l = 3$
- When $w = 1$, $l = 4$, and so on

Scientists often use tables of values to express relationships. For example, this table shows how a spring's length (l) depends on how much weight (w) is attached to it.

Weight w (pounds)	Length l (inches)
0	3
1	4
2	5
3	6
4	7

Understanding how to substitute ordered pairs from a table into an equation will help you choose the correct equation.

Tips to Remember:

> 1. Understand   2. Decide   3. Solve   4. Look back

- Ask yourself whether you have solved a problem like this before.
- Think about the relationships between the variables. Which variable is the dependent variable? Which operation do you use to relate the units or data in the problem?
- Think about the strategies you have learned and use them to help you solve a problem.

Solve.

1. Which equation below shows the same results as the table?

$w + 3 = l$ $w - 3 = l$ $3w = l$ $w \div 3 = l$

Think: Substitute some ordered pairs from the table in each equation.

_____

_____

Answer _____

_____

2. Suppose a spring is 9 inches long. Use your formula to tell the weight that was attached to it.

Think: Spring length is l and weight is w.

_____

_____

Answer _____

_____

332   Unit 11 Lesson 6

Circle the appropriate equation for each situation.
Explain why you chose the equation.

3. This table shows the weight in pounds of some containers of water. Which equation shows the same result as the table?

Gallons g	2	4	6	8
Weight w	16	32	48	64

$g + 8 = w$ $g + 14 = w$ $8g = w$

_____

4. Which equation shows the same result as this table?

x	y
-2	-1
0	0
2	1

$2x = y$

$\frac{x}{2} = y$

$x + 1 = y$

$x - 1 = y$

_____

5. The number of times a cricket chirps per minute depends on the temperature. When the temperature is **72°F**, the cricket chirps about **58** times a minute. When the temperature is **80°F**, the cricket chirps about **60** times a minute. Which equation models this situation?

$y = 2x - 100$ $y = \frac{1}{4}x + 40$

_____

6. A salesperson who uses her own car to make deliveries collected **$9** for driving **50** miles. Which equation could be used to show how much she would be paid for an **80**-mile trip?

$\frac{9}{x} = \frac{50}{80}$ $\frac{x}{9} = \frac{50}{80}$

_____

7. The sum of two numbers f and s is **14**. Which equation shows how s depends on f?

$s = f - 14$ $f \cdot s = 14$ $s = 14 - f$

_____

8. Maris is **5** years older than Carl. Carl is **2** years older than Rory. Which equation shows how Maris's and Rory's ages are related?

$M = R + 5$ $C + R = M$ $M = R + 7$

_____

Extend Your Thinking

9. Write a problem that could be modeled by a one-variable equation. Then write a problem that could be modeled by a two-variable equation. What is the difference between the situations?

_____

10. Explain your method for choosing the correct equation in problem **5**. Which words or phrases helped you choose the equation?

_____

Name _____

Graphing Linear Functions

You already know how to graph ordered pairs in the coordinate plane using tables and rules. Both the table and graph at the right represent the equation $y = 2x - 3$.

The equation $y = 2x - 3$ is a **function**, because for each value of *x* that you substitute in the equation, there is exactly one *y* value. For example, for $y = 2x - 3$, when $x = 2$, then $y = 2 \cdot 2 - 3$, or 1.

The ordered pairs of the equation $y = 2x - 3$ all lie on the **same line**, so the equation is called a **linear function**.

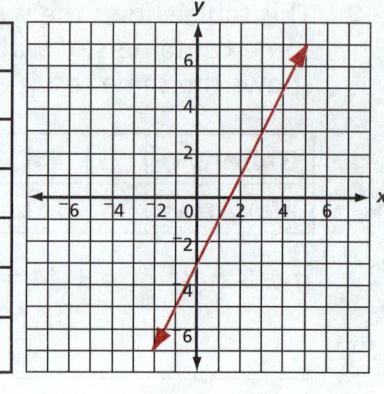

$y = 2x - 3$	
x	y
0	⁻3
1	⁻1
2	1
⁻1	⁻5
⁻2	⁻7

Circle the equations that define linear functions.

1. $y = 3x + 7$ $y = {}^-x^3 - 2x + 1$ $y = |x|$

2. $y = \dfrac{1}{x}$ $y = 0.25x - 2$ $y = \dfrac{-3}{4}x^2 - 8$

Complete the table of values for each function. Then, graph the linear function in the coordinate plane.

3.

$y = x$	
x	y
0	
1	
2	
⁻1	
⁻2	

$y = x - 3$	
x	y
0	
1	
3	
⁻1	
⁻2	

$y = 2x + 1$	
x	y
0	
1	
2	
⁻1	
⁻2	

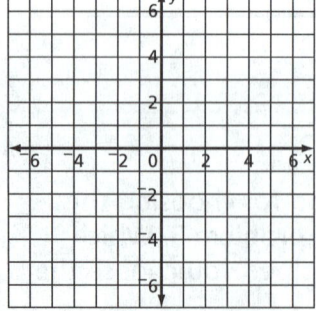
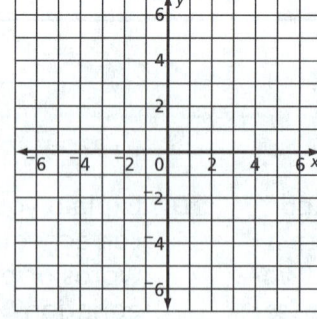

4.
$y = {}^-2x$	
x	y
0	
1	
2	
⁻1	
⁻2	

5.
$y = \frac{1}{2}x - 1$	
x	y
0	
1	
2	
⁻1	
⁻2	

6.
$y = \frac{2}{3}x + 2$	
x	y
0	
1	
2	
⁻1	
⁻2	

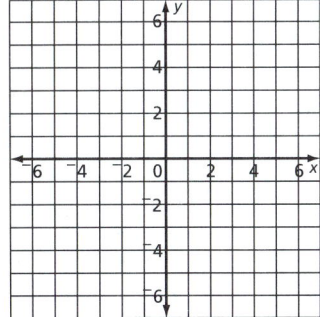
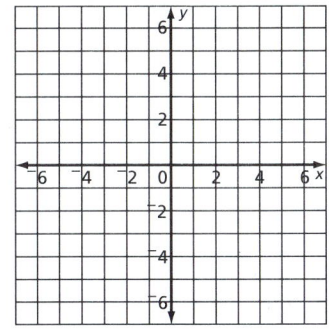
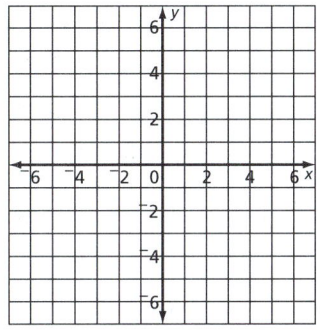

Problem Solving Reasoning — Use graph paper to draw a coordinate grid. Solve.

7. Plot the points (1,2), (1,⁻3), (1,5), and (1,⁻6). Connect the points in order. Are the points part of a function? Will its graph be a linear function? Explain.

_____

 Quick Check

Write the coordinates of the image point.   Work Space

8. The point **(1, 2)** translated **2** units right and **4** units down.

   _____

9. The point **(1, 2)** reflected over the **y**-axis. _____

Complete the table of values.

10. $y = x - 5$

x	y
6	
5	
7	
10	

11. $y = x + 2$

x	y
1	
0	
3	
5	

12. Which is the independent variable, *x* or *y*? _____

13. Graph the equations in exercises **10** and **11** in the coordinate plane. State whether the graphs are the graphs of linear functions or not. _____

Unit 11 Lesson 7 335

Name _____

Slope of a Line

The slope of a line is its steepness. Imagine that the line in the graph below is the side of a hill. You can see that the slope is very steep. The **slope of a line** (abbreviated as *m*) is the ratio of the change in the *y* values to the change in the *x* values between any two points on the line.

$$\text{slope} = \frac{\text{change in } y \text{ values}}{\text{change in } x \text{ values}}$$

The graph at the right shows the line $y = 2x - 3$. Two points on the graph are **(0, ⁻3)** and **(2, 1)**. The *y*-values change from ⁻3 to 1. The *x*-values change from 0 to 2.

$$\text{slope } (m) = \frac{1 - (^-3)}{2 - 0}$$
$$= \frac{4}{2} \text{ So, } m = 2.$$

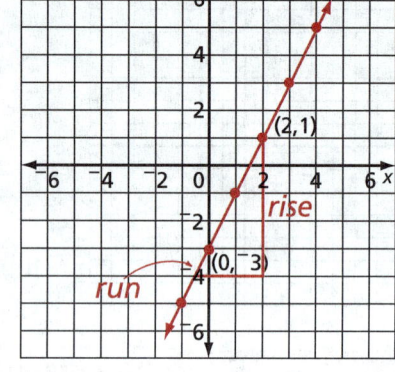

The change in the two *y*-values is called the **rise**. The change in the two *x*-values is called the **run**. You can think of slope as

$$\text{slope} = \frac{\text{rise}}{\text{run}}$$

It does not matter which two points you select on the line. The slope remains constant. For example, the points **(3,3)** and **(10,17)** are both on the line. The slope of the line is

$$\text{slope} = \frac{17 - 3}{10 - 3} \quad \text{or} \quad \text{slope} = \frac{3 - 17}{3 - 10}$$
$$= \frac{14}{7} \text{ So, } m = 2. \qquad = \frac{^-14}{^-7} \text{ So, } m = 2.$$

Notice that the slope of the line is the same as the coefficient of *x* in the linear function $y = 2x - 3$.

Find the slope *m* of the line.

1. $y = 4x + 3$ $y = -\frac{3}{5}x - 2$ $y = 1.2x + 5$

   $m = $ _____ $m = $ _____ $m = $ _____

2. $y = ^-5x + 1$ $y = \frac{4}{3}x + 2$ $y = ^-2.7x - 2$

   $m = $ _____ $m = $ _____ $m = $ _____

3. $y = 2$ $y = x - 5$ $y = x$

   $m = $ _____ $m = $ _____ $m = $ _____

Name _____

Find the slope *m* of the line shown on the coordinate grid.

4.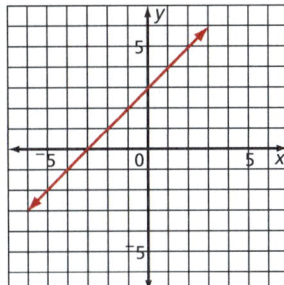

   m = _____

5.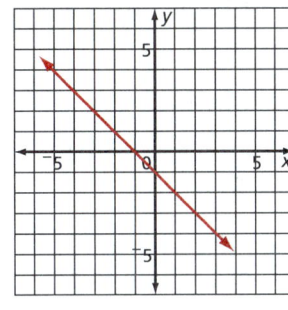

   m = _____

6.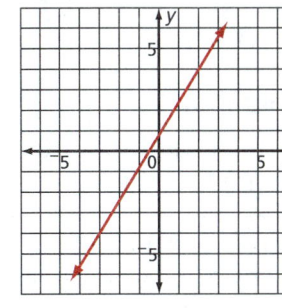

   m = _____

7.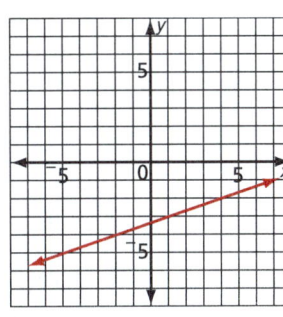

   m = _____

8.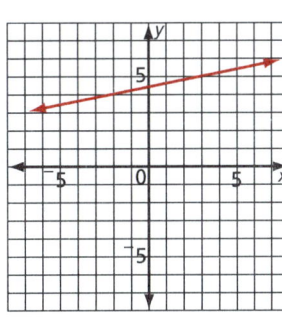

   m = _____

9.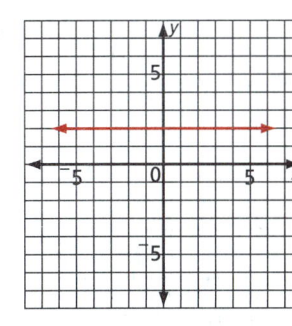

   m = _____

10. Graph each of the following linear functions using the values $x = 0$, $x = 1$, and $x = 2$ on the coordinate grid.

    $y = x$ $y = 2x$ $y = 3x$

11. How is the steepness of the graphs related to the coefficients of *x*? _____

12. At what point do all the lines meet? _____

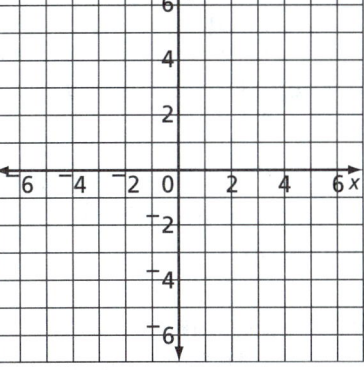

Test Prep ★ Mixed Review

13. Sue has used a grid to draw a geometric figure that is symmetrical about the *y*-axis. One of the points of the figure is (⁻3, 4). What are the coordinates of its matching point?

    A (3, ⁻4)   **C** (3, 4)

    B (⁻3, ⁻4)   **D** (⁻3, 4)

14. A rectangle *ABCD* has been drawn on a grid, and its translation image is *EFGH*. *C* is the point (3, 2) and *A* is the point (0, 4). If point *G* (the image of point *C*) has coordinates (8, 4), what are the coordinates of the point *E*?

    F (0, 6)   **H** (5, 6)

    G (6, 5)   **J** (5, 4)

Unit 11 Lesson 8   **337**

Name _____   # Direct Variation

You know that sometimes two numbers can vary in direct proportion to each other. For example, if you always leave a **15%** tip, then the amount of your tip is in direct proportion to the cost of your meal.

The table shows some values for this relationship.

This pattern can be written as **y = 0.15x**. *Direct variation* is another way of talking about direct proportions.

Cost of Meal	Amount of Tip
$1	$.15
$2	$.30
$3	$.45
$4	$.60
$5	$.75
x	$0.15x$

> Two variables *x* and *y* form a **direct variation** if they are related by a linear function of the form $y = mx$, where m is a non-zero constant called the **constant of variation**. It represents the rate at which the function is changing.

• Tell whether the relationship is a direct variation. If it is, state the constant of variation.

a.
x	6	7	8	9
y	9	10.5	12	13.5

Each *y* value is **1.5** times the *x* value. This is a direct variation, and the constant of variation is **1.5**.

b.
x	4	5	6	7
y	9	11	13	15

The values are related by the equation $y = 2x + 1$.

This is not a direct variation. The ratios $\frac{y}{x}$ are not constant, so there is no constant of variation.

• A variable *k* varies directly with *t*. When $t = 5$, $k = 40$. What is the constant of variation?

You know that this is a direct variation, so

$$k = mt$$

Substitute for *k* and *t*. $40 = m(5)$

Divide each side by 5. $\frac{40}{5} = \frac{m(5)}{5}$

Simplify. $8 = m$

The variable *k* is changing at a rate that is **8** times that of *t*.

State whether the relationship defines a direct variation. If it does, state the constant of variation, *m*.

1. $y = 3x$ _____ $y = \frac{1}{2}x$ _____ $y = 5x + 1$ _____

2. $y = 2x^2$ _____ $y = 0.6x - 2$ _____ $y = \frac{3}{4}x$ _____

Find the constant of variation.

3. $y = 9$ when $x = 3$ _____ $y = 210$ when $x = 30$ _____ $y = 5.6$ when $x = 0.7$ _____

4. $y = 9.6$ when $x = 4$ _____ $y = 16.74$ when $x = 5.4$ _____ $y = 1\frac{3}{4}$ when $x = \frac{1}{2}$ _____

Name _____

Latoya, Carlos, and Paula read at different rates. Paula reads **0.5** page per minute, Carlos reads **1** page, and Latoya reads **2** pages. You can write these relationships as

$$p = 0.5t, \quad p = t, \quad \text{and} \quad p = 2t$$

The variable **p** is the number of pages and **t** is the time spent reading, in minutes. These equations are all direct variations.

The equations are graphed at the right. Notice that the constant of variation equals the slope of the line. You can use the graph to estimate answers about the friends and their reading rates.

About how many pages will the three students each read in **5** minutes?

You can look at each graph at **t = 5**. You find that Paula will read about **2.5** pages, Carlos will read about **5** pages, and Latoya will read about **10** pages.

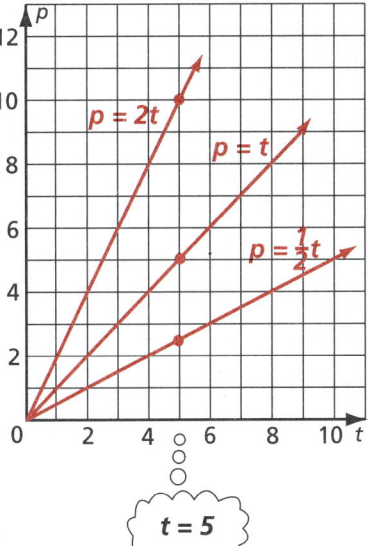

Graph the direct variation.

5. $C = 3.14d$

6. $s = 5t$

7. $y = \frac{1}{3}x$

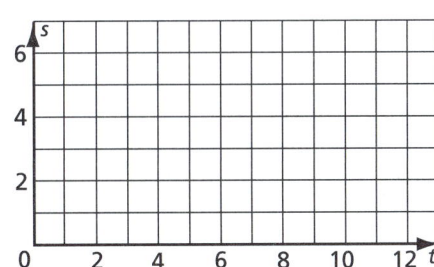

Problem Solving Reasoning Solve.

8. A car averages **27** miles per gallon of gasoline. Find the constant of variation and use it to find the number of miles it will travel on **15** gallons.

_____

9. A book has **48** lines of type per page. Find the constant of variation and use it to find the number of pages that **312** lines of type will fill.

_____

Test Prep ★ Mixed Review

10. Pat repairs appliances. She charges $75 to check out the appliance and, after that, $50 per hour (h). Her total charge (C) can be written as a function: $C = 50h + 75$.

What does she charge after $5\frac{1}{2}$ hours?

A $350   C $300

B $325   D $275

11. If you were to draw the graph of Pat's total charges function, what would the slope of the graph be?

F 75   H $5\frac{1}{2}$

G 50   J 0

Unit 11 Lesson 9

Name _____

Problem Solving Strategy: Write an Equation

This graph shows how the total amount Jayne is paid (**P**) depends on the number of lawns (**n**) she mows. How much will she earn if she mows **80** lawns during the summer?

It's not always possible to extend a graph or table to answer a problem. One way to solve this problem is to write an equation that relates the variables.

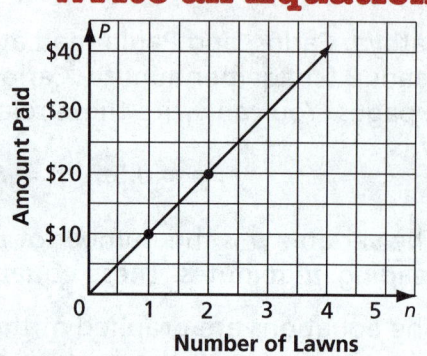

---

1 Understand As you read, ask yourself questions.

- What do you already know?

    Jayne is paid each time she mows a lawn, so **n** is the independent variable.

    The graph is the graph of a direct variation of the form $y = mx$. Some ordered pairs on the graph are **(1, 10)** and **(2, 20)**

- What do you need to find?

    _____

---

2 Decide Choose a method for solving.

Try the strategy Write an Equation.

- Let **n** be the number of lawns Jayne mows and **P** be the total amount she is paid.

- Find the value of **m**, the constant of variation. _____

Write the equation. _____

---

3 Solve Use the equation to solve the problem. **Solution:**

Remember to keep your equal signs aligned.

---

4 Look back Check your answer.

Use some other ordered pairs from the graph to check your equation.

Write your answer as a full sentence.

Answer _____

340 Unit 11 Lesson 10

Name _____

Use the Write an Equation strategy or any other strategy you have learned to solve these problems.

1. An Internet provider includes a service charge of **$18** per month (*m*) on the bill. How much will a customer pay in service charges (*S*) from April through December?

   Think: How many months is it from April through December?

   _____
   _____

2. A mobile phone company charges its customers a flat fee of **$10** per month and **$.19** for each minute or fraction of a minute (*x*) of use. In the month of May, Jana used her mobile phone a total of **82.5** minutes. What was her monthly bill for May (*y*)?

   Think: What operations will you use in your equation?

   _____
   _____

3. Saul is paid **$15** each time he mows his neighbor's yard (*n*). If he mows all summer he will also get a **$50** bonus. From June through September, Saul mowed the lawn **25** times. How much did his neighbor pay him (*P*)?

   _____

4. Star Bank automatically adds a **$5.00** bonus for opening a new savings account. Saul opened a new account in September and deposited **$100**. If the bank pays **0.3%** per month interest on deposits, how much does Saul have in his account at the end of September?

   _____

5. The ordered pairs show how the score (*s*) depends on the number of questions answered correctly (*n*). If Toria answered **25** questions correctly, what was her score?

n	0	4	8	10
s	0	16	32	40

   _____

6. The table shows how far (*d*) a car that is traveling at a constant rate of speed goes in *t* hours. How long would it take the car to travel **150** miles?

t	0	0.5	4	6
d	0	27.5	220	330

   _____

7. The *y*-values for a function are one less than twice the difference between the *x*-values and 3. If *x* = 3, then what is the corresponding value for *y*?

   _____

8. The *y*-values are one half of the difference between the *x*-values and 4. If *y* = 3, then what is the corresponding value for *x*?

   _____

Unit 11 Lesson 10

Non-Linear Functions

A function in *x* and *y* is a rule that generates ordered pairs. For each *x*-value you substitute into the rule, there is exactly one corresponding *y*-value. You have learned to use ordered pairs for linear functions. However, not all functions are linear.

Think about this formula for the area of a square: The area of a square is $A = s^2$, where *s* is the length of a side.

Look at the table of ordered pairs at the right. For each *s*-value, there is exactly one value for *A*. The formula $A = s^2$ is an example of a function. The area *A* depends on the length of a side *s*; so, *A* is a function of *s*. Notice that there are no negative values in the table, since there is no square with a side that is a negative number.

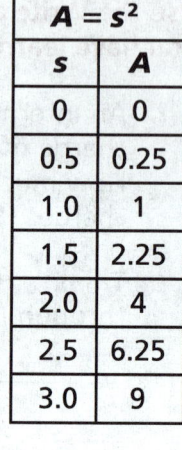

$A = s^2$	
s	A
0	0
0.5	0.25
1.0	1
1.5	2.25
2.0	4
2.5	6.25
3.0	9

In the graph of this function, the horizontal axis is the *s*-axis and the vertical axis is the *A*-axis. Remember that you can use different scales for the axes.

You can see that the area of a square with side **1.5** units is **2.25** square units. From the shape of the graph you can see that $A = s^2$ is the graph of a **non-linear function**.

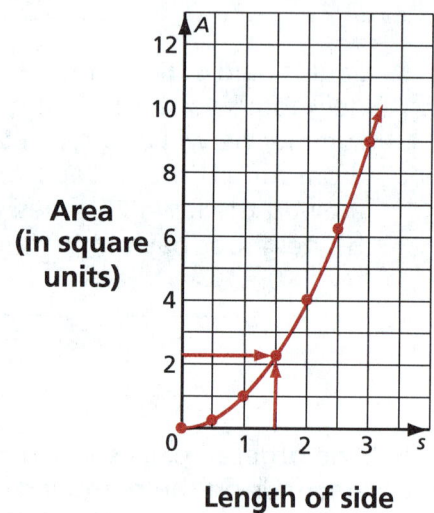

Length of side

Suppose that *s* could be a negative number. If $s = {}^-1$, then $A = 1$; if $s = {}^-2$, then $A = 4$, if $s = {}^-3$, then $A = 9$. If we plot the points $({}^-1, 1)$, $({}^-2, 4)$, $({}^-3, 9)$, the graph would be a curve called a **parabola** that is symmetric to the *y*-axis, and non-linear.

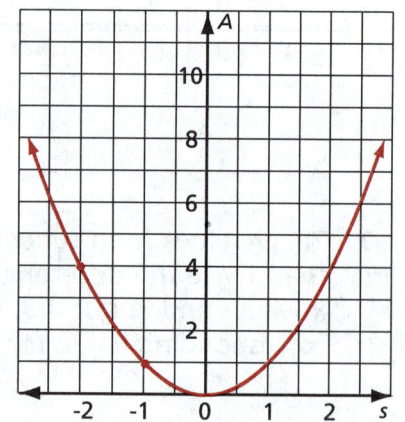

342 Unit 11 Lesson 11

Name _____

The volume of a cube is $V = s^3$, where s is the length of a side of a cube. Again, notice that there are no negative values of s in the table, since volume cannot be negative. The values of V increase very rapidly as the length of a side increases. Choosing an appropriate scale for the graph is difficult because of the rapid increase in V. In the graph, the horizontal axis represents the length of a side s and the vertical axis represents the volume V.

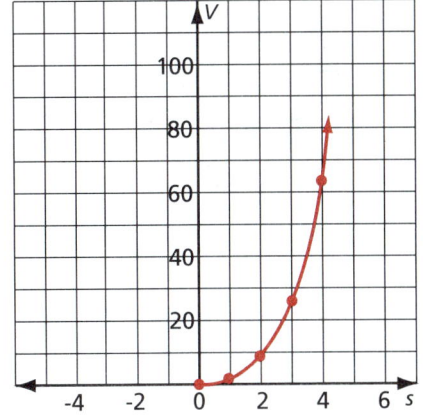

$V = s^3$	s	0	1	2	3	4	5
	V	0	1	8	27	64	125

If s could be a negative number, then the graph at the right represents $V = s^3$. It is a non-linear function that decreases very rapidly as s decreases.

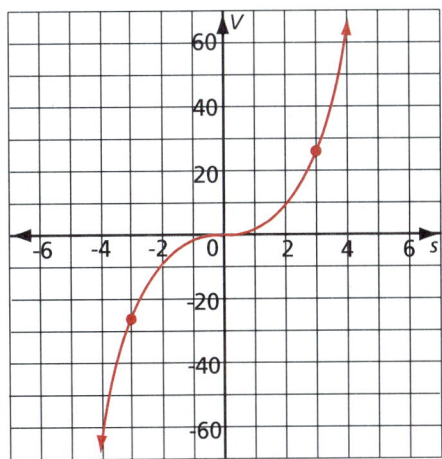

$V = s^3$	s	0	1	2	3	4	5
	V	0	1	8	27	64	125

Complete the table of values for the function. Graph the function on a coordinate grid. State whether the function is linear or non-linear.

1.

$y = x^2$	
x	y
0	
-1	
1	
-2	
2	
-3	
3	

_____

2.

$y = 2x + 1$	
x	y
0	
-1	
1	
-2	
2	
-3	
3	

_____

3.

$y = x^3 - 1$	
x	y
0	
-1	
1	
-2	
2	
-3	
3	

_____

Unit 11 Lesson 11

The following problems involve formulas that you have used in this unit. Select appropriate values and complete a table. Graph the function on a coordinate grid. State whether the function is linear or non-linear.

Area of a Circle

4. 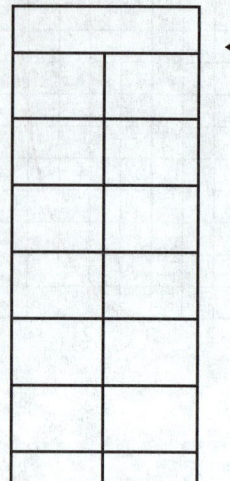 ← Formula

Circumference of a Circle

5. 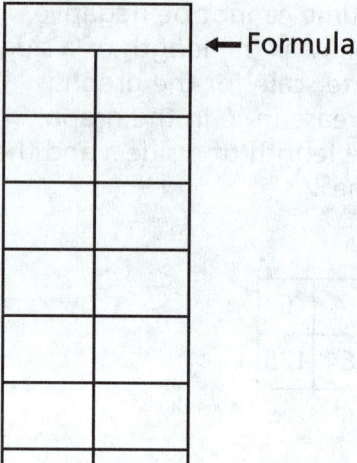 ← Formula

Perimeter of a Square

6. 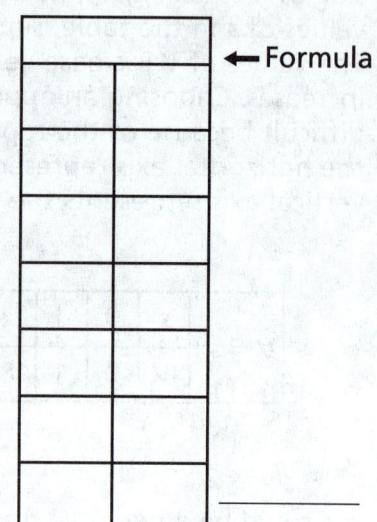 ← Formula

---

Problem Solving Reasoning — Complete.

Two variables *x* and *y* form an **inverse variation** if there is a positive number *k* such that *xy = k*. Here are two tables that relate rate (*x*) and time (*y*).

A

x	y
24	0.5
12	1
6	2
3	4

B

x	y
24	1
12	2
6	3
3	4

7. Which table shows an inverse variation? What is the value of *k*?

   _____

8. Use your answer from exercise 7 to extend the table of ordered pairs (be sure to include some negative values for *x*) and graph them. State whether the function is linear or non-linear.

   _____

   _____

 Quick Check

Work Space

Find the slope of the line.

9. $y = 3x - 8$ 10. $y = 0.2x + 18$ 11. $y = 3x$

   _____   _____   _____

Find the constant of direct variation.

12. $y = 10$ when $x = 2$ 13. $y = 3$ when $x = 5$

    _____   _____

14. Is the graph of $y = \frac{2}{3}x^2 - 1$ linear or non-linear? How do you know? _____

Name _____

Unit 11 Review

Translate the given figure according to the directions given.

1. Right 6 units, Down 4 units

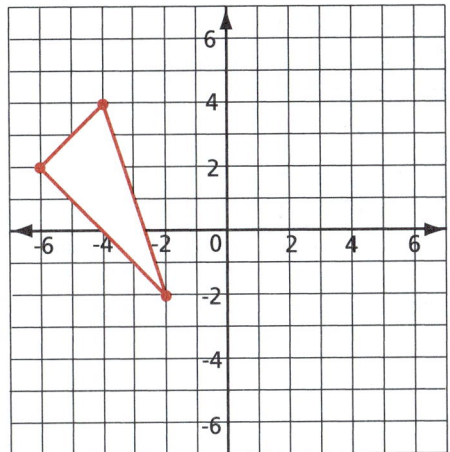

2. Left 5 units, Up 3 units

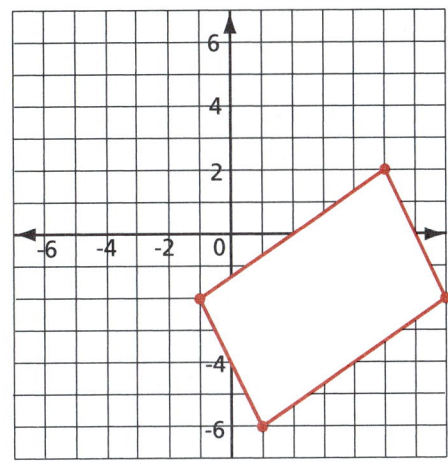

Reflect the figure over the given axis.

3. Reflect over the *y*-axis

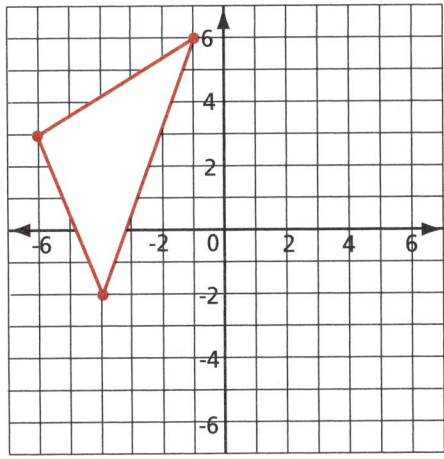

4. Reflect over the *x*-axis

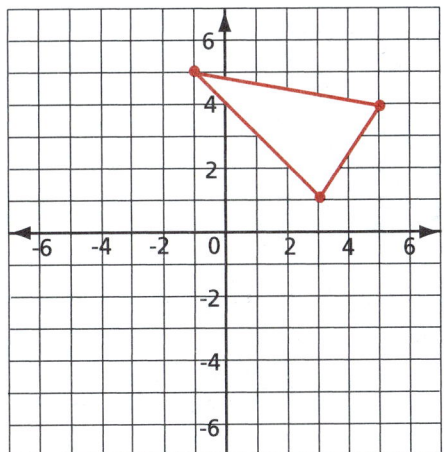

Complete the table of values for the given function. State whether the function is linear or non-linear.

5. $y = 4x$

x	y
2	
3	
0	
⁻1	

6. $y = \frac{-2}{3}x$

x	y
0	
3	
⁻3	
⁻2	

7. $y = {}^-x + 2$

x	y
4	
⁻2	
1	
0	

8. $y = x^2 + 1$

x	y
1	
0	
⁻2	
⁻1	

9. $y = x^3$

x	y
0	
⁻2	
1	
⁻1	

Unit 11 Review   345

On the grid below, complete the figure so it is symmetric to the given axis.

10. Symmetric about *y*-axis

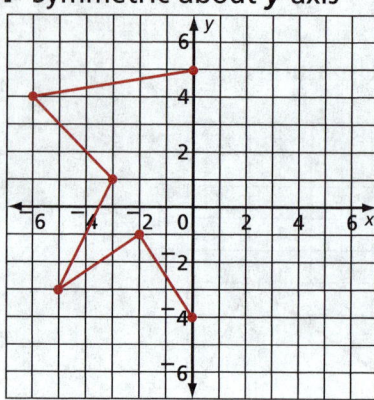

11. Symmetric about *x*-axis

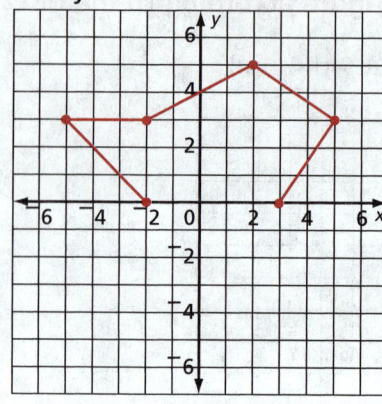

Graph the linear function on the coordinate grid.

12. $y = 2x - 5$

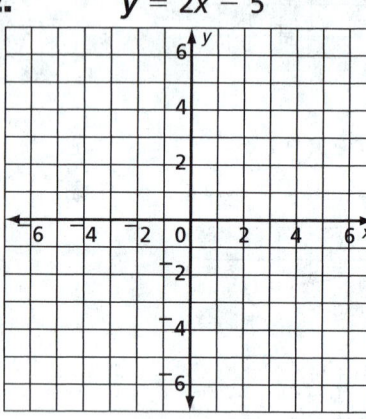

13. $y = -x + 2$

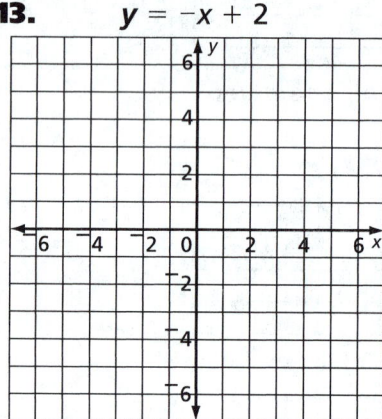

Find the slope of the linear function.

14. $y = 3x - 7$ _____   **15.** $y = -\dfrac{4}{5}x + 2$ _____   **16.** $y = -x + 3$ _____   **17.** $y = \dfrac{1}{3}x - 4$ _____

Find the constant of variation.

18. $y = 15$ when $x = 3$ **19.** $y = 2$ when $x = 10$ **20.** $y = 13$ when $x = 4$ _____

The figures are similar. Find the missing lengths.

21.

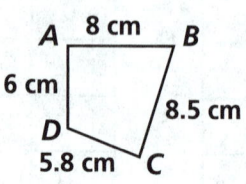
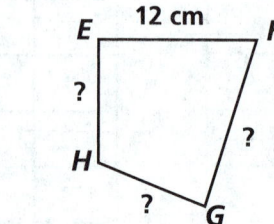

$\overline{FG}$ _____

$\overline{GH}$ _____

$\overline{HE}$ _____

346   Unit 11 Review

Name _____

Find the slope of the line.

22.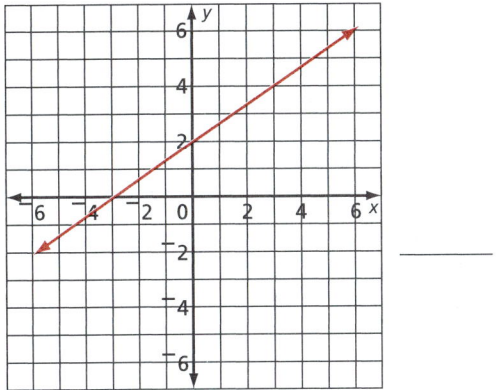

23.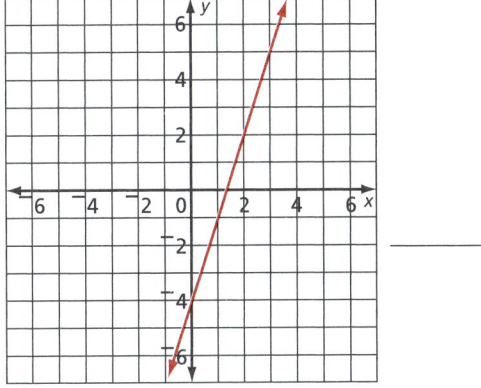

Graph the non-linear function.

24. $y = 2x^2 - 3$

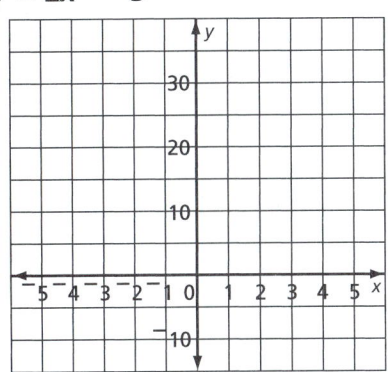

25. $y = x^2 + 1$

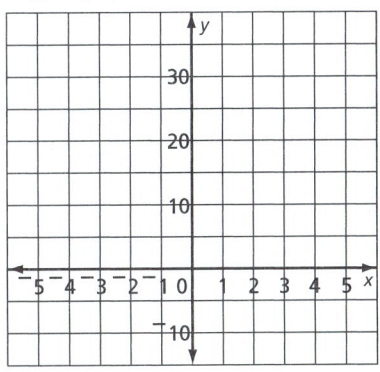

Solve.

26. A map has a scale of **1** inch:**50** miles. Two cities are $2\frac{3}{4}$ inches apart on the map. What is the actual distance between the cities? _____

27. Practice times depend on the age of a student. The average practice time for a **5** year-old is about **13** minutes, while that for a **12** year-old is about **34** minutes. Choose the equation that shows this relationship.

$y = 3x - 2$ $y = x + 5 + 12$ $y = 12 - 3x$ $y = 5x + 13$

Write an equation to solve the problem.

28. The ordered pairs are part of a function that shows how much an office spent per day for paper. Write an equation that shows how the ordered pairs are related. _____

x	0	1	2	3
y	0	$20	$40	$60

Use your equation to find out the paper cost for **250** days. _____

Unit 11 Review **347**

Cumulative Review ★ Test Prep

1 Steve is a paint supplier. He charges a flat rate of $30 for use of his spray-painting equipment and, after that, $13 per gallon ($g$) for latex paint. So his total charge (C) can be written as a function: $C = 13g + 30$. If you were to draw the graph of the function, what would the slope of the graph be?

A 30 **C** $\frac{30}{13}$

B 13 **D** $\frac{13}{30}$

2 A triangle ABC has been drawn on a grid, and its translation image is $\triangle DEF$. A is the point $(3, 6)$ and B is the point $(1, 3)$. If point D (the image of point A) has coordinates $(8, 9)$, what are the coordinates of the point E?

F $(4, 5)$ **H** $(9, 3)$

G $(6, 6)$ **J** $(9, 8)$

3 A light-year, the distance traveled by light in 1 year, is about five trillion, eight hundred seventy billion miles. Which of these is the closest to that number?

A 5.87×10^{10} **C** 5.87×10^{8}

B 5.87×10^{12} **D** 5.87×10^{18}

4 What is the value of the expression: $|{-30}| + {-25} \div {-5}$?

F 25 **H** -25

G 35 **J** -30

5 The differences of the four times p subtracted from three is at least seven. What mathematical sentence best represents this?

A $3 - 4p = 7$ **D** $3 - 4p > 7$

B $3 - 4p \geq 7$ **E** Not here

C $4p - 3 \geq 7$

6 Fourteen feet from the corner of a rectangular playing field Tina fixes one end of a 15-ft rope to a peg on the side line. Then, keeping the rope fully stretched, she moves toward the goal line until her end of the rope can be pegged exactly on the goal line. How far from the corner is that end of the rope?

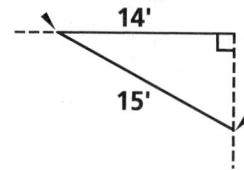

F 1 ft **H** 14.5 ft

G 5.4 ft **J** 29 ft

7 If a cylindrical container can hold 65 ft³ of water, how much water could it hold if the radius remained the same but the height were doubled?

A 260 ft³ **C** 105 ft³

B 130 ft³ **D** 65 ft³

8 A CD player was marked down from $98.98 to $84.99. About what was the percent of discount?

F 10% **J** 50%

G 15% **K** 86%

H 18%

348 Unit 11 Cumulative Review

Tables of Measures

Metric System

Prefixes

kilo (k)	= 1,000	
hecto (h)	= 100	
deka (da)	= 10	
deci (d)	= 0.1	= $\frac{1}{10}$
centi (c)	= 0.01	= $\frac{1}{100}$
milli (m)	= 0.001	= $\frac{1}{1,000}$

Length

1 kilometer (km)	= 1,000 meters (m)
1 meter	= 10 decimeters (dm)
1 decimeter	= 10 centimeters (cm)
1 meter	= 100 centimeters (cm)
1 centimeter	= 10 millimeters (mm)
1 meter	= 1,000 millimeters
1 millimeter (mm)	= 0.001 meter

Capacity

1 kiloliter (kL)	= 1,000 liters (L)
1 centiliter (cL)	= 0.01 liter
1 liter	= 1,000 milliliters (mL)
1 milliliter (mL)	= 0.001 liter

Mass

1 metric ton (T)	= 1,000 kilograms (kg)
1 kilogram	= 1,000 grams (g)
1 centigram (cg)	= 0.01 gram
1 gram	= 1,000 milligrams (mg)
1 milligram (mg)	= 0.001 gram

Area

100 square mm (mm^2)	= 1 square cm (cm^2)
1 square m (m^2)	= 10,000 square cm
1 hectare (ha)	= 10,000 square m
1 square km (km^2)	= 1,000,000 sq m

Volume

1 cubic cm (cm^3)	= 1,000 cubic mm (mm^3)
1 cubic m (m^3)	= 1,000,000 cubic cm

Customary System

Length

1 foot (ft)	= 12 inches (in.)
1 yard (yd)	= 3 feet
1 yard	= 36 inches
1 mile (mi)	= 5,280 feet
1 mile	= 1,760 yards

Capacity

1 cup (c)	= 8 fluid ounces (fl oz)
1 pint (pt)	= 2 cups
1 quart (qt)	= 2 pints
1 gallon (gal)	= 4 quarts

Weight

1 pound (lb)	= 16 ounces (oz)
1 ton (T)	= 2,000 pounds

Area

1 square foot (ft^2)	= 144 square inches ($in.^2$)
1 square yard (yd^2)	= 9 square feet
1 acre (A)	= 4,840 square yards
1 square mile (mi^2)	= 640 acres

Volume

1 cubic foot (ft^3)	= 1,728 cubic inches ($in.^3$)
1 cubic yd (yd^3)	= 27 cubic feet

Other Measures

Time

1 minute (min)	=	60 seconds (s)
1 hour (h)	=	60 minutes
1 day (d)	=	24 hours
1 week (wk)	=	7 days
1 month (mo)	≈	4 weeks
1 year (yr)	=	12 months
1 year	=	52 weeks
1 year	=	365 days
1 leap year	=	366 days
1 decade	=	10 years
1 century	=	100 years

Counting

1 dozen (doz)	=	12 things
1 score	=	20 things
1 gross (gro)	=	12 dozen
1 gross	=	144 things

Geometric Formulas

Triangle

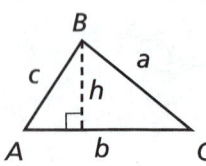

Perimeter:
$P = a + b + c$

Area:
$A = \frac{1}{2}bh$

Square

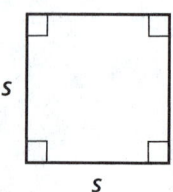

Perimeter:
$P = 4s$

Area:
$A = s^2$

Rectangle

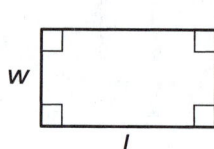

Perimeter:
$P = 2(l + w)$

Area:
$A = lw$

Parallelogram

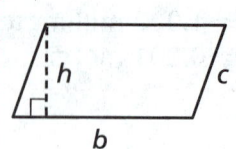

Area:
$A = bh$

Trapezoid

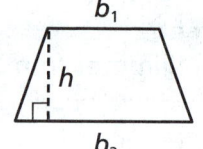

Area:
$A = \frac{1}{2}h(b_1 + b_2)$

Circle

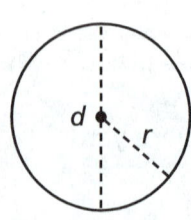

Circumference:
$C = 2\pi r$

Area:
$A = \pi r^2$

Rectangular Prism

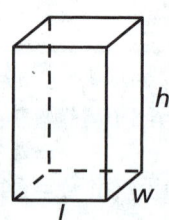

Surface Area:
$SA = 2(lw + wh + lh)$

Volume:
$V = lwh$

Cube

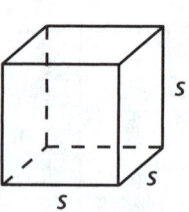

Surface Area:
$SA = 6s^2$

Volume:
$V = s^3$

Cylinder

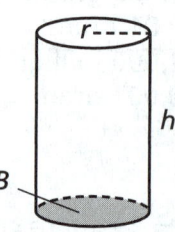

Surface Area:
$SA = 2\pi r^2 + 2\pi rh$

Other Formulas

	Distance (D) traveled	Simple Interest (I)	Percent (P) of a number
r = rate (in decimal form) t = time p = principal b = original base number	$D = rt$	$I = prt$	$P = br$

Symbols

=	is equal to	%	percent	⊥	is perpendicular to
≠	is not equal to	°	degree	~	is similar to
<	is less than	∠A	angle A	≅	is congruent to
>	is greater than	$\overline{AB}$	line segment AB	5^4	5 to the fourth power (5 · 5 · 5 · 5)
≈	is approximately equal to	$\overrightarrow{AB}$	ray AB	π	pi
n, x	variables	$\overleftrightarrow{AB}$	line AB	$^+5$	positive 5
$0.\overline{37}$	0.37373737... (repeating decimal)	△	triangle	$^-5$	negative 5
$a:b$	the ratio of a to b	∥	is parallel to	$P(A)$	the probability of A

Equivalent Fractions and Percents

$50\% = \frac{1}{2}$	$16\frac{2}{3}\% = \frac{1}{6}$	$90\% = \frac{9}{10}$
$33\frac{1}{3}\% = \frac{1}{3}$	$83\frac{1}{3}\% = \frac{5}{6}$	$14\frac{2}{7}\% = \frac{1}{7}$
$66\frac{2}{3}\% = \frac{2}{3}$	$12\frac{1}{2}\% = \frac{1}{8}$	$11\frac{1}{9}\% = \frac{1}{9}$
$25\% = \frac{1}{4}$	$37\frac{1}{2}\% = \frac{3}{8}$	$9\frac{1}{11}\% = \frac{1}{11}$
$75\% = \frac{3}{4}$	$62\frac{1}{2}\% = \frac{5}{8}$	$8\frac{1}{3}\% = \frac{1}{12}$
$20\% = \frac{1}{5}$	$87\frac{1}{2}\% = \frac{7}{8}$	$5\% = \frac{1}{20}$
$40\% = \frac{2}{5}$	$10\% = \frac{1}{10}$	$4\% = \frac{1}{25}$
$60\% = \frac{3}{5}$	$30\% = \frac{3}{10}$	$2\frac{1}{2}\% = \frac{1}{40}$
$80\% = \frac{4}{5}$	$70\% = \frac{7}{10}$	$2\% = \frac{1}{50}$

Square Roots

Rational approximations are rounded to the nearest thousandth. Exact square roots are in red.

Number	Positive Square Root	Number	Positive Square Root	Number	Positive Square Root	Number	Positive Square Root
N	$\sqrt{N}$	N	$\sqrt{N}$	N	$\sqrt{N}$	N	$\sqrt{N}$
1	1	26	5.099	51	7.141	76	8.718
2	1.414	27	5.196	52	7.211	77	8.775
3	1.732	28	5.292	53	7.280	78	8.832
4	2	29	5.385	54	7.348	79	8.888
5	2.236	30	5.477	55	7.416	80	8.944
6	2.449	31	5.568	56	7.483	81	9
7	2.646	32	5.657	57	7.550	82	9.055
8	2.828	33	5.745	58	7.616	83	9.110
9	3	34	5.831	59	7.681	84	9.165
10	3.162	35	5.916	60	7.746	85	9.220
11	3.317	36	6	61	7.810	86	9.274
12	3.464	37	6.083	62	7.874	87	9.327
13	3.606	38	6.164	63	7.937	88	9.381
14	3.742	39	6.245	64	8	89	9.434
15	3.873	40	6.325	65	8.062	90	9.487
16	4	41	6.403	66	8.124	91	9.539
17	4.123	42	6.481	67	8.185	92	9.592
18	4.243	43	6.557	68	8.246	93	9.644
19	4.359	44	6.633	69	8.307	94	9.695
20	4.472	45	6.708	70	8.367	95	9.747
21	4.583	46	6.782	71	8.426	96	9.798
22	4.690	47	6.856	72	8.485	97	9.849
23	4.796	48	6.928	73	8.544	98	9.899
24	4.899	49	7	74	8.602	99	9.950
25	5	50	7.071	75	8.660	100	10

Glossary

A

absolute value The distance of a number from zero on the number line, regardless of direction

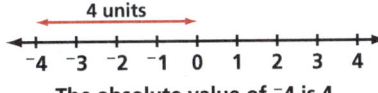

The absolute value of ⁻4 is 4.

acute angle An angle whose measure is between 0° and 90°

acute triangle A triangle with acute angles

addend (see *addition*)

addition The arithmetic operation that combines two numbers
Example: 23 ← addend
+ 13 ← addend
36 ← sum

addition property of equality If two expressions are equivalent, then adding the same number to each forms two more equal expressions.
Example: If $n - 7 = 10$, then $n - 7 + 7 = 10 + 7$

additive inverse (see *opposites*)

adjacent angles Two angles that share a common vertex with a common side between them

alternate interior angles (on a tranversal) Pairs of angles that are on opposite sides of the transversal and interior to the lines

altitude A segment of a triangle, parallelogram, or trapezoid that is perpendicular to the base. In a triangle one endpoint is the vertex opposite the base.

amount due The amount you pay back to the bank; that is, principal plus interest

angle A geometric figure formed by two rays with a common endpoint called the vertex. The angle below can be named either ∠ABC or ∠B.

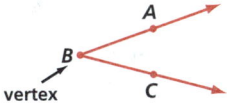

angle bisector A ray that divides an angle into two adjacent angles of equal measure

arc Two points on a circle and all the points of the circle between them.

$\overarc{AB}$: minor arc
$\overarc{ACB}$: major arc

area A measure of a region or a surface. A square is used as a unit.

associative property of addition The grouping of the addends does not change the sum
Example: $(37 + 95) + 5 = 37 + (95 + 5) = 137$

associative property of multiplication The grouping of the factors does not change the product
Example: $(25 \cdot 5) \cdot 2 = 27 \cdot (5 \cdot 2) = 270$

average A measure of central tendency. It is computed by adding all the items of data and dividing by the number of items.

axis (see *x-axis*, *y-axis*)

B

bar graph A graph that uses lengths of bars to represent the data

base (number) That part of the percent equation that represents the entire original amount.
Example: 25% of 16 is 4.
rate (*r*) × base (*b*) = percentage (*p*)

base (of a power) The number that is used as a factor when evaluating powers
Example: $3^4 = 3 \cdot 3 \cdot 3 \cdot 3$
The base is 3.

base (of a space figure) (see *cone, cylinder, prism, pyramid*)

binary operation An operation, such as addition, that is performed on two numbers at a time.

bisector A point, line, or ray that divides a figure into two parts of equal measure.

box-and-whisker plot A graph that shows how data are distributed by using the median, quartiles, maximum and minimum values

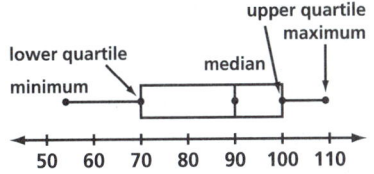

C

capacity The maximum amount of liquid that a container can hold

center (see *circle, sphere*)

central angle An angle whose vertex is the center of a circle

central tendency The most representative numbers of a set of data

chord A segment with its endpoints on a circle.

circle A plane figure that has all of its points at a fixed distance from a given point called the center

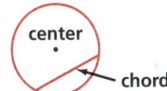

circle graph A pictorial representation of data that uses sections of a circle to show the information

circumference The distance around a circle. It is about 3.14 times the length of the diameter.

closed curve A curve that has no endpoints. If it does not cross itself, it is called a simple closed curve.

Glossary 353

cluster Several items of data grouped into a small interval

coefficient (of a monomial) The numerical factor in each term containing a variable
Example: for $3x^2 + 2x - 1$, 3 is the coefficient of x^2, 2 is the coefficient of x.

collinear points Points that lie on the same straight line

combinations A collection of objects in which order is not important

commission The part of the total selling price that is paid to the salesperson

common denominator A denominator used when adding two or more fractions with unlike denominators.
Example: Some common denominators of $\frac{1}{2}$ and $\frac{1}{3}$ are 6, 12, 18, 24, . . .

common factor A number that is a factor of two or more whole numbers
Example: 1, 2, 3, and 6 are common factors of 12 and 18.

common multiple A number that is a multiple of two or more whole numbers
Example: Common multiples of 3 and 4 are 12, 24, 36, . . .

commutative property of addition The order of the addends does not change the sum
Example: $3 + 4 = 4 + 3 = 7$

commutative property of multiplication The order of the factors does not change the product
Example: $3 \cdot 5 = 5 \cdot 3 = 15$

compass A geometric construction tool used to draw arcs and circles

compatible numbers Two numbers that form a basic division fact. For example, 5 and 30 are compatible numbers

complementary angles Two angles whose measures total 90°

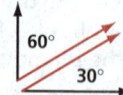

composite number A number with three or more factors
Example: 9 is composite, because its factors are 1, 3, and 9.

compound event The combination of two or more single events
Example: Rolling a "4" on one number cube and then rolling a "6" on another

cone A space figure with one flat, circular surface and one curved surface

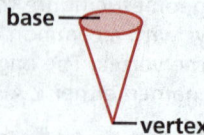

congruent figures Figures that have exactly the same size and shape. In congruent polygons, *corresponding angles* are congruent and *corresponding sides* are congruent.

constant A numerical term in a polynomial

constant of variation (see *direct variation*)

coordinate Each number of an ordered pair
Example: (4, 6) has a first coordinate of 4 and a second coordinate of 6.

coordinate plane A grid with number lines used to locate points in a plane

coplanar Two or more points, lines, or figures that are in the same plane

correlation (of scatter-plot points) A relationship between the x- and y-coordinates of points on a scatter plot such that both coordinates increase (positive correlation) or both decrease (negative correlation).

corresponding angles (on a transversal) Two angles in the same position in relation to two lines and a transversal

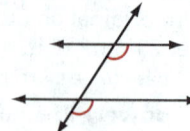

cross product property In a proportion, if $\frac{a}{b} = \frac{c}{d}$, then $a \cdot d = b \cdot c$

cross products The products obtained by multiplying the numerator of one ratio by the denominator of the other.
Example: In the proportion $\frac{5}{7} = \frac{2.5}{3.5}$, the cross products are equal: $5 \times 3.5 = 17.5$ and $7 \times 2.5 = 17.5$

cube A rectangular prism whose faces are all congruent squares

customary system of measurement The system of measurement currently used in the United States

cylinder A space figure with two congruent circular bases joined by a single curved surface

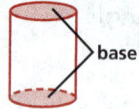

D

data Numerical information

decimal A number that uses place value to indicate parts of a whole. The decimal point separates the whole number digits from the digits representing parts of a whole.
Example: The decimal

3.67

decimal point

represents the number three and 67 hundredths.

denominator The numeral below the fraction bar in a fraction. It tells how many parts are in the whole.

dependent events Two or more events such that the results of one influences the results of the others
Example: Suppose the numbers 1, 2, and 3 are each written on a slip of paper. Choose one number, and without putting it back, choose a second number.

diagonal A segment joining two vertices of a polygon that is not a side

diagonal (of a polyhedron) A segment that joins two vertices that are not in the same face

diameter A chord of a circle that passes through the center

difference (see *subtraction*)

digit Any of the symbols used to write numerals. In the base 10 system, they are 1, 2, 3, 4, 5, 6, 7, 8, 9, and 0.

dimensional analysis (see *unit analysis*)

direct proportion A relationship between two quantities such that both increase simultaneously. For example, the distance (*d*) traveled by a car during a fixed time (say, 2 hours) increases as the speed (*s*) increases. $d = 2 \cdot s$

direct variation A linear function of the form $y = mx$. The non-zero number *m* is called the *constant of variation* and represents the rate at which the function is changing.

discount A reduction in the original or list price of a product

distributive property The same answer is obtained whether you add (or subtract) first and then multiply or multiply first and then add (or subtract).
Example:
$3 \cdot (20 + 7) = 3 \cdot 20 + 3 \cdot 7 = 81$

dividend (see *division*)

divisible A number is divisible by another number if there is no remainder when they are divided.
Example: 4, 16, and 640 are all divisible by 4.

division An operation that divides a set into equal sets
Example:
quotient → 10 R5 ← remainder
divisor → 6)65 ← dividend

division property of equality If two expressions are equal, then dividing each by the same non zero number forms two new equal expressions.
Example: If $a = b$ and $n \neq 0$, then $a \div n = b \div n$

divisor (see *division*)

double-line graph A line graph that compares two sets of data by using one line for each set

E

edge (see *polyhedron*)
endpoint (see *ray, line segment*)

equally likely Outcomes of an experiment that have an equal chance of occurring
Example: A spinner is divided into 6 congruent sections. Each section is an equally likely outcome of a spin.

equation A number sentence that says that two expressions have the same value. It may be true, false, or open.
Example: $3 + 7 = 10$ is true; $3 + 7 = 7$ is false, and $3 + n = 10$ is open.

equiangular Having angles of the same measure

equilateral triangle A triangle with three congruent sides

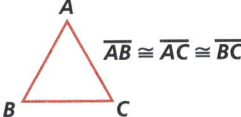

$\overline{AB} \cong \overline{AC} \cong \overline{BC}$

equivalent fractions Two or more fractions that represent the same number.
Example: $\frac{1}{2} = \frac{2}{4} = \frac{3}{6} = \frac{4}{8}$

estimate To find a approximate solution mentally by using numbers that are close to the original numbers and easy to work with mentally

evaluate To find the value of an expression

even number A whole number that is divisible by 2

event Any outcome or set of outcomes of an experiment

expanded form A number written so that each digit is expressed as a power of 10 instead of by its position in the numeral
Example: The expanded form of 316 is

$3 \cdot 100 + 1 \cdot 10 + 6 \cdot 1$

experimental probability An estimate of the probability of an event based on the results of an experiment

exponent A number that tells how many times a base is to be used as a factor
Example: 3^4 represents the product
$\underbrace{3 \cdot 3 \cdot 3 \cdot 3}_{\text{4 factors}}$

exponent form A number expressed as a power
Example: Exponent forms of 64 are 2^6 and 8^2

expression A combination of numbers and symbols of operation (or grouping) that represents a mathematical quantity
Examples: $(7 + 3) \div 5$ or $6 \cdot n$

F

face (see *polyhedron*)

factor (see *multiplication*)

factor tree A diagram used to help factor a composite number into its prime factors

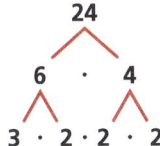

formula A general rule or relationship expressed in symbols.

fraction A number such as $\frac{1}{2}$ or $\frac{3}{4}$ that is used to express a part of a region or set

function A rule that tells how to perform one or more operations on a set of numbers so that each input value has just one output value. The rule is usually expressed as an equation.
Example: The equation $y = 3x - 7$ states that *y* is a function of *x*, and also expresses the rule of the relationship.

G

gap A characteristic of data. It is a significant interval that contains no data

graph A pictorial representation of a data set or equation

greatest common factor (GCF) The greatest number that is a factor of each of two or more numbers.
Example: The greatest common factor of 24 and 30 is 6.

H

hemisphere Half of a sphere.

heptagon A polygon that has 7 sides

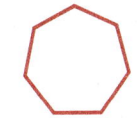 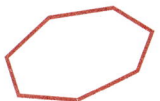

regular heptagon   irregular heptagon

hexagon A polygon that has 6 sides

regular hexagon
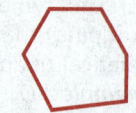
irregular hexagon

histogram A type of bar graph. The categories are consecutive intervals along a number line. The intervals are all the same size with no gaps between them.

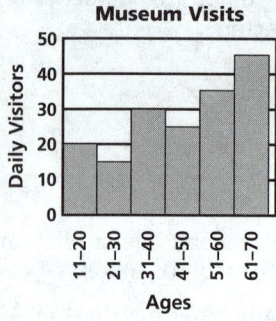

horizontal line A line that is parallel to the horizon

hypotenuse The side of a right triangle that is opposite the right angle

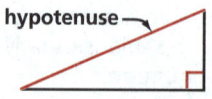

I

identity property of addition Adding zero to any number equals that number.
Examples: $7 + 0 = 7$ and $n + 0 = n$

identity property of multiplication Multiplying one by any number equals that number.
Examples: $10 \cdot 1 = 10$ and $n \cdot 1 = n$

image (see *reflection*)

improper fraction A fraction in which the denominator is either greater than or equal to the numerator

independent events Two or more events whose outcomes do not affect each other
Example: Two tosses of a coin when you are recording "heads" or "tails"

inequality A number sentence that states that two numbers or expression are not equal
Examples:
$3 + 6 < 10$ read "Three plus six is less than 10."
$5 + 7 > 10$ read "Five plus seven is greater than 10."

integer The set of numbers containing all the whole numbers and their opposites

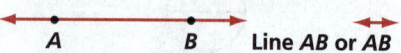
negative integers — zero — positive integers

interest The amount of money charged for a loan, or earned on a savings account. Interest that is allowed to accumulate and be added to the principal at regular intervals is compound interest. Otherwise it is simple interest.

inverse operations A numerical operation that undoes the results of another operation

inverse proportion A relationship between two quantities such that as one quantity increases, the other decreases. For example, the time (*t*) taken by a car to travel a fixed distance (say 10 miles) decreases as the speed (*s*) increases.
$t = \frac{10}{s}$

irrational number A number that cannot be expressed as a ratio of two integers
Example: An infinite non-terminating, non-repeating decimal such as $\sqrt{2}$ or π.

isosceles triangle A triangle with at least two congruent sides

L

least common denominator The least number that is a common denominator of two or more fractions. It is the least common multiple of the denominators of each of the fractions.
Example: The least common denominator of $\frac{1}{2}$ and $\frac{2}{3}$ is 6.

least common multiple (LCM) The least number that is a common multiple of two or more numbers
Example: 12 is the least common multiple of 3 and 4.

like terms (See *terms of a polynomial*)

line A series of points that extends endlessly in two opposite directions along a straight path

Line AB or $\overleftrightarrow{AB}$

line graph A graph that shows changes over time using line segments

line of symmetry A line that divides a figure into two parts that are the same size and shape and are mirror images of one another
Example:

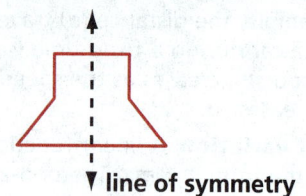
line of symmetry

line segment A part of a line that has two endpoints

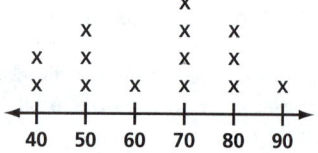

linear function A function whose ordered pair solutions lie on a straight line.

line plot A pictorial representation of a small set of data. Each data item is represented with an "X" placed above a number line

```
                    x
            x       x   x
    x   x           x   x
    x   x   x   x   x   x
    +---+---+---+---+---+→
    40  50  60  70  80  90
```

list price (marked price) The price of an item before any discount has been deducted.

M

major arc (See *arc*)

mean The average of a set of data. It is found by adding each item of data and dividing by the number of items.
Example: 4 is the mean of 2, 4, 5, 5.

median The middle point of the data when they are arranged from least to greatest. If there is an odd number of data items, it is the middle number. If there is an even number of data items, it is the mean of the two middle numbers.
Example: 4.5 is the median of 2, 4, 5, 5.

metric system of measurement An international system of measurement that uses the meter, liter, gram, and degrees Celsius as the basic units of measure

midpoint (See *segment bisector*)

minor arc (See *arc*)

mixed decimal A decimal, such as $0.83\frac{1}{3}$, that ends with a fraction

mixed number A number, such as $2\frac{2}{3}$, that is made up of a fraction less than one and a whole number

mode The number (or numbers) that occurs most often in a set of data. If every number occurs only once, the data has no mode.
Example: 5 is the mode of 2, 4, 5, 5.

monomial An expression consisting of a number, a variable, or the product of a number and one or more variables.
Examples: 5, n, $7xy$, $-3x^2$

multiple of a number The product of the number and any whole number.
Example: The multiples of 4 are 0, 4, 8, 12, 16, ...

multiplication An operation that expresses repeated addition of the same number
Example:
```
   12  ← factor
 × 4   ← factor
   48  ← product
```

multiplication property of equality If two expressions are equal, then multiplying each by the same number forms two new equal expressions.
Example: If $a = b$, then $a \cdot n = b \cdot n$

multiplicative inverse (see *reciprocals*)

N

negative exponent A number that tells how many times the reciprocal of the base is to be used as a factor.
Example: 3^{-4} represents the product $\frac{1}{3} \cdot \frac{1}{3} \cdot \frac{1}{3} \cdot \frac{1}{3}$

negative integer (see *integer*)

negative slope The slope of a line that goes downward from left to right.

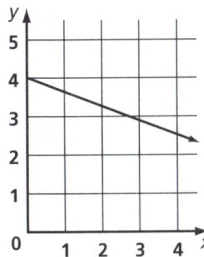

net A flat pattern that can be folded to form a space figure

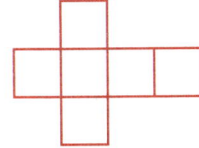

net price The price of an item after a discount has been deducted from the list price

net proceeds The difference between the amount of the sale and the commission

non-linear function A function whose ordered pair solutions do not lie on a straight line.
Example: $y = x^2$ and $V = s^3$

number line A line that has its points labeled with numbers (called coordinates) such as whole numbers, integers, fractions, and so on

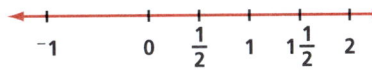

numeral A name or symbol for a number

numerator The number over the bar in a fraction. It tells how many parts of the whole are under discussion.

numerical expression An expression that contains only numbers and symbols of operation and grouping
Example: $(7 + 4) \cdot 6$

O

obtuse angle An angle whose measure is between 90° and 180°

obtuse triangle A triangle with one obtuse angle

octagon A polygon that has 8 sides

regular octagon   irregular octagon

odd number A whole number that is not divisible by 2

open equation An equation that contains a variable

opposites Two numbers whose sum is 0. They are also called additive inverses.
Examples: 2 and $^-2$ are opposites; so are $\frac{-2}{3}$ and $\frac{2}{3}$.

order of operations The rules that define the order in which the operations in an expression are to be evaluated. They are
1 First work within parentheses
2 Next evaluate powers
3 Multiply and divide in order from left to right
4 Finally, add and subtract in order from left to right

ordered pair A pair of numbers used to locate a point in a coordinate plane. The first number (x-value) is the horizontal distance from the origin; the second number (y-value) is the vertical distance.

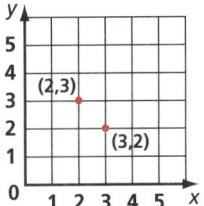

origin The point on a coordinate grid at which the two axes meet. Its coordinates are (0, 0)

outcome A result in a probability experiment

outlier An item of data that is significantly greater or less than all the other items of data

P

parallel lines Lines in the same plane that do not intersect

parallelogram A quadrilateral that has its opposite sides parallel and congruent

pentagon A polygon with 5 sides

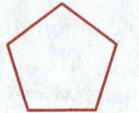 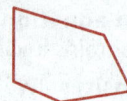

regular pentagon   irregular pentagon

percent A ratio that compares a number to 100
Example: 39% is $\frac{39}{100}$.

percent equation An equation of the form rate (*r*) × base (*b*) = percentage (*p*)

percentage The result obtained by multiplying a quantity by a percent

perimeter The distance around a polygon. It is found by adding the lengths of all the sides.

period Each group of three digits seen in a number written in standard form
Example: In the number 306,789,245, the millions period is 306, the thousands period is 789, and 245 is the ones period.

permutation An arrangement or listing of objects in which order is important

perpendicular lines Two lines that intersect to form right angles

pi The number used to tell how many times a diameter will fit around the outside of a circle; the ratio of the circumference to the diameter. Its value is about 3.14.

pictograph A pictorial representation of data that uses a single symbol to represent multiples of a quantity

place-value system A system of numeration in which the value of a digit depends on its position in the numeral

plane A smooth flat surface that extends indefinitely in all directions

plane figure A figure whose points are all in the same plane

point A location in space. It is represented by a dot.

polygon A closed plane figure composed of line segments that meet only at their endpoints.

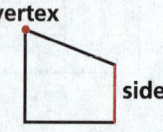

polyhedron A closed figure in space whose faces are all polygons

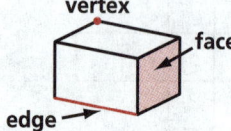 

polynomial An expression that is itself a monomial or is the sum or product of monomials.
Examples: 5   7xy   2(l + w)   πr²
3x² + 9xy − y²

positive integer (see *integer*)

power A number that can be expressed using a single base and exponent.
Example: 32 is a power of 2; it is the fifth power of 2.

prime factorization Expressing a number as a product of prime numbers
Example: 36 = 2 · 2 · 3 · 3 or 2² · 3²

prime number A whole number greater than 1 that has exactly two factors, itself and 1
Example: 2 = 2 · 1

principal (of a loan or savings deposit) The amount of money that is borrowed or deposited

prism A polyhedron that has two congruent, parallel bases that are joined by parallelograms. A prism is named by the shape of its bases.

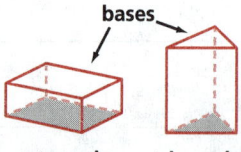

rectangular prism   triangular prism

probability A number between 0 and 1 used to describe how likely an event is to happen; a measure of chance

product (see *multiplication*)

proportion An equation that states that two ratios are equal.
Example: 3 : 4 = 6 : 8 or $\frac{3}{4} = \frac{6}{8}$

protractor A tool used to measure angles

pyramid A polyhedron whose base is a polygon and whose other faces are triangles that share a common vertex. A pyramid is named by the shape of its base

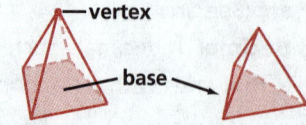

square pyramid   triangular pyramid

Pythagorean Property The square of the length of the hypotenuse of a right triangle is equal to the sum of the squares of the lengths of the other two sides.

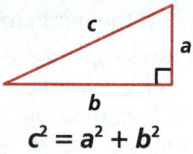

$$c^2 = a^2 + b^2$$

Q

quadrant One of the four sections of a coordinate plane formed by the axes. They are numbered counterclockwise starting from the upper right quadrant.

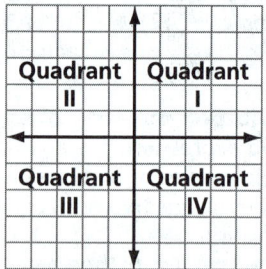

quadrilateral A polygon that has four sides and four angles

quartiles The three numbers in a data set that divide the data into four equal groups. The middle quartile is also called the median. The other two points are the upper and lower quartiles.

quotient (see *division*)

R

radius A segment from any point on a circle to its center; also the length of this segment

358   Glossary

range The difference between the least and greatest number in a set of data
Example: The range of the data 2, 4, 5, 5 is $5 - 2 = 3$.

rate A comparison by division of two unlike quantities, such as words per minute or feet per second

rate (in percent equation)(See *base*)

ratio A comparison of two like quantities using division
Example: 3 : 4, 3 to 4, or $\frac{3}{4}$

rational number A number that can be expressed as the ratio of two integers
Examples: $1.67 = \frac{167}{100}$ $^-5 = \frac{^-5}{1}$

ray A part of a line that has one endpoint. When naming it, the endpoint is used first.

A   B   Ray AB or $\overrightarrow{AB}$

reciprocals Two numbers whose product is 1. They are also called multiplicative inverses.
Examples: 2 and $\frac{1}{2}$ $\frac{^-3}{4}$ and $\frac{^-4}{3}$

rectangle A parallelogram that has four right angles

reflection A transformation that changes the position of a figure by flipping it about a line to form its mirror image
Example:

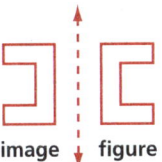
image   figure

regular polygon A polygon that has all sides congruent and all angles congruent

relatively prime Two or more numbers whose only common factor is 1

remainder (see *division*)

repeating decimal A fraction whose decimal expression shows a repeating pattern of digits
Examples: $\frac{1}{3} = 0.333333\ldots$
$\frac{1}{11} = 0.09090909\ldots$

rhombus A parallelogram that has all of its sides congruent

right angle An angle whose measure is 90°

90°

right triangle A triangle with one right angle

rise (see *slope*)

rounded number A number that is close to a given number in which the final digits have been replaced with zeroes.
Examples: 12,501 rounded to the nearest hundred is 12,500.
12, 501 rounded to the nearest thousand is 13,000

run (see *slope*)

S

scale drawing A picture or diagram that is an enlargement or reduction of another. Each distance in the drawing is in the same proportion as the corresponding distance in the original.

scale factor The ratio in a scale drawing or similar figures that compares the scale drawing dimensions to the actual dimensions

scalene triangle A triangle that has no congruent sides

scatter plot A graph of ordered pairs that shows two measurements for each item of a set

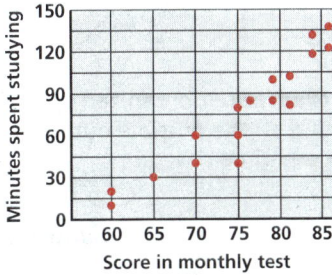

scientific notation A form for writing a number as the product of a number between 1 and 10 and a power of ten
Examples: $186.3 = 1.863 \times 10^2$
$0.0379 = 3.79 \times 10^{-2}$

segment (see *line segment*)

segment bisector A point, called a midpoint, that divides a line segment into two parts of equal measure

semicircle All points on a circle that are on the same side of a diameter, including the endpoints of the diameter; half of a circle.

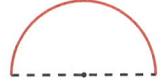

side (see *angle, polygon*)

similar figures Two figures that have the same shape but not necessarily the same size. In similar polygons, corresponding angles are congruent and corresponding sides are proportional.

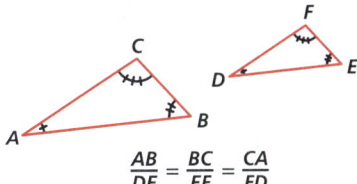

$\frac{AB}{DE} = \frac{BC}{EF} = \frac{CA}{FD}$

simplest form Either a fraction less than 1 in which the numerator and denominator have no common factors except 1, or a mixed number in which the fraction part is in simplest form
Examples: $\frac{5}{10} = \frac{1}{2}$ $2\frac{6}{9} = 2\frac{2}{3}$

skew lines In space figures, lines that are not in the same plane.

slope (*m*) The ratio of the difference in y-coordinates (the rise) to the difference in x-coordinates (the run) of any two points on a coordinate plane; it may be written $\frac{rise}{run}$

solution The value of the variable(s) that makes an open equation or inequality true.

space The set of all points

space figure A figure that is not entirely in one plane

sphere A space figure that has all of its points the same distance from a point, called the center.

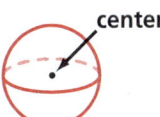
center

spreadsheet A computer program that creates tables or cells of values

square A rectangle that has all its sides congruent

square root A number such that its square is a given number
Example: 5 and ⁻5 are the square roots of 25 because $5^2 = 25$ and $(^-5)^2 = 25$. They are written: $\sqrt{25} = 5$, $-\sqrt{25} = -5$.

standard form A number that is expressed as a base 10 numeral
Example: 3,126 is the standard form of the number three thousand, one hundred twenty-six

stem-and-leaf plot A convenient way of arranging a data set in order from least to greatest by making the last digit of each number a leaf and making the other digits of each number part of the stem.
Example:

data set: 42, 37, 35, 48
56, 37, 42, 41

stem	leaves
3	5 7 7
4	1 2 2 8
5	6

straight angle An angle whose measure is 180°.

straightedge An unmarked ruler used as a geometric construction tool

subtraction An arithmetic operation that takes away a given amount
Example: 345
− 122
223 ← difference

subtraction property of equality If two expressions are equal and the same number is subtracted from each, then the two new expressions are equal.
Example: If $n + 7 = 10$, then $n + 7 - 7 = 10 - 7$.

sum (see *addition*)

supplementary angles Two angles whose measures total 180°.

surface area The total area of all the faces or surfaces of a space figure

survey A method of gathering data about a population by recording the results of specific questions

T

term (of a ratio) Either of the two numbers of a ratio

terms (of a polynomial) Each monomial that is part of a polynomial. If terms contain the same powers of the same variables, they are *like terms*. If terms differ in at least one variable or power of a variable, they are *unlike terms*.
Example:
$2x^2 - 4x$ $3y - 2x$ $7xy + 3xy$
unlike terms   unlike terms   like terms

terminating decimal The decimal expression of a fraction whose denominator can be written using only powers of 2 and 5
Examples: $0.1 = \frac{1}{10}$ $0.675 = \frac{27}{40}$

transformations The basic motions that can be applied to a geometric figure. Two kinds of transformations are reflections and translations.

translation A transformation that changes the position of a figure by sliding it in the same plane.
Example:

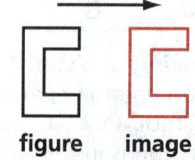

figure   image

transversal A line that intersects two or more other lines in the same number of points as there are lines.
Example:

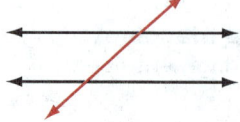

trapezoid A quadrilateral that has exactly one pair of parallel sides

tree diagram A organized way of listing all the possible outcomes of an experiment

Choice 1   Choice 2   Outcomes
red ⟨ white   1 red-white
       black   2 red-black
blue ⟨ white   3 blue-white
       black   4 blue-black

triangle A polygon that has three sides

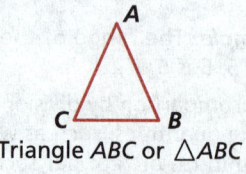

Triangle ABC or △ABC

U

unit A fixed quantity used as a standard for length, area, volume, weight, and so on

unit analysis (also *dimensional analysis*) A technique that uses units of measure in a computation to decide what unit is appropriate in the solution.
Example:
$\frac{65 \text{ mi}}{\text{hour}} \cdot 2.5 \text{ hours} \rightarrow 162.5 \text{ mi}$

unit price The cost of a single unit of an item or service
Example: $3 per pound for hamburger meat

unit rate A rate whose second term is a single unit, such as 50 miles per hour

V

variable A letter that is used to represent one or more numbers

variable expression An expression that contains one or more variables

variation (See *direct variation*)

vertex (see *angle, polygon, polyhedron*)

vertical angles Two "opposite" angles formed by two intersecting lines

vertical line A line that is perpendicular to a horizontal line

volume A measure of the space within a closed figure in space

W–X–Y–Z

whole number Any of the numbers 0, 1, 2, 3, . . .

x-axis The horizontal number line on a coordinate plane

y-axis The vertical number line on a coordinate plane

zero exponent The zero power of any nonzero base is 1; in other words,
$n^0 = 1$

zero property of multiplication Multiplying zero by any number equals zero
Example: $6 \cdot 0 = 0$